Screening THE TEXT

Screening
THE TEXT

Intertextuality in

New Wave French Cinema

T. Jefferson Kline

The Johns Hopkins University Press

BALTIMORE AND LONDON

The Johns Hopkins University Press
701 West 40th Street
Baltimore, Maryland 21211-2190
The Johns Hopkins Press Ltd., London

∞The paper used in this book meets the minimum requirements of the American National Standard for Information Sciences–Permanence of Paper for Printed Library Materials, ANSI Z39.48-1984.

Library of Congress Cataloging-in-Publication Data

Kline, T. Jefferson (Thomas Jefferson), 1942–
    Screening the text : intertextuality in new wave French cinema / T. Jefferson Kline.
        p.   cm.
    Includes bibliographical references and index.
    ISBN 0-8018-4267-0 (alk. paper)
    1. Motion pictures—France.   2. Motion pictures and literature.
3. Intertextuality.   I. Title.
PN1993.5.F7K57   1992
791.43'0994—dc20   91-36323

For the "magnificent Andersons"

Contents

Preface

The idea of this book grew out of courses I taught at Boston University on French film, and so I wish to thank all of my students for their thoughtful participation in the genesis of these essays. Likewise, my son Ethan and my daughter Chloë have, in their own academic development, prompted and challenged mine. I have been extremely fortunate in having excellent criticism from colleagues and friends at every stage of this book, and so I thank Charles Bernheimer, Ilsa Bick, Verena Conley, Joan De Jean, Chloë Kline, Mark Levy, and Bill Smith for their warm encouragement and suggestions. Most especially, I am indebted to Tom Conley, whose responses to this manuscript were delightfully insightful and inevitably right on the mark. And then there is Julie, without whose patience and love I would never have begun at all, and without whose bemused skepticism I might have "here and there exceeded the mark," as Browning says. I am grateful to my many colleagues at Boston University who provide the intellectual ferment I encounter every day and to those at the Johns Hopkins University Press who have helped to give this book its present form, especially Joanne Allen, for her expert and patient reading of the manuscript.

Screening THE TEXT

Introduction

Screening the Text

Un bon film ne me paraît pas parler un autre dialecte
que ma mère Littérature.
—*Eric Rohmer*

Film is always autobiographical in the sense that, for filmmaker and
spectator alike, the view (whether through viewfinder or from images
perceived in darkness) is a voyeuristic one. Because films recreate the
earliest primal scene experience or fantasy, they constitute a reposing
of our most basic and implicit questions about origins. Stanley Cavell
has written that the ontological conditions of the motion picture
reveal it as inherently pornographic, but given the relationship between cinematic voyeurism, the primal scene, and origins, a more
compelling argument can be made that film's pornographic conditions are ontological.[1] Baudry's cave dweller, displacing Plato's, rejects the reality of the outside world because of a profound regressive
need to recreate the illusions experienced in earliest life, be they
uterine or infant primal scenes.[2] The moviegoer will return again and
again to the "scene of the crime" precisely because it constitutes *re-
creation*.

The specificity of that re-creation depends very much on culture,
however. Some friends of mine reenact periodically a scene in which
she chooses a movie and he goes along with her choice and then finds
himself at the theater, groaning in disbelief at the film's lack of action,
plot, or normal character development. "French movie, Bill," she
chimes. "French movie, Bill," has become a refrain encapsulating a
perception of the (often unpleasurable) sense of cultural difference

1

that separates French from American cinematic expression. His lack of pleasure derives precisely from his failure to find a (historical) place for himself in the projected images.

What we glean so often from French cinema is the sense that *their* autobiography is somehow radically different from *ours*. Rebecca Pauly, paraphrasing Baudelaire, has characterized one aspect of this difference as the substitution of the *bibliothèque* for the *berceau* ("cradle") in French autobiographical writing. Indeed, students of French autobiography from Montaigne on have emphasized the *literariness* of this endeavor. Rousseau, for example, dates his first sense of himself to his earliest readings, Stendhal to the discovery of Diderot and D'Alembert's *Encyclopédie*, Sartre to the experience of hearing his mother read aloud. Indeed, Sartre writes hyperbolically, "Je suis né de l'écriture."[3]

Little wonder, then, that François Truffaut would claim that "in relation to American filmmakers, I believe we are all intellectuals,"[4] and Eric Rohmer would idealize the spectator as an "enlightened, cultivated amateur, possessing a taste for greatness, beauty, novelty, and profundity."[5] Cinema has always, of course, been "literary," if only in the sense that it wanted to tell a story, and "borrowed" from the novel not only many of the narrative techniques necessary to this project but most of its plots.[6] This aspect of film's literariness has been abundantly documented by film critics and historians alike, who have found ample evidence in cinematic adaptation of similarities of form and content between the two genres.[7]

The cresting of the *nouvelle vague,* however, beginning in France around 1958, brought an entirely new current to these waters.[8] Moving, paradoxically, in the wake of the new novel, the so-called new wave filmmakers self-consciously began their own break with tradition. Since French cinema in particular (and cinema in general) had been tied too closely to classic forms of narration and film production, these young theorists centered their attack on the work of such filmmakers as Claude Autant-Lara and on the tradition of the "well-made" and "literary" film. Film would no longer be the handmaiden of literature, but would stand as its rival. Searching for subversive techniques to break down the "normal" discursive function of traditional film, with its apparently seamless presentation of illusion, the new wavers (re)introduced the notion of rupture (borrowing from Eisenstein's theory of montage) and alienation (borrowing from Brecht).

In attacking the seamless illusion of reality presented by "well-

2

made" films, however, the new French cinema was asserting another aspect of its "Frenchness." Indeed, the "seamless illusion of wholeness" promoted by classic cinema sounds very much like the American description of the ego ideal, recently termed "a set of functions, more or less stable over time, governing synthetic and integrative functions . . . adapting the individual to his environment and the environment to the individual's needs . . . it has power, purpose and needs . . . for cohesion, continuity and self-esteem . . . subsumed within it."[9] Cohesion and continuity are precisely those features attacked by French cinema in the fifties in part because they no longer seemed pertinent. Lacan, whom Jeffrey Mehlman termed "the French Freud," had proposed another, less cohesive, nay, thoroughly discontinuous view of the ego.[10] Lacanian psychoanalysis theorized an unconscious structured like a language whose *moi* is merely the locus of a project of the recuperation of a (lost) wholeness. Little wonder that many French filmmakers found themselves increasingly uncomfortable with a theory of "seamlessness" and began to prefer a notion of film as discontinuity, rupture, project—an *écriture*. As an expression of the unconscious, film was to become increasingly the locus not only of conflict but of the subject(s) of repression.

Armed with such terms as "auteur" and "camera stylo," the new cineastes engaged directly in "film writing," rejecting the seamless interpretation of events that was implied by adaptation. In 1962, for example, Agnès Varda would declare, "I wanted to make a film exactly as one writes a book!"[11] The new French cinema thus sought to usurp rather than imitate the role of literature. But usurpation, "the absolute absorption of the precursor," no less than imitation, is a form of (oedipal) rivalry, betraying its own obsession with the authoritative model.[12]

If literature *qua* adaptation was repressed in their work, it had an uncanny way of returning in another form. So insistent was this newly implicit presence that one of the historians of this period of French cinema claims that "the cineastes of the new wave are rooted ['enracinés'] in literature," and Truffaut was later to complain of the "omnipresence of the book."[13] One of the forms of the return of this repressed element involved self-conscious theorizing. However much they rejected any notion of borrowing their *material* from the novel, the new filmmakers merely ended up borrowing the new novel's *program*. Coming as they did from the ranks of *La Gazette du cinéma, La Revue du cinéma,* and *Cahiers du cinéma,* their heavily theoretical bent subtly but forcefully confirmed a different but nevertheless entirely *literary* cast to the new project. In usurping the place of the writer, these filmmakers simply recast the meta-literary concerns of the 1950s into meta-cinematic ones.

Another, more insistent but also more paradoxical symptom of the repression of literary adaptation was the emergence of the book as object of attention, and the bookstore as the location of choice of their characters (see plate 1). Postwar French film abounds with such scenes as Charles Aznavour pausing to peruse a novel on his way through *Tirez sur le pianiste,* Jacques Demy's protagonist missing work in *Lola* because of his fascination with Malraux's *L'Espoir,* or Gérard Blain's purchase of Balzac's *Illusions perdues* in *Les Cousins.* At other times it is the haunting *absence* of books that is keenly felt: *L'Année dernière à Marienbad* feels very much as though it were a remake of Resnais's earlier documentary on the Bibliothèque Nationale, *Toute la mémoire du monde,* with all of the books (save one) missing. Truffaut's *Fahrenheit 451* is in some ways a metaphor for the whole of postwar French cinema's relationship to books: banned by decree, they remain cherished, embedded firmly in the minds of the principal players of the unfolding drama.

As endemic (and nearly epidemic) as is this obsession with the book, it has received but scant critical attention. Seen too often as the "other" of cinematic expression, tomes are mistaken too often as "tombs" of dead culture or simply moments of the auteur's graphic unconscious.[14] In fact, however, these allusions may function much as they do in literature, or as filmic allusions do in film: they institute a complex and highly mobile configuration of meanings, memories, and associations. The specific mobility of their presence derives most of all from the feature of repression that hovers over literature in general in these films. Filmmakers, as we shall have occasion to appreciate in these pages, may invoke one text to displace and/or repress another, thereby sublating literature into figures not reducible to semiotic components. It is often through such intertextual elements that French new wave film will tend to move meaning "elsewhere," into forms other than the ones that seem to be in evidence. In this sense, the texts screened come to function as screens in the sense that Freud gave to the term, as a memory "behind which lies a submerged and forgotten" phrase, event, or, in this case, text.[15] In this sense too, screening (out) seems always to involve a double movement away from and toward the object (of desire).

The essays in this volume, then, grow out of an awareness of the double bind of the book and work toward a fuller understanding of the conscious and often unconscious relationships that the French

4

PLATE 1.   Jean-Pierre Leaud and Marie-France Pisier make what is to become a routine stop at bookstores for the *dramatis personae* of the new wave, this one in Truffaut's *L'Amour à vingt ans*. (Courtesy of the Museum of Modern Art Film Stills Archive.)

new wave filmmakers developed to a constituted-and-then-repressed authority: the literature(s) that subtend their films. Each essay focuses on a text visibly screened to reveal a text screened (out), figuring ambivalence, misprision, or misrepresentation. What is remarkable in the configuration of these films by Truffaut, Malle, Chabrol, Rohmer, Bresson, Godard, and Resnais is the international range of the canon. Their fascination with American films is well known, of course, but it extends well beyond, to classical mythology, French literature both contemporary and classical, and Russian, Norwegian, German, and English writers and philosophers.

If I have engaged a set of films each of which has excited a lengthy and sustained critical debate, it is precisely because the subject of literary intertextuality has remained so marginal yet has so much to add to such a debate.

Every film, by its nature, inserts itself into the enormous unfolding context of cinema. No film, by nature, can escape insertion into the virtually limitless context of literary imagination. As Ellie Ragland-Sullivan wrote recently, "The fictions of an out-of-sight meaning system . . . determine the socioconventional meaning of contracts, pacts and laws from culture to culture. Meaning, then, cannot ultimately be identified with linguistic function only, for it is inherently relative, relational, structural and 'self-referential.'"[16] "Self-referential" having as it does in French culture such a resolutely *literary* connotation, we may imagine in the current project the beginnings of a "cinema without walls." Such is, I would submit, the *cinematic condition*.

Chapter One

Anxious Affinities:
Text as Screen in Truffaut's
Jules et Jim

I must confess that there is something I should like to
have explained. When we took the *camera obscura* to the
park yesterday you were too busy finding a truly picturesque view to have noticed what was going on
otherwise.
—*Goethe*

I still retain from my childhood a great anxiety, and the
movies are bound up with an anxiety, with an idea of
something clandestine.
—*François Truffaut*

Nowhere is the status of the text as an object for analysis at once more
translucent and more opaque than when it enters a domain that is
curiously parallel to the theory of psychoanalysis itself. If psychoanalytic theory originates from a strong desire to observe and represent
sexual origins, moving in a kind of specular play of speculation between analyst and analysand, so, it can be argued, is cinema born of a
need to interpret the world from a voyeuristic position for a spectator
who becomes mirrored in that world.

Cinema and psychoanalysis would thus share a common ontology
in what J. B. Pontalis calls "a desire for sexual knowledge coupled with
a sexual desire for knowledge."[1] Moreover, psychoanalysis and
cinema (co)operate in a kind of double articulation of reality and
fantasy: whereas the analysand realizes a discourse based on a representation of remembered and fantasized images, the cineaste represents in images a fantasy constructed as a photographic (i.e., real)

discourse. Both discourses are troubled and doubled by illusion and allusion. For the analysand, dreams and "screen memories" often simultaneously hide and reveal an absent presence at the nexus of a particularly tangled complex. In cinema that absent presence not only is constituted by the ontological nature of the medium but is itself often doubled by allusions to the "other scene" of literature. Because of its inevitable functioning as absent presence in cinema, the literary intertext thus occupies a place analogous to that of the dream in psychoanalysis, constituting a kind of "royal road" to understanding textuality. Indeed, if Pontalis is correct in ascribing to dreaming an unconscious attempt to "figure what is inaccessible while maintaining its inaccessibility," then screening a text would make it, likewise, "a particular type of object which makes present a certain absence and which doubles the invisible with the visible."[2]

If, as Freud also reminds us, the specific elements of a dream can be properly interpreted only through an understanding of their deeper associative connections to a "meaning" itself never entirely present, so too in film does the appearance of or reference to a literary text imply an entire system of meanings, whose interpretation can only be approximated by a combination of vertical (paradigmatic) and horizontal (syntagmatic) readings. Nor is the doubling that binds the dream (or intertext) to discourse (or filmic narrative) merely structural; Freud was categorical in his insistence that the figures of the dream function as doubles not only of the dreamer *but of each other*. It may be argued, by analogy, that when a text becomes a filmic intertext, it therefore undergoes an onirizing transformation in structure *and* in content. It follows, then, that the figure of the double at the heart of the intertext operates not merely at the level of structural analogy but also at the level of (psycho-)analysis.

François Truffaut's films make a particularly fruitful field for such an analysis, first, because Truffaut has said of the cinema, "I love the cinema because it's an indirect art . . . it conceals as much as it reveals."[3] Then, too, as François Ramasse noted recently, all of the new wave filmmakers were deeply rooted in literature, especially Truffaut, whose early work reveals "an obsession with books."[4] Indeed, *Jules et Jim* allows us to appreciate the force of Ramasse's term *obsédé*, for the film contains a complex of allusions to a panoply of literary and filmic texts that seem to persistently obtrude themselves on the director's consciousness and whose role in the work appears to be designed more "to reconcile ambivalent attitudes and therefore to consist of formulations or of statements which tend to cancel each other out" than to contribute to the narrative development of the work.[5]

While the most obvious literary allusion in *Jules et Jim* is Truffaut's adaptation of Henri-Pierre Roché's novel of the same title, that adaptation is certainly as much what Harold Bloom would term a "misprision" in the sense of a "misreading . . . an act of creative correction that is actually and necessarily a misinterpretation" as it is a "translation" of the literary antecedent.[6] For one thing, Truffaut collapses virtually all of Roché's women into a single character, Catherine, while at the same time virtually screening off the more violent and schizophrenic aspects of Roché's principal heroine, Kathe. Indeed, much in Truffaut's adaptation of this novel can be understood as a "screening" of the scene and implications of the figure of the double.

Truffaut reasserts in his film an equilibrium between Jim and Jules that is thoroughly lost in the second half of the novel. Close analysis of the film will demonstrate that these effects are profoundly linked and that Truffaut's repression of the double configuration in Catherine succeeds in diverting the viewer's attention from the analogous double structuration of the two male characters, which constantly risks revealing the "homosocial" nature of their relationship.[7]

It is uncanny that Truffaut's "screening off" of Catherine's potential doubleness without, however, totally obliterating it constitutes a remarkable analogy with the complex function of intertexts in the film as a whole. The dimensions and shape of Truffaut's "misinterpretation" of Roché's text can best be appreciated by analogy with the intricate arrangement of the other major intertexts in the film and, in particular, Mérimée's *Vénus d'Ille* and Goethe's *Elective Affinities*.[8]

Jules (Oskar Werner) and Jim (Henri Serre) bind their relationship most closely in their discovery of the Mediterranean statue, "a crudely sculptured woman's face wearing a tranquil smile which fascinated them ['les saisit']."[9] The narrator notes that for their pilgrimage to this statue "they had identical light-colored suits tailored for each of them," a detail that has the immediate effect of joining the two men in a specular relationship with each other at least as forceful as, if initially less obvious than, their individual or joint relationship to the statue.[10] This doubling surely evokes such precedents as Stevenson's *Dr. Jekyll and Mr. Hyde* and Dostoevsky's *The Double,* in which homosexual versus heterosexual and/or active versus passive oppositions are manifested through splitting of characters, and yet Truffaut never articulates such doubling at the anecdotal level of his film.[11]

When, subsequently, Catherine (Jeanne Moreau) appears to incarnate the idealized statue, the two are immediately bound to this "Frenchwoman who had an identical smile to that of the statue on the island. . . . The whole thing was beginning like a dream" (SC,

23/32).[12] This dreamlike double of a powerfully evocative "Venus d'île" cannot but evoke Mérimée's *Vénus d'Ille,* a fantastic tale of a kind of feminine Jekyll and Hyde—and of two countervailing views of women's sexuality.[13]

If Catherine's aspect expresses the "pride of a region that she had once incarnated as a child during a religious festival," Mérimée's statue wears an expression of "something ferocious . . . of infernal irony."[14] Those familiar with Mérimée's work will recall that the story centers around the

> admirable Venus, whose marvelous beauty is joined to an absence of any sensitivity. . . . If the model ever existed, [muses the narrator,] and I doubt that Heaven ever produced such a woman, I pity her lovers. There is in her expression something ferocious, and yet I've never seen anything so beautiful! It's Venus herself, entire, crouched on her prey! Her expression of infernal irony was perhaps accentuated by the contrast between her very brilliant eyes and the blackish patina that time had painted on the statue. Her brilliant eyes produced a certain illusion which recalled reality and life. I remembered that my guide had told me that she caused everyone who looked at her to lower their eyes. (VI, 194)

The narrator of *La Vénus d'Ille* instantly compares this recently unearthed statue, which bears the foreboding inscription CAVE AMANTEM, with the most beautiful virgin of the region, who is to be offered in marriage to the host's son. The narrator admires the living idol for the

> perfect naturalness of her responses and an air of goodness that was not, however, without a slight tint of malice and that almost in spite of myself caused me to recall the statue. In this comparison, I wondered if the statue's greater beauty was not due to her tigerlike expression; for energy, even when it is linked to evil passions, always evokes in us awe and an almost involuntary admiration. (VI, 202)

We may translate "l'énergie de la mauvaise passion" as unbridled sexuality, a characteristic so feared in women in nineteenth- and early twentieth-century literature as to consign them either to the brothel or to the asylum—or else, as in this case, to the realm of the fantastic. The unrepressed sexuality of the beautiful young bride in this story must be *projected* onto a statue.

Mérimée graphically portrays the consequences of such unbridled sexuality. Hindered by his wedding ring during a game of *jeu de paume* with some passing Spaniards, Alphonse conveniently places it

10

on the finger of the statue, only to discover, when he goes to reclaim the ring, that the statue has closed the fingers of her left hand over the band. "She seems to be my wife now," Alphonse naively exclaims, "since I have given her my ring! She doesn't seem to want to give it back!" (VI, 211). During the wedding feast, his father enjoins the groom,

> My son, choose the Roman Venus or the Catalan one, whichever you prefer. The rascal chooses the Catalan and he's got the better deal. The Roman is black, the Catalan is white. The Roman is cold and the Catalan inflames everyone that comes near her! (VI, 209)

As readers, of course, we understand that the choice has already and unconsciously been made by the young groom to attempt to have *both* of these beauties.

But this marriage to "the two faces of Venus" ends in disaster. On the morning after his wedding night, Alphonse is found lying half-clothed and livid across his broken bed, crushed horribly as if "embraced by a ring of iron"; beside the bed, of course, lies the diamond wedding ring, apparently dropped by the unearthed Venus as a signature of this double wedding. His "virgin" bride hovers hysterically in a corner—exactly the attitude consigned by Freud and Charcot to women whose sexuality was overly energized into "bad passions." The story corroborates Elaine Showalter's contention that until quite recently, the double figure in literature was limited to such tales as *Dr. Jekyll and Mr. Hyde,* which expressed in a manner which "hyd" and revealed a latent homoerotic sexuality and violence barely repressed in some men. Showalter argues that when women began to be doubled in twentieth-century literature, that doubling was constructed, not along the lines suggested in Stevenson's novel, but rather as beings in one of whose doubles (or multiple personalities) sexuality was "acceptably feminine," while in the other(s) it was unacceptable *for a woman,* that is, not specifically illicit or homoerotic but simply unrepressed, in other words, a "bad passion."[15] The parallelism evoked between male and female stories of doubles is, typically, unparallel.[16] The unrepressed sexuality of the beautiful young bride in this story is projected onto a statue. Unleashed, of course, this "other bride," whom Mérimée describes as exhumed from underground, does not evoke the traditional Venus, but, curiously, the Athlete of Morus, often named Germanicus! Her glance is full of "malice, even to the point of meanness," and her stare causes the narrator to lower his eyes in spite of himself. "Look what happens," Mérimée seems to be warning his (male) audience, "if we were even to imagine releasing the conveniently repressed, playful, athletic, masculine, and therefore 'malicious' side of women. Why, they would crush us with the force of their suffocating embrace." The very thought seems to be so chilling that it can only be rendered under the sign of the fantastic. The asymmetric parallelism that emerges from the comparison of stories of male versus female doubles suggests that whereas the unacceptable part of male sexuality that is "split off" in doubling tends to be homoerotic, the unacceptable part of female sexuality relegated to the "fantastic" is precisely that part of male sexuality that is repeatedly glorified in nineteenth- and early twentieth-century European fiction!

Now, Truffaut's use of the Mérimée intertext is most ingenious, for by reversing the terms of the original, he manages to mitigate or at least delay the force of the double configuration. Truffaut's statue is pure, beatific, perfect: apparently benign. Jules and Jim fall in love with *it* and only subsequently discover the real woman, whom they seek likewise to idealize. Catherine exhibits not only the *fierté* of Mérimée's statue but occasionally also the doubleness of the original statue: she is playful, once dresses like a man, is a trickster, is associated with both water and fire (her leap into the Seine and her brush with self-immolation) (see plate 2). Yet all of these signs are, as it were, repressed by her situation and her lovers. The playfulness of the *ménage à trois* assimilates most of the early "danger" signals into the funhouse of their relationship. Most of Jules-and-Jim's interaction with her is characterized by attempts to exclude and to neutralize her danger. She is, first of all, assigned to Jules, whose own (hetero) sexuality is so reduced as to be all but nonexistent. "Not this one, Jim," warns Jules (SC, 25/33) in a phrase strangely reminiscent of Mérimée's CAVE AMANTEM. It often seems, however, as though both of these men have elected to obey this taboo, for they frequently ignore her (e.g., twice at dominoes) and are almost always presented visually as a couple, with Catherine the "odd man out" (at the beach, on bikes, etc.). For the most part, Truffaut manages to suggest that Catherine's "problem" emerges in the course of the film's development rather than as the result of her psychologically double nature.[17]

Obviously, to reveal the double aspect of Catherine risks raising the issue of doubles in the film as a whole—opening a reinterpretation of this story of "two friends and the woman companion they share," who "love one another with tenderness and almost no harshness."[18] Truffaut's use of the narrative voice-over in the film functions, in this respect, in a most "reassuring" manner, always inscribing the actions of the characters we see within the comfortable limits of

12

PLATE 2.   Catherine (Jeanne Moreau) exhibits her playfulness in a race with Jules (Oskar Werner) and Jim (Henri Serre) in a lighthearted moment of Truffaut's *Jules et Jim*. (Courtesy of the Museum of Modern Art Film Stills Archive.)

friendship. Indeed, the narrator seems often to function as a "blinder," redirecting our attention from the rich and symbolic visual material on the screen to a more unidimensional story line.[19] Likewise, Truffaut's rephrasing the story twice within the narrative framework appears as a kind of hyperinsistence on this objectivity. Jim recapitulates the story of their friendship during their workout at the gym, and he tells Catherine an exemplary story of this friendship a second time just prior to the turning point of the film. Here again, the voice of the narrator insists on the traditional love triangle that has formed among them.

Retrospectively and retroactively, these versions take on a different tone and another kind of ambiguity, but only when considered in the light of the other elements of the adaptation. As doubles of each other, Jules and Jim might be interpreted as a "masculine-agressive" and a "feminine-passive" set of terms, where Jim's sexual activity contrasts with Jules's passivity.[20] Jim is frequently portrayed as getting out of bed to rejoin Jules (anticipating a more explicit configuration displayed in *Sunday Bloody Sunday*), and Jules as never getting into bed with anyone, in order to remain with Jim.

In contrast to a kind of Stevensonian *anecdotal* insistence on their double configuration, which would reveal the homosocial side of their relationship, Truffaut elects to represent this element visually and metonymically, as in the opening scenes, where the two friends play piggyback and then Jim dresses Jules in very feminine materials, or in the way in which Jim pointedly and gratuitously shifts their places in the cafe scene with Therese so that he comes to occupy the place of the man and Jules the place of the woman at the table.[21] Their status as couple is almost obsessively rehearsed in the opening segments of the film (see plate 3), and yet the director neatly manages to avert this interpretative stance first by deferring Catherine's status as double and then, when the double issue resurfaces, by "screening" the entire question behind another powerful intertext. Indeed, Truffaut focuses our attention so insistently on a copy of *Elective Affinities* that he virtually transforms the German text into a fetish (in the sense that behind it lies "a submerged and forgotten phase . . . of which it is both a remnant and a precipitate"), making the text perform like a "screen memory."[22]

The presentation of Goethe's text occurs during a scene in which Jules telephones Jim at the auberge near the chalet in Germany and asks his French friend to bring over his copy of *Elective Affinities* because Catherine absolutely has to read it that very evening. Jules adds, "Jim, Catherine no longer wants me. I'm terrified of losing her and that she'll disappear completely from my life" (SC, 71/83). Jules urges Jim to marry Catherine so that he (Jules) can continue to see her. "Don't think of me as an obstacle," Jules says, clearly asking Jim to interpret the transfer of the Goethe text as a kind of license for the transfer of women that is accomplished in Goethe's novella. It is worth recalling at this juncture Gayle Rubin's observation that "if it is women who are being transacted, then it is the men who give and take them who are linked, the woman being a conduit of a relationship rather than a partner to it."[23] The scene then shifts to the inn, where a closeup insistently frames the copy of *Elective Affinities* in Jim's hand. Another shift of scene brings Jim to the door of the chalet, where Catherine awaits him. Until this moment, Jules and Jim have been portrayed as "good friends" who view Catherine as an idealized woman and the relationship among the three of them as a kind of idealized platonic realm. The scene that next unfolds, however, subtly but insistently questions all of the assumptions and structures that have thus far governed the film.

PLATE 3.   Oskar Werner and Henri Serre enjoy a moment of play together in the opening scenes of Truffaut's *Jules et Jim*. (Courtesy of the Museum of Modern Art Film Stills Archive.)

Truffaut's camera follows Jim and Catherine from behind as she leads him inside. They turn toward each other, now in profile against the large windows that look out over the hillside (see plate 4). It is night, so that the exterior light silhouettes both of the faces in front of the window. As Jim traces Catherine's profile with his index finger, a large beetle on the glass behind them advances in a direct diagonal straight into the line of Catherine's lips and appears to disappear into her mouth an instant before Jim's lips meet hers.

Never was Walter Benjamin so correct as in his assertion that

the camera introduces us to unconscious optics as does psychoanalysis to unconscious impulses. . . . By close-ups of the things around us, by focusing on hidden details of familiar objects, by exploring commonplace milieux under the ingenious guidance of the camera, the film, on the one hand, extends our comprehension of the necessities which rule our lives; on the other hand it manages to assure us of an immense and unexpected field of action . . . [in which] an unconsciously penetrated space is substituted for a space consciously explored by man.[24]

15

PLATE 4. Jim (Henri Serre) and Catherine (Jeanne Moreau) turn toward each other, now in profile against the large windows that overlook the hillside. (Courtesy of the Museum of Modern Art Film Stills Archive.)

Surely an "accident" of shooting, Truffaut elected to keep this take of the scene in the final editing despite (or because of?) the disturbing presence of this large insect on the glass behind his lovers. This is, however, not the first allusion to insects in the film. Several scenes earlier, Jules tells Jim that marriage and motherhood have transformed Catherine from a *cigale* ("grasshopper") to a *fourmi* (ant) (SC, 54/67). Earlier Jules had expounded to Jim on his love of dragonflies *(libellules)* and his meanderings in the swamps in pursuit of them. "Perhaps one day I'll return to literature with a novel about love with insects for characters. I have a bad habit of over-specialization" (SC, 51/63). This curious juxtaposition of *amour* and *spécialiser* is immediately followed by, "I envy the spread of your 'éventail' Jim." The double entendre of *éventail* as range and, to follow the sexualized insect metaphor, as dragonfly wing, coupled with the term *ouverture*, is most suggestive. When the insect then appears on the window, it moves between Jim and Catherine and appears to enter her mouth with Jim's lips.[25] The moment seems to parallel an earlier one in

16

which Jim and Jules first view Albert's photographic slide of the idealized sculpture and Jim says, without consulting his friend, "We'd like to look at the preceding slide again," already assimilating Jules's desire to his own (SC, 18/27). In other words, the beetle on the window constitutes a return of the repressed doubling in the film thus far relegated to unconscious motifs and will now be directly repressed by the superposition of Goethe's *Elective Affinities* "over" the insect allusion.[26]

The visual insertion of Goethe's novella constitutes an attempt to impose an interpretation that would reassert a normative view of heterosexual arrangements at the very moment when the unconscious movement of the film threatens to open a meditation on doubles in a homosocial configuration. Truffaut may indeed be correct when he asserts that "every film must contain some degree of planned violence on its audience" and that he himself often risks "violating his public [by] making people see something they don't want to see," but he appears to need to "control" or contain that violence in this instance.[27]

Elective Affinities is indeed an ironic choice for a "normative" view since in 1809 it represented a socially daring departure from the rigidly conservative view of marriage.[28] Goethe introduced the chemical theory of attraction to justify the rupture of the classical notion of stability by new lines of desire. Freely mixing the chemical and social metaphors, Goethe argues that

> opportunity makes relationships, and where your natural substances are concerned, the choice seems to lie entirely in the hands of the chemist who brings these substances together. In these cases one can actually demonstrate attraction and relatedness; where four entities previously joined in two pairs are brought into contact, abandon their previous union and . . . seek one another out, attract, seize, destroy, devour, consume one another, and then emerge again from this most intimate union in renewed, novel and unexpected shape.[29]

It is doubly ironic, given Truffaut's "normative" use of this text, that Goethe originally introduces Ottilie as the unstable element in his social "formula" in order to compensate Charlotte for Eduard's exclusive attention to another man (the Captain). Yet as "chemist" of the "experiment" of 1809, Goethe "proves" that the more powerful heterosexual forces will create the "new unexpected shape" of what in Truffaut's time had become a much more traditional theatrical structure, the adulterous heterosexual couple or triangle.[30] Thus the introjection of the novella at a moment of ambiguity can be seen as

Truffaut's attempt to control the interpretation of Jules's legacy of Catherine to Jim, causing it to appear as a simple matter of triangular relationships rather than as the authorization of the control and exchange of women by men. The irony of Truffaut's "misprision" of Goethe lies in understanding the implications for homosocial linkage in this circulation of the woman, thus further exposing the male bonding so deeply embedded in this film. Despite its apparent design to screen off any "novel and unexpected shapes," Goethe's presence seems ironically to highlight them.

The outward and visible sign of the power of *die Wahlverwandschaften* is figured in Goethe's text by the body of Eduard and Charlotte's son, who, conceived while Eduard is desperately attracted to Ottilie, and Charlotte to the Captain, "aroused ever greater wonder and amazement (because) in his features and figure he was coming ever more to resemble the Captain, his eyes were becoming ever less distinguishable from Ottilie's" (EA, 248). "This strange affinity" reasserts the power of normative heterosexual attractions, which bind the forces of nature more powerfully than such commonly accepted laws as biological heredity. Perhaps this is why in Truffaut's arrangement the child Sabine comes to represent the double of her mother, for despite the imposition of Goethe's text, the film "hides and forever reveals" a complex arrangement of doubles.

Perhaps what is most ironic of all in Truffaut's use of Goethe is that the author of *Elective Affinities* uncannily and well before the letter—or the image, as our present case may be—alludes to the distractive force of the repressed. A stranger to Eduard's estate exclaims to his host, just as we might protest to Truffaut, "There is something else that detains me here, something I should like to have explained before I leave. When we took the camera obscura to the park yesterday, you were too busy in finding a truly picturesque view to have noticed what was going on otherwise" (EA, 245). If the "picturesque view" in *Jules et Jim* is "that of the friendship between two men who try to survive" and "the impossibility of the *ménage à trois*," "what is going on otherwise" in Truffaut's film, besides the triangular relationship, is precisely what Benjamin predicted it would be! The camera answers the director's attempt to mobilize a canonic text as an "authorized" version of events by capturing the insect that so insistently makes its way into the space between Jim and Catherine, reopening the question of unconscious doubling and consequently of homosocial bonding in this film in a way that can no longer be overlooked.

What is most uncanny in Truffaut's arrangement, however, is the way this "battleground" of conflicting intertexts is itself symbolically conflated in the emblematic documentary footage of World War I that erupts into the exact center of this film. In these scenes of war Truffaut makes use of a technique as old as cinema itself but one that Tom Conley has reinterpreted by terming it "collage," where

> the act of reference is caught in the glue that adheres one page to another. The eye cannot look through a text but arrests on the edge of the combination, affixes itself to what binds them and, in an instant, makes an imaginary montage of quotations that gain a plastic and very material substance they lacked before. Collage literalizes metaphor, turning the hidden moment of comparison into the sight of the bond that holds them together. . . . And no medium deals with collage better than film, where cuts and junctures of editing would be the medium closest to the objects fashioned by the . . . collage.[31]

Whereas Truffaut's sequence of documentary footage appears both to advance the narrative and to add realism, this celluloid footage "pasted over" Truffaut's "own" film is an exact replica *at the plastic level* of the intertextual screening of one text (Mérimée) by another (Goethe)—a move that is itself metaphorized at the level of content by the Franco-German conflict represented in these scenes, and perhaps as well at the meta-psychoanalytic level, where the Frenchman Truffaut battles vainly with the Germanic Freud's exposure of the system of repression. (We might more playfully term this level of the conflict screen-Mérimée versus screen memory.) In this process of "pasting over" a virtual concretization of the metaphors of screening and repression, Truffaut has reexposed the obsessive ambivalence that lies just below the surface of this film. The specific content of that ambivalence is itself metaphorized in these scenes as well. Because the process of collage requires "cutting and decapitation . . . of members from given works sliced and lopped off, then glued and bound back over each other," Conley argues that "collage binds the phantasm of the body to the register of seeing and reading."[32]

At the structural level, the documentary footage fills a gap cut out of the texture of Truffaut's fantasy. Within that gap, through the explosive scenes of war, Truffaut interposes first a shot of Jim saying, "I am afraid of killing Jules," and then one of Jules writing, "I lived in fear of killing Jim" (SC, 46–47/57–58). If, like the imposition of *Elective Affinities* on an otherwise problematic context, the documentary quality of this footage initially seems to refuse a metaphorical reading of these scenes, the violence of "flattened soldiers scampering up the barren hills of no man's land looking like insects" reevokes both the doubling and the homosocial bonding of the two protagonists.[33] Indeed, Truffaut once said of such scenes, "To make a fighting film, one would have to let man in the plural count for more than man in the singular, *and I can't imagine doing that*."[34]

Given the combination of collage as a decapitation and as a penetration of one text in/onto another, of the parallel confessions of fear and attraction of the two protagonists and the series of repeated explosions and violent physical penetration, these documentary scenes can be understood to reinforce the other images of doubling that permeate this film. Thus their status as documentary functions simultaneously as screen and, paradoxically, as concretization of the screened-off metaphor. Truffaut confirms this use of collage as screen by redeploying it in remarkably similar fashion in *La Chambre verte* (1978). As Julien Davenne, Truffaut himself plays a journalist obsessively devoted to his dead wife's memory because, as he says, "All my buddies died in the war. I am the only one left to keep their memory alive." *Their* memory is insistently evoked in the opening scenes of the film by the same documentary footage as that used in *Jules et Jim,* reintroduced by a series of slides of *libellules* (dragonflies!) and finally consecrated by a photograph of Oskar Werner as the beloved enemy soldier Davenne had killed during the war. Although in Henry James's text, "The Altar of the Dead," the death of the hero's wife is the principal motive in establishing a chapel to her memory, in Truffaut's "adaptation" she is but a pretext for celebrating the memories of his male friends. The film tends to insist on this homosocial arrangement both by the gratuitous introduction of the character Georges, a deaf-mute who "fills in" for the absence of Antoine Doinel and the wild child, and by the relentless rejection of the woman who attempts to break through Davenne's "mourning." The fact that Truffaut plays the part of Davenne and so actively references his *own* film history suggests that we are again in the realm of obsessive behavior and collage become thinly veiled screens for repressed homosocial feelings.

The eroticized violence of the war footage in *Jules et Jim* also evokes the erotic "heat" of the boxing scenes in which Jim immediately links the thrill of their stylized combat with its interpretation in the form of his reading from the novel of their friendship. Since that reading is taken from the pages of Roché's novel, it emblematically joins the intertextual structure of Truffaut's film to the intricate question of hiding and revealing the homosocial bond at its center.

In his use of documentary, then, Truffaut again demonstrates the way a classic technique of intertextuality may function as a rupture of the narrative line apparently to reinforce the purely anecdotal level of the work, while unconsciously countering the very message it was "intended" to propose. Truffaut's intertexts double as screens and subversions simultaneously and, as such, work to reinforce the major psychological premise of the entire work: that the homosocial bond signified in the double configuration is a subversive message that must be screened out at the same time that it repeatedly thrusts itself back into our consciousness through numerous visual and marginal elements that subvert the anecdotal level of the work.

All of these various "screens," which "forever hide and reveal" (Pontalis) a complex of psychic issues behind them, also clarify the nature of Truffaut's "misrepresentation" of the very text from which *Jules et Jim* was taken. In adapting the figure of Kathe for the screen, Truffaut elected to omit Roché's comparison of his heroine to Kleist's *Penthesilea*, by which Roché most forcefully signals the double nature of his heroine and, ironically, most aligns her with Mérimée's vengeful Venus.[35] Kathe is presented as a virtual changeling, evolving in a quasi-diabolical fashion:

> She passed from one extreme to the other with brusque attacks. . . . When she was torturing and tortured by her internal demon, she seemed to Jules to be a force of nature that expressed itself by cataclysms. A dark menace hovered over the whole house. (R, 92)

This behavior, too much for Jules ("She was not the kind of woman to tolerate him," notes Roché), is more readily accepted by Jim, who agrees to contend with Roché's version of *Penthesilea* for the duration of the work:

> One evening she read them her favorite passage from Kleist's *Penthesilea*, who feverishly massacres an Achilles disarmed and panting for her love. . . . Kathe said, "What could be more beautiful than red blood shed for love?" She added, "I am awash in the red of your heart, Jim, and I want to drink, drink, drink!" (R, 113)

Jim adds, "Her smile is nourished by milk and blood." And the narrator notes, "Kathe's lips were made for both."

The story of Jim and this "changeling" comes to usurp the place of the story of Jules and Jim of the title of the novel, with Jules relegated to the role of occasional observer with a role to play only when the two antagonists exhaust themselves in their struggles. Their story is hardly the one described by Truffaut in which "two friends and the woman companion they share, love one another with tenderness and almost no harshness." Truffaut's gloss, and indeed much of the film that results from it, function as a redirection of our attention away from Kathe's Jekyll and Hyde like metamorphoses from tenderness to taloned spirit. The Kathe of the novel changes with the suddenness of a thunderclap:

> From the most serene sky there would burst a thunderbolt and a frenzy of destruction took hold of Kathe. She craved combat and fresh blood. Her face was instantly ravaged by some doubt and took on a terrifying expression. Her angelic smile became a knife wound. . . . Jules considered these crises like some sacred evil, dangerous to her and everyone around her, almost like a "soul quake." (R, 135–36)

Ultimately, when Jules reflects back on her life with him, he instinctively inscribes her under the sign of the double:

> He imagined Kathe as he first knew her, before she had tasted blood, clever Kathe who would win races by starting on "two"! Kathe when she was generous, irresistible. Kathe when she was severe, invincible— Kathe–Alexander the Great. Kathe as wandering rose, Kathe whom he'd disarmed once upon a time by his complete surrender, Kathe who had attached him one fine day to her triumphal chariot. (R, 241)

But if Roché's Jules seems eager to understand the double in Kathe, François seems just as concerned to repress this aspect of his heroine, and to allow it play only at the most unconscious levels of his work. To Catherine are given the anecdotal materials of all of Roché's women save one, and her character, although occasionally surprising, is not portrayed as double until the final scenes of the film. By comparison with Roché's model, Catherine seems remarkably stable. This idiosyncratic adaptation of the Greek myth once again insists on the darker, murderous double of woman, which Truffaut elects to downplay until the very end of his film. Instead of portraying her as a double, Truffaut prefers to have his heroine evolve into a sexual profligate (like Jim), gun-toting and murderous (like the soldiers who punctuate the central scenes of the film).

Once this aspect is unleashed, however, Catherine's repressed side emerges full-blown, and she reveals behavior that is increasingly sexual, "immoral" (from the point of view of the male double standard that "regulates" the film), and, ultimately, "male." Only in driving Jim into the river in her car does she finally establish her doubleness as masculine (driver of the car) and feminine (reevoking her earlier ondinelike plunge into the river), while simultaneously alluding to the Venus d'Ille's metallic embrace through the analogy of the metal framework of the automobile, which ensnares Jim in its mortal enclosure.

But the double has been there from the beginning, hidden (but not quite) behind an idealization of the statue of a Venus that causes us to "avert our gaze," and behind a copy of Goethe that functions, as J. B. Pontalis would phrase it, like "a screen memory, a witness both insignificant and precious, mentally or physically manipulable, where forever is hidden and preserved that which must not be lost."[36] Ultimately, however, the superposition of Goethe over Mérimée cannot succeed in completely repressing the larger and more troubling unconscious messages of Truffaut's film.

Chapter Two

Remapping Tenderness:
Louis Malle's Lovers
with No Tomorrow

> Our working relationships are extraordinarily intimate.
> We cross *La Carte de Tendre* with great strides, observa-
> tion, the *coup de foudre,* tenderness, quarrels,
> reconciliations.
> —*Louis Malle*

> She took my arm and we began to walk again, though I
> had no idea in which direction we were going. This voy-
> age and the lateness of the hour troubled me; I was al-
> ternately carried away by pride and desire and brought
> to my senses by reflection.
> —*Vivant Denon*

If Stanley Cavell is correct when he argues that "the ontological conditions of the motion picture reveal it as inherently pornographic,"[1]
then Louis Malle's *Les Amants* would be the quintessential film (or
perhaps the quintessential "*si*nema"?). Graced at its release in 1958
with a "steamy reputation,"[2] the film caused "shock and indignation
not only in professionally virtuous circles but also among more liter-
ate and broad-minded people whose romantic sympathies tend to be
shocked by its matter of fact amorality."[3] In particular, Malle's explicit
filming of the night of love between Jeanne (Jeanne Moreau) and
Bernard (Jean-Marc Bory) represented a piece of cinematic voyeurism without precedent in the classic cinema. Ellen Fitzpatrick, of
Films in Review, was so shocked by this sequence that she vented:
"The script of *The Lovers* is an unbelievable contrivance to lead up to
one scene in which the camera records at length the facial reactions of

a woman during cunnilingus. . . . Louis Malle and his company should be ashamed of such low grade, anti-social money grubbing."[4] The film's very steaminess seems, sadly, to have condemned it to neglect by serious critics, stereotyping it as simply one more film in which a woman's body is offered up as object to a voyeuristic (predominantly male) audience. As such, *Les Amants* would be a most unlikely candidate to have served as "the beginning of the New Wave in France," as its author claimed.[5] In fact, *Les Amants* constitutes a remarkably complex meditation on the relationship between cinema and voyeurism, a meditation that becomes "visible" only when the film is read through/as a screen for a series of allusions, collages, and intertexts.

As several of the film's reviewers noted, Malle's film is loosely based on Vivant Denon's short prose text *Point de lendemain,* but it is far from clear whether any of those who thought to mention the novel actually read it or thought about the relationship it might entertain with the filmic text.[6] Only one, John McCarten, noted that Malle "advanced Vivant's plot in time to the present day, but," he quickly complained, "the characters and their dilemmas have an old-fashioned air."[7] In fact, however, Malle all but abandoned Vivant Denon's plot in favor of Louise de Vilmorin's altogether different scenario, and thus (as is so often true of the new wave filmmakers) the film-text relationship is centered on something other than the anecdotal. Dominque Vivant Denon's *Point de lendemain* (1777) recounts a most surprising—and ambiguous—night of love experienced by the young narrator at the invitation of an older woman. Indeed, the narrator is, for all intents and purposes, carried off by this woman and taken to the chateau of her husband, far from Paris:

> "Might you have any plans for the evening? I advise you to forget them. No questions, resistance is useless." . . . I am gagged and thrust into her carriage, and well out of Paris without having had the chance to inform anyone of my predicament. . . . Things were beginning to seem quite ominous. I demanded to know the meaning of this foolishness ["Je demandais avec plus d'instance jusqu'où me menerait cette plaisanterie"].[8]

After a most ambiguous night spent with his abductress, wandering the grounds of the husband's chateau, the narrator learns the next day, from Mme de T——'s "official" lover, that he has been made (without ever being specifically told so) to play the role of Madame's lover in a comic play destined to render her husband ridiculous. Thus his entire connection to Mme de T—— seems to be circumscribed by artifice and by limits that have been preestablished in concert with her official lover. Despite the fact that the narrator is a man, all the power in this text is concentrated in the hands of a woman. The narrator takes his leave the next morning as if from "a beautiful dream," searching for the moral of the story, but in vain.

Louis Malle's adaptation of this classic (but little-known) text seems as much dominated by his suspicions of literary texts as by the text itself. He recently claimed that "the scenario is, after all, only a rough draft, a skeleton without flesh, a pious dream. It contains everything but the essential. . . . You notice only the rigidity and imperfections in a written text. Rather than stick to it, you have to adjust it, change it, cut it and turn it inside out ['inverser']."[9] Perhaps more like Denon's narrator than he cares to admit, Louis Malle can only feel ambivalence toward a form that simultaneously dominates and inspires him. His own liberation from the authority of Denon's text takes an unusual "turn."

With the help of Louise de Vilmorin, Malle constructed a scenario that eschewed the deception fundamental to Denon's novel in favor of a more (at least more apparently) sincere love story. Jeanne Tournier (Jeanne Moreau) has been leaving her husband in their home near Dijon to spend weekends with her friend Maggie in Paris. There she meets Raoul (J. L. de Villalonga), a tall, attractive polo player much admired by the Parisiennes, and becomes his lover. When her husband, Henri (Alain Cuny), learns of the affair, he forces Jeanne to invite Raoul to their country house for the weekend. Jeanne and Raoul set out separately from Paris, she in her Peugeot 203 and he, with Maggie, in his Jaguar. Jeanne has the "misfortune" to experience an automotive breakdown and is given a lift by the passing Bernard (Jean-Marc Bory) in his 2CV. Henri obligingly invites Bernard to dinner and, because it is so late, to stay the night. After dinner, with a fishing party announced for early the next morning, Jeanne refuses Raoul's noisy entreaty to spend the night with him and descends to the salon to refresh herself with a glass of water and an earful of Brahms. Unable to sleep, she wanders out into the moonlight, encounters Bernard again, falls into his arms, and leads him back to her room in the villa, where they enjoy a night of lovemaking. At dawn, Jeanne kisses her sleeping daughter goodbye, and she and Bernard depart on "un long voyage dont les incertitudes ils connaissaient," leaving behind the stunned trio of husband, official lover, and friend.

At the anecdotal level, then, only the most superficial of similarities link Malle's film with Denon's text, a comparison that of course raises the question why Malle elected to adapt Denon's novel only to betray it. Nor do the questions stop there. If Malle's purpose was to replace the evocatively ambiguous story of *Point de lendemain* with a more classic love story, one may well wonder why the result obeys so minimally the rules of the genre. There is a remarkably contrived quality to *Les Amants,* and at least one critic argues that "this unbelievably flat film is hardly redeemed by a rather sympathetic but aesthetically tame love scene."[10] Neither character, in other words, seems to be developed so as to arouse the usual romantic identification by the spectator. Ultimately, there are "too many other things going on" to provide a classic fit to the genre of film romance. If there are connections to Denon's text, they are not immediately evident to the viewer (as evidenced by the "incertitudes" of the film's critics) and can only be accessed through the light shed by unveiling the other major intertexts of this film.

If *Les Amants* conforms but minimally to the demands of classic romance, it is undoubtedly not only because, as Malle himself said, "I don't believe in following the rules of genre,"[11] but also because its director has opted instead to follow the *Rules of the Game.* Malle has often cited his debt to Renoir: "During this period I conceived my desire to make films," writes Malle of his years as a collegian. "I could explain it in many ways—to say, for example, like so many other French filmmakers, that it was after seeing *Rules of the Game* at a ciné-club. Because it's true, Renoir's film made an enormous impression on me."[12] And he adds elsewhere, "*Rules of the Game* is one of the most inspired movies in all its details I've ever seen. . . . I've seen it around fifteen times."[13]

The presence of *Rules of the Game* in *Les Amants* is overwhelming. Malle's film, like Renoir's, is the story of an elaborate triangle in which the supposed lover turns out to be a disappointment and is ultimately replaced by one less heroic, less overtly romantic. Both films turn on the transition from Paris urbanity to the "simplicity" of the country-side, and in both the husband unexpectedly extends an invitation to the supposed lover to join the couple at their country home. The reappearance of Gaston Modot, who played Schumacher in *La Règle du jeu,* at the steps of the country house in *Les Amants* certainly recalls his earlier presence in Renoir's classic, and if Malle does not include a generalized reference to the servants' mirroring of their masters, he manages neatly to echo Madame de la Bruyere's ignorance about the "negroes" in pre-Columbian art[14] with Maggie's stupid rejoinder at dinner about Raoul's "friends" in Russia, Dostoevsky, Gogol, and

Tolstoy. Malle succeeds quite adeptly in following this scripted allusion to the lack of cultural literacy of the *haute bourgeoisie* by a visual mimicry of the stage business in the corridor of Renoir's *La Colinière:* where Renoir develops a choreography of cacaphonic *bonsoirs*, focusing briefly on Robert's congratulations to Christine for passing the "test" of good breeding with Jurieu, Malle visually mimics this same "test" by focusing on Jeanne in the dimly lit corridor of the Dijon residence as she resists Raoul's entreaties and then panning to the slightly ajar door of Henri, who has been eavesdropping on this "tête à test." In each film the evening is cut short by the promise of game at dawn the following morning, but Malle advances his expedition to a moonlit version in which the rabbits and pheasants are replaced first by fish, which are liberated by Jeanne and Bernard, and then by the lovers themselves.

In all, Malle leaves little doubt that *Les Amants* is to be read through the "grid" of Renoir's "dance on a volcano,"[15] the most devastating social critique of France's *haute bourgeoisie* filmed before the Second World War. By establishing this allusion to Renoir, Malle situates his film somewhere *between* Hollywood romance and social criticism. If the night of love between Jeanne and Bernard and the "manipulative" use of Brahms's romantic sextet cast the film in a romantic mold,[16] the allusions to Renoir disturb that mold without totally destroying it. We cannot escape the uneasy feeling that there is something "behind" the reality portrayed, yet precisely what must yet be defined. Malle clearly does not develop the satire to the extent that Renoir does in *La Règle du jeu;* or if he does, he manages a degree of understatement that displaces the object of the film's satire from a broad attack on bourgeois immorality and hypocrisy to some much more subtle problem. Indeed, one cannot escape the sense that Renoir's film serves as much to screen as to reveal Malle's message.

One of the ways in which this shift can be felt or measured is through the doubling of the husband and lovers in each film. If Renoir's Robert is obsessed with mechanical toys to the extent that he is blinded to his wife's existence, Malle's Henri is portrayed as a journalist one of whose functions is to photograph and report on the activities of his wife and her friends in Paris. When she returns from the capital, he hands her a copy of his newspaper in which Raoul and Maggie are captured on film. Unlike Robert, Henri's function might be compared to that of the classic film director: to observe and imprison Jeanne within the limits of his "viewfinder" (journal). When she visits his offices, she is portrayed passing beneath the ink-stained impression of a large hand on the wall above her—a menacing reminder of the ubiquity of her husband's reach. At dinner, Henri is able to serve up stories of their relationship that restrict and subordinate her emotional life to his own. The rules of Malle's game seem, in other words, to center much more on bourgeois male possessiveness of woman through economic and scopic means than on generalized hypocrisy or chaos. This other message seems to be reinforced by the remarkably claustrophobic camera work in the chateau: doors are constantly being closed behind the characters, seeming to imprison them in the spaces chosen by the husband.

As official lover, Raoul is a trivialized version of the already juvenile Jurieux: instead of a transatlantic solo flight, Raoul can provide only an amusement park flight, during which he gazes fatuously at his new consort. His heroics, like Jurieux's, open the film, but they have come rapidly down to earth: a polo game replaces Jurieux's risk of life and limb for his mistress. Jeanne is, according to Maggie, supposed to be grateful merely to be seen with the likes of Raoul.

And Bernard? If at first he plays the free spirit who liberates Jeanne from an unhappy marriage and a fatuous lover, his presence seems to begin and end under the sign of ambiguity. He begins by treating Jeanne with disdain and by making some unpleasant sexual innuendos about her presence beside the road. That is to say, he resembles no one so much as Jeanne's husband in their first moments together. This similarity is all the more curious since Maggie will accuse Raoul of acting like Jeanne's husband later in the film. Although Bernard acts the relaxed, unassuming vagabond, he is quick to remind Jeanne that he belongs to the snobbish Dubois-Lambert family, her well-to-do cousins. Though he is only a student, his interest in archeology and his ambition to dig for clues to the past align him rather closely with the "social" researcher, Henri. It is not surprising, then, that in the scene following the dinner at the country villa, Bernard willingly engages Henri in a discussion of the recently unearthed Vase de Vix. Nor should we overlook the fact that Bernard intervenes in Jeanne's life while she is en route to Dijon in her "deux cent trois," an automobile whose name is curiously reminiscent of the French phrase *jamais deux sans trois,* that is, that bad things always happen in threes. This coincidence would make Bernard but a mere item in a series, an interpretation that is certainly allowed by the title of the film and is bolstered both by the doubling suggested above and the large number of disturbing repetitions presented by Malle in this film.

When Bernard arrives to succor Jeanne, stranded in her 203, he does so in a 2CV, "deux chevaux" a car whose name suggests Raoul's

PLATE 5.   Bernard (Jean-Marc Bory) arrives in his "deux chevaux" to succor Jeanne (Jeanne Moreau), stranded in her "deux cent trois," in Louis Malle's *Les Amants*. (Courtesy of the Museum of Modern Art Film Stills Archive.)

only activity, horses (see plate 5). Moreover, Bernard treats Jeanne's car exactly as though it were an animal in need of a vet. These three, Bernard, Henri, and Raoul, engage in the kind of specular relationship more often reserved for women in Hollywood cinema.[17] When Jeanne goes to bed with Bernard, her passion is certainly not reminiscent of her feelings toward Henri, yet many of her actions seem oddly repetitive. At one point, midway through the night, Jeanne pushes Bernard away as they lie in bed, exactly repeating the gesture she had employed with Henri when he invaded her bedroom after drinking. When they arise at dawn, Bernard commands, "Hurry up, Jeanne!" and moments later the door opens and Henri repeats this command word for word. When we first see Jeanne and Raoul together after the polo game, they pause at a white fence blocking their way into the paddock. When, later, Jeanne meets Bernard in the moonlit gardens of the country estate, the couple pauses at a gate barring their way in a striking reenactment of the earlier romance. In yet another curious repetition, Henri assigns to Bernard the "green room" upon his arrival at the Tournier estate, while moments later Raoul intones an apostrophe to "the green memories of our childhood loves" ("le vert paradis de nos amours d'enfance").

The most uncanny of all of these visual doublings involves the towel that is "passed" from Raoul to Maggie to Bernard. In their first scene together at the polo grounds, Jeanne leans against Raoul as he pulls a towel around his neck. Jeanne and Bernard will create the next instance of this gesture when he steps from the bath after their night of love. She not only entwines him with a white towel but shrouds his head with it in a gesture that recalls René Magritte's painting *Les Amants*, of two lovers, their heads shrouded in such a way as to render them veiled and anonymous (see plate 6).[18]

This visual collage must strike us with all the force of a bad dream, for it functions literally as a nexus of a system of concerns in this film that lie, like a palimpsest, just *behind* the images presented. At this juncture it is worth interpolating a number of comments that Louis Malle has made about his work. Regarding the function of repetition as an element of montage, Malle has stated, "Montage is a series of moments which do not, in and of themselves, signify, but rather participate in an organic structure—the film. Cinema is an art of relationships, like music. Every frame is a note that, when combined with the others, contributes to the composition of the sequence."[19]

That is to say that Malle encourages a musical reading of his films in which the "sense" of the work is carried by repetitive elements structured as "themes and variations" and ultimately structured as melodic lines. Elsewhere, Malle has insisted on the symbolic value of even the most realistic images: "There are several levels: the real, the dream world of the characters and how they invent the people surrounding them in a completely different way. I'm very turned on by this way of looking at the world . . . that behind reality there's something else and we're looking for it."[20] As for the symbolic value of repetition, Malle is categorical: "Repetition," he says, "is death."[21]

The scene of Jeanne's shrouding of Bernard thus unites in a nucleus the themes of love, repetition, death, and veiling. Magritte's presence here invites a meditation on cinema and painting coupled with the artist's preoccupation with the veiling nature of love. In Magritte's *Lovers,* the two figures look more like prisoners to be executed than lovers. That painting, itself such a visual medium, should be used to evoke veiling and blindness suggests not only the meta-artistic function of his work but also a deep concern with the voyeurism at work in any portraiture and especially any image of love or eroticism. Malle's incorporation of the Magritte scene transposes these same concerns to his film. The connection between the repetition of this scene (in the

PLATE 6. René Magritte's *Les Amants*. (Copyright 1991 Charly Herscovici/ARS, N.Y.)

film's diegesis) with the explicit reference to death (in the use of collage) should surprise no one familiar with Freud's thinking on this subject in *Beyond the Pleasure Principle*.[22] The very title of Freud's major opus on this problematic (re)places the viewer in a position of cognitive dissonance vis-à-vis the film's romantic genre signs: love at first sight, the night of love, flight to happiness. Cognizant of this more ominous scenario "beyond" the "reality" of the anecdote, the viewer may also be increasingly aware of numerous signs that have, from the very outset of the film, undermined its romantic plot. A second look at the film reveals an unusual preoccupation with mirroring and the problematics of identity for Jeanne.

The decision to *leave her child behind* must also become cause for alarm for those who would insert this film in the romantic genre. Indeed, Malle was acutely conscious of the disruption of pleasure this detail involved:

> In *The Lovers* you have this very conventional woman and suddenly practically by accident, she discovers that all of the values she's been living with are totally absurd. She's a woman—*she's not a child*. She's

not an adolescent—so she does something absolutely extravagant: she runs away with somebody she's met the night before, which in those days was very much of a scandal. I remember one scene that really shocked people—the distributors asked me to cut it. It was when she was leaving the house at dawn and she went to her daughter's bed and said goodbye to her. And they all told me: "You're going to antagonize everybody, why don't you cut that scene out? *Let's forget the child.*" But that's what made it so interesting, that was the really shocking proposition in *The Lovers:* that she had a child and that she would leave anyway.[23]

One of the reasons this scene takes on such importance in the film is that Malle has already suggested the insidious connections that, in binding Jeanne to her child, create a problematic identity for the mother. When Jeanne returns from her first trip to Paris, her daughter notices that her mother's hairstyle has changed and exclaims, "You've had your hair done just like my doll!" This phrase echoes, but with an infantilizing difference, Maggie's claim that "Love agrees with you. You're unrecognizable!" Both comments propel Jeanne into a series of meditations on her identity that are always accompanied by searching looks into the nearest available mirror. The first of these is her near-fatal glance into her car's rear-view mirror on the way home from Paris, followed by the chilling words, "I'm dead" ("Je suis morte"). If this phrase normally connotes "dead tired," its denotation may well serve here as the second connotation. The allusion to Cocteau's celebrated *Orphée* (1950) is unmistakable. In that earlier film, Cocteau pointedly used the rear-view mirror of Death's limousine to serve as the agent of Eurydice's death. In *Les Amants*, Malle's lover seems to short-circuit the earlier scene by shifting the rear-view mirror to focus on her own face, so that she nearly becomes the agent of her own death. Malle so insistently focuses on this question and on mirroring in this film that we may conclude that indeed Jeanne's "I" has undergone some terrible debilitation.

To Henri's startling question "Pourquoi n'es tu pas triste?" of the middle section of the film, Jeanne responds only with an unhappy cast of expression in her final scenes with Bernard. Ultimately the landscape in which their final flight is filmed itself takes on a heavy symbolic value. The bleak fields ringed with cypress trees, the riderless white horse that appears (out of Cocteau's play *Orphée?*) in the field beside them, and the rather ominous deep take of the church steeple behind them all contribute to an eerie sense that this adventure has already passed beyond the mirrors in which Jeanne so insistently

33

looks, into the space of the rear-view mirror—Cocteau's well-known symbol for the realm of death and the unconscious. Jeanne's last words in the film are, "Don't look at me!" Surely, behind the scandal of Jeanne's adulterous departure with Bernard there is another scene, one (or several) in which the geography has become entirely symbolic and seeing and being "scene"—and indeed obscene—are intricated in a new way.

In his review of *Les Amants* for the *New Yorker,* John McCarten asserted that "the characters and their dilemmas have an old-fashioned air."[24] It is not at all clear what McCarten may have meant by this statement, since nothing in the setting, style of clothing, manner of acting, or camera work seems deliberately anachronistic. I would submit, therefore, that the presence of Madeleine de Scudéry's *Carte de Tendre* displayed during the credits that open the film elicited (perhaps unconsciously) this observation (see plate 7). Were the presence of this seventeen-century artifact intended to *situate* the action of the film, McCarten's comment might be entirely well taken. The fact is, however, that the map's presence here cannot so easily be justified, yet stands enigmatically for some orientation that must be understood. It is easiest to dismiss this decor as a signal for "old-fashioned," because for years *la carte* has been uncritically assumed to represent a merely precious representation, nay, repression of human feelings. Undoubtedly, Moliere's famous satire of the *précieux* ideology in *Les Précieuses ridicules* has much to do with our blindness about this social and political movement.[25] Nevertheless, it is remarkable that of all those who have to date written on this film, only one thought the presence of *La Carte de Tendre* worth noting. Richard Roud, writing at the time of the film's release, commented, "The film is firmly in that great French tradition which began with Mlle. de Scudéry's 'Carte de Tendre'—against which, by the way, the titles are superimposed."[26] Mr. Roud does not attempt to define exactly what tradition Madeleine de Scudéry actually begins, but his "by the way" is endemic, and, if I may be permitted, epidemic. The phrase "by the way" is utterly dismissive—the fact *and* the map are assumed to be marginal: "*by* the way"—yet profoundly, if unconsciously, symbolic; "by *the way*" may signify the mapping and remapping of sensitivities that was central to the *précieux*'s enterprise, one that will be shown to be central to this film. This reaction may be said to be epidemic when we understand that "by the way" also signifies (by coextension with the map) the marginal location of woman in cinematic discourse, a position from which until very recently she has been unable to reoccupy the center.

Thus, while the collage of *La Carte de Tendre* onto, or rather

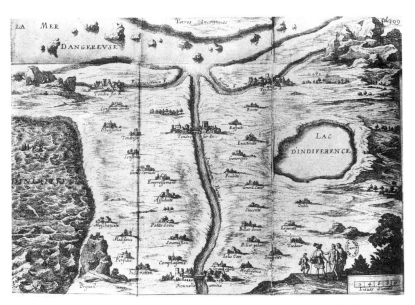

PLATE 7. *La Carte du pays de Tendre.* (Courtesy of the Harvard College Library.)

underneath, the titles of this film appears to reassure the viewer that Malle's film will enact a somewhat "old-fashioned" interpretation of human relationships, its presence anticipates the questions of feminine identity and voice so persistently alluded to in the mirrors and margins of this film. Recent criticism has, in fact, provided the first step in understanding the particular relevance of *la carte,* for far from serving as an innocuous pastime to the sensitivities of a group of "precious ladies," the map had, at its publication in Scudéry's *Le Grand Cyrus,* a powerfully political agenda. Of the *précieux* movement, Joan de Jean has elucidated "the often subversive role the most prominent of these female assemblies played in the political life of the *ancien régime*":

> Esteeming the level of politeness and wit there unacceptable, the marquise de Rambouillet . . . simply created an alternative space. . . . Within her blue room, the marquise created an alternative court, a new center of power, a place where power was exercised through conversation. . . . The salons were a world presided over by women. . . . *Préciosité* was much more than a literary moment of minor importance. It began as a feminist movement . . . and the précieuses made de-

mands of striking actuality: they sought for women what would today be termed control over their bodies.[27]

If the political relevance of *la carte* to Malle's *Les Amants* is not initially apparent, it is important to remember that the map is intimately connected to a revolution in discourse, and specifically discourse about the feminine body. If that discourse was historically restricted to "la chambre bleue," the map functioned, as did many maps of "nowhere" in the period, to perform a "semiotic transposition of a spatial organization of language, a discourse as space," that is to say, a utopia.[28] Louis Marin reminds us that just as Utopia was specifically unlocatable on a map of the Earth, its discursive status was intended to be ambiguous, sitting

> somewhere between yes and no, false and true, but as the double of figure, the ambiguous representation, the equivocal image of possible synthesis and productive differentiation. It points to a possible future reconciliation and a present acting contradiction of the concept and of history. . . . Utopia talks less about itself or the discourse it has . . . than about the very possibility of uttering such a discourse, of the status and contents of its enunciating position and the formal and material rules allowing it to produce some particular expression. . . . Produced in the distance between contradictory elements, it is the simulacrum of the synthesis, while yet signifying the contradiction that produced it.[29]

We should not miss the relevance of Marin's description of utopia as a *possibility of a discourse* and as a possibility of future reconciliation between conflicting ideologies. In a film whose central character is searching desperately for her identity *and* a discourse in which to present a possible identity, Marin's terms have a particularly powerful resonance. In her first presentation of the character of Jeanne, the feminine voice-off tells us,

> No, Jeanne Tournier knew nothing about polo; she simply went along with her friend, Maggie. Jeanne and Maggie, friends since childhood, had been born and raised in the provinces, but while Maggie had married in Paris and led a glamorous life there, Jeanne had remained behind in Dijon to become the wife of Henri Tournier, the publisher of the *Moniteur de Bourgogne*. Henri loved his wife but dedicated most of his time to this newspaper. Jeanne lived this way for several years. Encouraged by her husband, however, she had recently begun to spend

two weekends a month at Maggie's place in Paris. She enjoyed herself there, met all kinds of people, and received frequent compliments that reassured her.

Jeanne's identity as a provincial and wife has little to bolster it in any independent way. Thus, Henri may prefer his journal to his wife, but Jeanne can initially find no locus for her sense of self. She is "reassured" by the compliments she hears in Paris, an identity formed only by the sense others bestow on her. In this context, Maggie's contention that "love becomes you. You are unrecognizable ['méconnaissable']!" takes on ontological overtones. If love (or compliments in Paris) have the power to change her, Jeanne risks becoming simply an "other," even to herself. When she returns from Paris, her daughter compares her to her doll (another devastating commentary on Jeanne's identity). Henri, however, virtually obliterates her presence in the room with him until she directly intervenes in his pleasure, turning down the volume on the recording of Brahms that he uses to screen her out. When she discusses her experience in Paris, he interrupts her with such comments as "'Always' is a woman's word" or "You don't need style unless you're looking to be admired ['si tu ne tiens pas à être regardée']." In this last comment Henri deals a double blow to Jeanne's sense of self, first locating it within the gaze of others and then denying that there is any reason (now that she is married) to be looked at by others. Were she to follow this dictum, Jeanne would cease to exist altogether when Henri elects not to look at her, a tactic he pointedly chooses when she returns from Paris. Significantly, too, when he seeks to impress her with his powers of surveillance, he shows her a picture of her activities at the polo match in Paris from which she has been excluded! In the version we have just witnessed, Raoul receives the winner's cup in the presence of Maggie and Jeanne, but the *Moniteur*'s photo excludes the latter. Thus, almost immediately *Les Amants* centers on the relationship between identity, being seen, and being captured on film! Clearly, at the level alluded to by *La Carte de Tendre,* Malle's film addresses the very possibility of feminine subjectivity and feminine discourse. The presence of *la carte* at the outset thus constitutes at least an allusion to a utopian "solution" to Jeanne's impasse.

Marin's analysis of utopia suggests ways in which its "play" may be relevant to Jeanne's discursive impasse through the evocation of a *neutral space*—"neither masculine nor feminine. It is, rather, outside gender, neither active nor passive, but outside voice"—in which the possibility of a discourse may be conceived.[30] In arguing that "the neutral is the condition of possibility for producing and giving birth to the other side of the royal position of mastery and domination," Marin relates the utopian (in this case, the genre of *La Carte de Tendre*) not only to discourse itself but to a subversive discourse that seeks to engender the voice of the other in opposition to the established voice of mastery. Thus, to Henri's "You don't need style unless you're looking to be admired" the voice-off comments by noting that "Henri had seen nothing, noticed nothing." It is no wonder that Jeanne needs, pointedly, to consult a mirror both before and after this ontologically devastating encounter with her husband.

The question that haunts this entire film is, "Where will Jeanne find the discourse necessary to engender a real identity?" Again, the topos engendered by the utopian map may hold the key to our understanding of the way in which this might be conceived. It will not necessarily "take place" in the diegetic space of the film, for the power relationships are clearly established.[31] Now, as a figure aimed at consciousness raising, *La Carte de Tendre* can be read as an allegory of desire and of power, but in this case desire with a difference and power within deference. Claude Filteau reminds us that *la carte* aimed ultimately at establishing a contract (called "Nouvelle Amitié" on the map) that would give women as much to gain from friendship as men. Thus, the map itself signifies an egalitarian project couched in geometric and discursive terms:

> Designed by women, the map of tenderness is addressed to men. . . . Its code, in fact, is meant to imitate another code: that of "la conversation spirituelle" to which women alone hold the key. . . . Thus, the essence of the code can be learned by men only by a sort of "devenir femme."[32]

How may we then understand the application of *La Carte de Tendre* to *Les Amants?* It will be my contention here that in creating the order of discourse particular to this film, Louis Malle has, indeed, undergone something of the "devenir femme" implicitly necessitated by the map. Through his collaboration with Louise de Vilmorin, he seems to have created a film able to entertain a reaction to the male discourse that has dominated cinema from its earliest forms. And yet this more feminine reading of the map and film must first pass through and behind a superficial first impression to reach its *sub*versive power.

If we look again at the position of *la carte* in the film, we realize that it is a virtual collage, on which the name Jeanne Moreau first appears with no reference to her relation to anything (film, name of character, other characters) except the map itself. The impression established, whose pertinence will be appreciated below, is that the map is somehow the map *of* Jeanne Moreau, in the same way that a map bearing the word "France" would be assumed to be the map of that country. But the map itself functions as *collage*, whereby the "glue" that joins it together with the rest of this film has the potential to fix our gaze, in Tom Conley's words, "on the edge of the combination, affixes itself to what binds" map and film together, giving them "a plastic and very material substance they lacked before. Collage literalizes metaphor, turning the hidden moment of comparison into the sight of the bond that holds them together." In this sense, "collage binds the phantasm of the body to the register of seeing and reading." Conley also argues that since collage involves "cutting and decapitation . . . of members from given works sliced and lopped off, then glued and bound back over each other," this body phantasm reevokes castration as a problematic.[33]

That *La Carte de Tendre* should be the collaged element and the first element seen in this film is as uncanny as the allusion to Magritte's *Les Amants* discussed above. Although the drawing (see plate 7) classically functions as a political, symbolic, and utopic geography of this film (both in ways that have been discussed and in others yet to be introduced), its status as collage suggests its function as an analogue of the female body's exterior and interior anatomy![34] If Claude Filteau's interpretation of map as anatomy is limited to a "an anatomical dissection of the liver in which the agitation of the humors can be translated by the agitation of the seas,"[35] the author's own vocabulary betrays a much more erotic and voyeuristic program for the map in such terms as "the imaginary scene that channels the desiring look into this sort of window framed by the map and seems to organize the only possible opening into an inaccessible 'elsewhere.'"[36]

Encouraged by the no doubt unconscious doubling of Filteau's interpretation, we may read the map as a *coupe anatomique* not of the liver but of the female reproductive organs (see plate 8).[37] Moreover, in its particular framing and abstract design, the map bears striking resemblance to two other paintings by Magritte which mobilize remarkably voyeuristic (and sexist) views of the female anatomy: *Le Viol* (!) and *La Représentation* (!!) (see plates 9 and 10). Notably, in the first of these, the title suggests that the real rape of woman begins with the fantasmagoric substitution of body for mind; in the second, the exposed body foregrounds what Freudian discourse would undoubtedly label "castration" or "manque du phallus," in a frame that has

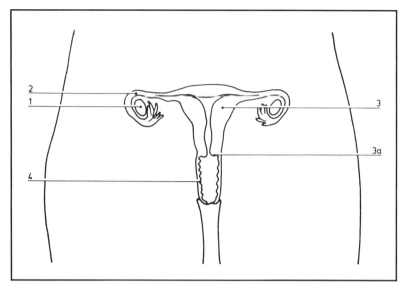

PLATE 8.   Anterior view of the female reproductive tract. 1, ovary; 2, fallopian tube; 3, uterus; 3a, cervix; 4, vagina. (Reprinted from *The Human Body on File,* ed. Ruth Swan [New York: Facts on File, 1983], 10.008.)

ironically decapitated the woman's head. The conjunction of these three topoi suggests a critique of a chauvinist ideology that equates loss of phallus with loss of mind. At this, most primary level of anatomical reading (which, I reiterate, responds to *la carte*'s status as collage and as "a challenge to men"), Malle's insertion of the map into the film evokes questions of interiority and exteriority, the separation of mind/discourse from body as scene, and the questions of lack, voyeurism, and the fetishization of the female body. If the map is pertinent to the discourse and problematics of *Les Amants,* it is in part because it unites in a single topos the interior with the exterior of the female body, for these have rigorously, if unconsciously, been split off from each other by the genre of Hollywood romance from its inception.

Indeed, Jeanne's position *within* the diegetic discourse of the film is much like that described by Kaja Silverman in her analysis of what she terms "dominant cinema." Women, argues Silverman, have suffered "anatomical deficiency and discursive inadequacy" from the earliest of Hollywood fiction films.[38] It is Silverman's contention that women's place in dominant cinema is the result of a complex arrange-

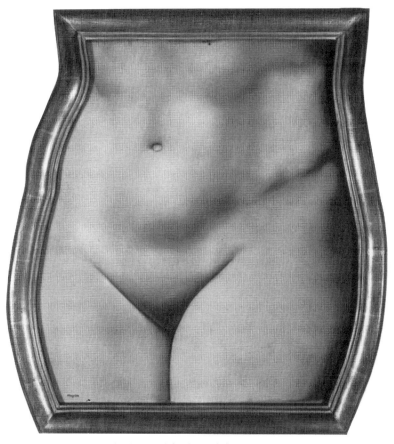

Plate 9.   René Magritte's *Le Viol.* (Copyright 1991 Charly Herscovici/ARS, N.Y.)

ment of male projection of lack. Silverman reminds us that Freud's theory of castration is too narrowly attached to the phallus and fails to link the later discovery of castration by the child to earlier losses. Lacan has, of course, argued that what Freud calls castration is really synonymous with all the early divisions experienced by the subject (whether male or female), including separation from the womb, from the breast, from feces, and, ultimately, from unicity of self in the mirror stage. Rediscovering that sense of lack in the oedipal phase, the male child merely projects onto the mother the lack he has already experienced. Thus, the normal male subject is constructed not on

41

PLATE 10.   René Magritte's *La Representation*. (Copyright 1991 Charly
Herscovici/ARS, N.Y.)

plenitude (the possession of the phallus) but rather on the denial of
lack and the projection of that lack onto the female. As Silverman
rephrases this, "The male subject proves his symbolic potency
through the repeated demonstrations of the female subject's symbolic
impotence."[39]

Cinema seems to have replayed this scenario in general terms, because like the child's entry into language (which, we remember, involves the subject's loss of self to the Other's order), cinema excludes the viewer from the point of discursive origin, evoking the isolation from the phallus (Lacan's "nom du père" or "the absent one," the paternal signifier upon which the child relies for his identity). Every frame line and every cut reevokes, according to Silverman, the male viewer's sense of exclusion from the site of production, arousing anxiety and fear.[40] It is her contention that the male viewer defends against this anxiety by identification with the male characters in the diegesis and by projecting his feelings of lack onto women in the diegesis in the form of a sadistic voyeurism, sadistic because it "excludes women from symbolic power and privilege; places her in a passive relation to classic cinema's scopic and auditory regimes. *Her* gaze is depicted as partial, flawed, unreliable and self-entrapping. Her words are even less her own than her looks." The male voice is always located at the point of textual origin, while establishing the diegetic containment of the female voice. Thus woman is confined "within" the story, while the male voice is allowed to move freely within and without this diegetic enclosure. The female voice is thus "identified with an intractable materiality and its consequent alienation from meaning," while the male subject "poses as the voice that constrains and orchestrates the feminine 'performance.'"[41]

In terms strikingly similar to the language used by Joan De Jean and Claude Filteau to describe the project of *La Carte de Tendre*, Silverman argues for a reorganization of the acoustic apparatus of cinema away from "a 'masculinization' of the female subject" and toward "a 'feminization' of the male subject—a much more generalized acknowledgement . . . of the necessary terms of cultural identity."[42] The topos of "devenir femme" of *La Carte de Tendre*, a kind of discursive neutrality sought, according to Louis Marin, by every topos of utopia, does indeed establish a case of "striking actuality" for *la carte*'s project.

Less immediately clear is the particular way that the project could be formed in terms of a discourse available to women in "dominant cinema." As Pascal Bonitzer has argued, the use of voice-off in cinema has, by definition, by its position in the acoustic ontology of the form itself as well as by its history of use in the medium, a kind of vested position of authority that is not open to diegetic contestation, since "it reflects from a place that is absolutely indeterminable. In this sense transcendent. . . . In so far as it arises from the field of the Other, this voice-over is assumed to know; such is the essence of its power."[43] Thus, as Silverman argues, "to disembody the female voice would be to challenge every conception by means of which we have known woman within Hollywood film since it is precisely *as body* that she is constructed there."[44]

There can be no doubt that it is in this confluence of Malle's use of *La Carte de Tendre* with the problematics of modern woman's (cinematic) identity that we can locate the most significant project of *Les Amants*. Indeed, *as body,* Jeanne Moreau seems entirely at peril in the world of her lovers, a world that allows her almost no access to a discourse that is not restricted or alienated. And yet *beyond* this con-fined and limited body and language, there is a voice-off: in a gesture that is rare in the Western romantic genre, a feminine narrator, one whose voice is disembodied, speaks with the kind of authority that transcends the particular limitations of body and discourse of the character. It is important to note that at no time in the film does this voice use the pronoun "I"; rather, she maintains her narrative distance and authoritative control.[45] Thus, at times when Jeanne is most de-based within the diegetic topos of the film, the voice-off maintains the (absent) presence to comment on that very debasement. The fact that this voice is Jeanne Moreau's produces an even more powerful effect, for her extra-diegetic status accords her a quasi-Brechtian distancia-tion on the events within the diegesis of the film. Immediately after the scene in which she returns to Burgundy from Paris for the first time, and in which Henri has just ridiculed her diegetic voice, the voice-off in turn condemns Henri for his obtuseness: "Henri had seen nothing, noticed nothing." If Henri attacks Jeanne's discourse within the film, the voice-off turns the tables and critiques the very qualities that would not only make Henri a "master" (his ability to control by surveillance) and a journalist (his perspicacity) but also confirm his status as male (the eye as phallus, the eye as the primary organ of cinematic voyeuristic enjoyment). Here the feminized voice-off plays a transcendent role, reorganizing the status of control and controlled within the diegesis. No longer simply interior to that diegesis, the voice-off plays with the plenitude of interior and exterior. These, we should recall, are precisely the terms evoked by *la carte*'s emblematic position in the film as well as by the allusions to Magritte's superposed collages of mind as body, and exterior versus interior anatomy of the sexual organs implied by, on the one hand, the map's evocation of the female reproductive system and, on the other, the frame and geog-raphy's visual evocation of the Magritte partial nude entitled *La Representation*.

At another entirely devastating moment in the film, following the dinner during which Maggie has rendered the feminine discourse truly imbecilic and Henri has instituted an authoritative lie that would subjugate Jeanne's desire and romantic life to his own, the voice-off intervenes again, from a position of greater (because extra-diegetic) authority than Henri's, to comment on Jeanne's position:

> Her universe was collapsing. With an odious husband, an almost ridiculous lover, Jeanne, who had believed herself in a drama, now found herself in a mere vaudeville show. She had a sudden desire to be someone else ["quelqu'un d'autre"].

Whereas Jeanne has no possibility within the diegesis of the film to reduce Henri to his proper place nor to restore Raoul to a position that would make her choice of him acceptable, the voice-off has the power to shift the very terms of the play from *drame* to *vaudeville,* thereby reducing Henri's seriousness to play and Raoul's ridicule to normal routine. What is more important, the voice-off establishes for the first time in the film a desire on the part of the female protagonist that goes beyond body and discourse to her very ontological status. She did not suddenly wish, we are told, for a *bon mot* that would put Henri in his place, or sexual satisfaction with Raoul, she wishes to be *someone else,* and it is precisely in the dynamics of that wish that the film turns. If granted, her wish would not masculinize her, but would reorganize the gender roles around her, for being someone else would mean for all to accept their common subjectivity and interdependence.

Perhaps Jeanne cannot exist without the ontological support of others and without the ontological tranquilizer of her frequent glances in the mirror, but neither can the male subjects in this film. Thus, when she leaves the chateau under the intensity of the moonlight, her encounter with Bernard is cast (again by the voice-off) in terms that accentuate both Jeanne's change of identity and her own equal control of the look. When Bernard first emerges from the darkness beside Jeanne, the voice-off notes, "You would have thought he was lying in wait for her ['la guettait'], and yet he seemed as if he didn't recognize her ['ne semblait pas l'avoir reconnue']." This time, Jeanne is "méconnaissable" not because love has worked some magic but more likely because she herself has desired this otherness—a shift of ontology that is crucial to this dynamic. As they walk side by side, Jeanne intones a hymn to the night: "Night is beautiful!" and Bernard imitatively adds, "Night is woman." Now this response is remarkable because it not only functions as an iterative gesture to Jeanne's words, reversing the normal order of discourse, but also develops a metaphor

45

that at once empowers woman and *removes her from a merely specular position!* The sense of the metaphor clearly establishes woman as she who surrounds and engulfs (rather than being surrounded by) man; but night also implies darkness, absence of the visual empowerment by which man governs woman's subjectivity (in traditional Freudian terms) and operates his voyeuristic pleasure, that is, cinema itself.

The next visuals reinforce this shift of discursive and political power, for Malle inserts a reference to *Le Rouge et le noir* that resubordinates Bernard *as student* to Jeanne as older woman in alluding to Julien Sorel's childish resolution to grasp Madame de Rênal's hand as the clock strikes ten or else to climb to his room and shoot himself.[46] In *Les Amants* this allusion to Stendhal is constituted by a mysterious ringing sound (subsequently revealed to be the sound of their glasses touching in the night) followed by a closeup of their fingers closing together. The voice-off again consecrates the sense of this visual allusion: "Love can be engendered by a glance. Jeanne felt her discomfort and her modesty dying away. She could no longer hesitate. One should never resist happiness." Given that the look referred to here is established by context to be Jeanne's and not necessarily Bernard's, Jeanne seems to take control of the scopic power, just as the voice-off has coopted the ordinarily male discourse. It is not Bernard who overcomes any hesitation and resistance to happiness here but very pointedly Jeanne as (tentatively) empowered subject. Most important of all, for the first time in this film a change in discursive power results in the "usurpation" of action by a woman.

If we return to the "source" of the film, Vivant Denon's *Point de lendemain,* and view it, too, through the optic of the utopian play offered by the presence of *La Carte de Tendre,* we should not be surprised to discover a similar dynamic at work in the novel. In Malle's rereading of Denon's text we can now discern a disdain for plot (undoing the traditional lines of authority of the adapted text) in favor of a reading of the novel that emphasizes both the feminine and the cinematic![47] If Denon (unlike Malle) employs a male narrator for his text, that narrator admits early on that he is entirely at the mercy of his more experienced abductress. As in Malle's film, their night of love is organized by Mme de T—— to figure a topology of female desire and discourse. Hers is an itinerary of tenderness rather than phallic desire and prefers the extension of discourse (on her terms) to rapid (or even eventual) consummation of love (a traditional end point in a male scenario).

After their brief introductions to Mme de T——'s husband, the lady takes the young narrator for a tour of the grounds in the moon-light:

> The night was glorious, half-lighting the objects around us as if to give more play to the imagination. The terraced gardens of the chateau sloped down to the banks of the Seine, whose many sinuosities created picturesque rustic islets that varied the landscape and increased the charm of this beautiful spot. (PL, 31)

This tableau alone could easily serve as the primary foundation for Malle's nightscape, which emphasizes the imaginary ("ne les voile que pour donner plus d'essor à l'imagination") over the realistic. Also, the word *voiler* takes on added significance when read in the context of (1) the question of veiling of truth practiced by Mme de T—— in the novel; (2) the issue of voyeurism and veiling of the woman's body posed by the traditional love novel; and (3) by extension, the questions of veiling raised in *Les Amants* and the Magritte paintings alluded to in that film. Here, "laisser entrevoir les objets" has a keyhole, voyeuristic connotation that applies equally well to Denon's and Malle's projects. Now, during their nocturnal wanderings, Mme de T—— begins to weave a spell of love on the young narrator. They enter a topography arranged by the woman, which seems always to move back and forth between the real and the imaginary, between the physical and the psychological:

> She had taken my arm and we began walking again, *but I was unable to tell what direction we were taking.* What she had just told me, . . . the traveling I'd done, and the late hour all confused me; I was by turns carried away by pride and desire and brought up short by reflection. Yet I was too moved to pay close attention to what I was feeling. . . . A few words from my companion brought me to my senses ["me firent *revenir à moi*"]. (PL, 39–40, italics mine)

Quite obviously, Denon has mixed exterior and interior maps here, in such a way that the confusion of their route is mirrored by the narrator's comings and goings between desire and reflection. We might dismiss this as a typical eighteenth-century conceit were it not that Malle's projection of the text gives it resonances with the problematics of both *La Carte de Tendre* and cinema as a medium. As the narrator moves in this "voyage" between desire and reflection, the traveler through "le pays de Tendre" moves between questions of exteriority and interiority realizable only within the discourse imposed by a "feminized" reading of the map. So, too, is the spectator in cinema transported between screen as desire and its reflection of our own desire.[48] Mme de T—— gets our narrator so lost in this labyrinth that he becomes simultaneously sighted and blinded by her stratagem:

> I felt one blindfold removed from my eyes, but I couldn't see the veil that still covered them . . . they (my captors) seemed distressed to have troubled me and to have perhaps gone too far in a tableau that might seem suspicious, since it was the work of a woman. (PL, 42)

In anecdotal terms, Mme de T—— has revealed the capriciousness of his current lover in Paris (and thus "stripped the blinders from his eyes") while at the same time cleverly blinding him to her own (entirely incomprehensible) intentions. Denon suggests that his narrator may indeed be undergoing some sort of transformation of point of view because of his submission to the new rules of feminine discourse. Nor can we, as "readers" of Louis Malle, fail to be struck by the analogy between Denon's language and that used by Baudry in describing the relationship between Plato's cave, Freudian theory, and the psychology of the cinema.[49] If Baudry is correct, Plato's prisoners of the cave actively prefer their "blindness" to the light of "reality" because of their need for the illusions of the cave and, in Freudian terms, their pleasure of regressing into a darkened and confining space in which they can recreate the dreams of infancy. Denon's older woman engages her childlike protégé in an incomprehensible voyage of illusions that parenthetically situates them on *La Carte de Tendre:*

> I understood nothing of what she was telling me. We set out on the highway of feeling and started from such a vertiginous place ["le reprenions de si haut"] that it was impossible to gauge our itinerary or destination ["d'entrevoir le terme du voyage"]. (PL, 42)

In this feminized voyage, the narrator loses his bearings, but as readers of *La Carte de Tendre,* we can easily identify that place as simultaneously "Les Terres Inconnues" at the very top of the map and, following the logic of "reprendre d'en haut," at the beginning of the text. Topology and discourse are intermingled in the utopian play of Mme de T——'s design. Needless to say, the emotion of this "hauteur" is dizziness. This same passage continues,

> In the midst of our metaphysical debate, I caught sight of a summer
> house. . . . What a pity that we did not have the key! In sweet conver-
> sation ["tout en causant"] we approached . . . and found it open. It
> lacked only daylight. But darkness had its own charms; moreover, I
> knew what charms were soon to embellish it. (PL, 43)

Again we find a remarkable confluence of the map and cinema: that
which necessitates a key but is already open to those who approach
"tout en causant." Its darkness promises the charms of those who will
enter in search of the ever-receding object of desire. This pavilion
seems to house a kind of magic lantern show!

> Less turbulent now, our inebriated senses left us speechless. . . . The
> darkness was too intense to make out any object, but through the
> transparent veil ["crêpe transparent"] of a beautiful summer's night,
> our imagination created an *enchanted* island. The river seemed covered
> with cupids ["amours"] playing in its eddies and the far bank peopled
> with lovers. (PL, 45, 47)

Notably, like the cinema, this pavilion proffers fantastic images of
lovers and precludes "l'usage de la voix." But Mme de T—— quickly
leads her young protégé away from this "dangereux séjour" where
"desire is ceaselessly reborn and we are powerless to resist" (PL, 48).

As if this first evocation of the cave of illusions is not sufficient,
Mme de T—— seeks out another space, this one even more elusive
and illusive than the previous one: "We wandered through a labyrinth whose key even my mistress had lost . . . 'What designs do you
have on me? What shall I become?'" cries the narrator (PL, 57), like
Jeanne, fearful for his identity. Heart beating "like an initiate in a new
rite before the celebration of a great mystery," the narrator begins to
"believe in sorcery" as the door of this new region opens. Like Jeanne
in *Les Amants,* the narrator is "no longer himself," but "ravi" by this
initiation—a position more feminine than masculine by traditional
genre standards. For the second time in *Point de lendemain,* we find a
remarkable complex of the utopian (nowhere) and the cinematic in
this

> vast prison of mirrors on which designs were so artistically painted
> that their *repetition produced the illusion of everything they represented.* I
> could discover no source of light, and yet a gentle and heavenly light
> penetrated each object according to its need to be perceived. This

pleasure palace ["ce lieu de délices"] was illumined as if by magic. (PL, 61)

The narrator's sole object in this magic space is to "adore" his guide, and hardly has he done so when he finds himself ushered out, as if at the end of a film! "Everything vanished with the speed that our waking destroys a dream" (PL, 65). Moments later, strolling in the gardens of the chateau, the narrator learns from the lady's lover that he has been but a pawn of Mme de T—— in an elaborate game staged for her husband. "I felt instantly my new role," he remarks. "Every word was loaded ['en situation']" (PL, 68). But the narrator is not the only dupe in this arrangement. The self-satisfied official lover, who vaunts his ability to "fix that woman," has been manipulated just as cleverly by Mme de T——. At the moment of taking his leave, Mme de T—— says to him, "Adieu, Monsieur, I return you now to your mistress in a condition more tender, more delicate, and more sensitive ['plus tendre, plus délicat, et plus sensible'] than I found you" (PL, 77). The narrator, in other words, has received an initiation into "le pays de Tendre." "I looked for the moral of this adventure but could find none" (PL, 78). The moral, to be sure, is not so easily locatable for a man, and outside the utopian space of her *chambre obscure*. In this very site, Louis Malle has reread Denon in such a way as to make the contrast of the exterior pavilion and the interior chamber into an opposition between masculine and feminine cinematic discourses.

Throughout the rest of their nocturnal adventure, it is Jeanne who very pointedly leads the way for Bernard through a terrain itself become doubly *hers*. Following the voice-off's statement of permission, Jeanne leads Bernard through a field that looks like nothing so much as the areas sketched on *La Carte de Tendre* to indicate uninhabited terrain. Their subsequent itinerary could easily be mapped entirely on *la carte*. Indeed, Jeanne leads Bernard to the banks of a river and then across a dam constructed to look very much like the bridge on *la carte* located in the town of "Nouvelle Amitié." There they enact a symbolic liberation of Henri's netted fishes, but not until Bernard looks to Jeanne for permission to do so.[50] Next, she leads him back across the river into a small boat, in which they drift downstream, presumably toward "Tendre sur Inclination." No trouble reaching this destination, which seems to include the chateau (now guarded by Henri's dalmatian), entered by the back door.

If Utopia is more clearly representable as a map than as a discourse, it is because maps do not topologize the fourth dimension. Utopia is not just a space outside of "known" space, it is outside of time as well.[51] Having stopped the clock, Jeanne leads the film's viewer through a reorganization of scopic dominance. For the first time in cinema, a love scene does not concentrate on a woman's body, but on her face and hands (the opposite visual representation to Magritte's *La Representation*). When the lovers undress and dress, the camera captures the man rather than the woman in this act. The scene's eroticism does not focus on, or end on, (male) orgasm but rather on tenderness, laughter, generalized touch. Most of the words in the scene are Jeanne's, not Bernard's. As in the exterior night scenes, the topos of the bedroom registers a significant shift in scopic and discursive dominance unseen in previous romantic films yet predictable in utopian spaces.

It is worth noting here, however, that virtually every reader of *la carte* has misread the ultimate direction of the lovers' progression. Filteau, for example, graphs the various important regions of the map in apparent ignorance of the fact that the "Inclination Fleuve" flows *toward*, and not away from, "La Mer Dangereuse," a direction that would entirely reverse previous "comfortable" interpretations of this topography, which locate its goal as "Nouvelle Amitié." The *précieuses* evidently understood all too well that it is *after* reaching "Tendre sur Inclination" that the real test of a relationship begins, and for this reason they labeled the waters beyond it "La Mer Dangereuse." Indeed, after their night of love Jeanne and Bernard set out again, and the voice-off comments,

> They were leaving for a long voyage they knew would be uncertain. They did not know if they would ever again regain the happiness of their first night together. Already at this dangerous hour of the morning ["à l'heure *dangereuse* du petit matin"] Jeanne had been plagued with self-doubt. She had brought little with her, but she regretted nothing.

At the far shores of "La Mer Dangereuse" on *La Carte de Tendre* lie "Les Terres Inconnues." It is very likely that in conceiving a utopia of relationships in which women might stand to gain as much as men, the *précieuses* felt unable to chart any specific course beyond the trajectory from "Nouvelle Amitié" to "Tendre sur Inclination." Beyond lay either marriage or social opprobrium, both entirely controlled by a patriarchal set of laws that radically alter the set of guidelines established within the utopia of "Tendre." The night of love for Jeanne and Bernard is punctuated by "l'heure *dangereuse*" (an adjective that is rarely applied to this noun in French literature) and leads only to the "incertitudes" of broken conventions. It is thus hardly surprising that Jeanne should burst into tears and Bernard wish that it could be "night all the time." This is undoubtedly, too, partly the cause of the imagery of death that surrounds these final scenes: their repeated passage into mirrors, the white riderless horse by the side of the road, the church tower, Bernard's repetition of Jeanne's earlier glance into the car's rear-view mirror, and, most significantly of all, Jeanne's attempt to stop time altogether by stopping the pendulum of the clock in her bedroom.[52]

Jeanne's penultimate line in the film is thus, "It's crazy, but I am no longer myself" ("C'est idiot, je sais, mais je ne suis plus moi-même"). Bernard could well say the same (although the film does not go quite that far, nor is it his film). It is this metamorphosis in Jeanne that allows her final command, "Ne me regardez pas!" to be directed with a newfound authority to the film's voyeuristic audience. If the film reduces "les amants"—Henri, Raoul, and Bernard—from positions of authority to mere items in a series, it is primarily to accommodate the radical shift in register that is produced in the utopian play of Jeanne's reordered space. That would also explain the ubiquity of the mirrors in the final scenes of *Les Amants*. Louis Marin reminds us that

> from the neutral state to neutral discourse we see that by overcoming the conflicting oppositions through the use of synthesis whose discursive neutrality allows for the neutralization of the opposites, a position of judicial force is reproduced. An authoritative position of speech and ideological organization are created that subject the conflicting parties or polemical discourses [in this case male vs female discursive power]; yet this position is the simple "hypostacized" reflection of them. These present parties would seem to turn on themselves, unrecognizable, to display the mirror image of their opposition.[53]

Several years after completing *Les Amants,* Malle confessed that he had wanted to work on "a classic theme of utopia" but that it was merely "un joli rêve."[54] "Utopia," he explained, "is essentially a moral lesson. It is a kind of mind game which consists of saying 'You live in a society that doesn't satisfy you. So here is a better system.' Ever since Plato, utopias have been conceived in troubled times by idealists in search of a golden age" (54). This suggests that unlike the narrator of Denon's novel, Malle *has* found the moral in the work and has re-exposed it through a powerful reinterpretation of *Point de lendemain.* Indeed, Malle appears to have attempted, like the ideal reader of *La Carte de Tendre,* a "devenir femme," which would make him more like Jeanne than like Denon's narrator. During his work of filming, he once said, "Our working relationships are extraordinarily intimate. We cross *La Carte de Tendre* with great strides, observation, *coup de foudre*, tenderness, quarrels, reconciliations. This passionate complicity of a few weeks is easier for me with women and adolescents" (67).

To be sure, Malle knows that for the spectator, "a film is someone's dream projected onto the screen in a darkened hall. The spectator, alone in all the world in his seat, is a voyeur. He watches the images, he adds to these his own fantasies, his mood of the moment, and makes them his" (69). But Malle also strives to open his spectator to something new:

> The cinema I love is not addressed to either logic or reason. It touches us, invades us, provokes us, it is a deforming mirror in which the spectator looks at himself. My characters . . . no longer follow social rules and thus cast a new and lucid light on society, because they're outside it. . . . I have an intimate conviction that I will never be for established order. (70)

This conviction is intimate undoubtedly for two reasons: Malle's belief concerns intimacy because it seeks the establishment of new rules within some utopian ideal of human relationships. But it is intimate also because he identifies so closely with his films and, curiously, with the character of Jeanne in this one. Having fought his distributor to keep the scene in which Jeanne enters her daughter's room to say goodbye at the conclusion of her night of love, Malle unwittingly confessed to a similar pattern in his own life. "I try to live between my films, I take the time to love. I have two children, and I never tire of looking at them and touching them. And then, I'm off again . . . I try to keep this dream alive" (72).

"My characters," he adds, "follow solitary paths. They are almost always marginal, or have broken off from others. Whether historic accident, rite of passage, interior crisis, something always happens to them to make them leave their path ['ils sortent de leur route']" (70). Malle's own break with the accepted rules of the game of discourse, whether itself an historical accident, a rite of passage, or an interior crisis, certainly allows him and his viewers to go "off road" into the "devenir femme" called for by *La Carte de Tendre*. Perhaps, after all, he has one too many *elles* in his name to be simply *male*. Perhaps that *elle* is *Louise* de Vilmorin, who wrote the screenplay for *Les Amants*. Whatever the cause, Malle has rewritten cinema—and literature—in ways that lead from "Tendre sur Inclination" to "Les Terres Inconnues."

Chapter Three

Rebecca's Bad *Dream: Speculations on/in Resnais's* Marienbad

> *Marienbad* is a fairly opaque story of the sort we experience during our crises of passion, in all our emotional life. . . . The unconscious is also a spectacle; perhaps the fundamental spectacle.
> —*Alain Resnais*

> I used to think I was one step beyond . . . in another world from the others. I dreamed once about a little girl who fell under the bed. They looked for her but they couldn't find her. She was in another dimension . . . . She screamed, but nobody heard.
> —*Sandra, a victim of incest*

As one of the most intriguing cinematic reconstructions of "terres inconnues" ever attempted, Alain Resnais's *L'Année dernière à Marienbad* has challenged and baffled its viewers since its release. Indeed numerous hypotheses have been advanced as to the meaning of the images. There is a tendency in much of the writing on *Marienbad* to follow Alain Robbe-Grillet's lead in believing the images to be nothing more than images and their reality only the reality of film.[1]

Now one scenario concerning Marienbad concerns an attempt at persuasion that seems to have no precise location in time and even less so in space. It seems to center on a discourse begun but interrupted, one that involves, at every turn, a question of mirrors and a radical questioning of identity. Marienbad *may* have been the location, but this is uncertain. When reference is made to a beginning point, that point suddenly loses its hold on reality and merges, as if by magic, with some later point. The words that were supposed to have been uttered are nowhere to be found. The words that are found appear in some way alien to the logic of chronology. And looking for them seems only to lead to a trace, absence, and confusion. What might have been originary refers back to something no longer there. What is assumed to have been there as originary and founding can no longer be trusted. Games have been played that lead only to more confusion. Those who might have been trusted must be doubted. Authority and authorship are mere figures in this play of mirrors from which no logical egress seems possible.

This scenario was not composed by Alain Robbe-Grillet with Alain Resnais; it is, uncannily, the "history" of Lacan's text "The Mirror Stage." Lacan himself claims that in 1936 he gave a paper on the topic of the mirror stage at the International Psychoanalytic Conference in Marienbad but that in the tenth minute of his presentation he was interrupted by Ernest Jones and never finished his talk. Elsewhere, Lacan claims that the Marienbad experience brought him and his colleagues "to the heart of a technical and theoretical resistance within international psychoanalysis."[2] Ellie Ragland-Sullivan reports that despite the appearance of the essay in the index of the *International Journal of Psychoanalysis* of January 1937 under the title "The Looking-glass Phase," no text in fact appears, only the words "J.Lacan (Paris)."[3] Jane Gallop reports, "Upon consulting the 1937 journal, one realizes that the French bibliography is not just ambiguous, but ironic. The other papers from the congress are summarized there, but one finds nothing at all *under* the title, 'The Looking-glass Phase.' No version, no translation, not even a summary."[4] Gallop argues that the difficulty of situating the chronology of this text "point[s] to some slight difficulty about the 'beginning' of the *Ecrits,* some trouble about where (and how) to begin reading" (RL, 76). The question, she argues, is far from trivial since it concerns the "germ" of Lacan's entire thought, "but 'the essential' is always 'quite imprecise on certain points.'" "'The Mirror Stage' is the place to begin a study of Lacan's work," she concedes, "yet not only does *Ecrits* not begin there, but it turns out that 'there' may be a difficult place to locate exactly, a lost origin, one might say" (RL, 76). This is because the very subject of "The Mirror Stage" is "in some way alien to the logic of chronology." Gallop resumes this alien logic as follows:

> In the mirror stage, the infant who has not yet mastered the upright posture and who is supported by either another person or some prosthetic device will, upon seeing herself in the mirror, "jubilantly as-

sume" the upright position. She thus finds in the mirror image "already there" a mastery that she will actually learn only later. The jubilation, the enthusiasm, is tied to the temporal dialectic by which she appears *already* to be what she will *only later become*. . . . The mirror stage itself is both an anticipation and a retroaction. (RL, 78)

Now, this confusion of temporality is intimately related to the confusion of identity that comes about in the mirror stage. If the unity of identity that is there formed is made up out of "le corps morcelé"— the "vision of a body in bits and pieces"—it remains unclear whether this formation is a "constitution" or a "restitution." While what is important to Lacan is "that [the ideal formed in the mirror stage] situates the agency of the *ego* . . . in a line of fiction," that formation seems, according to Gallop, to be "at once anticipatory and retroactive" (RL, 80–81). That is to say, from whatever position one assumes, there always seems to be a confusion about the chronology of the subject's coming into being. Gallop again:

Lacan says that the infant "anticipates the maturation of his power." Yet . . . the anticipation is much more complicated than a simple projection into a future. . . . It at first appears that the infant is inscribed in an inevitable developmental chronology and merely "anticipates" a later moment in that development . . . [but] since the self was founded upon an assumption of maturity, the discovery that maturity was prematurely assumed is the discovery that the self is built on hollow ground. Since the entire past and present is dependent upon an already anticipated maturity—that is, a projected ideal one—any "natural maturation" . . . must be defended against, for it threatens to expose the fact that the self is an illusion done with mirrors. (RL, 83)

Now, Lacan himself argues that

the mirror stage is a *drama* whose internal impetus lunges forward from insufficiency to anticipation—and which, for the *subject captivated by the lure of spatial identification, machinates the succession of fantasies* which go from an image of the body in bits and pieces to a form which we will call orthopedic of its totality—and to the armor finally assumed of an alienating identity, which will mark with its rigid structure his entire mental development.[5]

One cannot fail to be struck by the uncanny resemblance between the problematics of Lacan's "Mirror Stage," both as text and as psychoanalytic speculation, and Alain Resnais and Alain Robbe-Grillet's film *L'Année dernière à Marienbad*. On the most obvious level, the film deals with a confusion of chronology—whether the couple in the film has met before or not—and a concomitant confusion about the ontology of the film's images—whether they represent "present," "past," or "future." Indeed, Resnais once said, "It seems to me that the ideal film would be one in which dream images would be mistaken for reality, and real ones for a sort of confused bad dream ['une sorte de cauchemar confus']."[6] The film itself has seemed to many as merely "a succession of fantasies . . . in bits and pieces." Ultimately, as I hope to demonstrate in the pages that follow, that confusion extends well beyond any speculation on the activities of the fictional personae to questions of the constitution of identity, both on the level of character and on the level of the film's own origins.

Marienbad was filmed by Alain Resnais in 1961 working from a scenario given him by Alain Robbe-Grillet. The film's events are pictured as "taking place" in a baroque chateau (actually a composite of the German chateaux of Nymphenburg and Schleissheim as well as studio constructions for the long dolly shots). There are, visibly, three primary "characters," named "X," "A," and "M" in Robbe-Grillet's scenario but never given names in the film. To differentiate film from scenario, I shall designate these three by the initials of the actors who speak their lines in the film: GA (Giorgio Albertazzi), DS (Delphine Seyrig), and SP (Sacha Pitoeff), respectively.

The film opens on a series of credits with, in the background, a voice that can be heard *only with difficulty and only intermittently* intoning a rather hypnotic monologue:

> Once again I walk on, once again, down these corridors, through these halls, these galleries, in this structure—of another century, this enormous, luxurious, baroque, lugubrious hotel—where corridors succeed endless corridors—silent deserted corridors overloaded with a dim, cold ornamentation of woodwork, stucco, moldings, marble, black mirrors.

> Une fois de plus, je m'avance, une fois de plus, le long de ces couloirs, à travers ces salons, ces galeries, dans cette construction d'un autre siècle, cet hôtel immense, luxueux, baroque, lugubre, où des couloirs interminables succèdent aux couloirs, silencieux, déserts, surchargés d'un décor sombre et froid de boiseries, de stuc, de panneaux moulurés, de marbres, glaces noires.[7]

Although the "story" of the film cannot be rendered without to some degree distorting it, it involves GA's rather constant attempt to convince DS that they have met before, perhaps last year, perhaps at Marienbad. Her reactions seem to range from disinterest to fear to hysteria. Occasionally, SP intervenes in the picture, often to invite GA or others to engage him in either a game of nim or dominoes, at other times to question DS about her activities, plans, or feelings. GA's persuasion moves from a quiet suggestion to a rather exaggerated insistence, yet frequently involves denials and confusions, and then ends on a quieter note. Begun as a description of the interior of the hotel, his monologue concludes with a description of the exterior gardens:

> The park of this hotel was a kind of garden à la française without any trees or flowers, without any foliage. . . . Gravel, stone, marble and straight lines marked out rigid spaces, surfaces without mystery. It seemed, at first glance, impossible to get lost here . . . at first glance . . . down straight paths, between the statues with frozen gestures and the granite slabs, where you were now already getting lost, forever, in the calm night, alone with me.

> Le parc de cet hôtel était une sorte de jardin à la française, sans arbre, sans fleur, sans végétation aucune. . . . Le gravier, la pierre, le marbre, la ligne droite, y marquaient des espaces rigides, des surfaces sans mystère. Il semblait, au premier abord, impossible de s'y perdre . . . au premier abord . . . le long des allées rectilignes, entre les statues aux gestes figés et les dalles de granit, où vous étiez maintenant déjà en train de vous perdre, pour toujours, dans la nuit tranquille, seule avec moi.
> (ADAM, 165/181)

L'Année dernière à Marienbad has generated an enormous amount of critical attention, much of it sympathetic, some of it remarkably perceptive, yet virtually all of it dedicated to the conviction that no interpretation of the images of the film can—or even should be—attempted other than the recognition that the film is dreamlike and merely an exercise in the meta-cinematic.[8] If this is the only way to look at the film, one could only conclude that it is, as Neal Oxenhandler argues, merely "a brilliantly executed aesthetic maneuver" or, as William Pechter claims, "a cinema of beautiful images without meaning . . . a paradigmatic instance of artistic self-defeat."[9] Marie-Claire Ropars-Wueilleumier argues that the "insoluble contradiction" of the film renders impossible a single interpretation and appeals instead to "the consciousness of all possible realities."[10] Yet for all the critical diffidence about interpreting *Marienbad*, there is nevertheless a specific form to the film, to GA's "persuasion" and to DS's reception of and resistance to his persuasion. In addition, several other elements in the film demand another look. No one could claim, writing thirty years after the film was produced, and working in the shadow of such an important body of criticism, to have discovered a *definitive* interpretation of the work; and yet, using evidence in the film that has received little or no attention, as well as the cultural and psychoanalytic awareness that we have evolved since the film was produced, I hope to bring to light some important aspects of *Marienbad* that so far have been left obscured.

The juxtaposition of the film with the Lacanian problematic alluded to in the opening paragraphs of this essay brings most immediately to light the metaphor of the mirror and the role of that metaphor in the "drama" of identity. Whose identity? is of course the question that must first be posed. If at one level the film is structured like a dream, as Resnais himself has observed,[11] then a powerful case can be made for the film's figuration of a *composite* process of identity formation. Just as Freud long ago made a case for interpreting all of the personae of the dream as projections of the dreamer, so Nick Browne has suggested that "the role of the [film] spectator is to be in several places at once."[12]

This notion was initially blunted by Robbe-Grillet himself, who took pains to focus his screenplay through the "eye" and "ear" of the "unknown," which "register" all the data presented. "The hero" (Robbe-Grillet's term) presents a "past" to the woman, and she begins to accept it, nay, already *has* accepted it. Thus there has been a tendency to see *Marienbad* as *his*.[13] But Resnais, whose *film* it is, after all, not only has expressed doubt about that point of view in his extra-filmic interviews, he *engineered* it in the fabric of the film itself. Whereas Robbe-Grillet claims that "A" has "already given in long ago" (ADAM, 12/13), Resnais argues "that the character escapes from all control and all prediction ['le personnage échappe à tout contrôle et toute prévision']," the term *personnage* having a much more global rather than gender-specific sense here.[14] Elsewhere, perhaps in reaction to Robbe-Grillet's assertions, Resnais muses, "Everything is perhaps in the mind of the woman on the eve of having to make a decision, and she makes a kind of assemblage of all of the elements ['un rassemblement de tous les éléments']."[15] And again, "Evidently we never know whether the images are in the mind of the man or of the woman. . . . One can imagine that ultimately everything is narrated by her."[16] Or, he elsewhere concedes, "perhaps there is only one character."[17]

These interpretations (for Resnais is only one—certainly a privileged one but nevertheless just one of the interpreters of *Marienbad*) seem to jar against the apparent use of voice-over. Traditionally, as we have appreciated in the discussions of *Jules et Jim* and *Les Amants*, voice-over narration is tightly linked to point of view. But not always. Bresson was to experiment with an unreliable narrator in *Pickpocket* in ways that robbed the technique of its authoritative function. Resnais took explicit issue with the link between voice-over and narrative authority by giving the voice-over role to Giorgio Albertazzi, whose Italian accent "disqualified" him from assuming the position of narrator: "Since he is speaking in a language that is not his native tongue ['sa langue maternelle'], he is necessarily speaking to someone else ['il s'adresse à quelqu'un d'autre']. Otherwise, if it were an interior monologue, he would obviously be speaking his own language."[18]

Resnais also took pains (and in this he followed Robbe-Grillet's scenario to a great extent) to undermine the authority of GA's voice both by weakening it on the sound track and by undermining its narrative assurance. In the opening sequence, for example, we can hear GA's voice intoning the opening monologue, as I noted above, in such a way that we can only barely and intermittently make out his words. Moreover, the speaker undermines his own potential authority by referring to himself initially almost anonymously as "he who advances" ("celui qui s'avance") or "his own ear" ("sa propre oreille") rather than as "I." His frequent repetitions—"Une fois de plus," "les pas de celui qui s'avance," "aucun bruit de pas ne parvient à sa propre oreille"—promote a sense of a consciousness enmired in compulsive behavior. When he does finally enunciate "I," it is in such a context of repetition—"entre ces murs chargés de boiseries, de stuc, de moulures," and so on—that our faith in the "normality" of this "I" is severely shaken. A sense of "I"'s dependence on "you" emerges most powerfully from this opening monologue, since "I" never speaks without reference to "you": "je m'avançais, comme à votre rencontre," "j'étais *dèjà* en train de vous attendre," "je me trouve maintenant, devant vous." It is immediately as though this "I" could not even constitute itself without this "you." The final monologue confirms to a great extent this sense of interdependence: "Le parc de cet hôtel . . . où vous étiez maintenant *déjà* en train de vous perdre, pour toujours, . . . seule avec moi" (italics mine). In the midst of the continuity of "I"'s concern (signaled by the repetition of the opening discourse at the conclusion of the text) emerges a *radical discontinuity* signaled by the repeated use of the imperfect tense (implying the acquired characteristic of being) and the introjected adverb *déjà* (suggesting duration of being) coupled with "I"'s expression of existential lack. These terms seem exactly to reproduce the (Lacanian) problematic of the formation of the ego in the mirror stage, a combination of already and not yet that undermines every assurance of origin and leads to the inevitable and irrevocable alienation of the *moi* in its incorporation of the other, "a feeling of Oneness, which is already made up of two beings."[19]

This self/other construction is reinforced again when Resnais introduces the staged play. Here the actor on stage appropriates not only GA's discourse ("forever—in a past of marble, like these statues, this garden carved out of stone—this hotel itself ['pour toujours— dans un passé de marbre, comme ces statues, ce jardin taillé dans la pierre—cet hôtel lui-même']" [ADAM, 25/30]) but also his accented voice so thoroughly that it is impossible for the spectator to realize that there has been a shift (or doubling) of personae. This is all the more true inasmuch as GA's image has not yet appeared to the viewer. He is thus *misrecognized* in our first perception of him—again, a process exactly analogous to that (metaphorized) in Lacan's mirror stage. We see not an actor playing a role (a concept that itself is now problematized) in a film but an actor playing a role in a play in a film, whose voice and discourse have been borrowed from an (as yet not fully existent) *other* role. To insist: since Albertazzi has not yet made an appearance in the film, he does *not yet* have a self, and yet his purported self as constructed by language has *already* been appropriated as if it existed. Where to begin? asks Jane Gallop. Indeed. When the actress in the play-within-the-film then exclaims, "I am yours" ("Je suis à vous"), she enunciates a statement at once obvious and impossible: being ("Je") is not yet, or if it is, it already incorporates an as-yet-unformed other ("vous"). Small wonder that the play actress speaks this line without the slightest emotion or direction toward a possible interlocutor (see plate 11). Not surprisingly we see DS immediately after the actress in the play has finished her line, almost as if the actress on stage has addressed her speech to her counterpart in the hall. Rather than a moment of ecstatic union, it is a statement of tragic existential and psychological doubleness. As such it anticipates and mirrors (another a-chronological impasse euphemistically categorized as prolepsis) the condition and "development" of GA and DS outside the play.

For mirrors are, at every stage of this film, the thing by which we catch the unconscious of the "king." The camera moves along mirrored halls throughout the duration of the work. When we catch sight of GA for the first time, we still do not get to attach a voice to the face.

PLATE 11.   Stage actors playing roles in the play in Resnais's *L'Année dernière à Marienbad*. (Courtesy of the Museum of Modern Art Film Stills Archive.)

He stands to the side, and the camera catches *through a huge mirror* a couple, who (since we have no clue as to the identity of either GA or DS yet) might well be the film's "heroes" engaged in the following exchange:

> HOMME: The others? Who are the others? Don't be so worried about what they are thinking.
> FEMME: You know perfectly well. . . .
> HOMME: I know you said you would listen to no one but me [*"vous prètendez n'encouter que moi"*].
> FEMME: I'm listening to you. . . .
> HOMME: Then listen to my complaints. I can't stand this role any longer [*"Je ne peux plus supporter ce rôle"*]. I can't stand this silence, these walls, these whispers you're imprisoning me in ["où *vous m'enfermez"*].
> FEMME: Don't talk so loud, please don't ["je vous en *supplie"*].
> HOMME: These whisperings, worse than silence, that you're imprisoning me in ["où *vous m'enfermez"*]. These days, worse than death, that we're living through here side by side, you and I, like coffins laid side by side underground in a frozen garden ["Ces journées, pires que la mort, que *nous vivons ici côte à côte, vous et moi,* comme

deux cercueils placés côte à côte sous la terre d'un jardin figé lui-même"]. . . .
(ADAM, 30–31/34–35)

This conversation again expropriates *avant la lettre* the conversations that take place (and used to?) between GA and DS. Seen through the mirror, the subject of discourse *is* the mirror: "Vous m'enfermez!" he repeats, mimicking the mirror's metaphor of the construction of self as other, incorporating other in an alienating specular movement:

> Others give identificatory shape to a *moi* that, paradoxically, seeks the meaning of its own alienation through others' (ego ideals) and in language. . . . Tension, anxiety, conflict, ambiguity and oscillation . . . have their explanation in the nonpeaceful coexistence of the specular *moi* of narcissism, aware of but divided from the Other(A) from which it was formed, and forced to verify itself through others. . . . The subject of reality reconstruction or subjective perception—the *moi*—is elusive, kaleidoscopic, and evanescent, whereas the subject of meaning and speech—the *je*—seeks to "translate" the *moi* while adhering to cultural stipulations. . . . Lacan's *moi* is inherently paranoid because, given *the specular logic* peculiar to it, the *moi* can only experience itself in relation to external images and to the gaze of others. . . . The subject's identity is both fixed and continually *en jeu*.[20]

This may be one reason why games of all kinds punctuate *Marienbad* as film and as space: GA can never "win" at the games proposed, nor can he stop playing. It may also be the reason that Resnais himself calls his film "un film miroir" and elsewhere says, "We are only others" ("Nous ne sommes que les autres").[21] It also goes a long way toward explaining GA's loss of voice-over authority in another domain (the failure of the images to conform to his description) as well as his success at other times in "persuading" DS to conform her movements to fantasized (or remembered?) scenes.[22]

Norman Holland long ago likened the structure of *Marienbad* to that of the Freudian unconscious, concluding that the film represents "a perfect symbol for possibilities which are not true possibilities, choices which are not true choices."[23] If we extend his meditation beyond a generalized description of the Freudian id to a dynamic of the Lacanian *moi*, it is possible to account for the struggle between GA and DS as one involving the fragmented and alienated *moi* as it works at its own constitution borrowing from past and future to bolster an account of its origins.[24] The "persuasion" could then be understood as taking place between parts of the *moi*, on the one hand a piece that insists on a previous fusion of self and other, opposed to yet trying to convince another part, by seduction or by force, of the "truth" of that origin. The lack of origin (or doubt about originary fusion of a nonproblematical self) accounts for the number of images proposed by GA that simply do not materialize: there never was a last year at Marienbad.

The apparent triumph of this persuasion (in scenes in which DS conforms to his suggestions) would imply relative success in binding of self and other into the project of a coherent self in the mirror stage. This would explain the tendency of the two members of the couple to feel at times "as if there were only you and me" ("comme s'il n'y avait eu que vous et moi"), as if the only thing that mattered was the work of the development/anticipation of the *moi* out of the fragments it was/will have been. "Yes, no, I don't know" ("Oui, non, je ne sais pas"), responds the sense of fragmentation that feels only the alienation of this construction.[25] At the moments in which there is most insistence on (sexual) fusion, that is, allusions to the bedroom, DS tends most insistently to look either into the camera, into the bedroom's enormous mirrors, or at a mass of *duplicate* photographs—all elements of the look that simultaneously confirms and denies the self's wholeness.[26] At one point she presses her body so insistently against the mirror that it would seem as if she wanted to obliterate the separation implied in the specular (see plate 12). Lacan, we remember, emphasized the crucial importance of the ambiguity of inside/outside, boundary/nonboundary distinction underlying the process of introjection and projection. GA's frustration, on the other hand, is expressed as aggressiveness: in the discourse of coercion, in fantasies of rape, and even in two fantasies of murder, one a composite of scenes in the shooting gallery and an image of DS that is connected via montage to GA's aiming and firing a pistol, the second, SP's shooting of DS in the bedroom. "After the mirror stage," Ragland-Sullivan notes, "aggressiveness is specifically related to separation/recognition dynamics and is at the base of the paranoiac structure of the human subject."[27]

A narcissistic subject that is constantly menaced by its own otherness, the *moi* seems forever "at a loss." In this interpretation of the film the couple who compose the principal persona of *Marienbad* never separate, never really join, and never specifically *find* themselves in any originating fantasy: the film ends more or less where it began, in a seductive monologue in which GA appeals to DS in the garden "où vous étiez maintenant en train de vous perdre, pour toujours, dans la nuit tranquille, seule avec moi" (ADAM, 165/181). The oxymoron,

PLATE 12. Delphine Seyrig presses her body insistently into the mirror in
Resnais's *L'Année dernière à Marienbad*. (Courtesy of the Museum of Modern
Art Film Stills Archive.)

"alone with" constitutes the establishing and final figure of this extended meditation on the subject.

But we have far from exhausted *our* subject, *Marienbad*. If the
uncanny coincidence with Lacan's lost (y)ear at Marienbad has alert-
ed us to (one of) the underlying structures of Resnais's film, it does
not exhaustively explicate other levels of the work. It does not explore, beyond the vague and general outlines proposed, some specifics of Resnais's images. It does not, for instance, explain the insistent
poster advertising the film's play, ROSMER. To attempt to understand the place of *Rosmer* in *Marienbad*, it is necessary to look further
at the origins of the film itself and at the "collaboration" that produced it. To turn our own gaze on the origins of the film, that is, the
working relationship between Alain Robbe-Grillet and Alain Resnais, is to recognize another thoroughly *uncanny* structure: a replica-
tion of the very dynamics of the film itself!

If the film is, at one level, a story of an attempt at persuasion—by one partner to share or control the other partner's fantasies—so too, then, was the collaboration of the two Alains. Resnais has always teamed with an established writer, be it Duras, Semprun, Cayrol, or, in this case, Robbe-Grillet, claiming that he himself "doesn't know how to write."[28] But his collaboration with Robbe-Grillet was decidedly different. Resnais admits that he did not know Robbe-Grillet's work when the idea of the collaboration was proposed and that he read the new novelist's work rapidly, in the space of six days,[29] a circumstance that prompted one commentator to argue that their collaboration "may have depended entirely on a *malentendu*."[30] When they met, Robbe-Grillet proposed four different possibilities for a film, and Resnais says that he chose "the most sentimental and most austere."[31] The potential *malentendu* could only have grown from there. Robbe-Grillet went off and composed the project entirely on his own. Although Resnais has always liked making a film from an idea provided by a well-known writer, he has also specifically rejected the idea of working from an already written book. "If the book already exists," he insisted, "it no longer seems interesting ['ça ne m'amuse plus']."[32] "Personally, I don't like adapting films from books," he added elsewhere.[33]

What Robbe-Grillet brought back to Resnais was a book, complete down to the last detail, whose finished version has been published as Robbe-Grillet's *L'Année dernière à Marienbad*. Not only had the novelist produced a finished product but he had violated another of Resnais's known requests: "I always ask my scenario writers not to think about film technique ['ne pas penser à la technique cinématographique'] but to remain faithful to their own idiom. For the same reason, I have a lot of trouble getting interested in a scenario that's already done. . . . It's dead matter ['une matière morte'], you simply can't dream it ['on ne peut pas rêver dessus']."[34] The "book" provided was, as we now know, a scenario, complete with the most minute instructions on camera movement, lighting, field of view, decor, and sound track indications.[35]

Under the circumstances, it is difficult to understand how Resnais could have accepted Robbe-Grillet's text—undoubtedly the filmmaker felt that it was too late to refuse it. Whatever his reasons and feelings at the time, he entered the project with as much tact as genius, for during the filming and in the immediate aftermath he was careful to avoid revealing any negative feelings and abstained from any major disagreements or differences of interpretation with his new novelist collaborator. It is only in the light of numerous statements made in the intervening years that we can understand just how confining was the arrangement proposed by Robbe-Grillet. "I often had the impression," Resnais confided to *L'Arc*, "of merely serving as electronic robot in making the film ['de faire office de robot-electronique dans la confection du film']."[36] He also confided to one interviewer, "We were all obliged to follow a path we couldn't escape from. . . . We were sort of prisoners . . . not free. I am persuaded that we don't ever make the films we want to make. ['Nous étions tous obligés de suivre un chemin dont nous ne pouvions pas nous échapper. . . . Nous étions en quelque sorte prisonniers . . . pas libres. Je suis *persuadé* qu'on ne fait pas les films qu'on veut']."[37]

By contrast, Robbe-Grillet's comments sound almost ecstatic:

As far as I'm concerned, at least, . . . to think of a screen story, for me, is already to conceive it in images, with all the detail this involves, not only of gestures and setting, but of the placing and movement of the camera and the sequence of shots in editing. Alain Resnais and I were only able to collaborate because, from the outset, *we both saw the film in the same way; and not in the same broad outlines, but exactly,* in the way it would be built up as well as in the details of its construction. What I wrote might have been something he was already thinking. . . . It is necessary to stress this point, since this kind of *complete agreement* is something unusual. . . . Resnais adhered as nearly as possible to the set-ups and camera movements of my shooting script, not as a matter of principle but *because we both saw them in the same way.* . . . Naturally he had done a great deal more than respect my intentions: he had realized them.[38]

Given the objections to Robbe-Grillet's procedure voiced subsequently by Alain Resnais, it is difficult to understand how the novelist could have believed in such a perfect union. This entire "scenario" begins to bear an uncanny resemblance to that of the film itself! Let us listen to Robbe-Grillet's version of the scenario itself:

The entire film is, in effect, the story of a *conviction:* it has to do with a *reality which its hero creates out of his own words and vision.* And if this obstinate secret conviction finally prevails, it is after a perfect maze false trails. . . . Within this shuttered and stifling world, all seem victims of some kind of spell . . . a sense of inevitability that it would be as useless to attempt to change their smallest detail as it would be to try to run away. . . . As for the past which the hero forcibly introduces into this closed vacuum of a world, one has the impression that he is making it up here and now as he goes along. . . . This is essentially the record of a *communication between two people . . . one of them putting suggestions and the other resisting, until they end in agreement, as if this is how it had always been.*[39]

Like the characters in his own script, Robbe-Grillet put suggestions to Resnais, suggestions that the filmmaker perceived as so detailed as to imprison him in their inevitability. Afterwards, Robbe-Grillet called this relationship "perfect communication," but Resnais evidently experienced it more in the manner of the character of Delphine Seyrig in his film. If Robbe-Grillet termed the scenario a "conviction," Resnais preferred to see it as a "seduction."[40] He even seems to have sensed the mirrored effect in their film and their own relationship:

> When things really go well, I think we succeed in getting in the relationship scenario-writer-director something approaching the relationship between film and spectator. . . . We are two spectators, in a sense, who must succeed in *seducing* each other. This seems a rather healthy approach ultimately, since we are creating a spectacle and it's play ["on fait du spectacle et que c'est le jeu"].[41]

Just as he sees his film as the story of a seduction, he views the film's origins in the same terms. In instinctively taking the women's point of view in describing the film, Resnais seems to end up consistently recording his own relationship to the scenariste: "As for the seduction, the doubt and hesitation is an expression of the fear and inhibition that any [one] feels before being seduced."[42]

Robbe-Grillet's "seduction" seems to be (like his other films) long on conviction and short on sensitivity. In a joint interview with *Cahiers du cinéma,* the novelist repeatedly gave his version of the film's meaning without looking to his collaborator for corroboration. Thus, for example, he sees the film in resolutely masculine terms rather than feminine—or joint—ones; he argues that "we know absolutely nothing of their lives," nor do we need to. Robbe-Grillet's spectator must "let himself be carried along" by the images and must "agree to get rid of all those preconceived ideas, psychological analyses, more or less vulgar schemes of interpretation, which bad films repeat *ad nauseam,* and which are themselves the worst of abstractions."[43] Curious that he cared so little for the opinion of Resnais, who stressed "the use of psychoanalytic themes introduced consciously. . . . I am very familiar with the value of such work in psychoanalysis ['j'en connaissais très bien la valeur en psychanalyse']."[44] For his part, Resnais noted that "Robbe-Grillet was suspicious of . . . and refused to follow the play of feelings, even reproached me for having introduced psychology where it had no place."[45] In the famous *Cahiers* joint interview, amidst the general bonhomie engendered principally by Robbe-Grillet, Resnais remarks quietly, "We don't share the same tastes at all, and we occasionally encounter violent disagreements about a book or a film, or a way of life ['Nous n'avons pas du tout les mêmes goûts et il arrive que nous nous opposons violemment, sur *un livre,* sur *un film,* sur un mode de vie']."[46] Under the circumstances, it is hard to justify Jacques Brunius's dismissal of the difference of interpretation between the two Alains as a "trifle."[47]

Indeed, from our present perspective, it would be utterly baffling if there were no evidence of difference between two men whose careers have taken such radically divergent directions. Resnais's work, from his earliest documentaries to his most recent films (e.g., *Providence, Le Roman de la vie, Mélo*), portrays sensitively the attempts of his characters, more often than not women, to come to grips, through the work of the imagination, with the complexities of their past. The two films between which *Marienbad* was sandwiched have as their central figure a woman, a contextualization that tends to bring DS to the fore in *Marienbad.* In all of Resnais's work, no matter how "intellectual" or "academic," a moral purpose, or at least a moral question, can be detected in or immediately behind the film's unfolding.[48]

For all of his novelty and new novelistic brio, Robbe-Grillet's theory and practice eschews, and vehemently so, moralistic or ethical considerations. His most sympathetic critics speak of the author's "moral absence from his work," his "lack of ethics."[49] Games without rules, locks without keys, become the ruling aesthetic of films that feature increasingly sadomasochistic adolescent reveries.[50] Mireille Latil-Le Dantec summarizes the novelist-turned-filmmaker's work thus:

> If it is true that we never trod on virgin ground, but always seem to follow in our own tracks, Robbe-Grillet seems particularly prone, as a writer of fiction, to borrow from his own store of properties, from which he drags out the same names . . . the same places . . . the same sounds, the same equivocal objects (double rings, blinds [jalousies], ropes, chains, whips, gags) used in the same scenes (rape, murder, torture), the same characteristic silhouettes. . . . And this *desituated* ["désitué"] point of view of a consciousness without a subject, a convenient alibi for the spectator-voyeur, casts doubts on Robbe-Grillet's methods.[51]

Naturally, Latil-Le Dantec finds the two artists radically opposed in their approaches to what she terms the current crisis of expression. Robbe-Grillet's distanced, amoral position, with its trend toward increasing pornography and violence, has been compared by one critic to "the bomber pilot dropping his cargo of destruction . . . 'like Rice Krispies.'"[52] So consistently violent is the tendency of Robbe-Grillet's work that another critic concludes: "From the first scene of *Marienbad* [on] . . . the characters coalesce and fall together until in the end we realize that there is only one character in all these films: Robbe-Grillet himself."[53] As for Resnais, "the very word 'violence' evokes for me an unacceptable idea. The useless suffering imposed on men [and, *a fortiori*, on women] by other men. Oppression. I cannot accept violence."[54] And elsewhere he insists, "I think I have always had a great aversion to violence."[55] In the composite of *Marienbad* we have what amounts to a bad coupling of two radically opposed personalities, much like the way that, in the most disparate elements of the personality, "contradictory impulses exist side by side without neutralizing each other or drawing apart [but] combine in compromise formations."[56]

If the incorporation of one Alain by another, altogether *other* (alien?) Alain at first seems uncannily like Lacan's version of the mirror stage in the development of the alienated self, it has, thanks to Alain Resnais, a second, more poignant and potentially more political meaning. For given the rigidity of the scenario handed him by Robbe-Grillet, Resnais had to find ways to express his own originality as an image maker within the overall confines and limitations of the situation.

True to form, Robbe-Grillet attempts to move the interpretation of *Marienbad* in the direction of violence, both by the inclusion of violent scenes in the scenario (deleted by Resnais) and by his discussion of the film as a variant of his violent novels:

> In *Marienbad,* the important thing is always a kind of hollow at the heart of reality . . . just the way the principal act, the murder, is missing ["en creux"] from *Le Voyeur.* Everything is recounted up until this "hole," and again after the "hole," and an attempt is made to bring these two accounts together to cover this disturbing gap ["faire disparaitre ce vide gênant"]. But just the opposite happens: the gap invades and fills everything. In *Marienbad* . . . the event that the young woman was struggling to deny [in this case the rape, which was excerpted by Resnais from the film] has by the end contaminated everything.[57]

Not only did Resnais refuse to shoot the rape scene, considered by his collaborator to be so contaminating, but he subtly managed to convert the "hole" in Robbe-Grillet's mental text into a gap of his own. In the space between the words of Robbe-Grillet's scenario and Resnais's cinematic images, Resnais interposed—or to use his own term, improvised—a number of radical departures from the original.[58] Resnais has twice stated that a film is only "born" when it takes on its own life: "What is important are the successive skids ['dérapages'] in each scene from which the film will be born. The excitement enters when, suddenly, the meaning of the film begins to change ['le sens du film commence à changer']," establishing a difference from what was written.[59]

Those "dérapages" are often subtle and include primarily deletions, for example, the rejection of Robbe-Grillet's "rather swift and brutal rape scene" (ADAM, 146/164), for which Resnais substituted the brilliant scene in white of DS in which she seems repeatedly to welcome the viewer with outstretched arms. Resnais's visual restructuring of the statue scene and his refusal to "animate" one of the photographs of DS constitute other departures from the scenario. In general these changes can be seen as a reduction of the "mechanization" of the narrative process.[60] Robert Benayoun terms these changes "fruitful incidents of filming . . . which introduce into the authors' project a new series of disturbing factors."[61] Evidently Robbe-Grillet judged them disturbing enough to protest to Resnais, "I wrote *L'Année dernière,* period. You filmed *L'Année dernière à Marienbad:* This is a betrayal."[62]

The most disturbing factor of all is undoubtedly Resnais's insertion of an allusion to Ibsen's *Rosmersholm,* not once, but twice in the film.[63] Robbe-Grillet's scenario called for "a theater poster for a play with a foreign, meaningless title ['un titre étranger, sans signification'], the rest of the poster illegible except, perhaps, for a line in larger letters: Tonight only . . . ['Ce soir, unique représentation de . . . ']" (ADAM, 20/24). The choice of Ibsen might at first seem arbitrary (on my part *and* on Resnais's) but for a number of compelling elements.[64] Resnais, as a former student of acting and ardent thespian, knew Ibsen's work well. When he recruited Delphine Seyrig for the film, he found her in New York performing in Ibsen's *An Enemy of the People,* so that she was immediately associated with the playwright's work.[65] Nor was Resnais the least bit oblivious to the implications of literary allusions in his work. He once said,

> I am flabbergasted to see that *everything* you do during the shooting is always perceived by somebody! . . . That's why I am fastidious or meticulous when I am shooting. . . . I have understood that the title of a book in a library behind [one of my actors] will be debated . . . and so I have to have *the right book* that he could have read and little details like that. . . . Really I can't complain because a lot of people have *understood what I tried to convey.*[66]

Ibsen conveys a remarkable detour away from the direction Robbe-Grillet attempted to impose on the work.[67] Resnais somewhat subversively claimed, apropos of *Marienbad,* "I always try, when there is a lot of systematization in a film, to briefly say the opposite. I like to undo the entire design of a film with a detail, a zest for the irrational [*'par un détail,* un zeste d'irrationnel']."[68] *This* "detail" engenders an entire rereading of the film.

Published in 1886, Ibsen's *Rosmersholm* introduces a woman into the world of Norwegian politics and the traditional male *holm* in a way that very nearly revolutionizes both. Rebecca West, the stage directions inform us, is "in charge of Rosmer's household," that is, she *is* Rosmersholm in ways that immediately transcend the traditions of housekeeper. Indeed, the traditional housekeeper's role is occupied by Madam Helseth, giving Rebecca an anomalous role that defies normal assignment. As the play unfolds, a dark secret is revealed: Rosmer's wife, Beata, in despair had thrown herself from a bridge into the river. Her suicide hangs over the house. As Rebecca herself says, "They cling to their dead here."[69] And a second secret is about to be revealed. Because his own children have turned against his conservative views, Rector Kroll (Beata's brother) urges Rosmer to become actively involved in politics. Despite the aggressive politicking of the rector, Rosmer reveals his own conversion to radicalism, a stunning about-face for one of his family's stern traditions:

KROLL: But—the faith of your fathers—?

ROSMER: It is mine no more. . . . I have given it up. I had to give it up.

KROLL: But you have a duty towards the traditions of your race, Rosmer! Rosmersholm has, so to speak, radiated morality and order from time immemorial—yes, and respectful conformity to all that is accepted and sanctioned by the best people. . . . It would lead to deplorable, irremediable confusion if it were known that you had broken with what I may call the hereditary idea of the house of Rosmer.

(R, 273, 288)

The play thus turns on the conflict of, on the one hand, tradition, morality, conformity, heredity, and racism versus, on the other hand, democratic principles (radicalism) and the intrusion of the feminine. For it turns out that Rebecca has been the principal agent in transforming Rosmer's views of the world.

> How beautiful it was when we sat in the twilight, in the room downstairs, helping each other to lay out our new life-plans! You were to set resolutely to work in the world—the living world of today, as you said. You were to go as a messenger of emancipation from home to home; to win over minds and wills; to create noble-men around you in wider and wider circles. . . . *That is what you must do.* . . . Live, work, act. Don't sit here brooding and groping among insoluble enigmas. (R, 299)

Rosmer's immediate reaction is to propose that Rebecca become his second wife. He has, of course, confused her political seduction with an emotional one and as a result confesses his utter dependence on her. But her purpose, as both Kroll and Rebecca come to understand, was more political. Kroll directly accuses Rebecca of misuse of her power:

> I believe that you are at the bottom of [this change in Johannes Rosmer]. . . . Whom could you not bewitch if you tried? . . . You simply wanted to get a footing at Rosmersholm—to strike root here. . . . You are dangerous to people that you want to get into your power. It is easy for you to weigh your acts and calculate consequences—just because your heart is cold. . . . Well you have gained your end. You have got him and everything into your power. But in order to do so, you have not scrupled to make him unhappy. (R, 313, 314)

Faced with accusations about her morality and Rosmer's collapse, Rebecca herself confesses,

> I wanted to take my share in the life of the new era that was dawning, with all its new ideas. . . . We two, I thought, should march onward in freedom, side by side. Ever onward. Ever farther and farther to the front. But between you and perfect emancipation there rose that dismal, insurmountable barrier . . . the gloom of such a marriage. . . . But I saw quite clearly where your deliverance lay—your only deliverance. And then I went to work. . . . It was I that lured—that ended in luring Beata out into the paths of delusion . . . that led to the mill race. (R, 321, 322)

Rosmer, in awe, tells her, "Assuredly you were the strongest at Rosmersholm. Stronger than Beata and I together" (R, 331). Rebecca thus emerges as the most powerful figure in the play—up to the point that Kroll makes his insinuation about her relationship to Dr. West. From that moment on, Rebecca loses her strength and her conviction, as if she had been struck down "like a storm on the sea [which] seizes you and whirls you along with it, wherever it will. There is no resisting it" (R, 330). From Kroll's assertion on, Rebecca confesses that Rosmersholm has "broken me utterly and hopelessly.—I had a free and fearless will when I came here. Now *I have bent my neck under a strange law.* . . . My old fearless will has had its *wings clipped* here. It is *crippled!*" (R, 328, 331, italics mine). Unable to account rationally for the change, she cries, "Now, when all life's happiness is within my grasp—my heart is changed, and my own past cuts me off from it. . . . *And innocence? Where am I to get that from?*" (R, 333, italics mine).

Resnais spoke of how he denied "toute la construction d'un film par un détail, un zeste d'irrationnel." Surely *Rosmersholm* is just such a deconstructive detail. The presence of the play counters the force of Robbe-Grillet's scenario first by portraying the potential power of a female figure and then by "explicating" the undoing of her power. Ibsen's play, especially as interpreted in Freud's celebrated essay, demonstrates the utter destructiveness of the incestuous seduction, thereby robbing Robbe-Grillet's scenario of its "innocent" erotic pleasure. Clearly, Resnais knew of Freud's interpretation of *Rosmersholm,* for he told Bernard Pingaud,

> For me, the characters are real beings. They have their own latent and mysterious life. . . . *Marienbad* describes the hesitations, the madness, the anguish, and the moments of great happiness that accompany any passion. . . . Realism doesn't exclude ambiguity, on the contrary. . . . One wonders if it isn't a dream, imagines the best and the worst. I was working entirely within psychological realism! Of course, when I say "psychology" I'm not limiting myself to conscious or present behavior. There are images that inspire or prevent action. . . . Others derive from fantasy and the unconscious. A more or less stereotyped unconscious. *Marienbad* is composed of just such images. Like many filmmakers, I have considered adapting *Gradiva*. I read everything of Freud's that was available at the time. The unconscious is also a spectacle, perhaps the fundamental spectacle.[70]

The Freud that was available included an essay on the incest motif in *Rosmersholm*.[71] Freud, building on Otto Rank's *Das Inzest-Motiv in*

Dictung und Sage (1912), inquires what should have caused the otherwise highly successful Rebecca suddenly to abandon her gains and her happiness. In his investigation Freud concentrates on the fact that Rebecca "*understated her age by a year,* so that her confession is incomplete . . . hence her explanation of her renunciation *exposes one motive only to conceal another*" (SF, 326, italics mine). When Kroll insinuates that Rebecca "has a past," she believes that he is accusing her of already having had sexual relations with her "benefactor," Dr. West, before meeting Rosmer. But Kroll's accusation is otherwise: he reproaches her for being Dr. West's *daughter,* hence of "bad origins." When Rebecca is forced to confront both hypotheses together, she is overwhelmed by the evidence that she is a victim of incest. Freud notes that Rebecca "can still retain her composure for awhile, for she is able to suppose that her enemy is basing his calculations on her *age,* which she has *given falsely* on an earlier visit of his. But Kroll demolishes this objection by saying: 'Well, so be it, but my calculation may be right, none the less, for Dr West was up there on a short visit *the year before* he got the appointment.' After this new information she loses her self-possession" (SF, 327). In other words, the play within *Marienbad* is *also* based on a confusion about time, and about whether and when a seduction is to have taken place! After adducing the textual proof of his conclusion about Rebecca's incest, Freud concludes, "After she has learnt that she has been the mistress of her own father, she surrenders herself wholly to her now overmastering sense of guilt" (SF, 328).

It is only after proving convincingly that this scene of seduction *has actually taken place* that Freud initiates some reflections that have enormous bearing not only on Ibsen's work, and by extension on *Marienbad,* but also *on his own position on the seduction theory.* Freud sees Rebecca's renunciation of all she has ever wanted and worked for as *in fact* a case of multiple motivation, in which a deeper "motive comes into view behind the more superficial one. *Laws* of poetic economy *necessitate this way of presenting the situation,* for this deeper motive *could not be explicitly enunciated.* It *had to remain concealed,* kept from easy perception of the spectator or reader; otherwise *serious resistances,* based on the most distressing emotions, *would have arisen,* which *might have imperilled* the effect of the drama" (SF, 329, italics mine). What Freud has managed rather neatly in this explanation of *Rebecca's* motives is an implicit conflation not only of Ibsen's *presumed motives* with hers but also a *projection* of his own concerns onto both! Rebecca's motive, as we shall see below, has a great deal to do with the trauma, distortions, and repression commonly experienced by victims of father-daughter incest and as such goes a long way to explicate the specific images of *Marienbad*. A short examination of Freud's own unconscious motives will contribute, I believe, to the force of my analysis of the role of *Rosmersholm* in *Marienbad*.

To claim, as he did, that it was Ibsen's motive to conceal the presence of incest in the film is hardly credible, for Freud begins his essay by terming the playwright "a great dramatist, who loves to pursue problems of psychological responsibility with unrelenting rigor" (SF, 324). Indeed, Ibsen's mockingly sinister portrayal of Kroll as the spokesman for "morality and order from time immemorial— yes, and respectful conformity to all that is accepted and sanctioned by the best people" could hardly have been calculated to endear him to his bourgeois and respectable audience. No, Freud's attention to concealment constitutes a projection of his own difficulties with the subject of incest. We must remember that ten years before composing the essay on Ibsen, Freud had been forced to abandon his theory "about the genuineness of the infantile sexual scenes" in the face of "serious resistances," which had arisen "based on the most distressing emotions" and which "might have imperilled the effect of" the un- folding drama of psychoanalysis itself.[72] Indeed, according to Jeffrey Masson, Freud wrote to Wilhelm Fliess that because of his belief in the seduction theory, "I am as isolated as you could wish me to be: the word has been given out to abandon me, and a void is forming around me."[73] Ten years *after* composing the essay on Ibsen, Freud con- fessed, "I was at last [i.e., in 1896] *obliged* to recognize that these scenes of seduction had *never* taken place, and that they were only phantasies which my patients had made up or which I myself had *perhaps* forced on them. . . . When I had *pulled myself together*, I was able to draw the right conclusions from my discovery: namely, that the neurotic symptoms were not related to actual events but to wish- ful phantasies, and that as far as the neurosis was concerned psychical reality was of more importance than material reality."[74]

The Ibsen essay contains a curious about-face. After taking such pains to prove the *fact* of paternal seduction—this in the face of his own official denials of that very fact—he *repeats* the assertion (SF, 330) and then lamely covers it over with a kind of official disclaimer, while again *asserting the reality of the original seduction:*

> The practising psycho-analytic physician knows how frequently, or how invariably, a girl who enters a household as servant, companion or governess, will consciously or unconsciously weave a day-dream, which derives from the Oedipus complex, of the mistress of the house

> disappearing and the master taking the newcomer as his wife in her place. *Rosmersholm* is the greatest work of art of the class that treats of this common phantasy in girls. What makes it into a tragic drama is the *extra* circumstance that the heroine's *day-dream* had been preceded in her childhood by a *precisely corresponding reality.* (SF, 330–31)

Although he makes every attempt to marginalize the fact of seduction (as an "extra circumstance") and to separate this fact from the "precisely corresponding" mental event in later life, Freud in fact *returns to his own repressed* theory. This is a stunning "slip"—or "paraphasia," as Freud himself termed it—allowed presumably by "the laws of poetic economy," by which Freud unconsciously meant to include his own foray into the "safe" realm of literature.

If I have insisted on Freud's "mistake," it is because that "error" is consistent with recent clinical evidence to the effect that, in fact, father-daughter incest is an all too common event, one whose traumatic effects are potentially disastrous on the subsequent psychosexual development of the female victim.[75] Judith Herman has demonstrated that a history of incest inflicts "lasting harm" on the victim, including institutionalization or prostitution, "impairment in sexual self-esteem . . . sexual difficulties in adult life and a tendency toward repeated victimization in adult life. . . ." She notes that "a history of incest is associated with some impairment of the normal adult mechanisms of self-protection . . . . Symptoms include guilt, shame, feelings of inferiority and low self-esteem, anxiety, imitative ritualized sexual behavior, hostile or aggressive behavior, . . . depression, somatic complaints and 'promiscuous' behavior and a 'masochistic search for punishment,' accompanied by an intense fear of parental abandonment. . . . The victims' most common complaints . . . included . . . a 'repetition compulsion' with respect to abusive relationships."[76]

We are very close here to a composite portrait of DS in *Marienbad*. Seen in this light, DS's ambivalent behavior becomes much more understandable: she is, at least apparently, afraid of GA (hence her repeated "Laissez-moi, je vous supplie") yet unable to leave him; his intrusions, which include suggestions of sadistic violence (e.g., the montage of GA pointing a gun at the camera, presumably at the shooting range, and the image of DS as if *she* is the target),[77] the images of her death by shooting, and the eight repetitions of her white-plumed body giving way to the invasive presence of the camera, all communicate the impairment of her mechanism of self-protection, coupled with a repetition compulsion with respect to

ニング

abusive relationships. In addition, Chasseguet-Smirgel sees the broken glass as a symbol of rape and mutilation.[78]

To read the entire film from DS's point of view, however, as the allusion to *Rosmersholm* so strongly invites us to do, understanding it in the light of the psychodynamics of paternal incest, is to inject a considerable dose of unpleasure into an otherwise purely voyeuristic and sadistic scenario.[79] If the consciousness that "dreams" this entire scenario is not his (as so many critics have assumed) but hers, as Resnais himself has suggested (both explicitly and implicitly through *Rosmersholm*), then the film takes on an entirely different topos. Instead of a story of "conviction" as Robbe-Grillet has suggested, the film becomes an allegory of uncertainty—the fragmentation of the *moi* hypothesized by Lacan is here portrayed as greatly compounded by the intrusion of the incestuous father into the psychic world of the victim. *Marienbad,* in other words, far from being "just" an image of the "mirror stage," becomes a mimesis of the bleakness of the "obsidian mirror,"[80] of an identity that can no longer rely on any certainty because of the traumatic experience of exploitation and violence exactly there where security and sustaining care are necessary.[81]

For incest, as numerous victims of this abuse have testified, is not merely an isolated (and isolatable) traumatic event: it leads to a devastating reorganization of the victim's identity in ways that are psychically crippling. Judith Herman notes that "the struggle to accept and master the disappointment engendered by the incest taboo is a requisite step in the child's maturation; without it, the child *fails to develop the separate identity* and the internalized sense of social morality which are essential characteristics of well-adapted adults. . . . Many stated that they knew they could never be 'normal.' The sense of being an outsider, cut off from ordinary human intercourse, often reached extreme proportions. . . . The incest secret formed the *core of their identity*."[82] So ingrained is this secret, and so hidden even from the victims themselves, that "they seemed doomed to repeat their mistakes." For others, the presence of the past is terrifying: "The memory of incest was intrusive and often paralyzing. Some women complained of disturbing '*flashbacks,*' or memories of the incestuous sexual acts, in the midst of their love-making."[83]

One of the victims of incest who suffered from such flashbacks as "shadows over every event of my adult life" has told her story in *The Obsidian Mirror*.[84] Molested by her grandfather, raped by her stepfather, and abused by an uncle, Louise grows up learning only self-hatred and yearning for death as "a wonderful, familiar place" (OM, 10, 41). Because the men who abused her act as if nothing has happened and later deny their actions, the victim not only feels shame and guilt as the core of her being but feels that her body does not belong to her and that her past is so clouded in doubt and darkness that it is unfathomable (OM, 16, 87, 110). "Feelings chase each other in a circle. . . . Memories come in bits and pieces. . . . Pictures swirl together in oddly shaped puzzle pieces but the pieces don't fit together. The puzzle has pieces that don't have a place" (OM, 19, 124, 69). This certainly conforms to the spectator's first impression of *Marienbad*. The pieces that float in the darkness of Louise's "obsidian mirror" include: "sitting shaking and crying and waiting for the doorknob to open my room at night" (OM, 81); "checking myself into a hospital and letting someone else take care of me" (OM, 80); "childhood rooms which haunt me," (OM, 88); "sitting like a statue unable to move. My voice frightens me when it tells secrets. . . . The incest has become part of me, absorbed into my skin, my vagina, my mind" (OM, 88); "my mouth forms a scream but no sound comes out. . . . I hear a sound inside of me—a scream. . . . My mouth opens as if to make a scream, but I quickly close it again. I see the child in me screaming. It scares me" (OM, 38, 61, 156). "I repeat the same reactions I had as a child whenever I am scared now, even though the situations are different. Unless I remember what happened, I'll *never know the difference between the past and the present. I* still believe that nothing is safe and that I am powerless" (OM, 74). In short, out of the darkened glass that holds the repressed horrors of her earliest memories, Louise's mind produces images that are nearly identical to those in Resnais's film.

In DS's "dream," *Marienbad,* all of the figures take up symbolic positions in a *drame* that seems endlessly to *repeat* the originary figures that, together, compose the fragments of her *moi.* If GA and SP are both present in this imagined space, it does not necessarily mean that they are contemporaneous in the construction of her being, for dreams, as Freud so insistently reminds us, mix our earliest memories with yesterday's events.[85]

Taken as a composite of the paternal, the two principal male figures present unmistakable characteristics: GA's voice seems always present, not always comprehensible or clear, but always there to remind her/us that what is happening in the present has already happened before. His discourse centers on the present's compulsive repetition of a past event; his first words are "Une fois de plus . . . ," and his attention is focused on the labyrinthine nature of the decor she must attempt to sort out. Resnais's camera constantly tracks along endless corridors that have no "solution" in reality, for the film's decor is an imaginary montage of two different chateaux as well as a studio constructed for the film's duration. Moreover, the camera focuses on marginal details—molded panels or decorated ceilings—deliberately refusing the eye's attempt to find its way. In his attempt to convince DS that it does not really matter where or when they first met, Marienbad and/or Friedrichsbad are blended together, different years are conflated. GA serves as the ever-present insistence on *something* in her past that is partially exhumed every time the question of sexuality is raised, yet simultaneously he functions to blur or obstruct her access to those memories. For the incest victim, in other words, the incestuous father functions exactly like a screen memory (and, remarkably enough, like *Rosmersholm* itself), which simultaneously hides and reveals its secret.

It is no wonder that one of the first sentences to filter through the silence of the dream is, "Don't you know the story? It was all anyone talked about last year ['On ne parlait que de *ça,* l'année dernière']. Frank had convinced her he was a *friend of her father's* and had come to *keep an eye on her.* It was a funny kind of eye, of course. She realized it a little later: the night he tried to get into her room" (ADAM, 37/43). The *ça* may well refer directly to the unconscious force at work here— the id—but the reference to paternal violation could not be clearer. Throughout the film, GA will continue to blur past and present in increasingly insistent terms. That his voice folds into that of one of the characters in the stage play (itself an allusion to the incest motif) further serves to make his presence a reduplicative image that emerges everywhere she/we look. The condensation here of *Rosmer* with the actress's words, "Maintenant, je suis à vous," creates a composite meaning, collapsing Rebecca's suicide into DS's own surrender to GA's wishes. For the incest victim, to belong to a man is to *reex-perience* morbid feelings, because the *moi* that might have emerged is so radically split off from any positive images.

SP seems to function as a symbol of more present images: he fulfills the role of consort (appearing in the corridor to inquire when DS will dress for dinner, rushing to her side when she drops the glass, or sitting on her bed when she seems overwhelmed). He is nonetheless figured as a menacing and very controlling persona, one who insists on domination in the "play" of social interaction in the salons and whose barely repressed violence is figured in the series of flashes to the shooting gallery. The game of nim, at which he "could lose, but always wins," is, of course, triangular, symbolizing the perduring reversed oedipal configuration to which her incest victimization condemns her (see plate 13).

PLATE 13.   Giorgio Albertazzi and Sacha Pitoeff engage in the triangular game of nim in Resnais's *L'Année dernière à Marienbad*. (Courtesy of the Museum of Modern Art Film Stills Archive.)

As for DS, she figures herself (since we have taken her point of view) as a constantly marginal, barely reflected, and frozen figure. Indeed, it is undoubtedly because of her own insistent marginalization of her "self" (a trait common to most incest victims) that it has been so difficult to see this film as representing her point of view. When we first catch sight of her in the theater, she is merely "one of the crowd." She (barely) mirrors the actress on stage, who nevertheless is the first to enunciate DS's text:

> No, this hope—this hope is now without any object. This fear of losing *such a link, such a prison, such a lie,* has passed.—This whole story is already over now. It came to an end ["Elle s'achève"]. (ADAM, 24/28)

In her story, which has always already happened before it begins, every connection is a prison and a lie. After all, what is a story which is already over yet continues to be played out, in which every "new" gesture feels as though it has already happened, in which seduction is perceived as a form of violence, in which the present partner can only reenact a previous victimization, if not the incest victim's entire psychosexual life? DS's voice, already appropriated, can function only as a simulacrum of this one.

Our second glimpse finds her standing beside a door frame, once again symbolically marginalized in her *own* dream. The anonymous couple, who are first perceived *through a mirror* (doubtless projections of her own feelings), rehearse the morbidity of her inner feelings: "These whisperings, worse than silence, that you're imprisoning me in. These days, worse than death, that we're living through here side by side, you and I, like coffins laid side by side underground in a frozen garden ['Ces journées, *pires que la mort,* que nous vivons ici côte à côte, vous et moi, *comme deux cercueils placés côte à côte sous la terre d'un jardin figé lui-même*']" (ADAM, 31/35). The immobile garden anticipates the many views of the "jardin sans fleur" (ADAM, 165/181) which symbolizes her deflowering and which Chasseguet-Smirgel has, quite appropriately, interpreted as a scene of the general petrification of her being.[86] DS enacts that petrification herself in her many poses—almost always frozen with a blank expression, often her hands crossed protectively over her breast. In one scene she sits in the margins of the image in an almost fetal position.

Generally her dream never seems to exist without the invasion of his look and his words, which seem always to insist on the past yet always to confuse the specifics of that past. He frequently assures her that she was waiting for him, but she always tries to deny this (ADAM, 82). As a representation of the original scene of incest, she finds herself most often mechanically obeying the insistent scenario he provides. For example, when they dance, he is portrayed staring intently at her face, but her own look is turned away. In her own mind, that scenario more and more frequently connects up to scenes of violence, e.g., the montage of GA in the shooting gallery with an image of her own face, stricken with fear. Louise Wisechild's memory of being raped by her stepfather also contains violent elements:

> Sleeping brings repeating dreams of Don's hunting rifle propped against the twin bed in my room. Hunting season, early morning, before light. In the middle of the night he'll come shoot me. . . . He lifts the gun from the opposite bed as he leaves my room, stroking the barrel after ripping me. . . . His eyes are remote. I don't know what he's thinking. He says nothing as if nothing has happened, as if he's not there at all. . . . This couldn't happen. (OM, 68–69)

As the violence in *Marienbad* accelerates, the discrepancy increases between GA's quietly insistent voice and the film's images. "Vous m'avez répondu," he says, but she does not comply. He describes a walk in the gardens (but the image shows DS sitting watching a card game) and includes in his (unimaged) scene the "recollection" that the heel of her shoe broke and that "I suggested going to find you another *pair* ['J'ai même proposé d'aller vous en chercher une autre *paire*']" (ADAM, 81/93). The word *père* is of course evoked. The paternal is ubiquitous in her universe. GA's voice attempts another time to locate them in the garden, but again the image refuses to conform. He is *there,* but he functions in an increasingly split-off way. Significantly, GA speaks to DS via a mirror in several of the later scenes. "Nous sommes émiettés," Resnais once said: we are but fragments.[87]

If Resnais has so insistently argued that his films are about *imagination* rather than memory, it is because he fully understands the functions of repression, of screen memories, and of compromise formation in the evolution of memory.[88] Here a compromise forms around DS's ambivalence: her attraction to and need of the paternal figure, coupled with her fear and psychic injury.

As the images progress toward the moments of greatest trauma, GA describes seeing panels in the hotel's corridor, commanding: "BE QUIET!" ("TAISEZ-VOUS!"). This is a specifically oneiric element, since no written announcement would take this form in French, and signifies the paternal command of silence around the subject of incest. Louise fears that "in the middle of the night he'll come shoot me. He knows where I live. He'll know I told about what he did" (OM, 68).

DS's "Laissez-moi" devolves increasingly into "Je ne sais plus," as her confusions about what actually happened intrude on her present fantasies. These culminate in a series of moments bearing an uncanny resemblance to those shared by many incest victims: "sitting like a statue unable to move" (OM, 88); "my mouth forms a scream but no sound comes out" (OM, 38); "rooms which haunt me" (OM, 88); "sitting shaking and crying and waiting for the doorknob to open my room at night" (OM, 81). Resnais's camera catches DS frozen in place, at three different points emitting a high piercing scream which no one seems to hear (the first is drowned out by explosions and a cut to the shooting gallery, the second by a cut to a snowscape, and the third by a cut to DS *alone* in her bedroom). Finally we see DS sitting in her bedroom, waiting for the door to open. The fear of being shot is actualized in the imagery *by DS,* who imagines her white-plumed body shot and lying on the floor, but GA's voice corrects, "No, I want you alive!" Her reverie begins to include sexuality: while the string players perform in the hotel's music room, DS stands by a fountain in the garden and GA fondles her breasts. Her expression remains fixed and distant. The image returns to the concert. Uncertain of her memories and desires because robbed of her very being by the trauma of incest, she can only say, "Yes, no. I don't know any more ['Oui, non. Je ne sais plus']" (ADAM, 105/120). GA rejoins, "That's not true. . . . You've forgotten everything ['Ce n'est pas vrai. . . . Vous avez tout oublié']," enacting the incestuous father's fallacy of the double excuse: "It didn't happen, and besides, you've forgotten it already."

If, in GA's version, there is a rape—"I took you, half by force ['Je vous ai prise, à moitié de force']"—he quickly corrects himself: "Probably it wasn't by force ['Probablement ce n'était pas de force']" (ADAM, 115–16/132). The images do not help: Resnais shows DS, arms outstretched, as the camera invades her bleached out room eight successive times. Does she "accept" the rape? Louis Wisechild remembers with immense shame that during one of her stepfather's violent sexual assaults she experiences orgasm. Her immediate reaction is anger and disgust at herself. "What is wrong *with me* that I had an orgasm with him! And for years after that I was sexual with men I didn't like. I wanted to use them. . . . I didn't care about them at all. . . . This is so fucked up" (OM, 159). In *Marienbad,* GA's voice becomes hysterical:

> No, no, no! (violently:) That's wrong! . . . It wasn't by force. . . . Remember. . . . For days and days, every night. . . . All the rooms look alike. . . . But that room, for me, didn't look like any other. . . . There were no more doors, no more corridors, no more hotel, no more garden. . . . There wasn't even a garden any more.

> Non, non, non! (Avec violence:) C'est faux! . . . Ce n'était pas de force. . . . Souvenez-vous. . . . Pendant des jours et des jours, chaque nuit. . . . Toutes les chambres se ressemblent. . . . Mais cette chambre-là, pour moi, ne ressemblait à aucune autre. . . . Il n'y avait plus de portes, plus de couloirs, plus d'hôtel, plus de jardin. . . . Il n'y avait plus, même de jardin.
> (ADAM, 147/165)

His story, now so thoroughly imbricated in her version that it *becomes* history, is full of contradictions and denial. No clarity seems possible. It is very much like their versions of the statues: while GA argues that the couple on the pedestal represents "some precise scene," he nevertheless confesses that he does not really know and that it might as well have been "vous et moi, aussi bien" (see plate 14).

84

PLATE 14.   The apocryphal statue evokes conflicting interpretations from Delphine Seyrig and Giorgio Albertazzi in Resnais's *L'Année dernière à Marienbad*. (Courtesy of the Museum of Modern Art Film Stills Archive.)

Later he revises his version to claim that the man is trying to protect the woman from danger and then argues that *even if she sees it differently, their versions are not incompatible* (ADAM 65/74). SP gives yet another version (just as apocryphal, since the statue, as we know, was completed by Resnais's crew especially for the film) in which the telescoping of different time periods and the question of treason are prominent (ADAM, 69/79). Both versions converge in their effect of robbing DS of her version and of confusing real and imagined versions of the same event.

The film ends enigmatically, to be sure, but achieves closure only after the dream has included an imagined violent end for GA: he appears to have fallen from the collapsing balustrade overlooking the flowerless gardens. Subsequently, Resnais returns to the allusion to *Rosmer* and the play of incest, suggesting in a way that we have been inside Rebecca West's traumatic dream. As GA's insistent voice fades, his final words are "où vous étiez maintenant déjà en train de vous perdre, pour toujours, dans la nuit tranquille, seule avec moi." DS is always "alone with," for in that oxymoron are contained the seeds of both Lacan's mirror-stage construction of an identity formed of a self and an alienated other, as well as the traces of the incestuous father's pervasive presence in the fragmented self of the incest victim. No resolution seems possible, given the terms of the construct. The film's symmetrical patterning, as Roy Armes has noted, constrains the second half of the work to "constitute a mirror-image of the first."[89] The text returns, like the repressed itself, to occupy the screen as a sign of both the reality and the fictive nature of the images we have witnessed. But also the danger of the repetition compulsion encountered in the damaged self is that it will tragically repeat the same over and over again.

The arrangement in the film is constructed specifically to deny visual pleasure (especially of the kind found in later Robbe-Grillet films) and to substitute an *unpleasurable* experience of doubt, anxiety, and trauma. In so doing, Resnais manages to *undo* his own dependence on the absolute authority implied in Robbe-Grillet's overly detailed (and overtly violent) scenario. "J'essaie toujours," he had said, "quand il y a un systématisme dans un film, de brièvement dire le contraire. Je nie toute la construction d'un film *par un détail,* un zeste d'irrationnel."[90] If there were ever a detail that undid the entire system that contained it, the introduction of the allusion to Ibsen is just such a detail. It does not foreclose other possible meanings of the film (certainly the male gaze will always find some pleasure in such stories), but it does add a level that allows us to understand every element in the film as a consistent scenario. It may be that my evocation of the incest motif will encounter "serious resistance, based on the most distressing emotions . . . which might imperil the effect of" my essay.[91] But I will leave the last word to Resnais himself: "Pour moi, les personnages de mes films sont des êtres réels. Ils ont leur vie à eux, latente, mystérieuse. . . . Le réalisme n'exclut pas l'ambiguïté."[92] That ambiguity may not be pleasurable, but as Resnais says elsewhere, "As soon as you delve into the unconscious, an emotion may arise. . . . I find it interesting to explore this universe, from the point of view of truth, if not that of morality. . . . My desire is to provoke in my spectator some change, however small, however delayed. . . . My goal will have been achieved if, for example, two weeks after seeing one of my films, my spectator experiences a kind of click in the face of some event apparently unrelated to the subject of the film. . . . I want to provoke some sort of reflection, perhaps anger, bitterness, whatever it takes to produce some reflection."[93] I believe Resnais has attained his goal.

Chapter Four

In the Labyrinth of Illusions: Chabrol's Mirrored Films

> The boy began to enjoy his thrilling flight and left his
> guide to roam the ranges of the heavens, and soared too
> high. The scorching sun so close softened the fragrant
> wax that bound his wings . . .
> —*Ovid*

> What was he in this world of contending ambitions? . . .
> a poet whose thoughts never went beyond the moment,
> a moth flitting from one bright gleaming object to an-
> other . . . meaning well, doing ill.
> —*Balzac*

Claude Chabrol's *Le Beau Serge* has been called "the film that started
the New Wave."[1] Despite our current uncertainty as to exactly what
the new wave was, *Le Beau Serge* nevertheless seems at first glance an
unlikely candidate to be the film that "started it all." And with twenty-
five years of hindsight, Chabrol himself seems a less and less likely
candidate to be a new wave leader. Indeed, he himself once said that
"there is no new wave, there is only the sea ['il n'y a pas de nouvelle
vague, il n'y a que la mer']."[2] His work since 1959 has been singularly
lacking in direction, and more often than not Chabrol "accepts the
narrative conceptions of the moment" and does not impose his own
creative stamp.[3] Films such as *Les Godelureaux* now strike us as frivo-
lous, while others, such as *Le Tigre aime la chair fraiche,* seem too
blatantly commercial to merit their "auteur" a place in the cinematic
pantheon that honors Chabrol's contemporaries Godard, Truffaut,
Rohmer, Resnais, and Malle. It does not help much that Chabrol

often uses interviews as occasions for putting on a "clown's mask" and seems entirely untroubled by self-contradiction and silliness.[4] And yet, given another look, *Le Beau Serge* may arouse our interest partly because it initially seems so unlike the productions of Chabrol's contemporaries in the *Cahiers* crowd and partly because of the unusual relationship it maintains with Chabrol's second work, *Les Cousins*.

At its unveiling, *Le Beau Serge* was generally categorized as a piece of realism, prompting one reviewer to label it "a gray, realistic, incoherent study of contemporary French provincial life."[5] Robin Wood and Michael Walker concur that "when *Le Beau Serge* first appeared it looked like an attempt at developing a French neo-realist school, with Chabrol shooting entirely on location, using the real inhabitants of a real village, showing a consistent concern to represent the surface details of the environment and the people's lives with the greatest possible fidelity." And although they initially claim that "it is as germinal to Chabrol's oeuvre as *A bout de souffle* to Godard's,"[6] they end up either relegating it to the realistic genre from which they had claimed to rescue it or casting it into a vaguely religious mold.[7]

The film recounts the return of a native son to his village of Sardent and his thoroughly misguided attempts to help his old friend, Serge. When François (Jean-Claude Brialy) arrives from Paris, he finds the village very much as he had left it but the people changed. Some, like the butcher, have died; others have grown up and turned out far different from what he had expected. In particular, François discovers that Serge (Gérard Blain), who had wanted to be an architect, is now a truck driver for a lumber company, extremely embittered and ravaged by alcoholism.

François himself is sick, recovering from a bout of tuberculosis, and contents himself with wandering about the town. He quickly falls in with Marie (Bernadette Lafont) and climbs to her house on the hill for an afternoon of easy pleasure. He also visits the local priest (Claude Cerval) and rebukes him for not doing enough to save his parishioners. Finally, learning that Serge's first child had been born a "mongolien" and had quickly died, François attempts to console his friend and advises him to leave his wife, Yvonne (Michèle Meritz), to avoid further bitterness.

This piece of advice, coupled with François's attentions to Marie (whom Serge had once bedded), create tensions between the two and eventually lead to a nasty fight during an evening of dancing, in which François is severely beaten. François retires to his room for many weeks until the night that Yvonne is to give birth to her second child, an event generally expected to produce disastrous results. Roused by a neighbor, he hurries out into the snowy night, helps Yvonne into bed, races for the doctor, and then hunts down Serge, who is hopelessly drunk and lying in a sty, and literally drags him home to witness the birth of a son. As the cries of the infant break the lugubrious silence of the peasant cottage, François sinks down (presumably) to his death and Serge laughs hysterically. The final image of the film focuses on Serge's smile but loses focus to produce the visual effect of a horrible, grinning skull.

Realism of some detail there may be in this film, but the work hardly fits a neorealist classification;[8] many disturbing elements interfere. The fragmentary view of the village, the elliptical nature of the characters' lives, and above all the enigmatic relationship between the two protagonists create an uneasiness that is not easily calmed.[9] Too many ambiguities haunt the end of the film to permit a realist interpretation. Although critical response to the film has been (understandably) slight, the two major studies of Chabrol attempt a "Christian" reading of the work but ultimately renounce any attempt to produce a coherent sense of the plot. Joel Magny's strategy is particularly instructive, especially since his study of Chabrol's work is otherwise so perceptive. Although his symbolic reading "is evidently set in a Christian framework," Magny attempts two different religious interpretations without entire success. The first, "undoubtedly faithful to the conscious intentions of the author, at the time a practicing Catholic," nevertheless "remains obscure." The second, "an esoteric kind of symbolism," also remains "susceptible to as many objections as the first." Magny concludes: "The result is a film that is more confused than really ambiguous for which a Christian interpretation nevertheless works because it is shared, a priori, by most of the audience."[10]

This "orthodox" interpretation of the work accounts only with difficulty for the several highly unsatisfactory encounters with the village priest, the remarkably skeptic "I believed . . . ['J'ai cru . . .']" voiced by François as he collapses at the end of the film, and the nebulous death's head that seems to vitiate all of his efforts.[11] Although I admire Magny's candor, I am not ready to label the film "confused" simply because it does not so easily offer itself to interpretation. Nor can Magny be blamed; Chabrol's own statements on the "readability" ("lisibilité") of his films are ironically highly ambiguous: "I like to show that things are infinitely more complicated than they seem. A film has to be easily understood at the outset. It is better that its façade appear to be smooth ['lisse']."[12] In other words, Chabrol delights in presenting simple appearances designed to hide deeper complexities. It is hardly surprising that the film was mistakenly labeled realist or that an "obviously" Christian interpretation fails to account for all of its ambiguities. Another approach would seem imperative.

Indeed, a satisfactory understanding of *Le Beau Serge* begins to emerge by reading it together with its cousin, *Les Cousins,* for the two films share too many doubled configurations to be entirely understood separately. Chabrol has informed us that he wrote *Les Cousins* before *Le Beau Serge* but did not shoot it first because of financial considerations. His own version of the two films' interconnection intends "the universe of *Le Beau Serge*" as "the arrival of a 'Christic' character in a socialist-communist rural peasant community—in any case one that is anti-clerical. The universe of *Les Cousins,* the arrival of a young man from the provinces into a right-wing Parisian world. I used the same actors to make a nice little binary statement."[13] Jean-Claude Brialy plays the more sophisticated city cousin in both films and Gérard Blain the naive country cousin. Jeanne Perez has virtually the same role in each film: the city concierge, who knows everything, and the innkeeper in Sardent, who spreads François's secrets throughout the village. Raymond Durgnat reports that Chabrol told him, "Now I'm cured of curés in the cinema: I closed the church Gérard Blain tried to enter in *Les Cousins* by way of revenging myself for *Le Beau Serge*."[14] Although it is not at all clear in what way the *Cousins* sequence constitutes a "cure for curates," it is at least evident that the two films constitute an intricate continuity for their author.

If some have seen in this *jumelage* the retelling of Horace's and La Fontaine's fables of the country mouse and the city mouse, such references tend to oversimplify rather than develop the themes of the two works.[15] In searching out the motifs that emerge from the superposition of the two works, I find myself uncannily reoccupying the position Chabrol took up to survey Hitchcock's work. Chabrol found himself on the verge of seeing too much, or at least more than he felt Hitchcock would have wanted him to see:

> I hope Hitchcock will forgive me for having tried to clarify ["mettre au clair"] this important motif in his work (the image hidden in the tapestry . . . which can't be expressed in words) that he tried so carefully and prudishly to hide ["tant de soin et de pudeur à cacher"]. My excuse is that this project will perhaps permit us to dissipate a misunderstanding that would engender misreading ["à dissiper un malentendu qui engendrait la méconnaissance"].[16]

A curious justification! Chabrol sounds like no one so much as his own character François might sound explaining his attempt to "understand" the problem Serge has not asked him to explore. More to the point, Chabrol's descriptions of Hitchcock's methods (the careful and prudish attempt to hide a motif) are virtually mirrored in the opacity of Chabrol's prose: the enterprise will perhaps help to dissipate a misunderstanding that would engender misreading!? If there were ever a phrase whose own labyrinthine opacity might in and of itself engender misunderstanding and misreading, Chabrol has enunciated it here. Finally, Chabrol's gesture of excuse to Hitchcock sounds all too much like a displacement, for "mettre au clair" is an apt term for the cinema itself, and Chabrol's own cinema bears a remarkable resemblance to this aspect of Hitchcock's. Chabrol frequently reminds us how appearances can be misleading *and* revealing, and indeed Paul in *Les Cousins* reminds his cousin and the viewer, "One must not trust to appearances ['Il ne faut pas se fier aux apparences']."[17] The entire quotation thus reads as a kind of encrypted invitation to a reading of Chabrol's own work. As we shall appreciate in a moment, the quotation holds yet another clue to understanding Chabrol.

In mobilizing a general appreciation of Hitchcock, Chabrol situated the matrix—"figure mère"—of his Hollywood counterpart's films in the immobilized photographer in *Rear Window.* If the conclusion is unsurprising, the phrase "figure mère" is nevertheless revealing as a methodology.[18] It immediately recalls Chabrol's own pun "there is no new wave, only the sea ['la mer']," and provokes the question, What is the matrix or "figure mère" of Chabrol's own cinema? The answer, like that for Hitchcock, is "hidden in the tapestry" of Chabrol's films. To find it we must take another look at and around the margins of Chabrol's work.

One of the most remarkable features of that work is the mirroring accomplished in Chabrol's first two films. If *Le Beau Serge* recounts the arrival of the Parisian cousin in the provinces, *Les Cousins* presents the corresponding voyage in the other direction. Just as the "first" film opens with a bus ride, the "second" opens with a taxi ride. Charles (Gérard Blain) enters the world of his cousin Paul (Jean-Claude Brialy), taking up residence with him in their uncle Henri's darkly mysterious apartment. Charles feels no more at home there than François had in Sardent. Paul's world is inhabited by strange figures: Clovis (Claude Cerval), an older "friend" who loves violence; members of L'Association, a student club in the Latin Quarter; and various hangers-on who are always ready to party. Like François in *Le Beau Serge*, Charles meets a woman, Florence (Juliette Mayniel), who captures his attention, and, again like François, he loses her to his cousin. When he makes a date with her to meet after his three o'clock class at the Sorbonne, she comes to the apartment at three and is "redirected" into Paul's arms. Charles remembers that he has come to Paris to study law, like his cousin, and, unlike Paul, spends most of the rest of the film holed up in the deepest recesses of the apartment reading law and writing letters to his mother. Paul never studies, counting on his "excellent command of the principles of law" to help him through the exams. When the crucial moment arrives, Paul is passed (thanks to Clovis, who for a fee provides the answers), and Charles is flunked. Angry and frustrated, Charles tears up a year's worth of notes and his student identity card and hurls them into the Seine. Returning to the apartment, he loads one chamber of a revolver, aims the gun at his sleeping cousin's head, and pulls the trigger. The gun's chamber is empty. Paul is saved by chance; Charles will not be so lucky. After a night asleep at his desk, Charles is confronted by Paul, who histrionically aims the pistol at him and fires, killing him instantly. As in *Le Beau Serge*, the film ends in this mirrored figure of violence in which the visitor dies and the native son's death is prefigured by a final visual.

There is an additional commonality between these films that to date has gone largely unnoticed and yet does more to link Chabrol's work with that of his fellow sailors in the new wave than any other aspect of his films. When François arrives in Sardent, he very pointedly unpacks a collection of books from his suitcase and deliberately places his library on a shelf. We do not see this library again, it turns out, until *Les Cousins*. There it is figured as a *librairie* next-door to the apartment and becomes a refuge for the innocent Charles. Charles has just met Florence in the depths of L'Association, and, smitten, he rushes outside to follow her only to discover her in the company of another man. Dejectedly he enters a bookstore where the clerk, played by Guy Decomble, the schoolteacher of *Les 400 coups*, perceives in him a kindred spirit:

> LIBRAIRE: What would you like, Monsieur, something unusual, a novelty?
> CHARLES: I'm not too fond of that kind of thing. I'm leaning toward something by Balzac.
> LIBRAIRE: You're from the provinces.
> CHARLES: Does it show?

LIBRAIRE: Not really, but reading Balzac at your age is a sure sign of a provincial. Look at your friends, what do they read? That bunch next-door buys only murder mysteries. I tried to give one of them a copy of Balzac's *Le Père Goriot*. He very nearly threw it at me. . . . Murder mysteries and pornography. They claim they need to relax.

CHARLES: You look like you've given up completely.

LIBRAIRE: And with good reason! There are so many things to read, a lifetime wouldn't suffice. To see them wasting their time like that. . . .

CHARLES: You're right. I've spent the last ten years of my life reading. I find it most enjoyable.

LIBRAIRE: Look here, these days people should read Dostoevsky. He writes about everything that's wrong with us. They laughed at me.

CHARLES: You seem very bitter.

LIBRAIRE: And for good reason! When provincials are the only ones who buy Balzac any more . . . but when I say "buy," understand me: I'm going to offer you your Balzac free of charge. So, go ahead and choose. I like you.

CHARLES: That's very nice of you, but I can pay for it.

LIBRAIRE: Why? I can make it up on all the trash novels I sell. And besides, what I make on Balzac is so minimal compared to the enormous pleasure I'll get from giving it to you that I'll come out way ahead. So choose. . . . Have you read *Les Illusions perdues?* No? Then steal it. I won't look. Go on. Hurry up and take it!

CHARLES: You're a strange book dealer! You'll end up broke.

LIBRAIRE: It's because you love books. Your eyes are full of the treasures you've read. But now you're going to live in a strange world. You'll see![19]

Throughout this conversation, Chabrol's camera has kept both characters in close proximity, occasionally changing positions, but always tightly linked. Once they step outside the shop, however, the figure of Paul intervenes between them, and the intruder exclaims, "What a weird idea to be talking about books! They're furious. They can't play without you." The book dealer suddenly turns to Paul and asks, "Is this your brother?" "We're cousins," replies Paul. "It's all the same," responds the merchant cryptically. Charles will return twice more to this father figure when his problems with his "brother" become unbearable.

The advice to read Balzac's *Les Illusions perdues* merely confirms, in a way, what we *have* been doing from the outset of our encounter with these films, for Chabrol's work has often been compared to that of the nineteenth century's father of realism.[20] *Les Illusions perdues*, however, turns out to entertain an uncanny relationship to Chabrol's film(s).

The reader will immediately remember that Balzac's novel also deals with a pair of "brothers," David Séchard, the dry, studious brother, identified with life in the provinces, and Lucien (Chardon) de Rubempré, the prodigal "thistle," who is carried by the first favorable wind to Paris to seek his fortune. Lucien constitutes a kind of condensation of Chabrol's cousins, for his sojourn in Paris presents a constant choice between poetic success, which can be earned only through studious celibacy, and social success, which is quickly got by games of influence and profligate excesses. Like Charles, Lucien also comes to depend on book dealers, but he metamorphoses into a Paul-like extravagant, gaining influence through social brilliance and parties rather than through hard work. Balzac's *viveurs* are doubled by Paul's Association in *Les Cousins,* and the composite figure of Madame de Bargeton and Coralie is doubled by Florence.[21] The crowning moment of *Les Illusions perdues* comes at a supper given by Lucien and Coralie, much like the soirée given by Paul, but that very supper hides the seeds of Lucien's downfall. Soon afterward he is shot and wounded in a duel, falls into a fever, and quits Paris. In the meantime, his extravagances bring about the downfall of his provincial brother, David.

It is tempting to perceive the many similarities between the two works as a clever allusion affording the viewer a proleptic appreciation of Charles's impending fate. And yet, as is all too often the case with Chabrol, appearances may be deceiving. Where there is a "surface lisse," we have been warned to regard "things" as "infinitely more complicated than they seem."[22] For one thing, the circulation of Balzac's novel is disquieting: it is the only example in all of new wave cinema of a text that is *returned*.[23] And it is returned at a highly charged moment in *Les Cousins*. Charles has just "tragically" missed his rendezvous with Florence, leading to her involvement with Paul. When he returns to the apartment after vainly waiting for her near the Sorbonne, he is met by Paul and Florence, descending a staircase that is positioned exactly like the one Brialy and Bernadette Lafont use when stealing away (from Gérard Blain) in *Le Beau Serge*. In that film, Serge "*a beau* aimer Marie"—he loves Marie *in vain*. In *this* film, Blain is still the odd man out, and upon ascending the staircase to view the scene he might have had with Florence, he finds only a movie projector running, creating a disturbing flicker on the blank screen near the bed. Charles is too late to catch (or enjoy) the scene of sexuality directly and will ultimately displace his erotic feelings into violent ones. His immediate reaction, however, is to venture back to the paternal book dealer next-door and return the copy of Balzac he had "stolen." This is a most curious act, and as the most enigmatic moment of the entire film, it suggests itself as a "hidden figure of the tapestry" that hides and reveals the film's "figure mère."

The enigma, of course, resides in Charles's decision to abort the reading, thereby ignoring the advice this paternal figure has offered. Has he read the novel? We cannot know, but we do know that in returning it, he seems to be turning his back on exactly the kind of prolepsis that might save him. This is made all the more evident by the way Chabrol's camera focuses on a series of titles turning like haunting reminders of his plight in the display window of the bookstore as Charles exits. Such titles as *L'Outrage, La Menteuse, Le Château de ma mère,* and *Le Malheur d'aimer* seem almost to call out for Charles's attention. Literature's "lessons for life" constitute one of its figures of authority. The difficulty lies in interpreting that authority. Our interpretation must begin in the nexus of parallels revealed by this otherwise marginal scene.

In returning Balzac, Charles ironically reenacts the very moment that signals the failure of Lucien—rejection of paternal advice. Like Charles, Lucien finds himself thrown into a most mystifying world. The usual supports have disappeared, and the woman that had promised to serve as his guide has betrayed him. With Madame de Bargeton's rejection, Lucien must find another guide through the maze of false trails and dead ends that constitute Parisian society to the outsider. Lucien is fortunate enough to meet Daniel D'Arthez and to benefit from his fatherly advice.

> Your story is mine, monsieur, and the story of ten or twelve hundred young fellows besides who come from the country to Paris every year. . . . There is no cheap route to greatness. . . . The words of genius are watered with tears. The gift that is in you, like an existence in the physical world, passes through childhood and its maladies. Nature sweeps away sickly or deformed creatures, and society rejects an imperfectly developed talent. Any man who means to rise above the rest ["Qui veut s'élever au-dessus des hommes"] must make ready for a struggle and be undaunted by difficulties. A great writer is a martyr who does not die ["un martyr qui ne mourra pas"]; that is all. . . . Unless you have within you the will of genius, unless you are gifted with angelic patience, unless, no matter how far the freaks of fate have set you from your destined goal, you can find the way to your infinite ["le chemin de votre infini"] . . . you had better give up at once. (IP, 66, 68/228)

In inviting Charles to read *Les Illusions perdues,* the book seller has invited his new protégé to recapitulate exactly this moment of the novel, that is, to have literature stand in for him as the ultimate authority. Daniel's advice is not only good advice, it has a distinctly mythical ring to it. In identifying his own and Lucien's fate with that of thousands of others, D'Arthez allegorizes their experience, and he reinforces this level of his discourse by comparing society's rules to natural laws and by referring to the young poet's struggle as "la destinée." But this is not just any myth: it is very specifically the myth of Icarus and opens our reading of Balzac to the mythic substructure of that text, remarkably enough, the same one that subtends both of Chabrol's films as well as the very relationship between literature and film.[24] "Qui veut s'élever au-dessus des hommes" describes the metaphorical flight that Lucien is about to undertake on the "chemin de [son] infini." Daedalus, of course, gives similar advice to his son:

> Next he prepared his son. "Take care," he said,
> "To fly a middle course, lest if you sink
> Too low the waves may weight your feathers; if
> Too high, the heat may burn them. Fly half-way
> Between these two. And do not watch the stars,
> . . . Set your course where I shall lead."[25]

Balzac seems to spread his novelistic wings to incorporate this Icarian figure within the larger labyrinth of his depiction of Paris, without ever betraying the rigorously realistic vein of the work. Indeed, it is just such a composition of the transcendental and fantastic with an insistence on realism that characterizes Balzac's own genius. Vautrin may inhabit the Maison Vauquer in all its Left Bank seediness, but when necessary he metamorphoses effortlessly and inexplicably into more powerful figures. There seems always to be such an escape hatch from everyday realism somewhere in Balzac's novels. If not figured as the back of a closet as it is in C. S. Lewis's work, that fantastic gap is no less constant a figure in the French novelist's work.

Despite Balzac's own taste for the excesses of the fantastic, Lucien-Icarus is severely punished for disobeying D'Arthez's solidly middle-of-the-road advice against excess. Whereas in the provinces Lucien is portrayed as "a young swan whose wings provincial life had not yet clipped," once in Paris this "angel with many-colored wings ['ange aux ailes diaprés']" (IP, 108/274), "handsome as a Greek god" (114/279), is too "surprised . . . by the sharp contrast of heights and of depths" (149/320) to avoid a fall. Rather, "he had no definite aim . . . a moth flitting from one bright gleaming object to another ['il allait de lumière en lumière comme un papillon']" (344/522) and

96

finally is portrayed as "a fallen eagle ['un aiglon qui tombe'] . . . plunged into that dreadful sea of Paris ['jeté dans cette affreuse mer parisienne']" (83/46).

Indeed, once the outlines of the cretin figure of the labyrinth begin to emerge, it is difficult not to see them everywhere. Balzac has served (perhaps like Charles himself next to Paul) as a kind of royal road to the "figure mère" of Chabrol's cinema. Between the "stealing" of the book and its return, as between the covers of *Les Illusions perdues*, lies a labyrinth of allusions to the Daedalus-Icarus myth, to the labyrinth itself, and to its first visitor, Theseus. Of course, Chabrol gives them a very different spin than did Balzac and, certainly, Ovid or Apollodorus.[26]

We should not be surprised by the presence of the Greek myth in Chabrol's work, for virtually his entire *oeuvre* constitutes an active rejection of the Christian one. Chabrol once claimed that "a film is made in the same way everything else is; that is, all films tell the history of the world from its origins to our times, more or less well, to be sure, but tell it they do."[27] In an article published in *Cahiers du cinéma* shortly after the appearance of his first two films, Chabrol set out to prove that there was in fact little difference in scope between a "small subject" such as "a quarrel between neighbors" and a "large subject" such as "the apocalypse of our times."[28] It is Chabrol's humor to turn both "large" and "small" subjects into "fool's traps," but along the way he has nevertheless suggested, doubtless in defense of his own cinema, that small subjects contain large implications, in fact, "the smaller the subject, the more grandly one can treat it." Ironically, although he disavows them, all of the elements he sarcastically groups as "Grands Sujets Humains," that is, love, virile fraternity, self-exploration, nostalgia, death, and godhead, are exactly the elements that compose *Le Beau Serge*. The film is clearly "un petit sujet . . . traité avec grandeur." That grandeur is perhaps most tellingly located in the construct Chabrol labels "my personal executioner—having descended into the depths of the abyss, man, he discovers the strength to climb back out." This abyss, whether its topology is vertical or horizontal, is but an alternate version of the metaphor of the labyrinth.[29] If we look again at Chabrol's statement about the "figure mère" of Hitchcock's cinema, we cannot miss the "figure mère" of Chabrol's lurking alongside: "cacher l'image dans la tapisserie." The labyrinth, we must remember, holds a nexus of conflicting powerful messages: it was constructed to be virtually unreadable so as to "hide" the monster at its center, yet it stands as one of the most important architectural accomplishments of the human mind and psyche. Plumbing its depths will more likely lead to impasse than to resolution, and the prize for finding its deepest level is the confrontation with the man-beast imprisoned within. Its architect is its prisoner (!), and the maze can only be fathomed with the help of the woman who holds the thread. It invites and repels exploration, it excites and denies flight. The monster at the center is a figure of incest and excess and must be carefully repressed yet constantly fed through the sacrifice of the flower of youth. That monster can only be "had" while it is asleep. It sounds, in other words, uncannily like the figure of the unconscious itself: a topos of opposites without contradiction, of bestial drives, of repressed hunger and the seat of the figure of the (incestuous) Other, accessible only through dreams. Virtually all of the myths surrounding the labyrinth (Daedalus, the Minotaur, Icarus, Theseus, Ariadne and Phedre) broach incestuous desire,[30] paternal interdiction, repression and expression of unbridled curiosity, desire for and rejection of the maternal.

There is an additional figure implied in the labyrinth that Ovid was careful to include in his version:

> Minos reached the harbour in the isle of Crete
> And, disembarking, paid his vows to Jove,
> A hundred bulls, and hung the spoils of war
> To adorn his palace walls. His dynasty's
> Disgrace had grown; the monstrous hybrid beast
> Declared the queen's obscene adultery.
> To rid his precincts of this shame the King
> Planned to confine him shut away within
> Blind walls of intricate complexity.
> The structure was designed by Daedalus,
> That famous architect. *Appearances*
> *Were all confused; he led the eye astray*
> By a mazy multitude of winding ways,
> Just as Maeander plays among the meads
> Of Phrygia and in its puzzling flow
> Glides back and forth *and meets itself* and sees
> Its waters on the way and winds along,
> Facing sometimes its source, sometimes the sea.
> So Daedalus in countless corridors
> Built bafflement, and hardly could himself
> Make his way out, so puzzling was the maze.
> (OM, 175–76)

Chabrol's own insistence on the deceptive nature of appearances is remarkably constant and figures not only in *Les Cousins,* where Paul tells Charles, "You can't trust appearances," but throughout his work. Joel Magny argues that "the initial givens keep changing throughout the film, and none is ever really what it appears to be. The most exemplary of Chabrol's heroes condense the most contradictory tendencies of the 'homo chabrolus.'"[31] Chabrol himself adds, "Cinema is vehicle for reflection. . . . I'm not saying that History doesn't exist, but simply that chance happenings seem designed to refute it ['la nier']. That's what's really sublime: the gods exist, they both complement and cancel each other out; truth is a marvelous mix of the two whose dosage remains beyond the ken of mortals. . . . This kind of poetic vision tells us much more about historical moments than do all kinds of analyses."[32] "Realism," Chabrol reminds us elsewhere, "is never reality. It's just a game of mirrors."[33]

So too, *Le Beau Serge* and *Les Cousins* constitute a game of mirrors in which each film seems, as mirrors do, to reverse the field of vision. If LA NIER are the words that characterize illusion's hold on history, they seem to hold another fascination for Chabrol. When François arrives in Sardent, he takes a room in the HOTEL CHAULNIER. As he (as well as the spectator) looks from the window of this room to the town square below, the camera catches a piece of the hotel's sign:

HOT-**EL**

CHAUL-**NIER**

is the fragment that appears in the frame. In the light of Chabrol's (and Balzac's) insistence on the labyrinth, this fragment could signify "AILE NIÉE" ("the wing[s] denied," a cryptogram of Icarus's fall). Given the nexus of overdetermination that accompanies the figure of the labyrinth, EL could also signify elevation and the heights to which François will attempt to rise before he falls. And given the position of women in both *Le Beau Serge* and *Les Cousins,* the phrase could well signal "ELLE NIÉE" ("woman denied"). Such interpretation might seem gratuitous were it not for three other elements. First, Chabrol has always insisted (and his collaborators corroborate this) that *nothing* is allowed in the field of his camera's vision that is not intended. Describing his and Rohmer's approach to Hitchcock, Chabrol stated,

> We started out with that old cliché: "But he couldn't have thought of all that!" Now I know from experience that one does think of "all that" and even more . . . for example, I am well aware that the placement of a pitcher one centimeter to the right or the left on a table has meaning. It's absolutely crazy, and in this kind of delirium, maybe we aren't so crazy as all that.[34]

Elsewhere Chabrol asserts, "I am extremely precise about what you see on the screen." His assistant Pierre Gailliard confirms, "He knows exactly what he wants. *Nothing* is left to chance."[35]

Second, in another scene of extreme intensity, Chabrol's camera centers determinedly on the word RICARD and then moves just far enough to the right to eliminate the R, leaving the word ICARD, a homonym for ICARE, the French Icarus. As for the verbal puns, Chabrol is known for his liberties with the *calembour,* and he told Jean-Claude Bonnet, a propos of another film, "I've never hesitated to make plays on words."[36]

Finally, the entire film resonates with the Icarian myth.[37] Fran-çois's experience in Sardent begins with the idea of the journey: an image of a bus traveling away from Paris. Once in Sardent, he seems, for most of the film, to concentrate on ascent, both geographically and morally. As he leaves the bus, Michel takes his suitcase and asks, "Shall we go up? ['On y monte?']" François and Michel then spend several minutes climbing toward the Hotel Chaulnier, and once there, François again climbs to an upper floor, from which he seems to dominate the entire town. During the major part of the film, Chabrol's camera is always situated in such a way that François ap-pears to be taller than or above those around him. Thus, both Michel and Serge constantly appear to be looking up at François. François's lightness is accentuated by the fact that he never accepts food. No less than five times in the first seven minutes of footage, someone offers him a meal, and each time he pointedly refuses. On his first day in town he rises with the sun and gambols about like a school boy, throwing a stick up in the air in such a way that it catches in the branches of a tree and does not fall back to the ground. This particular scene recalls the Ovidian detail that as Daedalus worked,

> . . . His boy stood by,
> Young Icarus, who, blithely unaware
> He plays with his own peril, tries to catch
> Feathers that float upon the wandering breeze,
> Or softens with his thumb the yellow wax
> And by his laughing mischief interrupts
> His father's wondrous work.
>
> (OM, 177)

Shortly after meeting Marie, he is again pictured in a long ascent up to her house in pursuit of pure desire. Chabrol occludes the scene of their lovemaking but carefully keeps the aftermath, in which Marie, sensing François's loftiness, quickly deflates her lover, saying bitterly, "You seem to look on us as if we were insects." François's only response: "I was afraid of dying."(!) Now, human beings take on the appearance of insects from either the social scientist's or the bird's-eye view. In *L'Espoir,* for example, Malraux compellingly describes the lines of the enemy as so many ants as seen from the planes of the Republican air squadron.[38] As for the social scientist's view, Rainer Werner Fassbinder thoroughly disparages Chabrol's objectivity in arguing that "Chabrol's viewpoint is not that of the entomologist, as is often claimed, but that of *a child* who keeps a collection of insects in a glass case and observes with alternating amazement and fear and delight, the marvellous behavior patterns of his tiny creatures. . . . His standpoint, in fact, varies."[39] There is a suggestion here that Chabrol projects his own, childlike view on the film's youthful voyager.

If breaking the paternal law constitutes Icarus's identity theme, then François's behavior is thoroughly Icarian: from his first moments in Sardent, he seems intent on transgression. Already during his first ascent to Sardent from the bus, Michel comments on François's smoking when he is sick, clearly countermanding his doctors' orders. His affair with Marie also foregrounds the figure of excess and the breaking of oedipal interdiction. Marie represents desire; her house's situation well above Serge's suggests that François-Icarus has suddenly flown too high. She is, after all, only seventeen and, despite Serge's marriage to Yvonne, symbolically "belongs" to *him.* François's affair is all the more troublesome since Marie tells him that Serge has said he is "the only friend he'd ever had." Once inside the house, Marie tells him, "My father is not here," clearly an invitation to break a taboo. In fact, however, her father is there, his totemlike portrait hanging conspicuously on the staircase, so that they must pass and rise above him to reach the locus of forbidden desire. Although the progression of François's fall is not marked in linear fashion, it is evident that his loss of control begins after this scene with Marie.

It is notable, too, that the next time we perceive François, he is entering the village church—not to pray, but to contend with and usurp the place of the spiritual father of Sardent. Serge has already chastised him for "always looking to be a goodie-goodie." His arrival at the church occurs only at the conclusion of the mass, and François proceeds, after the obligatory brush with the baptismal font, directly to the apse. There he ascends to the altar and, *dipping his fingers in the hot wax of the candles,* burns them as he snuffs out the light. This usurpation of the priest's function is followed by a conversation in which François not only disregards the priest's advice but upbraids him for lack of paternal authority:

> PRÊTRE: So, what are your plans? ["A quoi te destines-tu?"]
> FRANÇOIS: Earning lots of money.
> PRÊTRE: You used to talk of becoming a priest.
> FRANÇOIS: I got over it.
> PRÊTRE: It's as if the villagers here were sinking into quicksand. . . . Michel, Serge, they no longer believe in anything. . . . I haven't figured out how to draw them into the fold. I haven't even been able to keep the others in the fold.
> FRANÇOIS: There was something that maybe could have been done, and no one did anything.
> PRÊTRE: You have no right to criticize me!

Once outside the church, François and the priest encounter Serge, sprawling, as if a fallen angel, on the church steps. Serge taunts the father about his sermons, and the priest retorts angrily, "If I have preached to you, as you say, it's because you needed it so badly." And to both of them he complains, "You despise me, you don't even want to listen to me! And I wanted so much to help you." François's pride reaches new heights in this exchange. The paternal logos has clearly been rejected here, and the priest's words bear a curious resemblance to those of the book dealer in *Les Cousins*. François's revolt, of course, reaches its apex in the later scene with the priest in which the prelate tells him, "You're acting high and mighty! . . . Who do you think you are, Jesus Christ? . . . It's pride, pure pride." For the moment, however, the hot wax has been touched, the parental warning neglected. As François and Serge walk together after lunch, they pass a large body of water, and Serge says ominously and apparently a propos of nothing, "It's horrible underneath that water."

The third violation of a paternal injunction occurs as François meets old Glomaud (Edmond Beauchamp) in the village bar and the old man shouts angrily, "You come sniffing around my daughter!" To this François answers, "She's not your daughter." Again, whatever the eventual effect of this news on Marie (it unbinds the incest taboo between "father" and "daughter"), it immediately affords François the occasion for another dethroning of a father figure. To emphasize the fatal effects for François, Chabrol films the young man's pursuit of his elder down the hill and into a cemetery, where they struggle physically. Glomaud is downed temporarily, but the effect on François is that he takes to his bed.

To concentrate on the François-Icarus figure as I have so far done represents a necessary but partial step in understanding the larger configuration of the film(s). The pairing of *Le Beau Serge* and *Les Cousins* allows us to see that both identity and chronology are intricated in complex ways. Not only has Chabrol created confusion as to the temporal priority of these two works, he inserts in each film a visual "play" with time that metaphorizes the breakdown of fixed linearity. In *Le Beau Serge* this "play" is Yvonne's, who is pictured arbitrarily advancing the large grandfather's clock to a time that suits her immediate purpose.[40] There is little sense in the film of the passage of time, little apparent necessity of plot. François goes about his activities in Sardent with no announced purpose. Seasons change with no apparent regularity. The entire movement is more dreamlike than real. "I've always loved putting fantastic elements in my films," brags Chabrol. "Maybe they are not very obvious, but they are there nonetheless."[41] One of the effects of this temporal dreamscape is to collapse the temporal distinctions of the "plot" of the myth of the labyrinth.[42] There is a general sense that the story of Theseus and Ariadne precedes the flight of Daedalus and Icarus, simply because that is how Ovid arranges his version, but there is no foundation for such priority, nor does myth need to isolate these stories from each other: all of the elements of the labyrinth are imbricated *by the structure of the labyrinth itself*.[43] In other words, the symbolic structure of mythology subtends all linear arrangements of myth.

Such a scrambling of linearity accounts for two complex features of this narration. Although it is tempting to see François-Icarus's flight as taken from the labyrinth of Paris (following the model of Lucien in Balzac), especially since *Les Cousins* seems to constitute a Parisian labyrinth, there is every evidence here that Sardent itself reconstitutes another labyrinth and, indeed, that François's flight takes place against the constant backdrop of imprisonment. The cold, foreboding design of stone walls in the wallpaper of his room never lets us forget the labyrinthine predicament that drives him to flight. In the larger labyrinth of "confused appearances" (OM, 175), the higher Icarus flies, the more he is constrained by the limitations of his means. Height implies depth; excess, limitation; desire, repression. The more Icarus attempts to distance himself from the depths of the labyrinth, the more ironic is his resemblance to the monster who lies there. They become alike in unbridled desire, repudiation of the middle way, and the breaking of taboo. At his farthest deviation from Crete, Icarus is symbolically closest to the Minotaur.[44]

As enigmatic as Serge's behavior appears, its coherence begins "to emerge from the tapestry" when we understand him as the paradoxical opposite *and* double of François. Serge first emerges from directly behind François when the bus pulls away, revealing his presence in the square. As a figure he is constantly paired with old Glomaud, his father-in-law, and is sandwiched between this monstrous figure of incest and excess and his own stillborn son—another "monster."[45] Serge is terrified that all of his progeny will likewise be monstrous and resents Yvonne for this. In his turn, he seems gradually to metamorphose into a monstrous figure himself. Early on, however, we learn from Michel that Serge wanted to be an architect (which would figure him as Daedalus), and indeed he says to Glomaud, "I could transform your cottage into a palace." Nor is it simply coincidental that François passes Le Café Palace on his way to find Serge. These allusions to Daedalus might seem confusing until we recall that Daedalus himself has a double nature—benevolent and malevolent. If he is solicitous of Icarus, he is devastating to his nephew Perdix. Ovid recounts how Perdix as a twelve-year-old apprentice to Daedalus had used the backbone of a fish to model the invention of the saw and had also invented the compass. But "In jealous rage his master hurled him down / Headlong from Pallas' sacred citadel, / Feigning a fall" (OM, 179). He, too, in other words, possesses a double nature that brings him close to the Minotaur he seeks to escape in flight.

However much Serge may have emulated the architect, he has become a monster. He is characterized by excess: he drinks so much that he must be carted home in a wheelbarrow. He is pictured as drinking wine for breakfast—and for second breakfast. When he has drunk, he forgets his clothes and nearly leaves his house "tout nu." Behind the wheel of his truck, he turns into a menace and tries to run down François and Marie, a gesture that recalls the bull raging toward Theseus and Ariadne (see plate 15). François shouts at him, "You're completely crazy, no?" His appetites extend beyond alcohol to sex: he has, we learn, slept with Marie despite his marriage to Yvonne, and at the dance he unexpectedly grabs Marie and dances provocatively with her as Yvonne watches from the sidelines. When François exits the church in the scene already alluded to, Serge is *lying* outside. In another, more explicit version of this scene, Chabrol's camera focuses on twenty children playing soccer in the public square. The ball, strangely resembling a ball of twine, comes to rest directly in front of the sleeping drunkard who had till that moment remained hidden from our view. Serge leaps to his feet, the children scream in terror and scatter in all directions, and he pursues them wildly. In the context Chabrol has established, Serge takes on the Minotaur's role here. Moments later, he is seen staggering wildly up the hill muttering

PLATE 15.   Behind the wheel of his truck, Serge (Gérard Blain) becomes a menace to François (Jean-Claude Brialy) and Marie (Bernadette Lafont) in Chabrol's *Le Beau Serge*. (Courtesy of the Museum of Modern Art Film Stills Archive.)

incoherently, "This damned place ['Ce lieu maudit']. . . . Kids are born to die ['Les gosses sont nés pour mourir']." Later, in the dance scene, Serge will unleash his violent nature in an unprovoked attack on François and nearly kill him. Chabrol then pointedly focuses on François inching his way back toward safety along a strand of barbed wire—recalling Ariadne's thread of escape.

From the outset, however, Chabrol's portrayal of these antagonists has been double. Beyond (but not forgetting) their obvious reverse pairing in *Les Cousins,* the director uses throughout *Le Beau Serge* a mirroring strategy that links the two figures in a spectrum of specters. They emerge from the same visual ground in the first scene and repeatedly come back together in the film despite their antagonism. Immediately after telling Yvonne what a beast she is, Serge runs to the church and spies on François as he enters the sanctuary. In an unforgettable dissolve, Chabrol fades on a closeup of Serge as the image of the arched tympanum of the church emerges over his head, thereby creating a momentary sensation that Serge has "entered" the church with François. When François emerges, despite their very different physical positions, Serge lying and François standing, the priest directs his rebuke to the two of them indiscriminately: "Vous me méprisez. Vous ne m'écoutez pas!" Yvonne remarks to François, "From the moment he saw you, he has been coming and going as if he didn't know what he was doing." He becomes, in her words, *another*. This pairing of opposites is most directly figured in a sequence in which Chabrol elects to compose a parallel cut showing François and Marie ascending a hill, he in dark, she in light clothing, and Serge and Yvonne descending a hill, he in light and she in dark clothing. François is pictured placing Marie on a bed, and Yvonne repeats this gesture with the nearly inert Serge. Each of these paralleled sequences is filmed from angles that make it difficult initially to identify the personages, further clouding distinctions. At the conclusion of his final encounter with Marie, François hears precisely the imprecation he has previously directed to Serge, "You're completely mad!" After leaving her, François takes up exactly Serge's previous position at the corner of a building and spies on Serge as he leaves his garage. "Are you hiding now?" asks Serge, his question ambiguously phrased so that it may mean "*You*'re hiding too?" François responds, "I think there's been a misunderstanding ['malentendu'] between us."[46] He then proceeds to create one by insisting on projecting his own feelings on Serge: "You're not happy with her."

After their violent melee at the dance, Serge enters François's room and the two exchange regrets. François mentions how ugly he finds the relationship between Marie and Glomaud, but Serge retorts, "It's not disgusting. It's almost normal. Put yourself in her place ['Mets toi à sa place']. It's not horrible, it's normal. Everyone is like that ['Tout le monde est comme ça']. . . . We're stupid animals ['On est des bêtes']." Indeed, François already has put himself in the place of both Glomaud and Serge. Marie's response has been to call him crazy. Everyone *is* "comme ça," for *ça* is the figure they all share: the labyrinth of unconscious desires and motives.

All of these themes are masterfully woven together in the film's final sequence. François gets a chance to display his haughty moral superiority at the moment of Yvonne's childbirth. Opposites are brought violently together here: burning with fever, he races out into the snow to "save" Yvonne. He literally takes Serge's place, helping the pregnant woman into bed and running out for the doctor. To find the doctor, however, he must first invade the house of Glomaud, the monster of incest. Glomaud, however, magnanimously gives up his claim to medical help, a gesture that blurs his monstrous nature. François then finds Serge, insensate, in a stable *among the cattle,* exactly where we would expect to find him. In a visual (and physical) coupling of these doubled opposites, François drags his victim through the snow to deposit him at the feet of Yvonne. True to the paradigm of the myth, at the "height" of his prideful behavior François falls, presumably destroyed by this grandiose effort. Can his double survive him? The death's head that forms the last image of *Le Beau Serge* suggests that one cannot outlive the other. Both monsters must die, or as Chabrol will state in a later film: "The Beast Must Die ['Que la bête meure']." Serge's presence is not necessary here. His baby's birth does not depend on his presence. "Well, at least its not a giant," mutters the doctor matter-of-factly. No monster here, other than the one Serge had fantasized. Serge's monstrous behavior is simply a product of his own excessive fears projected onto the world. The myth is present, and endures, to express what is monstrous in all of us, often hidden within "the mazy multitude of winding ways" of our unconscious. Icarus does not escape the monster *or* the labyrinth by flight, but merely confirms them in himself. Lucien de Rubempré, of Balzac's *Illusions perdues,* does not escape the labyrinth of Paris by returning (like François) fever-ridden from Paris to the provinces. He merely shifts the locus of his destruction.

Chabrol illustrates this aspect of the myth by resituating his characters in another remarkable visual and moral analogue of the labyrinth: Paul's dark and trophy-laden apartment in Paris. Indeed, once the pattern of the labyrinth emerges in Chabrol's first two films, it is difficult not to belabor its presence. Minos, we recall from Ovid, had "hung the spoils of war to adorn his palace walls." Paul's apartment walls are covered with "a few trophies," animal skulls, rifles, spears, and pistols. Paul himself first appears clad most regally in a full-length velvet robe and bearing a telescope, the mark of a Mediterranean sailor-king. In regal manner and in pseudo-ancient speech, he greets his country cousin with the words, "Has Carlus had a good trip? Is he contented?" Everywhere in this apartment, made more complex by the system of *couloirs* and mirrors, we see small figurines of soldiers on horseback. As already mentioned, Paul's invocation of the pistol's murderous potential includes the words, "You mustn't trust appearances," a direct allusion to Daedalus's architecture and Chabrol's cinematic style. It is significant that when Paul leads Charles on a tour of Paris we see only a montage of the Arc de Triomphe, Cleopatra's Needle, and the Pantheon, reminders of the contributions of ancient civilizations to the culture of France's capital. Once introduced to L'Association, Charles witnesses Paul's kingly status there: Paul controls who shall be with whom (breaking up one couple to assign Martine to the lonely Philippe) and proclaims to one of the cardplayers, about to play his king, "Le Roi, c'est moi!" When Florence says to Charles, "So you're the famous cousin," Paul quickly corrects, "Cousin, yes, but *I* am the famous one!" Also, Florence will later be called "la princesse." When Charles finally sits down to join the card game, Chabrol uses an unusual direct overhead shot to focus on the seated players, bringing into view the tablecloth, whose pattern reproduces a Cretan mosaic pattern (see plate 16).

Where Minos is, there shall a Minotaur have been, to reverse the Freudian formula. The one is always representing and barely repressing the other in the myth. The *apparent* monster appears the minute Charles arrives on the scene. Clovis opens the door, a long knife in one hand, a handful of food in the other. This droll character (played by Claude Cerval, the priest in *Le Beau Serge*) considers violence and excess to be his professed traits. His name may refer to a Frankish king, but in the phrase "barbares ancêtres" proffered by Paul, one cannot help hearing something more primitive, with cloven feet. When Paul comments on Uncle Henri's excesses, Clovis exclaims, "O la vache!" The two conduct a mock bullfight and then proceed verbally to psychologically assault a young woman who arrives to tell Paul she is pregnant by him. During her visit, Clovis makes a show of breaking a glass and banging a poker against the cast-iron fireplace. "I am often brutal," he explains. When it is time to pay her off, Paul removes a roll of banknotes from a skull hanging on the wall; later Clovis will tell his "king" that *he* has taken care of things.

Upon his arrival at L'Association, Clovis continues his clastic ways, sweeping the chessmen from their carefully positioned sites in front of a player. Throughout the film, Clovis swaggers through this role, well supported in all by Paul. For each of the parties, he will supply a "sacrificial victim"—for the first, the count Archangelo Minerva, a kind of double, wildly seeking female victims but victimized himself during the course of the collective debauchery. For the second party, a slave in chains constitutes his contribution. When not furnishing victims for entertainment, he continues to break things—bottles, glasses, relationships. Paul lacks his purely predatory instincts, and so it is Clovis who ensures that Florence will be "deflowered" by Paul before she is able to consummate her affair with Charles. He literally drags Paul and Florence together, almost as if he were raping both of them. (Chabrol repeatedly insists on Clovis's

PLATE 16.   Charles (Gérard Blain) plays cards over a Cretan mosaic design in Chabrol's *Les Cousins*. (Courtesy of the Museum of Modern Art Film Stills Archive.)

homosexuality, a feature that in the France of 1958 connoted something of a sexual monster.)

Florence can at first be interpreted as Ariadne to Charles's confused Theseus. If he is to survive the Parisian scene, he must somehow decipher it. She seems to have the necessary thread, but even in his opening scenes with her something seems to be amiss. She possesses threads, all right, but seems to use them to hypnotize and then ensnare Charles rather than to open doors for him. She passes, in other words from, Ariadne to Arachne, the spinner of illusions—from Ariadne's thread to Arachne's threat.

As soon as he has met her, Charles seems to begin a metamorphosis of his own. Appearances in this film have cajoled us into seeing Charles as a tender innocent, eager to learn the ropes (threads?), and Paul as master of an evil empire. (Paul's playful rendition of Wagner during his party and his brutal anti-Semitic treatment of Marc, the Jewish guest, contribute to this impression.) But, like the gun whose *mise en scène* is so thoroughly marked by Chabrol, Charles's appearance is deceptive. His place in the apartment has already been signaled as a kind of ultimate depth in the maze of corridors. During the soiree thrown by Paul, Charles displays a marked aggressivity to Rameau and excuses himself with the remark, "Me, I'm not very civilized." With Florence at the party, he is a paragon of verbal inadequacy and chooses the staircase as his perch— a detail that is not only neither here nor there, a figure of transgression,[47] but one that has also served to situate the usurpation of François-Paul's position with Marie in *Le Beau Serge*. Evidently uncomfortable in the social mix within, he drags Florence outside to tell her, not about his love for her, but about his mother[48] and about how "bête" he is: "Am I beastly ['bête'], do I have a beastly ['bête'] face, a beastly expression ['une expression bête']? Do I say beastly things ['des choses bêtes'], in a beastly way ['d'une manière bête']? . . . I would cut my tongue out rather than exceed the limits of my beastliness ['Je me couperais la langue plutôt que de dépasser les bornes de ma betise']" (see plate 17). That is surely enough *"bête-ese"* ("beastiality") to last a lifetime.

Charles's inability to communicate with Florence reaches its climax in their *malentendu* about time. During Charles's absence, Clovis convinces Florence that "Paul will save her from Charles," as if the latter represents a real danger to her. When Charles returns, he accepts Paul's outrageous behavior as if it were normal: we can almost hear the actor Gérard Blain saying to Jean-Claude Brialy in *Le Beau Serge*, "It's not so frightful. It's almost normal. . . . Everyone behaves like that. We're animals, but no one gives a damn ['Ce n'est pas si dégueulasse. C'est presque normal. . . . Tout le monde est comme ça. On est des bêtes, tout le monde s'en foût']." Now he merely withdraws into his "lair" surrounded by pictures of animals, refusing more than grunts to Paul and Florence. They consider him "not very gallant." Late in the film, Florence makes another attempt to tame Charles, during the second of Paul's parties, but he brutally pushes her out. Immediately afterwards, Chabrol's camera performs two consecutive 360-degree pans in the dark room, suggesting the circularity of a cave.[49]

The final scenes of the film further emphasize Charles's "monstrous" qualities. Not surprisingly, he is failed by his examining committee, as if there were a penalty for alienation and provincialism. Upon learning of the results, he destroys the official symbol of his cultural identity, his student identification card; it floats away in the night and cold waters of the Seine. Returning to the apartment, Charles loads one bullet in the revolver and points it at Paul's sleeping head. One might be tempted, given the traditional and iconoclastic

PLATE 17. Charles (Gérard Blain) plays the monster with Florence (Juliette Mayniel) in Chabrol's *Les Cousins*. (Courtesy of the Museum of Modern Art Film Stills Archive.)

roles taken by Charles and Paul, to see Paul as the sleeping Minotaur of the myth, and in a sense this is not wrong. But Charles has by now laid as much claim to that role as anyone in the film. Failing to kill his victim, he falls asleep at his desk and wakes up to a sudden and brutal death at the hands of his cousin. Paul aims the "empty" gun at Charles and fires: the country cousin (sleeping bull) is dead. To the victor go the "spools": Paul has already enjoyed Florence (Ariadne and thread) and (presumably) seen a movie with her. Now he is left standing over the inert remains of the monster who came to occupy the depths of his living quarters and who would have killed him first if he could have. Charles has completed his metamorphosis into the Minotaur just as he reaches the end of his journey. Paul seems to have been transformed in the opposite direction. Now, only Paul is left "to tell the tale." Or is he?

At least two other levels of meaning trouble this film, each of which is occluded, if only partially. With Paul and Charles (like Fran-

çois and Serge before them) neutralized in a metamorphosis of opposites into each other, we must look again at the figures of myth and
literature. The commingling of references to Ariadne and Arachne
noted above produces a third allusion. It is particularly interesting
that Ovid himself felt so much connection between these two women.
Of Ariadne he writes,

> . . . The door,
> So difficult, which none of those before
> Could find again, by Ariadne's aid
> Was found, *the thread that traced the way rewound.*
>   (OM, 176, italics mine)

The "thread . . . rewound" could also be Arachne's spiderlike en-
trapment. Indeed, Arachne's story encapsulates Ariadne's! In her
competition with Pallas Athena,

> Arachne shows Europa cheated by
> The bull's disguise, *a real bull you'd think,*
> And real sea. . . .
> Neptune she drew, changed to a savage bull
> For love of Canace; and Neptune too
> Sired, as Enipeus, the Aloidae;
> Bisaltes' child he cheated as a ram . . .
> To all of them Arachne gave their own
> Features and proper features of the scene.
>   (OM, 124, italics mine)

What is wondrous about Arachne's weaving is that, on the one hand,
it seems to entertain an absolute, almost photographic likeness to the
things it represents; on the other hand, the *subjects* of her art are all
figures of godly *deception*, fantastical tales of how appearance is a mean
guise for a deceiving reality. Moreover, her subjects recall directly the
bull of Minos and the sea that will drown those in flight from this
"monstrous hybrid beast." In combining these two mythical roles,
Florence plays Ariachne,[50] the *doubled maternal figure.* Tom Milne
once wrote of "Chabrol's air of calm beauty" as "simply a web woven
by a schizophrenic spider to entrap the unwary, a mask which conceals, but never eliminates the abyss of reality underneath."[51] In her
very web of realism and deception, we again perceive the "figure
mère" of Chabrol's cinema: the labyrinth itself. It is thus not surprising that when Charles returns to the apartment after failing to find her

(thread), he finds not only Ariadne transformed but a projector, turning noisily, casting fluttering light upon a screen.[52] He is no more able to decipher these (blank) images than he has been to discover the "hidden figure in her tapestry," or to solve the labyrinth. This is his tragedy—and perhaps ours, as well. He turns his back on her for good.

Meanwhile, his immediate reaction is to return the copy of Balzac's *Illusions perdues* he had "stolen" from the sympathetic book dealer. What is the connection, we ask again? Why should Balzac now have to be screened out? The simple answer *might* be that Charles no longer believes in the possibilities opened up by Lucien: the provincial from the Touraine region whose father was but a chemist and who was able to come to Paris and succeed in writing virtuoso criticisms (under a pseudonym) that won him instant acclaim. But Chabrol does not believe in simple answers: smooth surfaces always hide complex subterranean arrangements, he has said.

The more complex and more likely role of Balzac in Chabrol's film(s) begins with autobiography, traverses the labyrinth, and ends in (partial) repression of the truth. Although Chabrol has asserted that he is "not at all of an autobiographical temperament," we may be permitted some doubts. His reasons are not terribly convincing, given the lives portrayed in *Le Beau Serge* and *Les Cousins:* "Je ne suis pas de tempérament autobiographique," he claims, "because I force myself to live the simplest, most tranquil, and most harmonious life; thus, my life isn't very interesting. I wouldn't have much to tell apart from the story of a guy who tries to avoid conflict. Autobiography being forbidden ['interdit'], punishable by deadly boredom ['sous peine d'ennui mortel'], I just have to ['je suis bien obligé'] turn to the biography of others."[53]

This self-imposed interdiction is all the more interesting inasmuch as Chabrol's biography resembles no one's so much as Lucien's! A native of Sardent, his father a chemist, he left the town (after having started a successful cinémathèque there) to make his fortune in Paris. Like Lucien, he falls in with the right crowd (for Chabrol it was the "bande à Rohmer," otherwise known as the *Cahiers du cinéma* group. The battles fought by the *Cahiers* group have more than a faint resemblance to those waged by the Classics and Romantics of Balzac's Paris in the early 1800s. Under the pseudonym J.-Y. Goute, Chabrol "composed a virtuoso piece ['bâtit un article de virtuose']," which won him immediate attention and led eventually to his filmmaking career and celebrity. Like Lucien, Chabrol became known for his gourmandise, "an art of living for and appreciating the present, like his taste for cinema, connecting his appetites with his artistic practice ['un art de vivre et de goûter de l'instant comme une attitude envers le cinéma, dans sa consommation comme dans sa pratique'].["54] If one replaces the word "cinema" with the word "poetry" here, the phrase might well be Balzac's. Gilles Delavaud adds, "There is a legend surrounding Chabrol: a desire to provoke, a taste for practical jokes, a certain cynicism that would lead him to rush his films . . . and to give top priority in his working day to the dinner hour ['volonté de provocation, goût de canular, un certain cynisme qui le conduirait à bâcler ses films . . . à privilegier dans une journée de travail le moment de la bouffe'].["55] The world of *Les Cousins,* like the village of Sardent, was "un monde que je connaissais bien personnellement."[56]

As if these similarities were not enough (to want to hide), Chabrol's own relationship to Balzac furnishes another uncanny parallel: Fassbinder may have claimed that "in Chabrol, France has . . . no twentieth-century Balzac," but Chabrol was fascinated, if not obsessed, by his novelistic predecessor. Certainly the Balzacian model was there in both of Chabrol's first films.[57] But Chabrol always rejected (or at least claimed to reject) adapting Balzac to the screen:

> One can't transpose Balzac's time. I broke my back trying to transpose *La Peau de Chagrin* to a modern setting, but I couldn't find a way. Anyhow, I would rather take an undeveloped idea—not something so completely developed and filled out. . . . As they are already perfect as literature, I don't know how one could impose images on them. It would all be too academic for me. No I prefer either to use an original script or to adapt a thriller.[58]

Chabrol confided to Joel Magny that "the weaker the adapted work, the less bothersome it is," putting a Bloomian spin on his relationship to Balzac: better a weak authority figure than a strong one in this oedipal play of "misprision" between literature and film. And in a gesture that recalls Charles's, he said, "I've a strong admiration for writers like Balzac, for example, but it would never occur to me to film one of his books. Or rather it did occur to me in the early days, *but I soon dropped the idea.*"[59] Like Charles returning the stolen *Illusions perdues* to its place on the shelf, Chabrol himself had dropped Balzac, with his "perfection," for a weaker writer. In Charles's gesture, then, we have one more significant autobiographical detail, another clue to the figure in Chabrol's own tapestry. The text of Balzac operates in *Les Cousins* exactly like a screen memory: it surfaces long enough to draw attention to itself and to allude to a psychic charge behind it but veils that element just enough to defy complete understanding. Eventually, like Charles's copy of Balzac, it is "returned to the shelf" of unused memories. It functions, in other words, like the labyrinth of repression!

In an early story, *La Musique douce,* Chabrol revealed a remarkable series of features about his creative imagination and methodology.[60] The story involves a man who has decided to take revenge on his wife for having humiliated him. After killing her, he stuffs her body in a bag in order to disguise it and ties it with a pink ribbon. Discovered because of this unusual tie, he confronts the court . . . only to awaken from a bad dream. The story ends with the protagonist awake, awaiting his wife's return, thinking, "He now knew what mistake he must not make." In a second story, *Le Dernier Jour de souffrance,* Chabrol had told of a paraplegic victim of the war living with his wife and son Jean. A childhood friend, now a doctor, administers painkillers that augment rather than diminish Paul's suffering. Paul realizes that the doctor and his wife are in league to kill him and one night confides his fear to his son. The son calms his fears and administers the fatal dose of "medicine" to his father. Returning to the others, he announces: "He's dead. . . . He *almost* understood everything ['Il avait *presque* tout compris']."

The first story uses the device of the dream (just as Chabrol will use the myth of the labyrinth in his films), but the lesson is complex. If the text's protagonist learns only that the visible ties to his violence must be repressed, as readers we can see that there is a strong misogynist drive within and beyond the dream. He wants to put his mother in the sack in which in utero he had to be humiliatingly confined. Better not to have an umbilical cord at all, better simply to get rid of it altogether. Chabrol himself would like to hide the image in the tapestry deep enough so that it cannot be traced back to his own desires and autobiography, but dreams and films *do* leave traces.

The second story is a kind of oneiric reversal of the first: in that schema the danger still lies in clues, and the designers of the plot realize that one must be careful not to let the "reader" see too much evidence. The victim in the story has *almost* understood. Chabrol should take care that the same will not be true for his own spectator. *Une surface lisse* will hide *des choses très compliquées.* "Every film is the proof that chaos does not exist ['Tout film est la preuve de la non-existence du chaos']," Chabrol argues naively (and paradoxically), "since it organizes chaotic elements ['puisqu'il organise des éléments chaotiques']."[61]

And yet the beauty of a screen memory (or a screened text) is that it hides *and* reveals. Balzac provides a most interesting screen for Chabrol in that the novel evidences a distanced pattern of mythological and psychological structures that Chabrol can claim to have "borrowed" (stolen?) from his perfect model. This "objective" use of the Balzacian labyrinth corresponds to the more distanced cinematic style Chabrol insisted on: an objective—emphatically nonsubjective—positioning of the camera. "The camera never expresses the point of view of a particular character," affirms Chabrol, "but its *own* point of view."[62] Elsewhere he adds to this fantasy that the camera is somehow independent of his own volition: "I don't like subjective shots. For me the camera should be an additional character ['un personnage supplémentaire']."[63] Such a strategy works very much as the figure of the labyrinth works, to keep the monster at a safe distance while allowing it to be perceived.[64]

What is buried, like that which is repressed, is bound to resurface in a configuration Freud called the repetition compulsion. In Chabrol's work, the monster secreted deep in the labyrinth has a habit of reappearing quite regularly. In *A double tour* (1959) Leda is killed by the deceptively quiet son of her lover. *Les Bonnes Femmes* (1959–60) involves the cruel death of Jacqueline at the hands of a man she has come to love and trust. *L'Oeil du malin* (1961) involves the murder of a wife by her jealous husband. In *Landru* (1962) a model husband and breadwinner is revealed to have callously slain numerous women to earn a living. *Le Scandale* (1966) centers on the mysterious death of Christine Belling. *La Femme infidèle* (1968) sketches the transformation of an otherwise quiet bourgeois family man into a jealous assassin. Charles Thénier becomes the killer beast in *Que la bête meure* (1969). In *Juste avant la nuit* (1971) Chabrol expressly imitates the opening scene of Hitchcock's *Psycho* to reveal his protagonist in the act of murdering a naked woman. But unlike the ethical scheme at work in Hitchcock's universe, in Chabrol's film no one—not the dead woman's husband, the murderer's wife, nor the Parisian police—is the least bit troubled by this murder. The protagonist ends up more confused by their very indifference than by his own guilt! In perhaps the most emblematic of all of his films, *Le Boucher* (1969), Chabrol recounts the story of a mild-mannered butcher in Périgord who is revealed to be a serial killer of young women in the region. Not content to leave it there, Chabrol resurfaced this same theme in *Les Fantômes du chapelier* (1982). Numerous other films of Chabrol's delight in similar transformations of apparently quiet, harmless men into savage killers. The body count of women who die violently at the hands of these monsters is difficult to calculate with exactitude, but it fulfills remarkably the cryptic sign in *Le Beau Serge*, "ELLE NIEE." Chabrol's own comments about monsters are curious indeed:

> The notion of the *monster* has always fascinated me—this definition by difference ["cette définition par la différence"]. Those we call monsters are often people who are apparently frighteningly banal ["d'une banalité effrayante"]. I am very interested by the relationship between the interior and exterior of such individuals, the non-rational elements in an otherwise banal universe, scenes in which people do the opposite of what's expected. . . . A monstrous scene wakes people up ["Une scène monstrueuse, ça réveille les gens"]. It makes them almost dream ["Ça les fait presque rêver"].[65]

This statement is disturbing in many ways, not the least of which is the tendency toward self-contradiction (e.g., it "wakes people up" and "makes them dream"). It is more than a little curious that Chabrol placed *himself* among those who are "d'une banalité effrayante" when he claimed that his own life was too boring to allow any interest in autobiography.[66] Even more curious that he should so constantly defend (both implicitly and explicitly) these "monsters of difference": just as in a dream, there seems almost never to be a moral judgment brought against the ladykillers who populate his films. Chabrol even argued that "one must beware of putting sanctions on monsters" for they can, he argues, play *useful social roles*.[67] Of Landru, Chabrol said, "We always consider geniuses as monsters" a phrase that suggests more than a little identification with his monstrous character.[68]

Elsewhere Chabrol mused, "I believe in the revelation of guilt . . . guilt is always transferred from the most guilty to the least guilty. It's never the other way around." Again we witness the theme of reversal and the deception of appearances that haunts the director. He adds, "I think it's an interior need that finds its equilibrium. . . . Internally, psychologically, I seek to maintain my equilibrium while my natural tendency is toward imbalance. So, the search for symmetry in things helps me in doing that."[69] So many imaginary sacrifices seem to be required to maintain this equilibrium that Jean-Louis Comolli suggests that "the real hero of Chabrol's film is not such and such a character, but rather the film itself, to which, one after another, the characters are sacrificed."[70] Thus the scene in *Les Cousins* in which Charles returns to Paul's apartment to find Florence (the flower) deflowered and the projector turning, flashing shimmering images on a blank screen, might be taken as an emblem of Chabrol's work. It should be recalled that the *auteur* of *Les Cousins* has said, "I put a lot of *projections* in my films, but it's not with an idea of having films within films. Perhaps I simply like projectors."[71] The scenario of projection does seem to have an obsessive fascination for him.

With such a scenario, it is little wonder that the labyrinth should emerge as the "figure mère" that Chabrol had hidden, but just barely, in the tapestry of his films. What makes it so difficult and so easy to perceive is that it constitutes the very metaphor of deceptive appearances. No wonder, either, that Chabrol's "great testament," his "definitive message," is: "Don't judge! One has to avoid judgments to avoid traps, but this is not always easy."[72] And so, we will not judge, but merely observe. . . .

Chapter Five

Pascal Victim:
The Hidden Text in Rohmer's
Ma Nuit chez Maud

> By knowing each man's ruling passion, we are sure of
> pleasing him; and yet each has his fancies, opposed to
> his true good, in the very idea which he has of the good.
> It is a singularly puzzling fact.
> —*Pascal,* Les Pensées

> The satisfaction of desire must therefore seem to be
> fortuitous.
> —*Eric Rohmer*

Ma Nuit chez Maud is a singularly puzzling film. No other film I know
so insistently centers on a single text, and certainly no other centers on
a text that is taken so explicitly as a point of contention. The narrator-
protagonist of the film (Jean-Louis Trintignant) tells his friend, Vidal
(Antoine Vitez) (see plate 18),

> It just so happens I'm rereading Pascal right now. . . . I have to say I'm
> disappointed. . . . First of all I have the feeling that I know him almost
> by heart. Second, it doesn't bring me anything: I find it rather empty
> ["je trouve ca assez vide"]. To the degree that I'm Catholic, or at least
> trying to be, what he says isn't at all parallel to my own conception of
> Catholicism ["dans le sens de mon catholicisme actuel"]. It's precisely
> because I am a Christian that I revolt against that kind of austerity ["je
> m'insurge contre ce rigorisme"]. Or, if that's what Christianity is all
> about, then count me among the atheists![1]

Pascal thus becomes the implied antagonist of the film, and remains so throughout the narrator's night at Maud's. So much so that

PLATE 18.   The narrator (Jean-Louis Trintignant) meets his old friend Vidal (Antoine Vitez) to discuss Pascal in Rohmer's *Ma Nuit chez Maud*. (Courtesy of the Museum of Modern Art Film Stills Archive.)

most of the critics who wrote on this film at its appearance in 1970 professed consternation that the film seemed "little more than a skeleton upon which to hang Rohmer's philosophical observations."[2] Indeed, the average spectator of the film (and by "average" one may postulate an educated French viewer) is likely to identify with Maud herself, who, when asked if she has read Pascal, responds, "Oh, sure: 'Man is a thinking reed' . . . 'the two infinites' ['Oui, "l'homme est un roseau pensant" . . . "les deux infinis" . . . euh']" (SCM, 71/75). Or, like Vidal, the spectator may remember having read Pascal's famous text on the wager. Indeed, Rohmer's camera directs the spectator's attention to this text when Trintignant is perusing a copy of Pascal's *Pensées* in the bookstore. Rohmer thus virtually identifies Pascal's work with—and limits it to—Trintignant's "Je trouve ça assez vide."

The only "dissenting" view presented explicitly is Vidal's flagrant "misreading" of Pascal's wager in which he "empties out ['il *vide*']" the Jansenist's terms of their theological content to a historical or Marxist one.[3] Vidal's introduction of this "heretical" variant on Pascal seems initially plausible enough to seduce us into considering it as a possible reading of the seventeenth-century Jansenist, yet such an interpretation cannot be sustained by the epistemological context of Pascal's work. Vidal's comments thus constitute a kind of warning to the spectator to proceed with caution given the likelihood of a misreading of Pascal. Yet it remains remarkably easy and entirely tempting for the critic to play Maud to Rohmer's narrator and to congratulate himself or herself on knowing a few passages from Pascal, applying them loosely to the film and letting it go at that.[4] The viewer would, however, entirely miss the enormous tension created between the film's narrator-protagonist and the film's "image maker."[5]

To do so would be to participate in the enstasis that characterizes the narrator,[6] to overlook the dialectic specifically established by Rohmer to differentiate between *Ma Nuit chez Maud* as *text* and as *film,* and to fail to appreciate the complexity of intertextual elements that animate Rohmer's cinematic masterpiece. And to miss this level of tension in the work would be to obscure an equally important debate that has characterized Rohmer's cinematic work from its inception: the ambivalence about a realistic versus a structured presentation of images.

"Why film a story when one can write it? Why write it when one is going to film it? Both these questions may seem trivial ['oiseuse en apparence'] but not to me," writes Rohmer in the introduction to his *Six Moral Tales* (SCM, v/7).[7] It is by now well known that Rohmer adapted *Ma Nuit chez Maud* from his "moral tale" of the same title written some twenty years previously.[8] If in Rohmer's view the stories had a "resolutely literary quality ['apparence'],'' they only achieved their "full meaning" when made into films (SCM, v/7). Story and film illuminate each other in curious ways. Each displays elements that are absent from its homologue, and these elements are instructive not only for the particular meaning of this story (and consequently for an adequate understanding of the role of Pascal—and other intertextual elements—in the film) but also for an understanding of the difference between literary writing and film writing.

Rohmer gives a first indication of the difference between graphic text and imaged one when he insists, "It is only on the screen that the form of these tales is fully realized ['accède à sa plénitude'], if only because a new viewpoint is added ['elle s'enrichit d'un point de vue nouveau']—that of the camera—that no longer coincides with that of the narrator" (SCM, x/12). What is remarkable in this particular adaptation is that wherever the filmmaker *adds* a perspective not "available" to the writer, he *subtracts* a corresponding piece of the written narration. The implication is inevitably that the cinematographic substitution *replaces* a textual element, that it is assumed somehow to be an adequation of that element.

The most striking example of this figure of substitution occurs (or rather disappears) in (from) the first paragraph of the story:

> In this story, I'm not going to tell everything. Besides, there isn't any story, really: just a series of very ordinary events, of chance happenings and coincidences ["une série, un choix d'événements très quelconques, de hasards, de coincidences"], of the kind we have all experienced at one time or another in our lives. The deeper meanings of these events will be whatever I choose to endow them with ["n'ont d'autre sens que celui qu'il m'a plu de leur donner"]. (SCM, 57/61)

Our first experience of this narrator is of someone who will not tell all in his account of events. Moreover, and paradoxically, after admitting that the story will have only the meaning he chooses to give it, the narrator adds, "My feelings, my own opinions and beliefs, will not intrude upon the line of the story, even though they are very much at the forefront of the events described ['Mes sentiments, mes idées, mes croyances n'entrent pas en ligne de compte, bien qu'il en soit ici longuement question']" (SCM, 57/61). In other words, this "resolutely literary" narrator begins by establishing an extremely slippery relationship to candor, point of view, and textual authority. In proposing to his reader that these are only random coincidences, he has already considerably shaped our attitude to conform to his own, for we are later to learn that as a character and as a lover, he has a resolutely "probabilistic" attitude toward events. Finally, he asserts that the events will have only the meaning he gives them, but he wants us to believe somehow that this meaning will have nothing to do with his own beliefs! As readers, we thus encounter several glaring contradictions before the story is a paragraph old! We implicitly expect narrators to be as truthful and complete as they can manage and to establish clearly whether point of view is to be objective or subjective. Thus, the story's opening statements constitute a prescription for narrative unreliability.

Now, none of these statements appears in the film. Thus there is no *textual* indicator to encourage the film's viewer to question the reliability of its voice-over narrator-protagonist.[9] It thus falls to Rohmer's camera somehow to replace the sense of unreliability established explicitly by the narrative strategy of the story. Fresh from his role in Robbe-Grillet's *L'Homme qui ment,* Jean-Louis Trintignant seems an ideal actor for this job of seemingly innocent narrator. His apparently naive demeanor is frequently undercut by the self-contradictory statements he makes throughout the film. His first words of voice-over narration are, "On that morning, Monday, the twenty-first of December, the idea suddenly came to me, in a brusk, precise and definitive way, that Françoise would be my wife ['Ce jour-là, lundi le vingt-et-un décembre l'idée m'est venue brusque, précise, définitive que Françoise serait ma femme']."

Our only evidence of his contact with her has been either in the church, where he glances at her from time to time during the mass, or in the street, where he tries vainly to keep up with her Velosolex in his Renault 16. The story confirms that the character makes this "decision" despite virtually no knowledge of her: "I know nothing about her as yet. I'm not even sure she's noticed my presence, yet somehow there is the overwhelming notion that she will be my wife ['l'idée nette, précise, définitive, qu'elle serait ma femme']." And he adds, as if aware of how silly this proposition must seem, "I know, it all seems too pat, the end all too moral. And yet I haven't the slightest doubt that that is precisely how it will turn out" (SCM, 59/63). In the light of Rohmer's later comedy, *Le Beau Mariage,* in which Sabine makes a similar and ultimately ridiculously unrealistic decision to marry without the knowledge of her prospective husband, we may appreciate the irrationality of such a statement from Trintignant. And yet, Rohmer's literary narrator attempts to justify this fantasy by recourse to his system of religious beliefs: "I refuse even to dignify that quasi-absolute confidence I have in my own destiny as superstition. I have always had, since my tenderest years, the certainty that God was with me. That explains why I have never attached any importance to whatever obstacles have stood in my way" (SCM, 59/63). Immediately following these "certainties," the narrator in the short-story version proceeds to undermine them: "That is as much as I intend to say about my motives and my beliefs. What I say from here on out ['mes propos ultérieurs'] will more than suffice to reveal them. I confess that I will not always speak with total candor to others, but the truth is that one can lie to oneself as well ['mais l'on se ment à soi-même aussi']" (SCM, 60/64).

Once again, the story makes explicit a degree of narrative unreliability that is omitted in the film. In the film version we are much more dependent on the succession of images to ascertain this issue for ourselves. Rohmer cleverly allows his film's narrator the entire freedom (as opposed to the "responsibility") to present Pascal with little

extra-diegetic interference and few narrative confessions of unreliability. Thus, in the film, Trintignant's unreliability will emerge
slowly and implicitly. First, during his long conversation with Maud
and Vidal, he presents himself via half-truths. When he narrates his
experience in church he first says, "The other day there was a girl a few
pews in front of me . . . " But when Maud interjects, "What about
that pretty girl ['cette jolie fille']?" Jean-Louis responds disin-
genuously, "I didn't say she was pretty. . . . But for argument's sake,
let's assume she was ['Bon, admettons qu'elle l'était']. Anyway, I
shouldn't have said 'girl.' I should have said 'woman.' A very young
woman with her husband." This revisionist approach to his memory
of the church cannot fail to evoke Robbe-Grillet's characters, who
invent the story as it unfolds. Here Jean-Louis begins by refusing the
adjective *jolie,* then affirming it, then denying that he was talking
about a girl at all.

As viewers, we know that he has already seen the very pretty
Françoise (Marie-Christine Barrault) in the church, followed her in
the street, and even decided to marry her! His refusal to name her—
understandable, perhaps, in the presence of so seductive and so beautiful a woman as Maud—has a disturbing quality to it. Our sense of
the *probability* of truth from Jean-Louis is thus immeasurably reduced. A few moments later, when Vidal suggests, "You're a ladies'
man ['Tu cours les filles']," Jean-Louis retorts, "No!" "You used to
be," returns Vidal. "Mais non!" insists our narrator-protagonist, only
to exclaim a few moments later, "I won't deny that I've had several
'mistresses,' . . . I'm not here to bore you with the story of my life.
He's not my father confessor. But I'm thirty-four, and I have had a
number of girls in my life ['j'ai connu pas mal de filles']. Nor do I
pretend that I should serve as an example to anyone. Not in the least.
Besides, all this proves nothing." And only seconds later he blurts out
to Vidal, "You're crazy. You force me to think of things that are dead
and gone ['Tu m'obliges à penser à des choses qui me sont complète-
ment sorties de l'esprit']. Perhaps I did chase my share of skirts in the
old days, but the past is the past ['J'ai peut-être couru les filles. Le
passé est le passé']." It is hard to imagine a character who changes his
"story" faster than does Jean-Louis. And this is hardly the only occasion of his unreliability.

Now Rohmer's *text* includes numerous examples of this unreliability, and many of these will be adopted *word for word* into the
dialogue of the film. It is important for any subsequent understanding of the relationship between the text and film of *Ma Nuit chez
Maud* to delineate here the textual examples of the narrator's unre-

liability. In the first place, Rohmer's narrator is never named, a fact that differentiates him from the other three major characters in the work and immediately creates a kind of vagueness about his civil status that is never entirely resolved.[10] But the extraordinarily revisionist nature of his narration creates an ongoing problem of credibility. The most constant of N's "revisions" of what we "know"—or at least believe to be true, if we are to accept any of his version of events—is his evasiveness around the subject of Françoise. Once again, it is Vidal who leads the "investigation" during their evening at Maud's (see plate 19):

> "I wouldn't be surprised if he were in love."
> I burst out laughing. "Now, that's news!"
> Maud, not taking her eyes off me, said simply, "Is she blonde or brunette?"
> "I seem to remember he prefers blondes."
> Maud wouldn't let go.
> "Come on, tell the truth. Confession's good for the soul. It's nothing to be ashamed of."
> "No, I tell you . . . I don't know anyone. I don't love anyone. Period."
> But Maud was not so easily put off.
> "Does she live in Clermont?"
> "No! . . . My 'no' meant that she doesn't exist. And besides, even if she did, I have every right not to talk to you about her."
> (SCM, 78–79/82–83)

This denial of the existence of Françoise in the face of Maud's specific questions about her occurs quite deliberately twice more in the tale (SCM, 91/94, 101/104). Not only will he not tell all to his reader, N insists on a politics of denial with Maud, an alarming fact since she specifically represents a level of truth-telling that is both exemplary and disarming in the story. By contrast, N is unable to make the simplest account without a steady obligato of revision:

> I've been in love, which is a whole other matter. I've loved two or three women in my life—well, say three or four. I lived with each of them for a long time, several years. I loved them, not madly perhaps, but loved them nonetheless. No, that's not fair, either. I did love them madly. And it was mutual. (SCM, 87/90)

This constant need to refashion his narration may have to do in part with his genuine uncertainty. He confesses to his reader, "But I de-

PLATE 19. "I wouldn't be surprised if he were in love," says Maud (Françoise Fabian) at dinner with Vidal (Antoine Vitez) in Rohmer's *Ma Nuit chez Maud*. (Courtesy of the Museum of Modern Art Film Stills Archive.)

cided that I would not waste time raking over dead coals, trying to analyze my actions, since I was far from convinced I knew why I had vacillated so ['Mais j'ai dit que je ne m'étendrais pas sur les raisons de ma conduite, *à supposer qu'elles me fussent tout à fait claires à moi-même*']" (SCM, 96/99, italics mine). Indeed, N will repeat this behavior with Françoise when trying to explain to her the role of chance in his relationships (SCM, 110/113). A wholly ironic Pascalian (because so sovereignly unconscious) overtone invades N's presentation of self, for it was Pascal who wrote, "The heart has its reasons, which reason does not know ['Le coeur a ses raisons que la raison ne connaît pas']."[11]

Whatever the reasons for his vagaries, however, N extends them to virtually every aspect of his narrative technique and behavior. Although he proclaims that one would never love one woman and make love to another, N (having already announced his future marriage with Françoise) climbs into bed with Maud, chases her to the bathroom door when the ambiguity of his gestures drives her from that bed, and "Before she was able to open the door I had reached her, taken her in my arms ['Au moment où elle met la main sur la poignée, je l'ai rejointe. Je l'enlace']" (SCM, 95/98). After leaving her apartment, he announces, "I would never be able to face Maud again. . . . I made up my mind not to join them for the outing and drove back to Ceyrat. . . . By the time I arrived home I had already changed my mind" (SCM, 96/99). Between this revised decision and his afternoon with Maud, he chances to catch sight of Françoise, runs after her, and in trying to start up a conversation manages yet another self-contradictory statement: "I followed you," he claims, "against all my principles ['en dépit de tous mes principes']," and only seconds later he confesses, "Anyway I don't have any principles ['D'ailleurs, je n'ai pas de principes']" (SCM, 98/101, translation mine). During the same afternoon, N recounts that despite his certainty about Françoise, he takes Maud in his arms and even proposes to her: "And what if I were to marry you? How does that strike you? ['Vous voulez bien?'] . . . Say yes! Look how well we go together, you and I." Maud answers by reflecting that N would be as marriageable as Vidal and that "he pushed you into my arms to defend himself against himself ['c'est pour se défendre contre lui-meme qu'il vous a jeté dans mes bras']." Whereupon N responds by taking her in his arms, kissing her neck, and blurting: "But I'm not 'in' your arms ['Mais je ne suis pas "dans" vos bras!']" (SCM, 101–2/104–5). Although the narrative effect is quite different from that obtained in Robbe-Grillet's novels, Rohmer's narrator nevertheless shakes our confidence in his believability both as narrator and as character.[12]

All of these particular self-contradictory moments are included word for word in the film; and yet the visual context created by Rohmer in his cinematic version will produce a very different overall effect. Again, what I will emphasize here is the way in which a substitution is made of a visual for a verbal event in enough cases to create a meditation on the way the film's narrator, Jean-Louis, has accomplished a kind of textual sleight of hand that both hides and reveals his relationship to Pascal in the first instance and to truth and love in the second. The interplay of *screened texts* in the film produces a relationship between theology and morality subtly yet powerfully played out in the ironic movement of the film. Ironically, this "screening" is done against the backdrop of Rohmer's claim that cinema does not "lie" in the way poetry does:

What is the equivalent of metaphor in film? . . . [For the poet] metaphor comes from language's inability to make a reality concrete. By comparing the incomparable, by systematically using the incorrect term, poets *have never ceased to lie* throughout the years, but the lie was more respectful of the secret essence of things than were the pale, flat, abstract expressions of ordinary speech. Whether by luck or misfortune, the *filmmaker is not familiar with this art of felicitous lying.*[13]

Many of the critics who have discussed this film have sensed a tortuous relationship between the narrator's antagonism to Pascal, his vaguely Jansenist belief in predestination, and the odd twist of coincidences that causes the film to end on so surprising and ironic a note as to force a complete reevaluation of the previous events of the story![14] Not one has adequately addressed this problem (after all the crux of the film!), because although the "image maker" of the film provides the viewer with enough evidence to understand the theological and moral issues in a completely "Rohmerian" way, there is a trap involved. As in so many of the other films addressed in this study, one text is presented as a screen for another.

When Rohmer, in seemingly innocent terms, asks, "Why film a story when one can write it?" he initiates a profound meditation on the nature of representation itself. One of his answers to this question is verbal: "Only the act of making films gave the stories and what they were portraying—characters, plot, dialogues—their full meaning ['La mise-en-scène seule a la vertu de les (les personnages, situations, paroles) faire être pleinement']. For one never makes a film out of nothing. To shoot a film is always to shoot *something,* be it fiction or reality, and the more shaky the reality, the more solid the fiction must be ['Car on ne tire jamais un film du néant. Filmer est toujours filmer quelquechose, fiction ou réalité, et plus celle-ci est branlante, plus celle-là doit affermir ses assises']" (SCM, v/7). But when does reality get "shaky" ("branlante"), and what does it mean to make fiction "more solid" ("affermir ses assises") as a "correction" of the shakiness of reality? Such questions are paramount for Rohmer, have been so from his first meditations on cinema, and serve as the real text for which *Ma Nuit chez Maud* serves as pretext. Reality becomes shaky when we consider the degree of projection that has characterized our understanding of perception since the beginnings of modernism.[15] Indeed, "projection" is simply another term for the grid or filter we erect on/in our perception of the world in order to "understand" what we have perceived. Projection is the organization the mind makes of the random or traumatic events presented to consciousness. *Narration* of events controls what would otherwise overwhelm us.[16]

A second answer to the question, Why cinema?—intimately related to the first—centers on questions of cinematic space and architecture. Jean-Louis is alone in the world. In the opening sequence of the film, he stands in a coldly isolated and visually sterile villa on the outskirts of Clermont Ferrand, gazing out his window at the winter landscape, the camera catching him from behind in an angle that assumes his point of view, yet stands just far enough behind him to enable the spectator to establish a separate and evaluative position. This particular position of the camera is crucial for the entire film, for it immediately distinguishes the viewer's place from that of the reader of the *Maud* story. As viewers we have a privileged access to the narrator's point of view yet are not entirely confined to it.

The importance of this position is immediately evident. Jean-Louis's pacing and confinement in his house cannot fail to evoke for us the Pascalian discovery "that the sole cause of man's unhappiness is that he does not know how to stay quietly in his room," this fact itself deriving from "the natural unhappiness of our feeble mortal condition, so wretched that nothing can console us when we really think about it" (P, #136). The immensity of the landscape ("un immense panorama" in the text [SCM, 58/62]) that confronts Jean-Louis certainly adds to this sense of isolation, and we are shortly to learn from his brief but unengaged conversations with lunch mates in another visually sterile modern building that he is a traveler, having moved from Vancouver to Valparaiso to Clermont Ferrand, the birthplace of Blaise Pascal. The shots of Jean-Louis driving into town confirm his voyager's status, and he ends up fixed firmly by Rohmer's camera in the Eglise Notre Dame du Port.

Rohmer offers his viewers in this first sequence a contrast between modern and Renaissance architectures—one that informed his first major theoretical essay on cinema, "Le Celluloid et le marbre."[17] Rohmer claimed in these essays that cinema is first and foremost "un art de l'espace," a spatial art.[18] Lest there be any confusion about this generality, he opened a meditation on the relationship between cinema and architecture that intimately links the two.[19] Rohmer had previously argued that cinema replaced poetry as metaphor, explaining, "Fully metaphorical is that which, in its particularity, uncovers the presence of the greater laws of the Universe [and] the constant parallelism between the phenomena of the various natural orders . . . [leading to] the idea of a hierarchical and ordered universe, in the light of the final end of history."[20] And if cinema is metaphorical in just this way, then architecture, he reasoned, must be the art closest to cinema. The other arts are merely "mirrors of the world—mirrors that distort to whatever degree we desire." Their function is "to reproduce or sing," but they can never be more than fragmentary; as "microcosms, they therefore give a false semblance of the world."[21]

The architect's work, by contrast with the "lesser" arts poetry, painting, and music, participates integrally *in* the world because it consolidates the ensemble of the other arts as well as the common materials around us. Architecture is "a creation conceived of in its totality, and not as isolated fragments." Cinema belongs alongside architecture, since "constructing its fiction of real elements, the author of a film is more a *demiurge* than a creator." Architecture is likewise "the recognition of an order I shall call *demiurgic* (since its etymology so invites)." Its geometry and mathematics, Rohmer contends, are integrated into a "coherent and esthetic system that gives rise to the highest feelings: the feeling of harmony between nature and men's work is the best—and perhaps the only—access to understanding the divine." Thus, film's metaphoricity (the parallelism of the various natural orders) and architecture's metonymicity (bringing different physical matters together into a coherent esthetic harmony) may alike lead us to and indeed may actually be *signs* of the divine order of things. No wonder, then, that the age of Romanesque architecture should evoke "le sentiment de l'accord parfait entre la nature et le travail de l'homme . . . la compréhension du divin," whereas modern architecture should produce "the hope of a new world, clean, bright, perfectly adapted to our pleasures and to our thirst for freedom."[22] Two styles, two modes of life.[23]

But here Rohmer's argument takes a most curious turn—and it turns, uncannily, on the same literary allusion that plunges Truffaut's *Jules et Jim* into a "tailspin": Goethe's *Elective Affinities*.[24] No sooner has Rohmer evoked the divine harmonies of cinema and architecture in the service of a "perfect order" than, like the narrator in *Ma Nuit chez Maud,* he finds himself unable to control the destabilizing role of desire. Even though "this (architectural and cinematic) contemplation attempts to be free of desire ['pure de désir']," such a noble ambition itself becomes, Rohmer recognizes, "excessive." Inevitably, it seems, a "mal interne" troubles the purest happiness:

> Notice how in some of the most beautiful novels the idea of happiness—a happiness verging on the absolute but undermined by some internal disturbance ["quelque mal interne"]—is associated with *a precise architecture.* I'm thinking . . . especially of Goethe's admirable *Elective Affinities*, the greatest *monument* of world literature. . . . It is hardly an accident ["ce n'est point hasard"] that we find Edouard occupied from the first page in architectural landscaping work . . . and that the novel's characters *mistake as the divine order what is merely the*

highest conception of human intelligence. . . . They are punished, not for pride or disobedience, but for having wanted to find God there where he wasn't yet entirely present ["d'avoir voulu trouver Dieu là où il n'était pas encore tout entier"].[25]

Goethe's *Elective Affinities* seems fast on its way to becoming a new wave litmus test. Just as Truffaut managed to bend it to his purposes in *Jules et Jim,* Rohmer here flushes out Edouard's *demiurgic* tendencies as architect and "metteur-en-scène" of the novel's universe. But suddenly the *demiurge* (so clearly a positive term in Rohmer's designation of architect and filmmaker) is tinged with foolishness. It is as if Rohmer were unconsciously critiquing his *own* project for having wanted to make of the highest form of artistic endeavor a form of the divine order. The phrase "Dieu qui n'est pas là où on a voulu le trouver" cannot have failed to evoke Pascal's "hidden god" for Rohmer,[26] for he immediately launches into a kind of parody of Pascal's famous thought on the "unhappiness ['malheur']" of "man [, who] does not know how to stay quietly in his room":

> "Perfect life" cannot be the subject of fiction since it has no void that fiction could fill. Art is nourished by unhappiness ["malheur"], and it is one of our misfortunes, boredom, which art remedies. . . . Imagine a man immobilized on a lounge chair; there is no novelistic subject more seemingly untreatable. But have him approach his window, allow him to contemplate on the opposite façade, as if he were a prisoner in Plato's cave, the fleeting and deceptive images of the life he has renounced. By this means, which Hitchcock employs in *Rear Window,* fiction takes on a new theme. . . . The hero, become spectator, forces us to take a salutary step back from the event. Art and life tighten their connection, and both profit from this perspective. . . . What would we do in an empty world if not people it with the fantoms of an imaginary life?[27]

Pascal's famous thought on the man confined to his chamber is written in the same style as the above passage ("Imagine. . . . Let man then contemplate. . . ," etc.) and includes, as diversion, the possibility of gambling as remedy for the boredom ("l'ennui") he experiences. "Give him enough to gamble," argues Pascal, and his passions will be stirred so much that he will forget his misery. Pascal constructs his argumentative strategy to lead us from man's unhappiness to the idea of gambling, from there to the wager, and ultimately to the need to gamble on the existence of God, that is, ultimate happiness. Rohmer's way is not so clear. In place of gambling, Rohmer offers to his solitary man . . . the movies! Pascal's wager is replaced by Plato's cave of illusions; the promise of the divine by the enjoyment of voyeurism! Rohmer has thus somehow managed to (mis)use the subject of architecture and cinema as a vehicle by which to anticipate the ironic religious intellection of *Ma Nuit chez Maud*.

If we imagine Pascal himself languishing in his solitary room in his native town of Clermont Ferrand, it is but a step to picture him leaving that room for the sanctuary of the Eglise de Notre Dame du Port. This extraordinary Romanesque edifice thus becomes doubly significant in Rohmer's film—for her designation as "Port," which can only designate "haven" in this landlocked countryside, and for her history: it was in this very church that Pascal was baptised.

Jean-Louis's "conversion" as recorded by Rohmer's camera is in marked contrast to Pascal's, for the "fire" that Pascal experienced in his conversion from science to religion on November 23, 1654, brought him a vision of the biblical burning bush, but Jean-Louis's fire comes from another source. As the priest intones the Pater Noster and asks his parishioners to join with him in asking God to "pardon our offenses and deliver us from evil," Jean-Louis looks pointedly to his right. One of Rohmer's contentions about the architecture of cinema was that "the screen reveals a space this is not closed *but is spilling over on all sides, like a landscape from a window or a room from a keyhole.*"[28] Nowhere in this film does the space "spill over" so much as it does insistently in this scene of Jean-Louis's gaze outside of our visual field. The equation of Church with keyhole voyeurism is disturbing, to say the least. Rohmer's camera obligingly follows Jean-Louis's gaze, however, and encounters Françoise. "So that henceforth we may be delivered from sin," pleads the voice of the priest, "let us pray, O Lamb of God that taketh away the sins of the world, give us peace." But the lamb occupying Jean-Louis's look (and consequently that of the viewer) continues three times to be Françoise. His look is so insistent that finally she turns and stares at the camera (i.e., at the viewer), and Rohmer obligingly does a reverse angle shot that grammatically fixes that look on Jean-Louis. This response from Françoise takes place against the audible words of the priest "Behold the Lamb of God that taketh away the sins of the world. Lord, I am unworthy to receive thee. Say but one word and I will be saved." This last sentence is so insistently repeated, punctuating the looks exchanged between the two, that confusion arises as to who is to play the sacrificial "lamb" in this drama.

During the following day Jean-Louis will announce to his viewers that "l'idée m'est venue brusque, précise, définitive que Françoise serait ma femme." The chronological juxtaposition of the church sequence and this announcement leaves little doubt as to the nature of Jean-Louis's "conversion." Rohmer utterly confuses his audience by a subtle reversal of the roles of the two architectures—Romanesque and modern—evoked in his essay on that subject. Ironically, it is chez Maud that Jean-Louis will come closest to articulating his religious principles: "I have converted," he will tell his friends (SCM, 79/82), but that conversion seems motivated by curious impulses. Its rigor seems to involve something other than purely *religious* dedication.

Rohmer virtually instructs his viewer in a "catechism" of Jean-Louis's faith. Immediately following the annunciation of his future marriage with Françoise, ironically "consecrated" in the very architectural space where we would least expect it, Jean-Louis is seen in a bookstore. Most viewers will recall that he flips through a copy of Pascal's *Pensées,* but in fact that is the second book that appears in his (and momentarily our) sightline. The first is a book entitled *Le Calcul des probabilités.* Only after speculating on probability theory does Jean-Louis take up Pascal's *Pensées* and turn to the pages on the wager, where we read, "'But that is what I am afraid of.' 'But why? What have you to lose? But to show you that this is the way . . .' ['Mais, c'est ce que je crains. —Et pourquoi? qu'avez-vous à perdre? mais pour vous montrer que cela y mène . . .']" (P, #418).

Thus to orient our reading of Pascal and the wager as merely a calculation of probabilities is to engender not only a misreading (like Vidal's in the subsequent scene of their first meeting in the Suffren Bar) but a particular misreading, for Jean-Louis has constructed his entire narrative and project around just this misreading of Pascal, one that involves a particular enstasis. To set Pascal up next to (indeed sequentially following) a calculation of probabilities encourages a reading that falls into line with all of Jean-Louis's statements about chance and deliberately (or unconsciously?) deflects our reading away from a complete reading of Pascal, deemed too rigorous for our narrator-protagonist. This *screened* Pascal is not only the author of some *pensées* that directly confront Jean-Louis's version of "faith" but also the author of another text that is just as rigorously denied (and ironically suggested) to us by the inflection of the *probabilistic* reading of *Les Pensées: Les Lettres provinciales.*

Pascal himself was tormented, as Vidal reminds us, by the conflict between his scientific history (as author of numerous treatises on mathematics) and the story of conversion. Even in his *Pensées* he is acutely aware of these two types of mentation. Indeed, one of the opening *pensées* dwells precisely on this difference:

> *Difference between the mathematical and the intuitive mind.* In the one
> the principles are palpable, but remote from ordinary usage; so that
> from want of practice we have difficulty turning our heads that way:
> but once we do turn our heads, the principles can be fully seen; and it
> would take a thoroughly unsound mind to draw false conclusions
> from principles so patent that they can hardly be missed.
>
> *Différence entre l'esprit de géométrie et l'esprit de finesse. En l'un les
> principes sont palpables mais éloignés de l'usage commun de sorte
> qu'on a peine à tourner la tête de ce côté-là, manque d'habitude: mais
> pour peu qu'on l'y tourne, on voit les principes à plein; et il faudrait
> avoir tout à fait l'esprit faux pour mal raisonner sur des principes si
> gros qu'il est presque impossible qu'ils échappent.*
> (P, #512)

The mathematical mind, Pascal is arguing here, is not always at work,
but once it comes into play, it will demand logic in every working of
its attention. Once in play, he warns us, even *a little* in play, it
cannot—certainly should not—escape our notice. In other words, it
takes work to produce a blindfold so thick that the mathematician in
us should not see the work of illogic and inaccuracy. The construction
of just such a blindfold, I would contend, is begun by Rohmer's
unreliable narrator-protagonist in the scene in the bookstore and
certainly continued in the church, where the act of "turning one's
head in that direction" takes on a decidedly un-Pascalian purpose.
Pascal notes further in this first *pensée:*

> With the intuitive mind, the principles are in ordinary usage and there
> *for all to see.* There is *no need to turn our heads,* . . . it is only a question
> of *good sight* . . . but . . . one needs *very clear sight ["la vue nette"] to see
> all the principles* as well as an accurate mind to avoid drawing false con-
> clusions from known principles. (P, #512, italics mine)

Clearly the emphasis on good sight cannot escape our notice in the
context of film, nor has it escaped Jean-Louis's, but the object of his
gaze has become *la femme* rather than *la flamme.* It is all right to be
intuitive if one is thorough in seeing all the principles and if one acts
according to all of these principles. And so, continues Pascal, "all
mathematicians would be intuitive *if they had clear sight* for they do
not reason incorrectly from principles known to them." Mathematicians, however (and Pascal should know, for he had lately been one),
are notoriously blind:

The reason why mathematicians are not intuitive is that *they can not see what is in front of them;* for being accustomed to the clearcut, obvious principles of mathematics and to draw no conclusions until they have clearly seen and handled their principles, they become lost in matters requiring intuition. (P, #512)

Jean-Louis's tendency to substitute a convenient system in place of perception becomes the underlying subject of this remarkable film, whose larger subject, as I have suggested, is projection and the problems of narration. As narrator of the story, Jean-Louis has the "responsibility" to show us everything that is pertinent to our understanding of that story. And yet his own blindness (caused at least in part by too much systematization) prevents him from doing just that. The moment in the bookstore in which he holds up to our view a copy of *Le Calcul des probabilités* next to the title page of Pascal's *Pensées* and the selected pages on the wager corresponds cinematographically to the moment in the graphic text in which Rohmer's narrator writes "Je ne dirai pas tout dans cette histoire." Rohmer has transposed the question from writing to seeing in the film and in so doing has brought the entire question into precisely the terms in which Pascal frames it in *Les Pensées.* Little wonder that he should state that "it is only on the screen that the form of these tales is fully realized. . . . Perhaps it also mirrors the anxiety of cinema ['Elle figure peut-être aussi celle du cinéma tout entier']" (SCM, x/12, ix/11).

In this single sequence, Rohmer has established (1) an examination of the difference between the mathematical (blind) and the mathematical-intuitive (sighted) mind; (2) a dialogue between Jean-Louis's limited and limiting version of Pascal versus a(n implied) more complete reading of Pascal; (3) a consequent meditation on the relationship between the unreliability of his narrator and the necessarily impaired reading of Pascal that results; (4) an opposition between his unreliable narrator and the (presumably more global) understanding of the film's "image maker"; and (5) a dialectic between writing and filming.

There is a second highly significant omission from the written narration in its filmic avatar, one that again centers on Pascal and highlights what is present and what is absent from Jean-Louis's avowed reading of the Jansenist. As graphic narrator, he writes,

Pascal is one of the writers who have made the biggest impression on my life ["qui m'ont le plus marqué"]. I thought I knew his work by heart; as I reread it, however, though I found the text familiar, it was no longer the same one I remembered ["ce n'était plus le même texte"]. The one I recalled had taken to task ["fustigeait"] human nature as a whole. The text I was reading now, after all these years, struck me as uncompromising and extreme ["quelque chose d'intransigeant, d'excessif"], passing judgement on me ["me condamnait"] on both my past and my future. Yes, a text written for and aimed specifically at me ["me visait tout particulièrement moi"]. (SCM, 58–59/62–63)

But the film's narrator omits this admission. We know only that in his discussions with Vidal and Maud, Jean-Louis "s'insurge contre le rigorisme" of Pascal. A series of surprising juxtapositions replace the textual confession that Pascal "me visait tout particulièrement." The first is the superposition of the two titles *Le Calcul des probabilités* and *Les Pensées*. Readers of *Les Lettres provinciales,* Pascal's most direct dialogue with "les hommes de bonne volonté" of his time, that is, the Jesuits, will recall that in this *other* text (cf. "ce n'était plus le même texte") Pascal attacks the Jesuits' theory of *probabilism*. That is, the text created by the dialogue of the calculation of probabilities (Jean-Louis's favorite pastime) and Pascalian "rigorism" is precisely *Les Provinciales* and not the text screened. But to discuss *this* text is to engage in a confrontation that indeed does "vise tout particulièrement" the narrator, and with such unrelenting good logic that he would be powerless to respond. It is, in fact, much easier for Jean-Louis to refute in general terms Pascal's inflexibility on such straw items as his pleasure in drinking Chanturgue wine than it is to explain why he uses the mass to find the "right" woman. And explain he must, were he reading *Les Lettres provinciales,* for Pascal directs one of his letters precisely to this activity! Escobar, one of the Jesuits most constantly attacked by Pascal for his probabilism, writes "that a wicked intention, like that of looking at women lustfully, combined with that of hearing mass ['comme de regarder des femmes avec un désir impur, jointe à celle d'ouir la messe'] does not prevent one from satisfying the obligation."[29] The opening scenes in the church represent an almost parodic cinematic transcription of this recommendation from Escobar, one of hundreds of ridiculously framed moral statements attacked by Pascal in the *Lettres provinciales*.

The *Provinciales* were conceived as a whole as a response to the doctrine of probabilism as it was advanced by the Jesuits of Pascal's time. This doctrine had, by the middle of the seventeenth century, become an elaborate justification for any and every kind of moral and immoral excess. The theory allowed that a "probable" justification for moral laxity could be found somewhere in a "doctor"'s opinion on the matter, or in a "probable" interpretation of that laxity. "A probable opinion," noted Pascal, irony dripping from his pen, "is one with a basis of some importance ['un fondement considérable']" (LP, 82/390). This "probability" was manipulated with such shameless dexterity by the Jesuits that, as in Freud's theory of the unconscious, opposites could mean the same thing: "The fact is . . . that both the affirmative and the negative of most opinions have some probability, in the view of our doctors, and enough to be followed with a safe conscience. It is not that the pro and the con are both right together in the same sense, that is impossible, but just that they are probable and consequently safe" (LP, 91/393). Thus, Jesuitical argument justified dispensation from fasting if, for example, one were too tired from chasing girls (LP, 86–87/388–89); it excused slander if the "intent" were to protect oneself; it allowed ambush and murder if one thought one's life were in danger. "We correct the viciousness of the means ['le vice du moyen'] by the purity of the end" (LP, 104/398).

Such moral relativism may be remarkably convenient for one who prefers to be "un homme de bonne volonté," but it is painful to confront. And so it is not surprising that Jean-Louis evokes but does not directly confront Pascal's "rigorisme," preferring to evoke his own "pureté de coeur" and engaging in the fine art of justification by "sufficient grace." Like Escobar and the other Jesuits attacked by Pascal in the *Lettres provinciales,* Jean-Louis tells Maud, "I don't aspire to be a saint. . . . I mean I can't become one. . . . I'm part of the world we live in, of this century ['Je ne veux pas être un saint. Et quand je dis "Je ne veux pas," je veux dire "Je ne peux pas." . . . Je suis dans le siècle']."

Maud, of course, is on to his Jesuitism. When he seems too willing to stay with her "against his principles," she says, "I thought Christians were judged according to their acts, and yet you don't seem to attach any importance to them" (SCM, 90/93). Thus Pascal might have addressed the *Pères jésuites* of his letters. Jean-Louis sidesteps the obvious moral dilemma by responding, "To acts? Of course I do. A great deal of importance. But for me it's not one specific act that matters, it's the totality of all one's acts that does . . . an overall choice, a certain way of living ['la vie dans son ensemble']." This is the same character who only minutes before has extricated himself from a difficult confrontation with his actions by arguing, "Le passé c'est le passé." And the same character argues that he intends to marry a practicing Catholic, yet when he is confronted by Maud's "I'm shocked. I thought that abstinence prior to marriage ['rester chaste jusqu'au mariage'] was a necessity for a true believer," he responds,

> We're talking about the past. . . . My Christianity and my amorous adventures are two very different things—contradictory ["contraires"] in fact. There's an obvious conflict . . . I have a very strong feeling that running after women is no worse, as far as one's relationship with God is concerned ["ça ne vous éloigne pas plus de Dieu"], than, I don't know, practising math. (SCM, 82–83/85–86)

All of this moral slipperiness causes Maud to exclaim, "I've never met anyone who disturbed ['me scandalise'] as much as you have. . . . You know what bothers me ['me chiffonne'] most about you? It's the fact that you're evasive ['vous vous dérobez']. You refuse to assume responsibility. On the one hand you're a shame-faced Christian, and on the other a bashful ['honteux'] Don Juan. Which is a bit too much ['C'est bien le comble!']" (SCM, 86–87/98–99).

To which Jean-Louis (eventually) responds,

> All I ask of grace is that it open up to me the possibility, however slight, of being touched by it ["de me faire entrevoir la possibilité d'être un saint"]. Whether I'm right or wrong, and going on the assumption that not everyone can aspire to sainthood, I think that there have to be people—and I count myself among them—who, given their nature, their aspirations, their talents and limitations, simply cannot aim that high. Take me: with all my mediocrity, my careful middle-of-the-roadism, my lukewarmism—all of which God despises, I know—I can still attain a kind of, not plenitude, that's the wrong term, a kind of fulfillment, again in the biblical sense of the term ["une certaine justesse, dans le sens où l'Evangile dit le 'Juste'"]. (SCM, 88–89/91–92)

As he proclaims this dubious ethical position, Jean-Louis moves about Maud's room. Once again, Rohmer takes great pains to establish a distance between Jean-Louis as narrator-protagonist cum philosopher, and the film's image maker. While it would be cinematically consistent with the narrator's position to take scenes including the narrator either from a third, "objective" position, which might have the effect of "objectifying" the narrator's authority, or from a shot-countershot alternation, which would put the viewer much more within the narrator's frame of reference, Rohmer does neither. Instead, he accentuates the independence of the camera in this sequence. When Maud asks Jean-Louis to hand her a cigarette lighter, the camera, independent of Jean-Louis's movements (he is situated on the other side of the room from the camera's point of view), makes a distinct search for the lighter, locating it on a table at some distance from the bed, then locates Jean-Louis, who approaches the table to take hold of it. With this "ironic" distance firmly and insistently established,[30] the camera then records Jean-Louis's movements from a perspective that accentuates his physical proximity to a painting on Maud's wall and to a table lamp nearby. The painting in question is of a white circle about twelve inches in diameter on a dark background. The newly established independent camera perspective creates a perspective in which Jean-Louis's head repeatedly approaches a position in which this circle would form a halo for the would-be, wouldn't-be saint yet never quite manages to achieve the effect. The lamp beside him adds to this ironic topography by projecting Jean-Louis's *shadow* onto the nimbic circle. The visual commentary proffered by the image maker leaves little doubt that Jean-Louis's ethical and moral position "misses the point." Or rather avoids the point.

"I find your Jesuitical thinking amusing," says Maud when she sees him again later that day (SCM, 104/107). And, indeed, it *is* amusing when seen in the light of the *Provincial Letters*. To side with the Jesuits against Pascal's rigorism can only be considered an invitation to ridicule by anyone who has read *Les Lettres provinciales*—which of course Jean-Louis would have done as a *lycéen* but which he has conveniently screened out. Rohmer subtly reminds his viewer of this text first through the juxtaposition of the *Pensées* and *Le Calcul des probabilités* early on and then in a variety of visual and verbal cues such as this one. Two others are worth mentioning as well.

When Jean-Louis succeeds in accosting Françoise in the street "contre ses principes" (which in any case do not exist), she accepts a ride home and then invites him to stay in an empty room in her villa since his car is stuck in the snow near her house. When he is alone with Françoise in her room, Jean-Louis begins all over again his anti-Pascalian discourse on chance, even pausing for a moment to ask, "Does it bother you that I keep referring to my luck? ['Ça ne vous choque pas que je parle tout le temps de ma chance?']" When he links his luck to the question of grace, she corrects, "But grace is something quite different. It has nothing to do with material success. . . . If grace were given to us like that to fortify our clear consciences ['pour alimenter notre bonne conscience'], if it wasn't deserved, if it wasn't anything more than an excuse to justify everything . . . " But Jean-Louis, anticipating an uncomfortable truth about his ethical position, interrupts: "You're a believer in predestination! ['Vous êtes très janséniste!']" (SCM, 109/112). Before retiring to his own bed, he leads

Françoise through a miasma of moral relativism in which he again adroitly substitutes luck for moral rectitude.

As he climbs into bed and reaches randomly for a book to lull him to sleep, Rohmer ironically makes it his "luck" to encounter yet another indirect reminder of Pascal's *Lettres provinciales* and his own Jesuitism. He pulls from the bookshelf over the bed a copy of *De la vraie et de la fausse conversion*. For the second time in this film, Rohmer insistently screens a text: *De la vraie et de la fausse conversion* hides and reveals a truth that has been tracking Jean-Louis from the first images we see of him. Maud had said to him, "I don't really subscribe to your 'love but under certain conditions only' business . . . the way you calculate, plan ahead, classify. The *sine qua non* for you is that your future wife be Catholic. Love will follow in due course" (SCM, 104/106–7). Aside from the fact that she virtually paraphrases what Pascal himself had written about the blindness of the overly mathematical mind, Maud's comment is doubly telling. Her criticism, when simply inverted, reveals Jean-Louis's true project. Not only does religion "add to love," as Jean-Louis had professed during their first five minutes together, "but love to religion as well." Religion is "un prétexte à tout justifier," especially for finding nice Catholic girls who will not threaten too much his natural timidity.

Jean-Louis's behavior with Françoise immediately bears out what Maud had said about his "Don Juanisme honteux." If Don Juanism consists, in part, in repeating the same gestures and the same lines to different women, Jean-Louis seems to be the past master of this art. In this respect he seems to be repeating Marivaux rather than Pascal. Jean-Louis's preoccupation with luck, his smarmy sense of morality, and his search for the ideal woman might as easily be called "le jeu de l'amour et du hasard" or "la double inconstance," if not "les fausses confidences," as *Ma Nuit chez Maud*.[31] These allusions to Marivaux are hardly idle play. To see Jean-Louis's activity as "marivaudage" is to understand the entirely parodic and ironic intent of the film, and to underscore his "unreliability" as a reader of Pascal. He manages to find himself alone with each woman because of the danger of driving in icy conditions—likely a sign of his moral slipperiness. With each he launches into discussions of Pascalian theology and manages "à coup de paradoxes" (his own term) to effect a discursive feint in which luck is substituted for ethical responsibility. With each he executes the gesture of rolling himself up in a blanket and then making an advance on the woman's bed, each time with dubious success. On the morning after his night "with" each woman, he reveals to each one the strength of his feelings, evoking from Maud, "I don't know you!" and from Françoise, "You don't even know me."

But as subtle as it is, the difference in their reactions alludes to the final irony of the film. For Jean-Louis has substituted a system of his own making for love and religion. Rather than following "all the principles," as Pascal would put it, he puts on blinders to some and follows only those that seem to serve his particular needs. Those needs seem to derive as much from fears as from either desire or, as again Pascal might put it, "the true good." Just as he is blind to the real ethical responsibility that Pascal might have inculcated in him had he chosen any other route than to screen out the moral discomfort of the *Provincial Letters,* he is remarkably insensitive to the realities of the two women with whom it is his "fortune" to spend the night.

Rohmer has again provided an extraordinary visual cue in his role as "image maker" of the film. C. G. Crisp has discussed the way Rohmer seems to have created a dichotomy between Maud and Fran-çoise that the critic feels is resolved in "the narrator's moment of triumph—of triumph over himself—when he rejects Maud and chooses Françoise . . . the moment of conversion from being a 'false' Catholic to being a true one."[32] Thus Crisp sees Maud as dark, lo-cated in the "grubbiness of an industrial city, . . . engaged in a worldly practice—medicine . . . at ease during the night-time. . . . She repre-sents the forces of anti-nature, the dark powers." Françoise, by con-trast, is, according to Crisp, blonde, associated with height, white snow, unworldliness, and purity. Crisp summarizes the resolution of this opposition as "the narrator's escape to Nature . . . an escape from the unrewarding complexities of an urban mechanized world to a Rousseauesque dream of rural peace and permanence . . . a release into the natural fluent order of things attained through a grace that passeth all understanding."[33]

While I agree that there *seems* to be such an opposition between these two women, this opposition is undercut by the stinging irony of the film's final scene. Only then does Jean-Louis understand that the woman he has chosen for her purity, Catholic ideals, and "natural-ness" is the very woman who had destroyed Maud's marriage by seducing her husband. Not a little of the film's irony lies in the fact that this probability has entirely escaped the fanatic of calculation, Jean-Louis, but need not have escaped the viewer's calculation of the probabilities of its occurrence. For Rohmer has, like the best directors of murder mysteries, provided all the clues necessary for the viewer to solve this "crime."

Maud had already told Jean-Louis that her husband had a mis-tress, "your type, that girl, very upstanding, decent, a good Catholic . . . no hypocrisy about her, nothing self-seeking. . . . she was crazy about him . . . but I don't think she would have gone so far as to marry him" (SCM, 93/96). Françoise fits this description precisely, coincidence enough in a small town like Clermont Ferrand and therefore of putable interest to a person nearly obsessed by probabilities. Among his first illustrations of probability with Vidal is, in fact (dare I say *coincidentally?*), "The probability of my running into someone whose address or place of work is unknown to me is, of course, impossible to determine." In the short story, the narrator adds, "Of course it was Françoise I had in mind" (SCM, 63/67). But Françoise has also told Jean-Louis that she is/was in love with a married man, and Vidal nearly falls over backwards when he encounters Françoise with Jean-Louis, a double take that would have elicited some curiosity in a person of *intuitive intelligence.*

Moreover, Françoise is absent from the services on Christmas Eve (quite against her custom and Jean-Louis's justifiable expectations), the very night that Maud's husband is back in town "pour voir la petite," a stunningly ambiguous phrase. The irony of this coincidence is that it twice causes Jean-Louis to lie to Françoise and grossly to misrepresent his relationship with Maud. For a person so single-mindedly committed to "fidelity" to a "blonde Catholic girl" he hasn't even spoken to yet, Jean-Louis ends up sacrificing this puritanical renunciation of Maud to the necessity of matching bad behavior with the very person whom he hoped to win over by his fidelity!! How can this can of worms be termed an effect of "grace that passeth all understanding?"[34]

I submit that instead of an effect of grace, we see the inevitable irony produced by a the superposition of a grid of Jesuitical hypocrisies onto life's complexities. For lying to Françoise about Maud's reputation is more than just a scheme to get her back (I intend this sentence to be doubly ambiguous), it is an injustice to Maud. The latter may be dark, worldly, a city dweller, and a night person, as Crisp quite rightly points out in establishing her apparent opposition to Françoise. But is she so different? Are the oppositions real? Maud may not be Catholic, but she embraces a "religion" at least equally principled to that espoused by her counterpart. She says,

> I know [that the irreligion of free thinking is actually a form of religion] but I have the right to prefer that religion to any others. . . .
> At least I'm faithful [to my religion]. . . . It's not "nothing." It's merely a much freer way of looking at problems. With a great many principles, in fact, often very strict principles, but without any preconceived ideas ["aucun préjugé"]. (SCM, 70/74)

Maud represents at the very least a degree of sincerity that is difficult to match in the universe of this film (and of Rohmer's cinema). Certainly the difference between Maud and Françoise is lost on Jean-Louis himself, as indicated by the parodic repetition of his Don Juanism. In addition, Rohmer has provided his viewer with yet another remarkable visual clue, one that borrows from and thus returns us to the Romanesque site of this film. During his night with Maud, Rohmer's camera carefully frames her lying in bed, head propped on hand, in exactly the pose adopted by the Romanesque sculptor Gislebertus's Eve (see plates 20 and 21). This pose might have been gratuitous had not the image maker placed in Françoise's room a photographic enlargement of this very sculpture! That Maud enacts and Françoise reproduces the figure of Eve suggests that there is more to this "moral tale" than just a parody of morals.[35] Indeed, one of the "hidden texts" of this film is, as we have already appreciated, the body of Rohmer's own writing about architecture and the cinema. If there is an opposition between the "contrived" Maud and the "natural" Françoise, it may indeed mirror a similar conflict in Rohmer's singularly ambivalent attitude toward the nature of cinema itself.

"How vain painting is, exciting admiration by its resemblance to things of which we do not admire the originals!" wrote Pascal (P, #40). How much more so cinema, we might argue. It is a dialectic engaged by Rohmer long before he began to work on *Ma Nuit chez Maud* or, for that matter, any of his films. In his earliest essays, Rohmer had articulated a position against *montage* and interpretation or manipulation of reality in the cinema. In "Cinéma, art de l'espace," Rohmer had criticized recent developments in cinema that had perverted the spectator's relationship to reality, so that it had become "more a deciphering than a viewing." "In learning to interpret," Rohmer had argued, "the modern spectator had forgotten how to see."[36] A staunch ally of André Bazin, Rohmer castigated those who would use cinema to tamper with reality, and he praised the seventh art for its unique ability to capture reality in its unvarnished truth, or as he phrased it, "to look at the world with our everyday eyes."[37]

In those early years of theorizing, Rohmer took the position that any cineaste who really looked at nature would be so "fascinated by his model [that] he would forget the order he had intended in his arrogance to impose on it and, in so doing, reveal the true harmony of nature, its essential unity."[38] C. G. Crisp notes that Rohmer's belief that "a humble documentary presentation of reality inevitably reveals an inherent order, which speaks of God" eventually came into conflict with his evolving experience as a filmmaker. As his writing progressed, Crisp notes, Rohmer's theory of an unvarnished realism encountered increasing dissonance vis-à-vis his beliefs in auteurism and in a literary and moral cinema. Crisp concludes that "if Rohmer

PLATE 20. Maud (Françoise Fabian) imitates the pose of the Autun Eve in Rohmer's *Ma Nuit chez Maud.* (Courtesy of the Museum of Modern Art Film Stills Archive.)

openly advocated a transparent realism that focused on God's greatness, he often most admired (and later praised) a psychological realism that focused on man's frailties. Whilst the former is predominantly visual and external, the latter is predominantly verbal and introspective, and the two are by no means always compatible."[39] It was, in fact, his preference for literary cinema that led to an about-face on the subject of realism. About the time he was making *Maud,* Rohmer wrote,

> The literary dimension is no less fruitful than the lyrical. . . . It is easier for the novelist to describe the mental world than the physical. For the filmmaker the contrary is true. But . . . we should be more and more curious to pierce the external shell of things, which the stark image presents to us. . . . In the realm of pure plastic expression, the portrayal of action, and even the presentation of life, the cinema has done wonders; but it has proved pretty restricting when it comes to portray-

PLATE 21. The Autun Eve. (Courtesy of abbé Denis Grivot, Maitre de la Chapelle de la Cathédrale d'Autun, and Giraudon/Art Resource, N.Y.)

ing reflection, a character's developing awareness of himself. . . . Purely visual cinema was incapable of exploring this realm.[40]

The problem for Rohmer, as for Pascal before him, lay in the very nature of the *deus absconditus*—the "hidden God."[41] Goldmann writes of Pascal's relationship to the divine,

> The hidden God . . . is an idea which is fundamental in tragic thought in general and in Pascalian thought in particular. It is a paradoxical idea: For Pascal, the hidden God is both present and absent, and not sometimes absent and sometimes present. He is always absent and always present. . . . God always exists but never appears. . . . But we must add that for Pascal . . . this hidden God is present in a more real and more important way than any empirical and perceptible being, and that his is the only essential presence that exists. . . . The central problem [thus becomes:] can a man still live in the hope of reintegrating moral and superindividual values in this rational and "silent" space?[42]

If, following this terrible realization of Pascal's, the absent presence of the hidden God would not be revealed in just any slice of life, as Rohmer had once proposed, then cinema would have to engage in an "arrangement" of life in such a way as to reveal God's presence to a skeptical world. "On ne tire jamais un film du néant," Rohmer had confessed. "Filmer est toujours filmer quelque chose, fiction ou réalité, et plus celle-ci est branlante, plus celle-là doit affermir ses assises." A reality that did not immediately reveal a divine purpose or harmony would indeed be more disturbing than not; fiction would thus have to "firm up" the deficient reality. Like Jean-Louis, Rohmer will not be able to "dire tout dans cette histoire." He will have to be selective and even secretive. Like Jean-Louis, he will be caught in a moment of ambivalence about how much to impose his own version of things on a world that might appear too chaotic if left to improvisation:

> The contemporary filmmaker—and this includes me—dreams of being the sole creator of his work ["l'auteur à part entière de son oeuvre"]. . . . Sometimes that omnipotence, instead of being an advantage and a stimulus, acts as a constraint ["est ressentie parfois comme un gêne"]. To be the absolute master of your subject, to be able to add to it or delete from it whatever you like, depending on the inspiration or exigencies of the moment, without having to account for what you do to anyone, is on one hand intoxicating and, on the other, paralyzing; that facility becomes a trap. . . . It is easier to compose images starting with a story than it is to make up a story on the basis of a series of images *shot more or less at random* ["tournées au bonheur de l'instant"]. Strangely, it was the latter method that tempted me at first. . . . But little by little I realized that this confidence in the role of chance ["les hasards"], which such a method required, did not fit in ["ne cadrait pas"] with what I had in mind, which was premeditated and very clearly defined. It would have taken a miracle in which, I must confess, I did not believe, for the various elements to come together in a meaningful whole exactly as I had conceived of them ["Il eût fallu un miracle, auquel on me pardonnera de n'avoir pas cru, pour que tous les éléments de la combinaison s'emboîtassent les uns dans les autres avec la précision exigée"]. (SCM, vi/8–9)

The preface of his *Six contes moraux* thus reads almost as if the narrator of *Ma Nuit chez Maud* or Pascal himself (!) had written it. As much as one would like to, one simply cannot count on miracles to make things come out right in a world in which God is "toujours présent et toujours absent." As a consequence, in imitation of his author the story's narrator writes early on, "My faith in my destiny did not make me fatalistic. I had made up my mind to put as much of myself into the undertaking as possible" (SCM, 60/64). So much for his professed believe in chance, grace, and predestination.

In imitating his own narrator in the matter of manipulating his story, Rohmer throws into question his own reliability as much as that of Jean-Louis. Just as Pascal wagers on the existence of God and Jean-Louis wagers on success in love with a blonde Catholic, Rohmer wagers on the truth value of his own fictional universe. But if Rohmer must compose fictions because reality is too "shaky," then perhaps we, as his audience, are just as much at risk with *him* as we are believing in Jean-Louis's stories. How to know the "true good" from "the idea he has of the good"? Rohmer shakes our confidence even more when he confesses that "in *Ma Nuit chez Maud* I committed myself without commitment through the character of Jean-Louis Trintignant, but it all remains very fuzzy ['très enveloppé'] in a very complex and ambiguous situation."[43] His narrative ends up functioning as a kind of tissue,[44] half revealing and half hiding, like Pascal's God himself, any moral certainty. The tragic irony inherent in the post-Pascalian universe becomes "a singularly puzzling fact" indeed in Rohmer's very probabilistic filmic one.

Chapter Six

Picking Dostoevsky's Pocket:
Bresson's Sl(e)ight of Screen

They want to find the solution where all is enigma only.
—*Pascal, in Bresson,* Notes sur le cinématographe

Hide the ideas, but so that people find them. The most
important will be the most hidden.
—*Bresson,* Notes sur le cinématographe

Like his contemporary Eric Rohmer, Robert Bresson has been called
a Jansenist, and this by none other than Jean-Luc Godard.[1] But if the
label has some usefulness in assessing the place of Pascal in Rohmer's
work, it seems to serve more as an easy "solution" to Bresson's "enigma" than as a real hermeneutic strategy.[2] Bresson's own allusion to
Pascal in his *Notes sur le cinématographe,* when juxtaposed to the more
playful hide-and-seek attitude toward ideas in his films, seems more
coy than transcendent.[3] The "purloined letter" effect may indeed be a
better critical tack than Jansenist labeling when one is confronted
with the deliberately enigmatic quality of Bresson's style, for his films
are so constructed as to appear nearly invisible at first viewing and
require an unusual effort of reconstruction for any satisfactory comprehension. The *cinematograph,* as Bresson was to label his work, is
difficult to see precisely because its author conceived it against all of
the norms of classical cinema. In reintroducing the normally dropped
syllable *graph,* Bresson accentuated cinema writing (*écriture*) at the
expense of *mise en scène.* "Cinematography ['Le cinématographe'] is a
writing ['une écriture']," Bresson writes, "with images in movement
and sounds" (NC, 2/12). Although this definition seems anodyne at

148

first glance, its implications are far from insignificant. The first corollary of the theorem is: "A film cannot be a stage show ['un spectacle']" (NC, 3/12). And insistence on the unspectacular nature of the cinematograph led immediately to a second corollary: "An actor in cinematography might as well be in a foreign country. He does not speak its language ['Un acteur est dans le cinématographe comme dans un pays étranger. Il n'en parle pas la langue']" (NC, 3/13).

Pickpocket constitutes a perfect emblem of Bresson's entire project: its very title is a foreign word, isolated from definite or indefinite article, ambiguous. That ambiguity is to remain in force throughout the film. Indeed, it was not only Bresson's actor who was to feel like a stranger in the world of his film: often his collaborators felt as much "in the dark" as his actors and critics. Leonce-Henry Burel, Bresson's cameraman for *Pickpocket,* was to say later, "I didn't understand what he was trying to say. As a matter of fact I don't think anybody has ever understood, really. Who is this pickpocket, why does he steal and so on?"[4]

Analysis of the opening sequence of the film immediately suggests the degree of difficulty that faces us as viewers. Following the title of the film, Bresson addresses a caveat to his viewer: "The style of this film is not a thriller. The author attempts to explain in pictures and sounds the nightmare of a young man forced by his weakness into an adventure in theft for which he was not made. Yet this adventure, by strange paths, brings together two souls which might otherwise never have been united." The French term for such a text is *prière d'insérer,* a technique belonging to a long literary tradition of confessional literature, including not only Montaigne and Rousseau but numerous eighteenth-century novelists, of orienting the reader's attention in a particular way. It must be noted that this tradition includes a subtradition of subversion: modern examples of this technique are more often traps for the unsuspecting reader than sincere helps to the reader's progress.[5] In this particular case, a reading of the film's "plot" has been offered that will conflict with the visual evidence to be presented. The immediate effect of this notice, however, is of distanciation: the lowering of expectations of genre (the word "style" substituted for "genre" is, I would contend, a most revealing substitution, for it is Bresson's style itself that undermines the expectations of the genre), the destruction of suspense by revealing the general outcome of the story, and the insistence on the *explanatory* nature of the work all contribute to a flattening of the viewer's emotion.[6] The very substitution of a *text* for *images* is itself a sign of Bresson's insistence on cinema writing. The titles and credits that follow this announcement themselves constitute a throwback to a style adopted at the outset of the movies and seem consciously to reject years of evolving techniques in presenting credits. In and of themselves they function as a rejection of an entire tradition of cinema and announce a return to origins.

Pickpocket's first image offers little relief from this insistence on *écriture*. We see a closeup of a hand (with no identification of its "owner") writing what is clearly a diary or journal entry: "I know that normally those who have committed crimes don't talk about them or that those who talk about such things haven't done them. And yet I have done these things ['je les ai faites']." This image is accompanied by a voice-off, establishing a narrative voice for the film that is to recur at regular intervals some sixty times in the film, four times accompanied by an image of journal writing. Although there is generally little carry-over from film to film in Bresson's works, the image of the journal writing accompanied by voice-over narration immediately evokes its homologue in *Journal d'un curé de campagne*. In both works the image of the journal produces a complex and often ambiguous effect, establishing simultaneously a link with and a break from traditional literary technique. As Nick Browne has pointed out in an essay on Bresson's *Journal d'un curé de campagne:* "Text is neither a simple commentary on the image, nor is image a simple illustration of the text. Disjunction, independence, interrogation, and even negation of the image, by the sense of the text, is as much a feature as illustration or duplication."[7]

One of the immediate ambiguities, as Browne points out, is that between past and present narration.[8] Although a journal normally suggests events that have already taken place recollected in a meditative spirit, in *Pickpocket* Bresson's camera catches the as yet unidentified hand in the present act of writing. The past tense employed in the journal writing contrasts actively with the present tense of the camera, creating a tension between *knowledge* and *perception* that constantly disturbs our ability to trust the narrator. That is, the journal entry itself ("je les ai faites") implies a knowledge of the events of the whole film that seems to be negated by our perception that the journal writing occurs in the same chronological period as the other events pictured, a fact reinforced by three other journal "entries" that occur in the present tense of the film. At the very least the *place* of the narrator becomes highly suspect. That suspicion invades at least one other level of the film. At numerous times the voice-over narrator will actively mislead the viewer, stating attitudes or facts that are directly or implicitly contradicted by the images we see.[9]

Now, because the journal writer's activity is exactly parallel to the inscription, or *prière d'insérer,* that opens the film, the narrator's and the "image maker"'s activities are implicitly associated.[10] If the narrator becomes discredited, there is at least a suspicion that this unreliability extends to the image maker himself. By extension, writing itself comes to be put into question in ways that will have a profound effect on our understanding of the film.

Bresson moves from this highly problematic view of textuality to yet another image, which, because of his editing, further complicates our understanding. The closeup of the hand writing the journal dissolves into a closeup of another disembodied hand, this one female, holding a sheaf of hundred-franc notes. There is at least a suggestion that writing and money will occupy similar positions in the universe of this film. This seems all the more likely inasmuch as the editing of the entire first sequence leaves the viewer caught entirely off guard. Bresson's camera focuses on various people in a crowd without identifying either the locale or any figure with whom the viewer may identify. Finally, the words (*off*) "For several days my decision has been made. But will I have the courage?" coincide with the camera's frontal view of Martin Lasalle. Yet he is so expressionless as to resist our attention and only retains it because of the series of looks exchanged with others in the crowd.[11] He turns, and the camera follows him from behind as he trails a mass of people (toward what end?) and stops, as they stop, finding himself directly behind a woman in a large brimmed white hat. Now as the character Michel faces the camera, the voice-off narrator (in reality, Michel's disembodied voice) says without a trace of emotion, "I should have just left ['J'aurais mieux fait de m'en aller']." The camera and editing now shift repeatedly from the actor's expressionless eyes to his hand as it slowly moves to unhitch the clasp of her alligator purse and removes another sheaf of French francs. The click of the clasp is immediately followed by the only facial expression Lasalle is to provide in the entire film: a wincing of his eyes, which has an almost orgiastic effect in the bleak facial desert of his expression. The hand movement and eye movement are accompanied by the sound of horses' hooves galloping by. We are at the Longchamps race track. Michel is a pickpocket.

The camera next follows Michel through the crowd, past some iron gates onto a wide alleyway, at which point he drones, "I was walking on air. I had conquered the world. But a minute later I was arrested ['Je n'avais plus les pieds sur terre. Je dominais le monde. Mais une minute après, j'étais pris']." But we do not see him taken; we see only two men walking behind him. A cut places Michel between two men in an automobile, and another cut places him (presumably) in the police station, where a detective is concluding their encounter with the words, "You're free to go ['Vous êtes libre']." Michel's eyes move to the sheaf of francs on the inspector's desk. The inspector hands him the money, and he stands as if to leave.

Bresson's camera work and editing in this sequence produce an effect of strangeness. On the one hand, with but three exceptions, the images we are privileged to see are virtually devoid of informational content (the three exceptions being the three images of money). On the other hand, again with those exceptions, the *actions* announced are not shown. Repeated viewings of this sequence lead to the impression that what Bresson has included in his film are those images that are normally consigned to the cutting-room floor. We do not see the horses racing. We do not witness the arrest of Michel. We do not hear the conversation between Michel and his captor. We experience only the transitions *between* those actions announced by the narrative voice-over. It is almost as though we were reading a sentence from which all of the adjectives and most of the substantives had been removed, leaving only prepositions and conjunctions.

As Alan Williams has noted, classic Hollywood cinema developed a "grammar" that was dedicated to making what is in fact an on-tologically discontinuous art form appear seamless.[12] Through careful editing of transitions, classic directors succeeded in minimizing the gaps between shots and scenes, artfully removing "unnecessary" transitions by a montage of actions that appeared to bridge those transitions. Such a grammar of continuity allowed film to concentrate on the significant actions and manage an economy of gesture without any apparent discontinuity of movement. Bresson's work, on the other hand, and *Pickpocket* in particular, seems dedicated to maximizing our sense of discontinuity. This is reflected not only in this first sequence but in many others as well. The most remarkable of these discontinuities occurs in the sequence when Michel accompanies Jacques and Jeanne to an amusement park. The scene begins with an invitation from Jacques, who stands at Michel's door. A cut to Jeanne outside is followed by a dissolve to the three friends sitting at a cafe table. Jacques says to Michel, "You're sad ['Vous êtes triste']." Michel responds, "Non." Whereupon Jacques accuses him, "You're not really living. You're not interested in the things others are ['Vous n'êtes pas dans la vie réelle. Vous ne vous interessez à rien qui intéresse les autres']."[13] Jacques and Jeanne rise from their seats, and Jacques asks, "Are you coming? We're going to take a plane ride." (A curious juxtaposition with the accusation just leveled.)[14] Bresson's camera focuses on Michel sitting alone at the table. Michel stands. Bresson's camera fails to follow Michel and instead remains trained on the empty table. A dissolve moves us away from and back to the empty table, undoubtedly to indicate some passage of time. Another dissolve moves us to an empty staircase. Michel passes through the frame and enters his room, cloaked in shadows. He leans over a pitcher in the corner, produces a handkerchief, and wipes blood off his hand. "I had run and fallen ['J'avais couru. J'étais tombé']," the narrator's voice-over informs us. Later we are to "learn" that Michel has apparently stolen a watch and/or encountered some violent adventure during the time Bresson's camera and editing have been riveted on the empty cafe table. The connecting pieces are again displayed in place of actions normally considered worthy of the viewer's attention. Again we are compelled to accept Bresson's substitution of the voice-over narrative account for visual proof. Inasmuch as the voice "belongs" to Michel, and inasmuch as he has much to hide in this film, we are entitled to doubt what we hear.

Both of these sequences illustrate a shift of emphasis in Bresson's new *cinematograph* away from the image whose value normally derives from its power of representation to images and sounds that have a purportedly neutral value and are meant to function merely as elements in a relational system.[15] Although Bresson never mentions his work directly, Saussure's linguistic theory underlies this new language of film. Bresson prescribed a

> cinematographic film, where expression is obtained by relations of images and of sounds, and not by a mimicry done with gestures and intonations of voice. . . . One that does not analyze or explain. That *recomposes*. . . . An image must be transformed by contact with other images, as is a color by contact with other colors. . . . No art without transformation. . . . Cinematographic film, where the images, like the words in a dictionary, have no power and value except through their position and relation. . . . No absolute value in an image. Images and Sounds will owe their value and their power solely to the use to which you destine them. . . . IN THIS LANGUAGE OF IMAGES, ONE MUST LOSE COMPLETELY THE NOTION OF IMAGE. THE IMAGES MUST EXCLUDE THE IDEA OF IMAGE. (NC, 5/16, 5/17, 11/28, 33/71)

Reference to Saussure's theory of linguistic value will help clarify the radical nature of what Bresson is proposing here. In his *Course in General Linguistics,* the Swiss linguist proposed that given the arbitrary nature of the sign, individual units of language had no intrinsic value. "Language," he proposed,

is a system of interdependent terms in which the value of each term results solely from the simultaneous presence of the others. . . . All values are apparently governed by the same paradoxical principle. They
are always composed: (1) of a *dissimilar* thing that can be *exchanged*
for the thing of which the value is to be determined; and (2) of *similar*
things that can be *compared* with the thing of which the value is to be
determined. Both factors are necessary for the existence of a value. A
word's content is really fixed only by the concurrence of everything
that exists outside it. . . . The value of any term is accordingly determined by its environment. . . . Concepts as well are purely differential
and defined not by their positive content but negatively by their relations with the other terms of the system. Their most precise characteristic is in being what the others are not.[16]

It suffices to substitute "image" for "word" or "phoneme" to understand how neutral Bresson would like his image to be: "*Images*
(phonemes) are characterized not, as one might think, by their own
positive quality but simply by the fact that they are distinct. *Images*
(phonemes) are above all else opposing, relative and negative en-
tities. . . . In language there are only differences . . . *without positive
terms*. The idea or substance that an *image* (sign) contains is of less
importance than the other signs that surround it. Proof of this is that
the value of a term may be modified without either its meaning or its
sound being affected, solely because a neighboring term has been
modified."[17]

Bresson is explicit in his substitution of *image* for *word*: "The most
ordinary word, when put into place, suddenly acquires brilliance
['éclat']. That is the brilliance with which your images must shine"
(NC, 56/116). And he adds, "See your film as a combination of lines
and of volumes in movement apart from what it represents ['figure']
and signifies. . . . To move people ['émouvoir'] not with images likely
to move us ['images émouvantes'], but with relations of images that
render them both alive and moving ['des rapports d'images qui les
rendent à la fois vivantes et émouvantes']" (NC, 44/92, 43/90). The
implications of this attempt to neutralize the value of the image become clear in the following passage from Saussure: "The value of any
term is accordingly determined by its environment; it is impossible to
fix even the value of the word signifying 'sun' without first considering its surroundings: in some languages it is not possible to say 'sit in
the sun.' . . . If words stood for pre-existing concepts, they would all
have exact equivalents in meaning from one language to the next; but
this is not true."[18]

No one doubts the cultural value that can be attached to images, for every civilization has its own particular icons of beauty. Nor can we forget the experiments in image contexture carried out by the Russian director Kuleshov demonstrating that the same photograph of an expressionless face could be "read" as happy or sad according to the surrounding images.[19] Bresson seems intent, however, on moving beyond these positions to a notion, borrowed from Saussurean linguistics, of the absolutely arbitrary nature of the image. Such a move goes counter to everything we know about the ontology of the photographic image, of course.[20] Because the camera replicates exactly the reality that stands before it, it has an iconic value that is lacking to the word. And yet, consistently to deprive individual images of their normal narrational and/or cultural contexts, as Bresson has consistently attempted to do, has a *transgressive* function that cannot be denied. "Cinematography," insists Bresson almost doggedly, "the art, with images of *representing* nothing ['de ne rien représenter']" (NC, 59/120). Re-presentation, in other words, is nothing but repetition; presentation, by contrast, is the essence of creativity. The "image orderer," as Bresson prefers to call the director, thus becomes a kind of god. "Cutting ['Montage']. Passage of dead images to living images. Everything blossoms afresh ['Tout refleurit']" (NC, 43/91). Out of dead, flat images, new life is given by the particular combinations dictated by the image maker. "An old thing becomes new if you detach it from what usually surrounds it" (NC, 26/57). However much this may sound like Proust's writing on the nefarious effects of "habitude," Bresson's application of the theory seems entirely antithetical to Proust's. The filmmaker's emphasis on "dead" and "flattened" images (as opposed to Proust's metaphors) will likely strike the filmgoer at first viewing as, in fact, deadening—mere absences, such as the cafe table from which Michel's absence is the only justification for the presence of the image.

The implications of this theory for the actor are no less severe. Indeed, Bresson excised the very word "actor" from his working vocabulary and substituted the word "model" in order to eliminate any possible "pollution" from "the terrible habit of theater" (NC, 2/12):

> The truth of cinematography ["Le vrai du cinématographe"] cannot be the truth of theater. . . . Nothing rings more false in a film than that natural tone of the theater copying life and traced ["calqué"] over studied sentiments. . . . The photographed theater or CINEMA requires a *metteur-en-scène* or director to make some actors perform a play and to photograph these actors performing the play; afterwards

he lines up the images. Bastard theater lacking what makes theater: material presence of living actors, direct action of the audience on the actors. (NC, 3–4/13–14, 5/16)

Like his attempt to "neutralize" the image, Bresson's attempts to "detoxify" his models of any theatricality is by now legendary. His theory of the "model" culled from his *Notes sur le cinématographe* can be synthesized as follows:

No actors.
(No directing of actors).
No parts ["rôles"].
(No learning of parts.)
No staging ["mise en scène"].
But the use of working models taken from life ["modèles, pris dans la vie"].
BEING ["ETRE"] (models) instead of SEEMING ["PARAITRE"] (actors). . . .
Model. Reduce to the minimum the share his consciousness has ["Réduire au minimum la part de sa conscience"]. Tighten the meshing ["l'engrenage"] within which he cannot any longer not be him and where he can now do nothing that is not *useful*. . . . Model. Preserved from any obligation towards the art of drama. . . .To your models: "One must not act either somebody else or oneself. One must not act anybody ['Il ne faut jouer personne']."
(NC, 1/10, 26/58, 29/63, 31/67)

This effectively *absent presence* was to be accomplished by a rigorous training requiring repetition of the model's lines until all theatricality had been eliminated.[21]

> Your models, pitched ["lâchés"] into the action of your film, will get used to the gestures they have repeated twenty times ["les ap-privoiseront à eux"]. The words they have learned with their lips ["ap-prises du bout des lèvres"] will find, *without their minds' taking part in this,* the inflections and the lilt ["la chanson"] proper to their true natures. A way of recovering the automatism of real life. (NC, 32/70)

Thus the model was to become a kind of blank that, like the other images in Bresson's creation, would draw its meaning from its juxtaposition with other images:

> Model. Enclosed in his mysterious appearance. He has brought home to him ["ramené à lui"] all of him that was outside. He is there, be-

hind that forehead, those cheeks. . . . Over his features, thoughts or feelings not materially expressed, rendered *visible* by intercommunication and interaction of two or several other images. (NC, 7/21, 22/50)

In the sequences from *Pickpocket* we have just discussed, it is clear that Bresson has achieved the unexpressive facial image in at least two different ways: first he has expanded the role of voice-over narration, removing from his protagonist the need to appear to speak, thus minimizing the facial movement that occurs in reaction to one's own discourse; second, he has instructed Martin Lasalle to avoid all facial play. Thus the only life that seems to occur is the montage of glances from one character to another.

Further, in order to keep the presence of the model as neutral an image as possible, Bresson worked to ensure that his models, both male and female, would be as "virginal" as possible. This meant, among other things, that Bresson not only used nonprofessional actors as his models but never used the same actor in more than one film. Marjorie Greene reports that when asked whether he would use Claude Laydu of *Journal d'un curé de campagne* in another film, Bresson responded (almost as if he were replaying Michel), "No. . . . How can I? For *Journal* I robbed him of what I needed to make the film. How could I rob him twice?"[22] Such solicitude, however, does not at all correspond to Bresson's usual treatment of his models.[23] Nor is the question of inexperience really convincing; as Jean-Luc Godard repeatedly pointed out to Bresson, it matters little whether one uses a trained actor or not if ultimately one trains his actors as intensively as Bresson does.[24] It is more plausible that Bresson, consciously or unconsciously, avoided professional actors precisely because of their inevitably *intertextual* nature. As Georges Sebbag has noted, "As handsome as a lightning rod, the professional actor captivates our attention. He incessantly exerts a kind of blackmail of reincarnation. Every time he slips into a new skin, he manages to carefully retain something of his familiar intonation and customary silhouette."[25] Marlon Brando, for example, brought to each of his films the persona he had developed in previous ones. Recent filmmakers have explicitly exploited this tendency: Bertolucci exploring Brando's various film personae in *Last Tango in Paris* and Truffaut Jean Dasté's previous avatar in *La Chambre verte*.[26] By using "virgin" models, Bresson effectively isolated his films from this intertextual phenomenon.

Bresson's theory and practice of the cinematograph, however self-contradictory the proposed justifications may be, do, taken as a whole, propose a radical departure from the traditions of representation and film acting so basic to classic cinema. His theory of the *combinatoire,* coinciding as it does with Saussure's theory of linguistics and the arbitrary nature of the sign, tends to break down linear narration and chronological and spatial coherence in favor of the purely relational function of the image. In such a "zero degree" climate, the film viewer must attempt whatever coherence she or he can derive from the accumulation and repetition of images. The introduction of any emotional or allusive material into such a "climate" would of course generate no little heat. Such is indeed the case with the allusions to Dostoevsky's *Crime and Punishment* that punctuate this film.[27]

Purely at the level of anecdote, there are numerous parallels between film and novel. At the most superficial level, both authors recount stories of men who commit crimes, are "cornered" by a sympathetic police inspector, and go to jail, where they are comforted by a woman to whom they had confessed their crimes. The stories' protagonists, Michel and Raskolnikov, are both students living in the poorest of conditions. Raskolnikov's garret, "under the roof of a high, five-storied house was more like a cupboard than a room. . . . It had a poverty-stricken appearance with its dusty paper peeling off the walls. . . . The furniture was in keeping with the room: . . . a painted table in the corner on which lay a few manuscripts and books; the dust that lay thick upon them showed that they had been long untouched. . . . It would have been difficult to sink to a lower ebb of disorder."[28] The dust on Michel's books, piled on a table in the corner of his slatternly room, attracts the police inspector's attention, causing him to run his index finger through it in a meditative gesture. Raskolnikov is, like his French counterpart, "above the average in height, slim, well-built, with beautiful dark eyes and dark brown hair" (CP, 4). Each receives an important letter from his mother and as a consequence develops an increasingly strained relation to her. Each decides, as an act of will, to commit a crime against a woman. Each seems to disdain the monetary gain from his crime and to be motivated instead by some other factor; each succumbs to "the condition that overtakes some monomaniacs entirely concentrated on one thing" (CP, 29). Each hides his stolen money "in a hole at the bottom of the wall" of his room (CP, 90). Each will return to the scene of his original crime and thereby ensure his capture (Raskolnikov to the old lady's apartment, Michel to the Longchamps racetrack). Each is haunted by repeated encounters with a police inspector who suspects him of the crime and who interrogates him about his theories of crime! To Porfiry Petrovitch, Raskolnikov exclaims, in reference to an article he has published on crime,

> I simply hinted that an "extraordinary" man has the right . . . that is not an official right, but an inner right to decide in his own conscience to overstep . . . certain obstacles, and only in case it is essential for the practical fulfillment of his idea (sometimes, perhaps, of benefit to the whole of humanity). . . . All legislators and leaders of men, such as Lycurgus, Solon, Mahomet, Napoleon, and so on, were all without exception criminals, from the very fact that, making a new law, they *transgressed* the ancient one, handed down from their ancestors and held sacred by the people, and they did not stop short at bloodshed either, if that bloodshed . . . were of use to their cause. . . . In short, I maintain that the majority, indeed, of these benefactors and leaders of humanity . . . must from their very nature be criminals . . . more or less of course. . . . You see there is nothing new in all that. The same thing has been printed and read a thousand times before. (CP, 254–55)

Early in *Pickpocket*, Michel encounters in a neighborhood cafe the police inspector who had confronted him after his arrest at Longchamps. To the inspector's question about his theory of crime, Michel answers, "It's not new! Men of talent and genius are free in certain cases to disobey the law. Society has everything to gain from this arrangement ['Elle n'est pas neuve! Les hommes de talent ou de génie sont libres dans certains cas de désobéir aux lois. Pour la société il y a toutes les bénéfices']." "Who will distinguish them from the others?" asks the inspector. "Themselves," responds Michel. "But they'd never stop," argues the policeman. "You want to turn the world upside down! ['C'est le monde à l'envers!']" "It's already upside down ['Il est déjà à l'envers']," retorts Michel. "It's a question of turning it right-side up ['Il s'agit de le mettre à l'endroit']." Thus, although the economy of the film does not allow for the same degree of development of this dialogue, Bresson repeats the essential terms of Dostoevsky's argument. And in both novel and film this initial conversation will be repeated, though in much abbreviated form, in a later scene: in the novel, in Raskolnikov's interior ramblings, and in the film, when Michel visits the inspector in his office (CP, 269). In both novel and film, criminal and police inspector meet one final time. Dostoevsky's version reads:

> No sooner had he opened the door than he stumbled upon Porfiry himself in the passage. . . . How could Porfiry have approached so

quietly, like a cat, so that he had heard nothing? Could he have been listening at the door?

"You didn't expect a visitor, Rodion Romanovitch," Porfiry explained. . . . "I was passing by and thought why not go in for five minutes. . . . I came to see you the day before yesterday, in the evening; you didn't know? . . . I came into this very room. . . . Don't you lock your door? . . . You are nervously irritable, Rodion Romanovitch, by temperament; it's out of proportion with other qualities of your heart and character, which I flatter myself I have to some extent divined. . . . No, Rodion Romanovitch, Nikolay doesn't come in! This is a fantastic, gloomy business, a modern case, an incident of today when the heart of a man is troubled. . . . Here we have bookish dreams, a heart unhinged by theories. . . . No that's not the work of a Nikolay, my dear Rodion Romanovitch!"

"Then . . . who then . . . is the murderer?" Raskolnikov asked in a breathless voice. . . .

"Why *you*, Rodion Romanovitch! You are the murderer." . . .

"You are at your old tricks again, Porfiry Petrovitch! Your old method again. . . ."

"What does that matter now? . . . I have not come to chase and capture you like a hare. . . ."

"If so, what did you come for?" Raskolnikov asked irritably. "If you consider me guilty, why don't you take me to prison?" . . .

". . . to arrest you directly is not to my interest. . . . What you need now is fresh air!"

Raskolnikov positively started. "But who are you? what prophet are you? From the height of what majestic calm do you proclaim these words of wisdom?"

"Who am I? I am a man with nothing to hope for. . . . But you are a different matter, there is life waiting for you."

"When do you plan to arrest me?"

(CP, 434–46)

Although much more succinct, Bresson's version maintains the essential features of Dostoevsky's:

VOICE-OVER: I hadn't heard him coming.
The Inspector enters Michel's room.
MICHEL: It's you!
INSPECTOR: I already came by three days ago. I waited around for you for a while.
MICHEL: I'd gone out to get some air.
INSPECTOR: It's unhealthy to stay cooped up in this little room ["enfermé dans cette petite chambre"] immersed in your books and notepads.

160

The Inspector crosses the room to Michel's table and draws his index finger through the dust on a book lying there.

MICHEL: I know you suspect me. If you think you are within your rights to arrest me, go ahead, arrest me! Put hand-cuffs on me! Otherwise don't push me to the limit. I don't want you constantly hanging around ["Autrement ne me poussez pas au bout. Je ne veux pas que vous continuiez à tourner autour de moi"].

INSPECTOR: I left you alone.

Michel throws a book on the floor. That's enough! Enough!

INSPECTOR: Don't shout. Calm down. Control yourself. Don't get crazy ["Ne vous mettez pas la tête à l'envers"]. And sit down. I came because I'm interested in you.

MICHEL: I don't give a damn about your interest.

INSPECTOR: . . . and to let you in on a little fact that I didn't know. . . . A complaint was lodged a little over a month ago . . . (we hadn't met yet) by a girl to the police in the neighborhood. . . . A small sum of money had disappeared from the home of an old woman living in her apartment building. The next day the complaint was withdrawn. Because often the guilty party turns out to be a relative or old friend who can't be arrested. Anyway, this lady had a son. Well, it's not really stealing to take money from one's mother. . . . Maybe they were living together. . . . And then a month later, the same young man is arrested at Longchamps at the racetrack. The matter is far from clearcut. So I release him. . . .

MICHEL: And who is this young man?

INSPECTOR: It's you!

Michel gets up. You're mistaken!

INSPECTOR: I'm not mistaken.

MICHEL: Curious method!

INSPECTOR: Forget about my method.

MICHEL: You're trying psychology on me, but you're not sure. . . . You kill me! This is really a killer! ["Vous m'assomez! C'est assomant!"] What do you want from me?

INSPECTOR: I wanted to open your eyes! ["Je voulais vous ouvrir les yeux!"]

MICHEL: They're wide open.

INSPECTOR: To yourself. But I was wasting my time. As for the future, for your future. . . .

MICHEL: What's it to you? Are you a prophet? Do you think my future is any of your business? ["Croyez-vous que mon avenir vous regarde?"]

INSPECTOR: Yes, it seems to be my business to an extent. . . . All I have to do is give the order and you will be arrested and sent to prison.

He gets up.

MICHEL: And what are your intentions? I *insist* on knowing them!!!

Although highly condensed, Bresson's version of this scene is surprisingly similar in its development, characterization (both police inspectors are calm, arriving at the accusation through a kind of quiet reason, while the accused becomes highly volatile), and vocabulary (the words "method" and "prophet," among others, are striking repetitions).

Ultimately both Raskolnikov and Michel return to the scene of their crimes, an error that lands them in prison. Finally, each bears his soul to a young woman (Raskolnikov to Sonya, Michel to Jeanne) who seeks him out in prison. There we witness a highly ambiguous final scene that may or may not be interpreted as a "conversion" of the criminal.

There can be no doubt that Bresson intended some reference to Dostoevsky's *Crime and Punishment* in *Pickpocket*. Indeed it can be argued that this novel was also the source of his next film, *Au hasard Balthazar*.[29] And yet, for all its apparent similarities to the Russian model, Bresson's film bears a highly ambiguous relationship to Dostoevsky's masterpiece. Put succinctly, there is just enough resemblance between the two works to cast Bresson's work into a perfectly Dostoevskian ambiguity but not enough to allow an interpretation of the whole of Bresson's film.

Bresson's previous experience in adaptation is well documented. In particular, his *Journal d'un curé de campagne,* adapted from Bernanos's work of the same title, was termed by André Bazin "the kind of fidelity . . . most insidious and the most penetrating kind of creative liberty." Bazin had already termed Bresson's adaptation of Diderot, *Les Dames du bois de Boulogne,* "a marvellously subtle play of interferences and counterpoint between fidelity and betrayal." As for *Le Journal d'un curé de campagne,* Bazin argued that Bresson's film "opens a new stage in cinematic adaptation. Until now, film tended to try to replace the novel as if it were an esthetic translation into another language. . . . But *Le Journal d'un curé de campagne* is something else again. Its dialectic of fidelity and creativity reduces, in the last analysis, to a dialectic between the cinema and literature. It is no longer a question of *translating* . . . but of building *on* the novel *by* the cinema, a work of another order. The film is no longer 'comparable' to the novel or 'worthy' of it, but rather an esthetic being which is like a novel *multiplied* by the cinema." Paradoxically, Bazin argued that the filmmaker's work was more literary and the novelist's more imagistic than its counterpart![30] Thus, even in a work whose title and dialogue were entirely maintained by Bresson, the question of adaptation was at best a highly charged, ambivalent, and even perverse venture.

So perverse, indeed, that although the relationship demands attention, virtually all of the critics who have noted Bresson's allusion to the Russian novel have elected to dismiss the matter. Thus, for example, Roger Tailleur dismisses *Pickpocket* as "Dostoievski written . . . by an abusive disciple."[31] Bresson himself seeks to problematize his relationship to his "model." In an interview with Paul Schrader he stated, "If I make a film from Dostoevsky, I try always to *take out* all the literary parts. . . . I don't want to make a film showing the work of Dostoevsky."[32] What he intended to *save* from the Russian novelist's work may be gleaned from a passage from *Notes sur le cinématographe:* "Proust says that Dostoevsky is original in composition above all. It is an extraordinarily complex and close-meshed ['serré'] whole, purely inward ['interne'], with currents and counter-currents like those of the sea, a thing that is found also in Proust . . . and whose equivalent ['pendant'] would go well with a film" (NC, 63/126–27).

We are truly at sea in this play of Bressonian ambiguities. It is not clear from the context what Bresson may mean by the term "take out"—he could either intend "to remove" or "to include." What is "the work" of Dostoevsky? Is it "un ensemble extraordinairement complexe et serré, purement interne"? Bresson claims numerous times in his *Notes* that his only interest is in the internal drama of his films. On the other hand, what is meant by the "pendant," the equivalent that would "go well" in a film, is also entirely ambiguous. What *is* clear is that the so-called psychological workings of *Crime and Punishment* have been entirely removed from *Pickpocket*. Bresson has effectively replaced Dostoevsky's entire polyphonic and dialogic structure[33] with a cinematographic and purely external display of the work of the pickpocket. One of the effects of this departure is to force our attention back on those aspects of the two works that do coincide. And we are forced, precisely, to consider why Bresson was at such pains to imitate Dostoevsky only in the two overlapping scenes (described above) and in the particular finale, that is, the proposal of a theory justifying the protagonist's criminal activity, the police inspector's cat and mouse game with the suspect, and the so-called conversion to love at the end of both works. What emerges as a *certainty* from the parallelism established by Bresson with the Russian novel is the *ambiguity* of the final scenes of both works.

Dostoevsky's "Epilogue," coming as it does after five hundred sixteen pages of unmitigated psychological turmoil and numerous subplots, involves Raskolnikov in a renewed debate over his "guilt": Raskolnikov "judged himself severely, and his exasperated conscience found no particularly terrible fault in his past, except a simple *blunder* which might happen to any one. He was ashamed just because he had so hopelessly, stupidly come to grief through some decree of blind fate and must humble himself and submit to 'the idiocy' of a sentence. . . . But he did not repent of his crime" (CP, 525). The question of guilt continues throughout the novel to hinge purely on the success of his venture: "Those benefactors of mankind who snatched power for themselves . . . succeeded and so *they were right,* and I didn't, and so I had no right to have taken that step" (CP, 526). In the last two pages of the novel, Raskolnikov is suddenly overcome by love for Sonya. "How it happened he did not know. But all at once something seemed to seize him and fling him at her feet. . . . He knew with what infinite love he would now repay all her sufferings. . . . Everything, even his crime, his sentence and his imprisonment, seemed to him now in the first rush of feeling an external strange fact with which he had no concern. . . . Life had stepped into the place of theory" (CP, 530–31). Taking up a copy of the New Testament that Sonya had given him, Raskolnikov asks himself, "Can her convictions not be mine now? Her feelings, her aspirations at least. . . ." Dostoevsky concludes his novel with the passage that has legitimized an eternal debate on the meaning of his novel:

> He did not know that the new life would not be given him for nothing, that he would have to pay dearly for it, that it would cost him great striving, great suffering.
> But that is the beginning of a new story—the story of the gradual renewal of man, the story of his gradual regeneration, of his passing from one world into another, of his initiation into a new unknown life. That might be the subject of a new story, but our present story is ended. (CP, 532)

The interpretations of this finale leave little doubt as to its ultimate undecidability. Some critics seize on the fact that Raskolnikov grasps the New Testament and wonders whether Sonya's convictions may not now be his. Thus, for example, Maurice Beebe argues that "the revelation that comes to Raskolnikov through love and humility 'in prison, *in freedom*' is inevitable because it is the obverse side, the *pro,* of the will-to-suffering, the *contra,* that has been throughout the entire novel his primary motivation."[34] Edward Wasiolek adds, "If we consider the beginning and end of *Crime and Punishment,* we find that Raskolnikov goes from pride to humility, hate to love, reason to faith, and from separation from his fellow men to communion with them. . . . Raskolnikov is the image of a man pursued by God, condemned by his nature to choose him, yet hating the choice he is forced to make." Yet even Wasiolek concedes that "the epilogue follows logically, but not artistically," from the rest of the novel.[35]

The problem is, of course, that the final two paragraphs do not specifically mention *religious* conversion and are remarkably vague about exactly what "renewal" may mean. Dostoevsky coyly commits the answer to a *never to be realized future*. Thus, even such critics as Konstantin Mochulsky and A. Boyce Gibson, who term Dostoevsky "the great Christian writer," do not see a religious conversion in the final pages of the work. "We know Raskolnikov too well to believe this 'pious lie,'" writes Mochulsky, who nevertheless finds a Christian meaning in the work.[36] Gibson argues that "there is no theology . . . and particularly no theodicy [in this] sidelong approach to a Christian interpretation of man."[37]

Michael Holquist, who makes perhaps the most cogent argument for a religious conversion in *Crime and Punishment,* manages this conclusion only by dividing the work into "two different and opposing types of plot and two different kinds of time, two different ways of understanding, two different modes of interpretation that their traditions presuppose." This dialogic structure permits Holquist the discovery of "a bond between the parts [of the novel] that derives from the direction of time in the two story types that define the novel. . . . The movement of the epilogue is analogous to the wisdom tale in that it points back to the inadequacy of answers that precede its concluding insistence on *another* realm . . . and to the reminder of another and greater mystery."[38] Yet, as convincing as Holquist's dialogic argument may be, it still does not resolve what a majority of critics see as Dostoevsky's decision to unbalance these two forces in such a way that "hope and belief play havoc with the imaginative logic of the work."[39] If there is a truly Christian presentation in Dostoevsky's work, he was not to develop it explicitly for another decade.

We have, in other words, in the model to which Bresson alluded in his film, "the immanence of a revelation which does not occur,"[40] a decidedly problematic (even modernist) analogy. I cannot but conclude that Bresson chose to highlight the ambiguous ending of a novel by a writer that was *not yet* a Christian apologist to convey, through a parallel ambiguity, that his own work was *no longer* comfortable with orthodox Christian solutions. In her study of Bresson and Dostoevsky, Mireille Latil-Le Dantec concludes of Bresson's *oeuvre* as a whole, "A new day can be discerned behind the tragedies of Dostoevsky. But the darkest night invades the final scenes of Bresson and engulfs the steps of an irresponsible criminal steeped in de-

spair. . . . The absurd reigns supreme, and with it a feeling of soli-
tude."[41] Precisely because it does mark such a turning point in
Bresson's work, the final scene of *Pickpocket* ends up producing a
mirror of the critical controversy surrounding Raskolnikov's sense of
renewal.

Indeed, the final scene of *Pickpocket* bears a disquieting likeness to
Dostoevsky's ambiguous epilogue. After delighting his viewers with
a carnivalesque display of the pickpockets' sleight of hand and digital
finesse, Bresson has his protagonist fall too easily into a trap he *knows*
has been set for him, with the result that he ends up in prison. Jeanne
arrives to visit him in jail, but at her first visit Michel remains cold and
aloof (see plate 22). Like his literary predecessor, "he judges himself
severely . . . but does not repent of his crime" (CP, 525):

> MICHEL: These walls and bars are all the same to me. I don't even no-
> tice them. It's the idea.
> JEANNE: What idea?
> MICHEL: I should have been more careful. I let myself get caught. The
> idea is unbearable!
> JEANNE: You're suffering.
> MICHEL: I confessed everything. . . . But I shall deny it all. Why did
> you come?
> JEANNE: You're all I have.
> MICHEL: You want me to tell you that I have acted badly and that you
> win . . . I don't need anyone.
> *Having returned to his cell,* MICHEL: There was something else that I
> hadn't said. Why live? I had decided nothing as yet.

In his notes for *Crime and Punishment,* Dostoevsky hesitated between
two possible endings for his novel, acceptance of suffering and suicide. Ultimately he seems to have kept both, assigning to Svidrigailov,
Raskolnikov's double, the option of suicide.[42]

After Michel returns to his cell, Bresson conveys, through a series
of dissolves, some passage of time. One of these dissolves produces
Michel holding a letter from Jeanne recounting the sickness of her
child and concluding, "I will come to see you again." The voice-off
narrator recounts, "As I read this letter, my heart beat violently." The
guard then leads Michel back to the visiting area. A shot-countershot
sequence displays Michel, expressionless, standing behind the bars
and Jeanne sitting. She stands. The narrator notes, "A glow illumined
her face." They kiss expressionlessly through the bars. The narrative
voice-off intones, "O Jeanne, to get to you what a strange path I have
had to take ['pour arriver jusqu'à toi, quel drôle de chemin j'ai dû

PLATE 22.   Michel (Martin Lasalle) remains impassively in jail in Bresson's
Pickpocket. (Courtesy of the Museum of Modern Art Film Stills Archive.)

prendre'].″ A final shot shows Michel and Jeanne standing on either
side of the bars, their cheeks pressed together through the bars, their
faces expressionless.

If Jeanne is illumined, Michel does not seem to be. His beating
heart *may* be a sign of love, but it recalls as much his first essay at
pickpocketing, when he notes the beating of his heart, as it implies an
emotion that has never seemed more unlikely in a fictional character
than in this automat. The ending is remarkably ambiguous, and like
that of *Crime and Punishment,* it has engendered a fierce interpretative
debate.

Those who look for transcendence and religious grace in Michel's
evocation of "le drôle de chemin" will find it there as surely as the
Christian critics find evidence of Raskolnikov's conversion in the
epilogue of *Crime and Punishment.* Paul Schrader, for example, argues that "at the close of *Pickpocket* Michel comes to an acceptance of
grace in the person of Jeanne. . . . The ending is a 'miraculous event.'
. . . This decisive action forces the viewer into the confrontation with
the wholly Other he would normally avoid. He is faced with an

167

explicably spiritual act which now requests his participation and approval. . . . It is a miracle which must be accepted or rejected."[43] Daniel Millar agrees that *Pickpocket* is "a spiritual drama," and Richard Roud avers that "what interested Bresson was the road to redemption, not the scenery along that road. . . . *Pickpocket* is an allegory of redemption."[44] Certain French critics are even more categorical: Amédée Ayfre writes, for example, "Grace is there, powerful, even while invisible. In fact there is nothing but grace, its sovereign omnipotence obscures everything else. . . . In the end only God knows."[45] Michel Estève concurs: "Bresson's films illustrate so well what Chantal de Clergerie, Bernanos's heroine, said: 'As for sin, we're all immersed in it, some enjoy it, others suffer from it, but, in the last analysis, we all have to break the same bread at the fountain's edge.' Only Jeanne's true love can deliver Michel and open man's soul to Grace. . . . The beauty of the last scene of *Pickpocket* evokes . . . the defeat of Evil and illumination by redemption."[46] What is regrettable in these several assertions is the rejection of visual evidence ("what interested Bresson was not the scenery along that road," "grace, while invisible . . . obscures everything else") in favor of the invisible and inexplicable.

On the other hand, critics such as Jean Sémolué can point to the fact that like Raskolnikov, Michel has considered and rejected theology: "I believed in God for three minutes," he has told Jeanne earlier in the film. Sémolué argues that "the asceticism evoked here is not necessarily of the Christian variety. . . . We have, rather, an impression of a lapse into ordinariness following on the collapse of Michel's personality. Bresson wanted to paint love as an explosion; one wonders whether we aren't witnessing his defeat, a splintering. . . . The last phrase is spoken in total darkness, the color of salvation in Bresson's ambiguous universe. . . . But I don't feel the plenitude in *Pickpocket*'s darkness. Michel's conversion to love seems more a conversion to resignation."[47] Even a critic who situates *Un Condamné à Mort* firmly within the context of grace notes that Bresson's other works do not incarnate that grace.[48] More bleakly, Louis Seguin writes, "In *Pickpocket* Bresson ends up alone, abandoned to his own resources, i.e., to nothingness," and Roger Tailleur adds, "With Bresson we enter the reign of the hyper-empty."[49] Summing up the undecidability of the ending of *Pickpocket*, Robert Vas notes, "We are further from understanding Michel's pilgrimage and the forces behind it than we have ever been in the case of past Bresson heroes."[50]

If it was Bresson's object to evoke the same ambiguity that reigns at the end of *Crime and Punishment,* he could not have made a better calculation, for the debate that rages about the spirituality of the film is only exacerbated by reference to the enigmatic ending of the Russian model. But the parallels with Dostoevsky's text are not limited to the anecdotal levels of the two works. In fact, despite his aversion to the psychological morass of Raskolnikov's interior debates, Bresson subtly and quietly adopted what Bakhtin has called the dialogic and carnivalistic aspects of Dostoevsky's poetics.[51] Indeed, the reason that the debates continue to rage about the ultimate meaning of the final scenes of both lies precisely in the dialogic structure of the two texts: at least two (and in Dostoevsky's case, many) points of view are presented for consideration. Thus it is no mere coincidence that Bresson included in *Pickpocket* a discussion of morality that throws established rules into doubt. If Michel tells the police inspector that his theory of the superman is "nothing new," he is recognizing that the same tension that existed in Dostoevsky's time between Hegel's *Philosophy of History* and Chernyshevsky's "anthropological principle of history" still resonates today between such thinkers as Nietzsche and Camus, on the one hand, and Marx and Teilhard de Chardin, on the other.[52] When the police inspector objects, "C'est le monde à l'envers," Michel interjects, "Il est déjà à l'envers. Il s'agit de le mettre à l'endroit." This direct allusion to Camus[53] hides another allusion to Dostoevsky: the upside-down, carnivalesque nature of his world.[54]

In assessing Dostoevsky's poetics, Mikhael Bakhtin discovered not only the polyphonic and dialogic structure of his novels but, alongside these, "the task . . . of destroying the established forms of the basically monological European novel."[55] Indeed, the most stunning of Bakhtin's discoveries is that these two are aspects of the same urge and intersect in Dostoevsky's "carnival attitude." This latter Bakhtin describes as

> deliberate multifariousness and discordance, a mixture of high and low. . . . The laws, prohibitions and restrictions which determine the system and order of normal, i.e. non-carnival life are for the period of carnival, suspended, above all the hierarchical system and all the connected forms of fear, awe, piety, etiquette etc. are suspended, i.e. everything that is determined by social-hierarchical inequality among people, or any other form of inequality. . . . Man's behavior, gesture and word are liberated from the authority of all hierarchical positions (of estate, rank, age, property status) which define them totally in non-carnivalistic life. . . . Eccentricity is a special category of the carnival attitude which is organically connected with the category of familiar contact, it permits the latent sides of human nature to be revealed and developed in a concretely sensuous form.[56]

169

Among the categories Bakhtin discerned in the carnival structure, he lists profanation and the mock crowning and subsequent discrowning of the king of carnival. He notes, however, that "carnival is functional not substantive: it absolutizes nothing: it proclaims the jolly relativity of everything." And, continues Bakhtin, because carnival emphasizes the borderline position between opposites, its spatial metaphors are thresholds and stairs: thresholds because they are neither in nor out, stairs because they symbolize the transition upward and downward.

These are precisely the elements shared between Dostoevsky's novel and Bresson's film, and they constitute, beyond the all too evident coincidences of plot, the deeper structural relationship between the two works. Both Raskolnikov and Michel are truly *eccentric* characters, most prominently in their disregard for social and hierarchical relationships, for family, and for social values as expressed through dress codes, dwelling arrangements, and money. What is more important, they seek to *profane* not only Christian values (Michel says cynically, "J'ai cru en dieu pendant trois minutes") but also canonical philosophical texts (Raskolnikov parodies Hegel; Michel Nietzsche, Camus, and . . . Dostoevsky).[57] Both characters see themselves as latter-day Napoleons, justified in rising above the law because of their "greatness," but in the context of their acts these fantasies are specifically carnivalesque: the mock crowning and discrowning of the carnival king. Michel parodies this apotheosis early in *Pickpocket* when he proclaims, "Je n'avais plus les pieds sur terre. . . . Je dominais le monde!" and seconds later he is arrested. And just as "Raskolnikov lives in essence on the threshold: his narrow room, the 'coffin' opens directly onto the stairway landing, and he never locks his door," so too does Michel "live" primarily in transitions between more settled spaces. If "the threshold, the foyer, the corridor, the landing, the stair, its steps, doors which open onto stairs, garden gates, and aside from this the city: squares, streets, façades, taverns, dens, bridges, gutters are the space in *Crime and Punishment*,"[58] so Bresson has trained his camera on stairs and on doorways, merely to try to catch Michel passing through *his* frame. The characters, the nature of their acts, the structure of their worlds, and the aesthetics of their authors[59] are all characterized by a single word: *prestuplenie* ("transgression," or literally, "overstepping").[60]

It is no accident that virtually all of Michel's transgressions occur at racetracks (a literary and cinematic topos for "le monde à l'envers"), on subway trains, while victims are getting into automobiles or crossing the street (see plate 23). The apogee of all of his activity takes La

PLATE 23. Virtually all of Michel's transgressions occur in a topos of transition in Bresson's *Pickpocket*. (Courtesy of the Museum of Modern Art Film Stills Archive.)

Gare de Lyon for its stage. Here Michel and his doubles enact the most carnivalesque scene of all: in the great Salle des Pas Perdus and on the train, newspapers are substituted for pocketbooks, hands fly into the most awesome variety of hidden places, and money, watches, wallets, and other valuables are moved so rapidly from hand to hand that the spectator is left dizzy and disoriented. Whereas Bresson's filming with but few exceptions has been remarkably passive until now, the camera leaps into the fray, seeking out the most hidden of gestures, moving rapidly from one subtle gesture to another. The editing likewise takes on a frenetic pace of cutting that itself breaks all the normal rules of film grammar. Everything is turned upside down and inside out. The pace and length of this scene make it abundantly clear that Bresson considers it the "crowning achievement" of his film. Certainly nothing else in the work, and especially not the markedly understated finale, can match it for interest or intensity.

Also, inasmuch as *transgression* is the modus operandi of both character and author in both *Pickpocket* and *Crime and Punishment*, I cannot fail to remark that the very voice-off narrator established to "orient" the viewer's understanding of the film, no less than the *prière d'insérer* inserted at the outset of Bresson's film, is himself part of this carnival. In the hierarchy of narrative authority, one should, traditionally, always be able to count on the narrator. That authority increases as the narrator is distanced from the world of the story: in cinema a voice-off narrator automatically commands our implicit respect, so much more so the image maker. Yet in *Pickpocket* that reliability is called into question repeatedly. We have already appreciated the fact that as image maker, Bresson avowedly destroys the normal cues by which viewers orient themselves in a fiction film and find coherence in its images. Bresson further undermines his authority as image maker in protesting the "weakness" of his character in an adventure "for which he was not made." Our experience of the film hardly corroborates these statements. In introducing a simultaneous voice-off narration and visual journal, Bresson introduces a confusion of point of view that is never resolved. But the most destructive because most obvious breakdown of narrative authority comes through the numerous misstatements pronounced by the voice-off narrator. Since Bresson's voice-over is integrated into the system or the psychology that motivates camera movement in the film by its strict identification with a character whose honesty is immediately in question,[61] the narrative authority is itself carnivalized, rendered topsy-turvy. Indeed Michel frequently omits or misstates information necessary to our understanding of events and in one case blatantly abuses in both voice-over narration and journal the credibility of the viewer.[62] In his last journal entry, Michel writes (and confirms by voice-over narration):

> During the two years I lived in London, I made some handsome strikes, but I lost the greater part of my gains on gambling or wasted it on women. I found myself in Paris again aimless and penniless.

This statement is so wildly out of character for Michel (gambling does not occupy his time in Paris, and his relationships with women are so tortured as to make the statement parodic) that it casts into doubt every other narrative statement he makes. And it is ultimately this degree of doubt that robs of its credibility and power the final voice-over statement of the film: "O Jeanne, pour arriver jusqu'à toi, quel drôle de chemin j'ai dû prendre." Because of this doubt as well, we are forced to turn elsewhere to understand the mystery and enigma of this film.

   If the parallel Bresson has established with Dostoevsky succeeds in revealing the carnivalesque nature of *Pickpocket* and ultimately in undermining the believability of Michel's conversion, it nevertheless fails to account for much of the rest of the film. Among the things left unexplained by Dostoevsky's presence in the film is the remarkable shift of registers between Raskolnikov's murder and Michel's pick-pocketing. Quite paradoxically and undoubtedly in a way that Bresson could not have foreseen, the allusion to Dostoevsky so fore-grounds the presence of an absent text that it appears to screen and virtually render absent a text that is very present in the film. Not a single mention has ever been made in the more than fifty reviews of *Pickpocket* nor in the dozen books that have been devoted to Bresson of the presence of Richard Lambert's *The Prince of Pickpockets* in this film.

While it may perhaps be futile to speculate on the reasons for the suppression of Lambert, that silence is all the more surprising given the insistence with which Bresson has foregrounded this study of George Barrington. The book is presented full-face (title page and frontispiece) to the film viewer when Michel returns to his room after his training at the café with his doubles and finds Jacques sitting on his bed. Jacques holds open to the camera the copy of *Prince of Pickpockets* and says, "Thieves are reprehensible and lazy people." Michel objects, "Barrington wasn't lazy. He spent entire nights reading." "Only to dupe rich people into becoming his friends. He stole from his friends. Do you find that acceptable?" questions Jacques. And he adds, with as much emotion as a Bressonian character can muster, "At least he was courageous. In his day they hung thieves. Now they just go to pris-on." Michel changes the direction of their debate: "Do you know what prison is?" "I can imagine," answers Jacques. "You can't imagine it at all ['Tu n'imagines rien du tout']."

Not content to leave it there, Bresson reintroduces the book in the second and third encounters between Michel and the police inspec-tor. In their second meeting at the cafe, the dialogue is as follows:

INSPECTOR: Pickpockets will never improve the condition of humanity.
MICHEL: I never said that. That's absurd.
INSPECTOR: One question: Do you believe there are many of these people among us?
MICHEL: Which people?
INSPECTOR: To whom more is permitted that the others. . . . Maybe you know a person like this?
MICHEL: If I knew such a person, I wouldn't come to tell you about it.

INSPECTOR: Obviously. *Takes* The Prince of Pickpockets *from Jacques.*
May I? . . . Barrington, never heard of him. Maybe he's one of these
superior men. . . . Come see me and bring this book.

In the scene immediately following, Michel sits outside the inspector's office holding a copy of the book. Upon entering the office he
says immediately,

MICHEL: I've brought you the book.
INSPECTOR: What book? Ah yes, Barrington. So this Barrington inter-
  ests you?
MICHEL: Everything interests me.
INSPECTOR: Of course, a young writer.
MICHEL'S VOICE-OFF: I thought I could discern sarcasm in his
  expression.
INSPECTOR: He manufactured hooks. *Holding up to the camera an il-
  lustration from the book entitled* Barrington Picking the Pocket of J.
  Brown, esq. This is how he inserted them into people's pockets.
  *Reaching in desk drawer, the Inspector holds up a crochet identical to that
  pictured in the book.* Look, a worker in Nurenberg made me fifteen
  of these.
  *Michel makes a gesture with the hook as if to cut his own pocket. The Inspec-
  tor closes the book and returns it.*
MICHEL: I have to leave. Keep it.
INSPECTOR: Good bye.
MICHEL'S VOICE-OFF: How could I have not realized. It was a trap.

Finally, when the inspector pays an unexpected visit to Michel's room
and directly accuses him, it is this same book that Michel throws to the
floor "in anger."

"It was a trap," thinks Michel. Indeed, the book can be read as
"trap" not just in the sense of diversion of attention but also, by an
easy extension of exactly the kind we make in the unconscious, as a
metaphoric displacement. We recall that the most egregious of
Michel's misstatements or lies is his assertion that he had gone to
England and has wasted all his money on women and gambling. Now,
The Prince of Pickpockets, like the title of Bresson's film, is in *English,* a
language that would presumably be difficult for Michel, Jacques, and
the Inspector. None seems to have difficulty reading it (i.e., translating its meaning into their own idiom).

The presence of *The Prince of Pickpockets* in Bresson's film effectively displaces the register of Raskolnikov's murder down to the
apparently trivial activity of the "vol à tire," as Bresson inevitably calls

this activity: theft by pulling. Murder, by its violent nature, its utter finality, and the extreme punishment meted out to the criminal, occupies our attention at a level that makes Raskolnikov's original motivation and ambition at least plausible. Picking pockets does not. It is, as Jacques correctly points out, a socially reprehensible and cowardly activity. So why would Bresson have shifted Dostoevsky's ethical register downward in a way that apparently trivializes Michel's status? Barrington himself suggests part of the answer to this question, for as reprehensible as the activity appears, he was a master at transforming it into something it was not! This in two ways. First, like Dostoevsky's Raskolnikov, he argues that by his actions he becomes the equal of the most powerful prince:

> Sovereigns seize on the territories of neighboring princes, whenever they think doing so suits their purposes, without scruple or remorse; people of fashion run in debt and never pay their creditors; bankers and brokers are seldom restrained by conscience in the interest they take, or the charges which they make; merchants, and traders of all kinds are not more scrupulous in the profits which they exact of their unwary customers; and as for lawyers of every denomination, their boundless rapacity is proverbial. The *mode* then of appropriating the property to oneself, and not the *act* of doing so, is the sole difference between the most powerful prince and the most opulent merchant.[63]

In this, Barrington doubles Raskolnikov's argument for the permission to crime. But Barrington's second activity is much more pertinent for its inclusion in Bresson's fictional universe: pickpocketing becomes the pretext for art. Because of the need to pass unnoticed among the finest peers of England, Barrington constantly played at being someone he was not. "Disguise made it difficult to identify him, and everywhere his deportment gave him the *prima facie* advantage of appearing sober and well-bred" (PP, 33). When caught, he repeatedly had recourse to the most extraordinary verbal pyrotechnics in the courtroom and numerous times so articulately and movingly defended his person that the jury was induced to pardon (PP, 110–79 passim). To one jury he exclaimed, "There is no joy but what arises from the practice of virtue and consists in the felicity of a tranquil mind and a benevolent heart" (PP, 183), a monumental hypocrisy, it turns out, since he was back in jail within days for the same illegal activities. What makes Barrington all the more interesting as a model for the character in Bresson's film is that he was a poet and an actor. He is known to have addressed a series of poems to one of the actresses in a theater troupe he joined to avoid detection. To Barrington are attributed as well the following verses intended to serve as a prologue for a play in New South Wales entirely produced by convicts:

> From distant climes, o'er wide-spread seas, we come,
> Though not with much éclat or beat of drum:
> True patriots all, for, be it understood,
> We left our country for our country's good. . . .
> But, you inquire, what could our breasts inflame
> With this new passion for Theatric fame;
> What, in the practice of our former days,
> Could shape our talents to exhibit plays? . . .
> And sure in Filch, I shall be quite at home.
> Unrivall'd there, none will dispute my claim
> To high pre-eminence, and exalted fame. . . .
> Sometimes, indeed, so various is our art,
> An actor may improve and mend his part: . . .
> Grant us your favour, put us to the test,
> To gain your smiles we'll do our very best;
> And, without dread of future turnkey Lockits,
> Thus, *in an honest way, still pick your pockets.*
>
> (PP, 245–46)

Barrington's equation of theatrical passion and picking pockets should not go unnoted. I am particularly struck by Philip Rahv's contention that Dostoevsky's novel "depends on the sleight of hand of substituting a meaningless crime for a meaningful one."[64] Bresson's explicit subject, coupled with his insistence on "hiding ideas so that they may be found" (NC, 42/85), suggests how much the Lambert text's invisible visibility may be a metaphor for Bresson's own cinematic activity. In his doubling of Michel's unreliability as narrator, Bresson has already suggested an underlying parallelism between their two arts. But the similarity goes much further.

Bresson once stated that "the subject of *Pickpocket* is in my view a pretext for creating 'cinematic material ["une matière cinémato-graphique"]."[65] But the pretext has a concretely metonymic relation-ship with the text. Bresson noted in *Notes sur le cinématographe*, "Your film, let people feel the soul and the heart there, but let it be made like a work of hands ['un travail de mains']" (NC, 12/30). And later he adds, "The things one can express with the hand ['Que de choses on peut exprimer avec la main']. . . . What economy!" (NC, 64/127). Sometimes, to be sure, unconsciously: Bresson (mis)appropriates Montaigne to the effect that "hands are often carried where we direct them not ['La main se porte souvent où nous ne l'envoyons pas']"

(NC, 68/133).[66] In any case, his conception of the cinema is "a hand
directing everything ['une main qui dirige tout']."[67] In response to a
question about the subject of his film, he expounded on "the wonder
of pickpocketing. Have you ever felt the disturbance in the air created
by the presence of a thief? ['le merveilleux du vol à la tire. Avez-vous
déjà ressenti le trouble que met dans l'air la présence d'un voleur?'] It's
inexplicable. But the cinema is also the domain of the inexplicable."[68]
"Those people," Bresson said of the pickpockets of Paris, "pull off
astonishing feats ['des choses merveilleuses!']." And Jean Sémolué
adds, linking this evocation of the pickpocket to Bresson's own work,
"All that remained was to organize those things into something no
less astonishing and marvelous than a well-constructed film, a beautiful object."[69] But somehow, for Bresson, this work of organization
had to be carried out on the sly. Indeed, the very way Bresson went
about his work on this film suggests this deeper connection to the
pickpocket: he has recounted how he began *Pickpocket* filming "in
hiding":

> They told me, "Hide, it's easy." I hid. I was soon discovered. We had
> to employ ruses ["Il fallait user des ruses"]. Shots made from hiding
> are not very precise. Crowds are chaotic ["un désordre"]. I used this
> chaos in certain scenes. The sequence in the station was shot entirely
> in the crowd, during the month of July as the rush was on to leave for
> vacation. It required an enormously mobile camera and the rapid de-
> ployment of our material. In short, I heaped difficulties on myself, not
> the least of which was working in all that bustle and noise.[70]

We can easily imagine Michel making this same statement when asked
to reveal his M.O. Elsewhere, in a moment of cinematic bravado,
Bresson writes, "Your camera catches ['attrape'] not only physical
movements that are inapprehensible ['inattrapables']" (NC, 53/110).
His favorite analogy for the camera is an aggressive one: "For me, the
word shot ['prise de vue'] signifies capture. One has to catch ['at-
traper'] the actor under the play of lights and surprise him ['le sur-
prendre'] and seize from him ['de capter sur lui'] . . . the rarest and
most secret things he can produce."[71] Of Claude Laydu, the priest in
Journal, Bresson claimed, "I robbed him of what I needed to make the
film."[72] Joel Magny has noted that Bresson imitates his characters not
only in this surreptitious activity of the pickpocket but in his very
obsessiveness:

> Prey to an idea, a desire, a vocation, the character ends up seeing the
> world only in terms of the goal to be attained: the only things that

matter are obstacles or aids to his quest, anything outside his path is a
matter of indifference and disappears. This is the state of mind, or better yet the point of view ["optique"], that Bresson wants to create in
the spectator.[73]

And in that optic Bresson films. Even to the extent of saying, like
Michel, "Laugh at a bad reputation ['Moque-toi d'une mauvaise rép-
utation']" (NC, 62/125). Like Michel, and Raskolnikov before him,
Bresson sees himself as a member of a group of solitary visionaries
able, nay, destined, to transgress the general rules because of a secret
superiority: "The future of cinematography belongs to a new race of
young solitaries who will shoot films by putting their last cent into it
and not let themselves be taken in by the material routines of the
trade" (NC, 62/124–25). As with Michel and Raskolnikov, the real
interest is not in material gain but in a goal that always remains
aggressively secret and mysterious. "Hide the ideas. . . . The most
important will be the most hidden" (NC, 18/42).

And what is this "most important, most hidden idea"? Louis
Malle was among the first to suggest the answer to this "enigma."
"Pickpocket is also an erotic film, 'le vol à tire' being evidently merely
a thinly disguised or transposed symbol of the sin of the flesh. The
cold expression and pursed lips of Martin Lasalle and his accomplices
evoke Don Juan and le marquis de Sade."[74] Robert Bresson is never
so passionate a filmmaker as when he is filming the orgy of pickpocketing in the Gare de Lyon. That orgy is exquisitely prepared by a
more private one, when Michel and his doubles are practicing their
art. Here Bresson lubriciously approaches his camera to a closeup that
eliminates faces and leaves only bodies prey to myriad hands that
reach inside clothing at both breast and crotch levels, unbutton but-
tons, pull out secret and preciously guarded objects (see plate 24).[75]
Although the scene in the Gare de Lyon is the apex of this frenzy—
Jean-Pierre Oudart calls it "a hysterical erotic relationship ['rapport
érotique hystérisé']"[76]—the most violently intrusive example occurs
just after Michel, waiting in the bank for his next victim, experiences a
failure of will. "I was stopped by fear ['J'ai eu peur']," he says as the
victim passes through the doors, "he got away ['il m'échappa']." But
typically for this narrator, he is wrong. Seconds later we see Michel
and his accomplice work the man over with a thoroughness that has
all the overtones of rape and is rendered all the more uncomfortable
for the viewer by the stop-action editing on certain hand movements
that, were they conducted so slowly, would surely have been detected
by the victim. The impression given by this "cooperative" camera

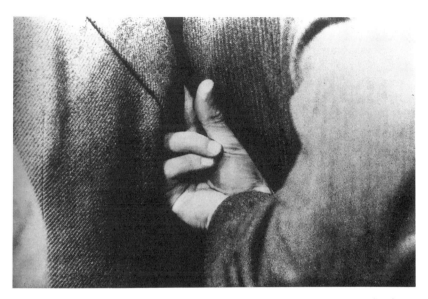

PLATE 24. Myriad hands reach inside others' clothing in Bresson's *Pickpocket*. (Courtesy of the Museum of Modern Art Film Stills Archive.)

work and editing is that the image maker enjoys a very Gidean complicity with the thieves in their most intimate activities.[77] Not that there is any *evident* pleasure to be gleaned here.[78] Even the ocular orgasm—Bresson uses the term "ejaculatory force of the eye ['force ejaculatrice de l'oeil']"!! (NC, 6/19)—witnessed at the racetrack in the opening scene is so transient and so ascetic that it seems to signify "erotic" without affording the pleasure normally associated with the erotic.

So much in this film is defense against just such an erotic pleasure that it is small wonder that the explanation of grace seems to have taken hold despite its lack of applicability to the character or to the intertextual supports that lend the film its major resonance. The defense begins, of course, with Bresson's very theory of the cinematograph: if no image has value, and if value is only relative, then we are cast into a world of fragments whose ultimate meaning is always "elsewhere" ("ailleurs"). The defense continues with Bresson's condemnation of psychology: "No psychology!" warns Bresson, in a general approach that sounds more like an illustration of Freud's theory of repression than anything else (NC, 39/83). "Apply myself to insignificant (non-significant) images. . . . Flatten my images (as if

179

ironing them ['comme avec un fer à repasser']), *without attenuating them*" (NC 6/18). But he seems to understand the visual effects of a repressive camera style: "Production of emotion determined ['obtenue'] by a resistance to emotion" (NC, 65/129). And for a director who will have no truck with psychology, Bresson appears to have an unusual interest in his own unconscious desires: "Your film begins when your secret wishes pass into your models ['Ton film commence quand tes volontés secrètes passent directement à tes modèles']. . . . Impose on it your urges, your orgies ['tes volontés, tes voluptés']" (NC, 43/90, 63/126).[79] In *Pickpocket*, however, the eye may see and the hand may reach, but the ego seems to be able neither to tolerate a direct expression of pleasure in that which is forbidden nor to forgo transgression.[80]

Pleasure in *Pickpocket* is always somewhere else. It must always be located in the fetish as replacement for the desired object. Of course, fetishism is always a kind of theater, as Joyce McDougall reminds us, a drama in which one's "I is a character, an 'actor' in the scene of the world, who, in private, in his internal reality, stages a more intimate theater whose repertory is secret." In all of us, "the I continually settles accounts with the past and so indefatigably reproduces the same dramas. . . . These psychic scenarios are always handicrafts ['artisanales'], sometimes however approaching real works of art." For some, psychoanalysis will be the stage in which these dramas are enacted, employing a cast of characters that the I has dredged spontaneously from the unconscious. For others, this "tireless rehearsal for an anonymous spectator" will be played out in a private drama of fetishism or a public drama of cinema—or both.[81] In this case, the I will often need others for its (private) theater:

> In the scenarios that derive from (the unconscious), the I attempts to expel and thereby externalize its intimate conflicts, but in order to accomplish this, it needs the cooperation of the other I's; those others will be called on to play the roles of various minor characters, derived from the internal world of the subject, having been designed by projection for these identifications of the expelled characters, and yet the subject has not the least suspicion that it has served as *metteur en scène* for these dramas, and the relational tensions that result from them.[82]

Now, to some extent this structure describes all creative artists, who draw from their imagination various aspects of their own personalities. But Bresson's application of this tendency is particularly marked. It is by now well known (both from his own writing and from the reports of his "models") that he worked to "wear down the actor, to make him die ['aplanir l'acteur, le faire mourir'],"[83] to reduce his players to virtual automatons. Those who have reported on his techniques, such as M. Monod, refer to the "slightly sadistic advantage gained through discomfiture of others" and to the fact that "Bresson played every part."[84] Bresson himself writes,

> Model. Reduce to the minimum the share of his consciousness ["sa
> conscience"]. . . . You will guide your models according to your rules
> ["à tes règles"]. . . . It would not be ridiculous to say to your models:
> "I am inventing you as you are." . . . The cause which makes him say
> this sentence or that movement is not in him, it is in you. . . . Models:
> mechanized externally, internally free ["intacts, vierges intérieure-
> ment"]. On their faces nothing willful. . . . Your film begins when
> your secret wishes pass into your models. . . . It is to you, not to the
> public that they give those things which it, perhaps, would not
> see. . . . A secret and sacred trust ["Dépot secret et sacré"]. Many peo-
> ple are needed to make a film, but only one who makes, unmakes, re-
> makes his images and sounds, returning at every second to the initial
> impression or sensation which . . . is incomprehensible to the oth-
> ers. . . . When I listen only to myself, I do wonders ["des merveilles"].
> (NC, 8–70/23–136 passim)[85]

Jean-Pierre Oudart goes so far as to assert that "the sadistic relation-ship between Robert Bresson and his actresses constitutes the re-pressed of the Bressonian fiction."[86] Beyond his repression of his actors, however, we have become aware of the many other fetishistic aspects in Bresson's work.

Now, fetishism itself, according to McDougall, usually derives from unmanageable fears deriving from the primal-scene experience, which result in what Freud has called *Verleugnung* ("disavowal"). But McDougall argues that this disavowal is compensated by the restruc-turing of the psyche around fantasies that replace the disavowed pa-rental genitals. The child "takes note and creates in an *autoplastic* way the fantasmatic means for dealing with this unhappy knowledge." This *reworking through fantasy* may include what McDougall calls "denuded representation," which screens not only the "empty sex" of the mother "but also the meaning of that which should have been attached to this discovery."[87] She notes,

> In these efforts to know nothing of the truth of sexual relations in or-
> der to be able to maintain the fictive introjection of the primal scene,

the pervert engages in a no win struggle ["un combat"] with reality. In this light, his erotic behavior is a sort of perpetual and compulsive *acting out*. For the subject has created for himself a mythology whose real meaning remains hidden, a text whose most important passages have been erased ["un texte dont on aurait gommé des passages importants"]. [But] these missing passages are not repressed, for in that case, they would have given rise to neurotic symptoms; they have been abolished, the subject having *destroyed* the meaning.[88]

In essence, McDougall is arguing that fetishism may take the form of a generalized fragmenting of reality into whose ellipses the disavowed meaning has slipped. The result is a recathected *collage*. Masud Khan writes, "One of the results obtained by the collated internal object in the psychic reality of the pervert is that this object gives him the possibility of instituting in his internal reality a paradoxical screen which protects him from the global invasion of his person by the intrusive omnipresence of the mother in his infantile experience."[89]

"Les idées les cacher, mais de manière qu'on les retrouve. La plus importante sera la plus cachée," writes Bresson. We may begin to perceive, if not exactly *what* is screened off, at least the means by which the "ideas" are hidden. Bresson's cinematograph is, as we have had occasion to note, a montage; but in the light of McDougall's analysis of fetishism and perversion, we can see that this montage comes more and more to resemble a perverse collage of individual images each of which has been carefully decathected. "Images chosen in prevision of their *inner* association," writes Bresson, "don't run after poetry. It penetrates unaided through the joins (ellipses) ['Elle pénètre toute seule par les jointures (ellipses)']" (NC, 25/55, 14/35). What is left between these significant ellipses is a system of fragments that, like the fetish, operate primarily by *synecdoche,* what Pierre Jouvet calls "meaningful fractions."[90]

This collage effect, in which each of the images loses its primacy of reference to be subsumed into an overall pattern, results perhaps less in a sense of overall composition than in generalized fragmentation. This again is consistent with the workings of fetishism in general and of the pickpocket, both film and character, in particular. Michel's real crime (like Meursault's in Camus's *L'Etranger*) is against his mother. As the police inspector points out, an identity has been established between the man who stole from his mother and the man who has been picking the pockets of women and then men in the racetracks, subways, streets, and stations of Paris. In both cases a violation that, rather than operating in the repressed realm of sexuality, has taken a "drôle de chemin," a displacement onto fetishized objects, fragments that are slipped deliciously from under the clothes of the other player in this drama into the hands of the fetishizer. The *real* thing has been disavowed. The pleasure is always elsewhere: in the hand, in the money, wallets, watches removed from the victims—fragments. Just as in the making of the film the pleasure itself is located in fragmentation, a pleasure of the fetishized eye. "My joy is in *making the film*," exclaimed Bresson to Marjorie Greene.[91] "La force éjaculatrice de l'oeil," he writes (un)cryptically in his *Notes* (NC, 19).

Perhaps this is why the final images of the film focus on Michel carefully separated from Jeanne by iron bars. Perhaps this is why Bresson confesses, "Shooting is going out to meet something. Nothing in the unexpected that is not secretly expected by you ['Rien dans l'inattendu qui ne soit attendu secrètement par toi']" (NC, 52/108). What a strange path, through Dostoevsky and George Barrington, Bresson has taken in order (not) to tell us his story.

Chapter Seven

The ABC's of Godard's Quotations:
A bout de souffle *with* Pierrot le fou

> If I become not then all of remembering will cease to
> be. Yes . . . between grief and nothing I will take grief.
> —*William Faulkner*

> Vloumb! Vloumb! There's no time to think! . . . The sit-
> uation's getting critical. . . . Confusion's at its height?
> . . . my memory's out of breath! . . . everything carries
> you off . . . everything drifts dreamward . . . everything
> yields . . .
> —*Louis Ferdinand Céline*

It was perhaps inevitable, given Hollywood's appetite for cooptation,
that Jean-Luc Godard's *A bout de souffle* would be transformed into a
remake twenty-five years after its explosive appearance in the cinemas
of Paris. It was just as inevitable, no doubt, that the film's story would
be returned to a circulation of cinematic language just as far within
the acceptable comfort level as Godard's film had stood outside it at its
inception. In this sense, Jim McBride's recuperation of Godard is as
natural and understandable as, for example, Madison Avenue's bor-
rowings from surrealism in the service of the very consumerism surrealism had sought to undermine. Pamela Falkenberg has staked out
what is at risk when she argues that McBride's remake "might be
characterized as . . . the opposition . . . in which the principles that
determine the classical art cinema are themselves negated."[1] And, as
Falkenberg also notes, to resituate *A bout de souffle* in Los Angeles as
an American crime melodrama is to introduce the American film into
an ironic circulation of simulation, for Godard's film of 1959 was

already based on the reality of classical Hollywood narrative cinema! Falkenberg captures the utter irony in McBride's practice by noting that already in Godard's film

> Patricia is Jean Seberg, an American movie star; Jean Paul Belmondo is the simulation of Humphrey Bogart. But Patricia also simulates Michel as Humphrey Bogart; she appears in Michel's shirt, his hat, and his dark glasses; finally, she even simulates the gesture (thumb across lips) that marks Belmondo's simulation of Bogart. Michel is the simulation from a distance of an American character, and Patricia simulates that simulation.[2]

Beyond the fifth-column anticipatory gesture already constituted by this circulation of simulation within his film, Godard must have anticipated McBride's recuperative gesture, for he harshly repudiated the "fascism" of his own film:

> *A bout de souffle*, is a film I've always been ashamed of when I saw it, although there are others of my films that I like seeing again. . . . *A bout de souffle* is a film that I just can't look at without beginning to perspire, to feel, I don't know, as if I'd been forced to strip naked at a moment that I didn't feel like it, and that's always seemed a bit strange to me. . . . It's a film that came out of fascism and that is full of fascist overtones ["un film qui sortait du fascisme et qui avait plein de teintes fascistes"].[3]

If the fascism of *A bout de souffle* is not immediately apparent, it may become so in the light of the other anticipatory gesture made by Godard to deflect the Hollywood cooptation of his work: *Pierrot le fou*.[4] I believe we may read this latter film as Godard's own remake of *A bout de souffle* constituted in order to articulate precisely the principle that McBride was to "violate" in *Breathless:* French cinema's ongoing revolt against the aesthetics of identity.

By comparing *Pierrot le fou* with *A bout de souffle* we may better understand in what way the earlier film could be considered "fascist" and exactly how the later film both gains its distance from *A bout de souffle* and anticipatorily subverts McBride's *Breathless*. Marie-Claire Ropars-Wuilleumier has noted of these two works that "from one film to the other, one form was destroyed and another tried to come into being," but this rupture can scarcely be observed at the level of anecdote, where "many similar givens allow the reconstitution of the same plot, of the same story or the same anarchistic adventure which unites for a moment a man whose strength is born of his inner certainty and an uncertain woman who will betray him and push him toward death."[5]

Indeed, the similarities between the story lines of these two works are remarkable. In both films a protagonist, played by Jean-Paul Belmondo, falls in love with a woman he knows only casually, runs off with her, moving from stolen car to stolen car, hoping to get to Italy, a scenario in which "the theme of the car" constitutes an "invitation du voyage et de fascination de 'l'ailleurs.'"[6] In both works the characters pass nonchalantly by cadavers. In each case the woman self-consciously explores her relationship to works of art (Seberg to Picasso, then Renoir; Karina to Renoir, then Picasso) (see plates 25 and 26), and both films involve men who constantly change names: Michel Poiccard goes under the alias Lazlo Kovacs in *A bout de souffle,* and Ferdinand "becomes" Pierrot in *Pierrot le fou.* Each film pauses to incorporate an interview with a film director (Jean-Pierre Melville, under the pseudonym Parvulesco, imitates Raoul Walsh in the first film, and Samuel Fuller plays himself in the second). In each, one character struggles to understand his or her partner: "I want to know what's behind your face. I've watched it for ten minutes and I see nothing . . . nothing . . . nothing," says Patricia, whereas Ferdinand will tell Marianne, "I try to know exactly who you are . . . I dunno if you're making things up or not ['j'sais jamais si tu racontes des histoires ou pas']."[7] In each, the hero and his moll temporarily hole up in a protected space from which she proceeds to betray him. And in each, the male protagonist entertains a fascination with death: "Between grief and death . . . grief's idiotic, I'd choose nothingness," argues Michel, and Ferdinand muses "I want to stop time." Both films end with the violent death of the male protagonist, in both cases a death "chosen" by that character.

Noting that *A bout de souffle* "is present as a double exposure in our memory while watching *Pierrot,*" Gilles Jacob worried, at the latter film's release, that Godard "remains tenaciously faithful to a universe closed in on itself. . . . *Pierrot le fou* offers us a remarkable retrospective. . . . It repertories, recapitulates. . . . Doesn't Godard have anything new to say? No, but what he says seems so important that he must repeat it over and over until he's satisfied. . . . The same images assault and solicit our imagination. The familiar obsessions remain."[8]

Perhaps. And yet despite these fundamental similarities of plot, any viewer of these two films will agree that *A bout de souffle* and *Pierrot le fou* belong to radically different moments, types, political statements, and even genres of film. Ropars-Wuilleumier notwithstanding, this difference is not simply a matter of style.[9] *A bout de*

PLATE 25.   Patricia (Jean Seberg) self-consciously explores her relationship to Renoir in Godard's *A bout de souffle*. (Courtesy of the Museum of Modern Art Film Stills Archive.)

souffle, like its successor, already displays a highly nervous style, using a hand-held camera, jump cuts, and highly self-conscious transition markers to accentuate its discontinuity and its break from accepted cinematic grammar. Indeed, the "breathless" style of Godard's first full-length fiction film has been amply documented.

The principal difference between these two moments in Godard's career may be sought elsewhere. Gilles Jacob notes: "We rediscover the theme of love that leads to death, tenderness and maladroitness, Godard's occasionally annoying taste for quotation . . . the need to make his spectator uneasy . . . the love of cinema and quiet references

187

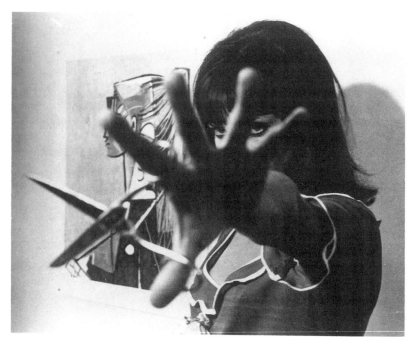

PLATE 26.   Marianne (Anna Karina) with scissors and Picasso in Godard's *Pierrot le fou*. (Courtesy of the Museum of Modern Art Film Stills Archive.)

to his own work."[10] I would submit that these last four items are part and parcel of a single tendency for Godard—quotation—and that within this particular characteristic we can discover a subtle but paradigmatic shift between *A bout de souffle* and *Pierrot le fou*, one that goes a long way in explaining the differences we feel between these two otherwise repetitive works. I should hasten to point out that if Godard's citations have been abundantly noted by his critics, their specificity has not only been ignored, it has been rejected. Dudley Andrew's exploration of the place of American B-movies in the unfolding of *A bout de souffle* and Ropars's essay on the graphic unconscious in the same film, while they seek to explore certain "intertextual" elements of the film, specifically proscribe any attempt to read specific allusions as having a particular significance.[11] Following Susan Sontag's lead, Andrew writes,

> Godard, it seems, had at least two uses for intertextual references. The
> first, stronger use, deepens the aesthetic and philosophical thrust of his

own effort by linking it to the low-art film noir with its excruciating ruminations about death and love. The second use, paradoxically involving elite novelists, composers and painters, is textual rather than structural. Godard splashes these names on his canvas to vary the tone and interest of his scenes. . . . He thought himself the first filmmaker . . . to drop names . . . to play disrespectfully, because offhandedly, with art. . . . An older form of criticism might have wrestled some of these references into an allegorical frieze. . . . [But] if literature is to appear in his films . . . it is as a thing apart. The hard edge of words confronts the engulfing image without being swallowed up. Literature sticks out of Godard's films, the way pieces of newspaper stick out of cubist collages.[12]

It is not immediately clear why Andrew should valorize allusions to "low-art film noir" as stronger than allusions to literature, nor why he should label only these latter as "elite" in Godard's fictional universe. After all, Godard was brought up in a bourgeois family in Lausanne in which reading out loud was a family tradition, and it provided him with an enduring interest in literature. His writing is full of references to literary works—Aragon, Malraux, D. H. Lawrence, Racine, Goethe—made in anything but an "offhanded" manner. We remember Truffaut's claim that "par rapport aux cinéastes américains, je crois que nous sommes tous des intellectuels."[13] Andrew himself is not above recourse to this "elite" allusionism, citing "Sartre's Roquentin, Camus's Meursault, and Jean Genet's perverse heroes" as models for Michel Poiccard and elsewhere arguing that both *Breathless* and *A bout de souffle* "acknowledge the need for mediation, for intertextuality, and forthrightly insist that the truth of any new cinema . . . is . . . established by . . . looking at other movies, at books, songs and representations of all sorts."[14] More tellingly, Andrew's own analysis of the imbrication of American B-movies in *A bout de souffle* is so sophisticated, so intricate, and so illuminating as to *inspire* rather than discourage a similar effort with the literary quotations in the work! Likewise Ropars, who claims in an early essay on Godard:

To reproach Godard either for his abuse of quotations or for taste for speeches is to fail to see that these phrases constitute objects and not meanings and that meaning can only be born of a global confrontation of all the objects perceived by the spectator at any given moment at the point of their convergence. . . . It is important that the spectator never retain one expressive element at the expense of another, but instead accept a global apprehension of all without attempting to understand them separately.[15]

To refuse meaning to any object in an of itself, but especially to an intertextual filmic element, seems a less than plausible approach. Nor does Ropars-Wuilleumier adhere to her own dictum, for she proceeds directly to "interpret the significance" of Elie Faure's statement on Velasquez that Belmondo quotes in the opening moments of *Pierrot le fou*. In another essay on Godard, Ropars argues that "the sign's graphic inscription causes it to oscillate between figure and significa- tion." Symptomatically, her analysis of the presence of Maurice Sachs's *Abracadabra* in *A bout de souffle* is frozen at the level of "the layout [which] seems to represent the sign's very mechanism. . . . There is suddenly a risk that the hieroglyphic combination may freeze up. . . . Isn't Abracadabra a sign too, albeit a cabalistic one, magic's actual formula, the power of the word as opposed to that of ob- jects?"[16] Or, I would ask, is *Abracadabra* not a text after all, capable of the same circulation of meaning as, say, the allusions to Westerns in this film? Thus, while I do not dispute Ropars's interpretation of these signs as objects, I do question any a priori restrictions imposed on Go- dard's quotations as "non-signifying" elements.[17] Ropars-Wuilleumier argues that

> the victory of cinema is affirmed in the defeat of articulated language, in the triumph of the unformulated ["l'informulé"], which becomes the truly unspeakable ["l'indicible"] once in a while, in rare moments of joy where the montage is lyrical. This lyricism, this harmony between being and language, can today be only instantaneous and ephemeral.[18]

But the potential functioning of literary intertextuality in cinema is in no way limited by this idealized moment of the "indicible . . . in- stantané et éphémère" but rather operates (as it always has) in a con- stant mobility moving back and forth within this more visual yet equally thought-provoking sphere. As Ropars-Wuilleumier herself notes of Godard's work, "Shots ['Prises de vues'] and articulations ['prises de mots'] operate in a like movement, which changes words into images and images into words."[19]

It is just such a moment that critical reflection on cinema recapitu- lates, and in such a space that Dudley Andrew, for example, discovers the vibrant resonances of the American B-movies in *A bout de souffle*. Likewise, it is in just this topos that I would propose to explore the several literary intertexts proposed by Godard in *A bout de souffle* and reinterpreted six years later in *Pierrot le fou*. I believe that it is precisely in this act of rein*script*ion, screening off old intertexts by new ones, that Godard constitutes the episteme of all of his work after 1965.

Dudley Andrew was, of course, "right on the money" in revealing the Americanism of *A bout de souffle*. Andrew notes that in working toward his own film through the apprenticeship of film criticism, "Godard may not have been sure of his subject, but he had certainly settled on a style. It would be 'American,' with speed, reflex, and a character who could go to the limit. In short, it would have a directness and honesty in theme and style, as opposed to the good taste . . . of the ruling French cinema of quality."[20]

Americanism, however, was gradually to become a code for a complex of issues that subtly but entirely govern *A bout de souffle* in ways Godard would later feel compelled to reject. For several years prior to the making of his own film, Godard had been extolling the virtues of American cinema. In 1952 he praised "the freshness and invention of American films" and extolled the "swiftness of action of American comedy which allowed the moment to be savoured to the full."[21] In Howard Hawks he admired "an increasingly precise taste for analysis, a love for this artificial grandeur connected to movements of the eyes, to a way of walking, in short, a greater awareness . . . of what the cinema can glory in, and a refusal to profit from this . . . to create an anti-cinema, but instead, through a more rigorous knowledge of its limits, fixing its basic laws" (G/G, 29–30).

The basic aesthetic laws of American cinema may well have been speed and freshness of action, but the philosophical underpinnings were remarkably different. J. P. Telotte has noted that however much American film noir betrays a "dis-ease with the nature of discourse in the modern world . . . a majority of *films noirs* generally follow the classical narrative model."[22] Godard complained that the failure of contemporary art was that "it has rejected for centuries the pride of the great masters, and indeed of humbler craftsmen: the *portrait of the individual*" (G/G, 30, italics mine). Along with this very classical taste for portraiture, the Godard of 1957 revealed a resolutely conservative (and anti-existential) appreciation for clarity and morality:

> Poor novel which makes ambiguity its ambition. Poor painting, fettered by fear of representation! In short I . . . deplore the too ambiguous morality of our time and its art. . . . Artistic creation does not mean putting one's soul in things but painting the soul in things . . . . The natural order corresponds to that of the heart and mind. . . . Art attracts us only by what it reveals of our most secret self. This is the sort of depth I mean. Obviously it assumes an idea of man which is hardly revolutionary, and which the great film-makers from Griffith to Renoir were too conservative to dare to deny. So, to the question 'What is Cinema?', I would first reply: the expression of lofty sentiments. (G/G, 30–31)

American film, as it turned out, seemed to respond, precisely at the level of portraiture and the idea of coherent character, to Godard's early desire for coherence and clarity—even as he sought to rejuvenate cinematic style. Thus, in praise of Hawks he writes, "All the freshness and invention of American films springs from the fact that they make the subject the motive for the *mise en scène*" (G/G, 25). He lauds Hitchcock's *The Man Who Knew Too Much* for having "as its sole mainspring—assuming one rejects metaphysics—feminine intuition. . . . We are touched by a grace which may only come to us in snatches but which minds more immediately lyrical are incapable of dispensing with such delicacy" (G/G, 38–39). Of *The Wrong Man* he gushes, "The beauty of each of these close-ups, with their searching attention to the passage of time, comes from the sense that *necessity is intruding on triviality, essence on existence*" (G/G, 49, italics mine). Of Nicolas Ray's *The True Story of Jesse James* Godard exclaims, "One must judge *Jesse James* on its intentions. . . . One recognizes Nicolas Ray's signature . . . by the compositions which somehow manage to make ideas as abstract as Liberty and Destiny both clear and tangible" (G/G, 60–61). Writing of Anthony Mann's *Man of the West* only months before he began shooting *A bout de souffle,* Godard notes, "It is the most intelligent of films, at the same time the most simple. What is it about? About a man who *discovers* himself in a dramatic situation and *looks* about him for a way out. So the *mise en scène* of *Man of the West* consists of discovering and defining at the same time" (G/G, 119, italics Godard's).

In short, what emerges from Godard's years of meditation on American cinema is an admiration for soul, the secrets of characterization, feminine intuition as a kind of metaphysics, belief in essence, and predefinition of character, revealed rather than formed by action. These are the "lofty sentiments" behind Godard's earliest cinematic expression. Indeed, so massive is the American belief in portraiture and character that the very terms of cinematic practice reflect it. Richard Roud thus finds himself caught between two very different epistemes in attempting to translate the French term *découpage* (an analytic and very French intent), for which he substitutes "construction" (a synthetic and very American solution) in the translation.[23] It is precisely the gap between *découpage* and "construction" as the necessity for a compromise formation that makes *A bout de souffle* at once so remarkable and so problematic for its author. The superposition of these Americanisms on a French landscape ironically allowed their easy recuperation by McBride in *Breathless* and necessitated their tortuous ob-literation (in the most literal sense of that word) by Godard in *Pierrot le fou*.

Meanwhile, in *A bout de souffle* Godard was busy incorporating the *quintessence* of American B-movies, including their taste for death and the style that "translates" this:

> I would go so far as to defy anyone to capture in a medium long shot ["plan général"] the extreme disquiet, the inner agitation, in a word, the confusion which the waist shot ["plan américain"], through its very inexpressiveness, conveys so powerfully. If one had to pin down a somewhat excessive taste for death in the American cinema, I would suggest that it lies in the fear of repose, in those moments where, in the panic of the heart, the slightest gesture reveals certain knowledge and, all at once, hatred, repentance, mockery and courage. The fact is, perhaps, that the most delicate *nuances of the soul* must be treated with greater emphasis, just as a gesture which draws attention to itself excuses the delicate from any need to be touched by it. (G/G, 28–29, italics mine)

Yes, Godard wrote, "'The Hollywood Machine' is very worn out and often goes wrong, nowadays, but it can still deliver the goods" (G/G, 72). "The goods" also get delivered, in *A bout de souffle,* by a strict adherence to the ethics, if not the aesthetics, of this machine. Despite the inventiveness of his style (to which I shall return), Godard rigorously wove his characters into a system of intertextual allusions both to the American film and to American literature.

Dudley Andrew has artfully unraveled this tapestry to reveal the "Hollywood love story" implicit in the long scene in Patricia's hotel room, the film's salutes to such films as *The Harder They Fall, The Enforcer, Ten Seconds to Hell, Whirlpool, Gun Crazy,* and Raoul Walsh's films in general, especially *High Sierra*. Andrew subtends this entire network with the observation that "the theme of the film, like the *essence* of its hero, is precisely the futile struggle to be original 'in the manner of' something or someone else. The notion of individuality and of forthrightness is as American as the movies, and as fully processed. Since there can be no escaping genre, since freedom is attainable only within or against genre, Godard the cinéphile embraces it. And he chooses the genre that most promoted and problematized freedom, the film noir."[24] *Pierrot le fou* was to demonstrate better than any other "thesis" could just how essentialist, processed, and thoroughly American this film was, by the *mise en scène* of an opposing epistemology. Meanwhile, Godard wallowed in portraiture and genre. "In *A bout de souffle,*" he wrote a few years later, "I was looking for the theme right through the shooting, and finally became interested in Belmondo. I saw him as a sort of block to be filmed to discover what lay inside" (G/G, 175–76). At the same time, and very much in keeping with this idea of classical portraiture, Godard toed the line on genre:

> What caused me a lot of trouble was the end. Should the hero die? . . . Finally I decided that as my avowed ambition was to make an ordinary gangster film, I had no business deliberately contradicting the genre; he must die. If the House of Atreus no longer kill each other, they are no longer the House of Atreus. (G/G, 174)

Beneath this avowal of his classicism of the period of *A bout de souffle,* one can sense the nostalgia for coherence and for unity of character and of action that are often disguised beneath a frenetic renewal of style. If the quick cuts, reverse camera directions, 360-degree pans, and general "cinematic hyperactivity"[25] give an initial impression of avant-garde technique, they ultimately and ironically function as the best possible style to define Michel's restless "automotive" character. Far from scrambling his portrait, they paradoxically affirm it. Any other style would have had an oddly jarring effect when matched to such a character. In other words, Godard is not yet at the point (that he will attain in *Pierrot le fou*) where stylistic disruption takes on an epistemological and revolutionary character. In contradistinction to the style of Raoul Walsh, for example, Jean-Luc Godard employs a hand-held camera to chase Belmondo down the streets of Paris and through the junkyards of its *banlieue.* But Walsh, we must remember, was filming Belmondo's ironic idol: the master of cool, who never broke into either a run or a sweat in the most pressured of situations, whose cigarette hung perennially from his lower lip, ever intact to the last particle of its fragile, glowing ash. Like *his* American idols, Walsh, Mann, and Ray (but so unlike the director he was later to become), Godard marries his style perfectly to the character he sets out to "discover," knowing all too well where and how he will end up because the genre has already determined it. Nothing could be more essentially classical.

The importance of Godard's quotations in this film should not be underestimated (see plate 27). Despite a general critical consensus that Godard's taste for citation is "abusive," that characteristic is not only a regular feature of his work, it is, in the director's own view, an integral part of his work:

PLATE 27. The importance of quotations in Godard's *A bout de souffle* should not be underestimated. Here Patricia (Jean Seberg) and Carl Zumbach (Roger Hanin) discuss a book. (Courtesy of the Museum of Modern Art Film Stills Archive.)

I improvise, certainly, but with material which goes a long way back. Over the years you accumulate things and then suddenly you use them in what you're doing. . . . One can make use of what one has already seen in the cinema to make deliberate references. This was true of me in particular. . . . This is much the same sort of thing as my taste for quotation, which I still retain. Why should we be reproached for it? People in life quote as they please, so we have the right to quote as we please. Therefore I show people quoting, merely making sure they quote *what pleases me*. In the notes I make of anything that might be of use for a film, I will add a quote from Dostoievsky if I like it. Why not? If you want to say something, there is only one solution: say it. (G/G, 172–73, italics mine)

Far from being "non-signifying" elements, Godard's intertexts are deliberate and carefully chosen. A close analysis of the three texts that are displayed for our view in *A bout de souffle* reveals how congruent

195

they are to the dominant (American) philosophical thrust of the film. During Michel's long scene with Patricia in her hotel room, she attempts to engage him in discussions of Faulkner's *The Wild Palms* and Dylan Thomas's *Portrait of the Artist as a Young Dog*. Later, at Beruti's apartment, Michel fingers a copy of Maurice Sachs's *Abracadabra* on which Lenin's words "We are all dead people on leave" ("Nous sommes tous des morts en permission") are exhibited as a publicity dust cover. Each of these three texts has particular resonances with the scenes in which it occurs as well as the larger movement of the film. Although neither of the latter texts is directly quoted by any of the principles in the film, their presence contributes to the literary mythologization of film that will be more thoroughly developed in the quotation from Faulkner.

We recall that Patricia surfaces a copy of Dylan Thomas's *Portrait of the Artist as a Young Dog* after she and Michel have made love under the sheets of her bed. This collection of stories of lost loves and thoughts of death by a Welshman who died tragically in America may, at one level, give a nicely adolescent spin to Michel's pursuit of this girl who claims he does not understand her. Thomas's characters are ever in search of the perfect (and always inevitably unknown) woman and never seem to achieve, always just brush real communication with the opposite sex. In this sense the stories contribute to the construction of Michel's character as a construct of unfulfilled desire.

That portrait of desire, however, comes remarkably close to another specific concern in *A bout de souffle* in the following passage from "Old Garbo," in which the "young dog" goes to the movies:

> She showed me to a seat. During the educational film, with the rude seeds hugging and sprouting in front of my eyes and plants like arms and legs, I thought of the bob women and the pansy sailors in the dives. There might be a quarrel with razors, and once Ted Williams found a lip outside the Mission to Seamen. It had a small moustache. The sinuous plants danced on the screen. If only Tawe were a larger sea-town there would be curtained rooms underground with blue films. The potato's life came to an end. Then I entered an American college and danced with the president's daughter. The hero, called Lincoln, tall and dark with good teeth, I displaced quickly, and the *girl spoke my name as she held his shadow*, the singing college chorus in sailor's hats and bathing dresses called me big boy and king, Jack Oakie and I sped up the field and on the shoulders of the crowd the president's daughter and I brought across the shifting-colored curtain with a kiss that left me giddy and bright-eyed as I walked out of the cinema into the strong lamplight and the new rain.[26]

We must remember that it is Godard's and not just Patricia's pleasure to place this quotation, not just Patricia's, and as such it represents the feeling of fraternity with another artist who, like himself, felt the pull of American cinema and the powerful identificatory fantasies at work therein. We will see the figure of the shadow at work in both of the other intertexts that punctuate this film. Nor must we forget that if filmic quotation runs across these texts like a shadow, literary quotation runs across the one film that is screened in *A bout de souffle*. Godard will substitute his own literary texts for the soundtrack of the film Michel and Patricia watch briefly before their flight from the theater on the Champs Elysées.

Maurice Sachs's *Abracadabra,* which appears "gratuitously" in the final scene between Michel and Patricia, again plays with shadows and a fascination with American cinema. Ropars has revealed one level of this title's "graphic ambiguity" by inserting it into the mobile play of graphic signs in this film, finding in it both a cabalistic sign and a rearranged alphabet that with the author's name suggests "death laughing (la mort se rit)." Her conclusion is that "at the end of his road, M, the uncultured hero who loves Bogart and has never heard of Faulkner, will leave the world of images and succumb to the order of books."[27] But Ropars's gaze does not penetrate beyond the cover of Sachs's novel. *Abracadabra*'s readers will take pleasure, as Godard undoubtedly did, in the resonances that play between film and its intertext. Like Patricia, the novel's heroine, Aurore, tries to warn her lover away: "I cannot love you. . . . You must not attach too much importance to me."[28] But for Daniel, "that of course only rekindled his obstinate and impetuous feelings. . . . 'If she will not love me, I prefer to die'" (Aa, 68, 85). And Daniel's fantasies about Aurore are whetted by the cinema:

> Sometimes at the movies, when he draped his arm over the back of her seat, he felt the delicious sensation of Aurore's neck touching for an instant his wrist. . . . It launched him into dreams of magnificent gifts, of immense sacrifices, and of travels together to the most exotic lands. . . . But she didn't want to leave Paris. (Aa, 69–70)

Just after the framing of *Abracadabra* in *A bout de souffle,* Patricia tells Michel, "It's sad to fall asleep. You have to . . . separ——," and Michel completes her phrase, "——ate." "To separate," continues Patricia. "They say 'sleep together,' but it's not true." "Sleeping together" will constitute the moment in *Abracadabra* when Aurore takes her revenge and disappears, and Daniel wakes to find himself the victim of a cruel illusion. Grain de sel, the fairy who comes to take the place of the absent Aurore, drags Daniel to the movies to help him forget her. Walt Disney, it turns out, is his favorite auteur, precisely because of his ability to understand the essence of things. "He never would have believed any man knew so completely the truest secrets" (Aa, 128). Both *A Portrait of the Artist as a Young Dog* and *Abracadabra* portray the American B-cinema as a model for their characters' fantasies and behavior, suggesting their linkage in Godard's film with the third major literary intertext.

The most developed allusion of the three, Faulkner's *The Wild Palms,* again situates American literature as the central referent. Patricia (Jean Seberg) is, above all, an American girl. As Arlene Croce notes, inviting a comparison with *Hiroshima mon amour,* "No one says, *'Tu es New York'; 'Tu es Paris,'* although it is implied at every second. . . . Patricia, the American, . . . is the triumphant actual artifact of a culture of which he, in his delusion, is the copy, the dupe."[29] She wears, in bold Gothic, "THE NEW YORK HERALD TRIBUNE" across her braless breasts and hawks this quintessentially American point of view with a classically American accent. When Michel visits her room, she pulls her copy of Faulkner from under the bed and asks, "Do you know William Faulkner?" Entirely in character, Michel responds, "No. Who's he? Someone you slept with? ['T'as couché avec lui?']" It has been asserted that Michel's particular ignorance of Faulkner somehow vitiates the significance of the work in this film, but Faulkner's text contains a rather startling pretext both for Michel and for Godard himself. In introducing one of the convicts who will play a major role in "The Old Man" thread of his story, Faulkner writes,

> He was in for fifteen years . . . for attempted train robbery. He had laid his plans in advance, he had followed his printed (and false) authority to the letter; he had saved the paper-backs for two years, reading and re-reading them, memorizing them, comparing and weighing story and method against story and method, taking the good from each and discarding the dross as his workable plan emerged, keeping his mind open to make the subtle last-minute changes, without haste and without impatience, as the newer pamphlets appeared on their appointed days as a conscientious dressmaker makes the subtle alterations in a court presentation costume as the new bulletins appear. And then when the day came, he did not even have a chance to collect the watches and the rings, the brooches and the hidden money-belts, because he had been captured as soon as he entered the express car where the safe and the gold would be. . . . So now from time to time . . . he mused with raging impotence . . . and cursed in a harsh steady

unrepetitive stream, not the living men who had put him where he was but at what he did not even know were pen-names, did not even know were not actual men but merely the designations of shades who had written about shades.[30]

Faulkner's Old Man resembles no one so much as Jean-Luc Godard in his attempt to construct his own enterprise on the basis of literary and cinematic models. The convict rages against books written by "uncorporeal names . . . whom he believed had led him into his present predicament through their own ignorance and gullibility regarding the medium in which they dealt and took money for, in accepting information on which they placed the stamp of verisimilitude and authenticity . . . and which on actual application proved to be impractical and (to the convict) criminally false" (WP, 23). Both convict and filmmaker have constructed their work on the basis of quotation, and in both cases the quotation has an uncanny way of betraying the erstwhile imitator. The betrayal (so keenly resented by Faulkner's Old Man) extends directly to Michel, who must pay with his own "life" for Godard's fidelity to this detective genre. What is more significant, however, is that in his very fidelity to the American B-movie genre, Godard will feel most acutely his own ultimate inauthenticity. He will look back on *A bout de souffle* with embarrassment, saying, "I felt ashamed of it. . . . Now I see where it belongs—along with *Alice in Wonderland*. I thought it was *Scarface*" (G/G, 175). For his part, Michel is caught in a double bind. When his American girlfriend pulls Faulkner out from under her bed, she does so to illustrate (or foreshadow) the fears she has just expressed:

> You know, you said I was afraid, Michel. . . . It's true: I'm afraid because I want you to love me. . . . And then, I don't know, at the same time, I want you not to love me anymore. (B, 86)

The Wild Palms, like so many of the American B-movie models Godard's characters are unwittingly following, recounts another ill-starred romance in which Wilbourne falls in love with Charlotte and whisks her off to a life of adventure. But their love culminates in her death from an abortion he has administered and his condemnation to fifty years of hard labor in the local penitentiary. Claiming to be pregnant with Michel's child, Patricia already understands the familiar plot lines of Michel's desire and, like some character from Pirandello, seeks to warn him of the impending tragedy of being a character in an imitation B-movie! Patricia's quotation "Between grief and nothing I will take grief" removed from context reads like a Sartrean passage on existential choice. When replaced in context, however, it has a distinctly American ring:

> But after all memory could live in the old wheezing entrails: and now it did stand to his hand, incontrovertible and plain, serene, the palm clashing and murmuring dry and wild and faint and in the night but he could face it, thinking, *Not could. Will. I want to. So . . . no matter how old. Because if memory exists outside of the flesh it wont be memory because it wont know what it remembers so when she became not then half of memory became not and if I become not then all of remembering will cease to be.*— *Yes,* he thought, *between grief and nothing I will take grief.* (WP, 324)

Those familiar with the novel will thus realize that in context the choice of grief is connected to essential being itself, to integrity, to a temporary but critical affirmation of the historical self, as established by memory, as central to the constitution of meaning and the very possibility of meaning. In refusing grief Michel appears to betray Faulkner, but ironically, in choosing death he enters into a double bind: his is exactly the path chosen by all the heroes he emulates. Almost in spite of himself he ends up being *essentially* American.

Well, almost. After he argues that "grief is idiotic ['la douleur c'est con']," Patricia will respond, "The French are idiotic too ['Les Français sont cons aussi']." Once under the sheets, Michel laughs, "C'est vraiment une rencontre franco-américaine" (B, 89). Perhaps the reason Godard felt afterward that *A bout de souffle* was more *Alice in Wonderland* than *Scarface* was that Michel is French. His (and Godard's) pretense of Americanism is rendered exceptionally ironic in the explicit reference to Robson's *The Harder They Fall* (1956).

Few commentators of *A bout de souffle* have failed to note that Jean-Paul Belmondo stops early in the film to admire a large picture of Humphrey Bogart displayed in a publicity poster for *The Harder They Fall*. The allusion seems to fit the same topos as other Americanisms in Godard's film: other references to American cinema, the interview with Jean Pierre Melville (masquerading as Parvulesco), whose own films, especially *Le Doulos* (starring Belmondo), are unabashed homages to the American gangster films and especially the American automobile, which seems to symbolize so much of America to French directors.[31] That Michel Poiccard's alias, Lazlo Kovacs, is the name of a Hollywood cameraman testifies to the shameless degree of Godard's own fascination for the meta-cinematics of this "rencontre franco-américaine."

But there is another double bind for Michel in this homage to Bogey, one that is even more ironic than his rejective adherence to Faulkner. Dudley Andrew reminds us that Belmondo had been a boxer before becoming an actor,[32] but it is crucial in appreciating this "lip service" to Bogart that Bogart was an actor before being a boxer. By this I mean that the reference to *The Harder They Fall* gets caught in that film's story of Bogart's exploitation and betrayal of Toro, the foreign boxer. Hired by Nick (Rod Steiger) to put out a lot of false publicity on Toro, an Argentine boxer with a chin of glass and a punch like putty, Eddie (Bogart) conveniently sets Toro up and sells him out. Throughout the film, Toro looks at Bogart with a doglike innocence and refrains, "You're my friend, Eddie. I trust you." In a marvelous reprise of *On the Waterfront,* Humphrey Bogart takes Marlon Brando's seat in the back of a limousine with Rod Steiger, the corrupt boss. Instead of Brando's "I coulda been somebody!" Steiger preempts Bogart's unvoiced objections to his exploitation of Toro with, "He'll never be anybody!" When Bogart, pricked more by his scandalized wife than by his own conscience, finally gets around to telling Toro that he's nobody and that he has to take a fall against the champ to survive, the game foreign boxer evokes his country's honor and takes a horrible physical and financial beating. George, the Afro-American trainer, has to explain things to Bogart: "Some guys can sell out and others just can't."

If Bogart ultimately tries to make good to Toro by sending him back to his native country with his own (meager) share of the purse, the trainer's "Some guys can sell out" nevertheless rings loud and clear as an epitaph for the film. And so it might for *A bout de souffle*. Again, I believe that Dudley Andrew is entirely correct in asserting that "we who have entered the theater after ogling production stills of Belmondo and Seberg must find our interest deflected from the story of the chase to the mythology of representation."[33] Godard is also right, however, in shamefacedly comparing that mythology to *Alice in Wonderland*. In "selling out" to a specifically American mythology, Godard was aping a culture whose mythology he could no more be comfortable in than Toro in Rod Steiger's prearranged ring. He would soon come to understand mythology in the Barthesian sense of ideology rather than as Lewis Carroll fantasy. In any case, Michel Poiccard as subject must die for this pursuit of mythology. It was François Truffaut who said of Godard, "He seemed to have from the outset a sort of disdain for total fiction, he has always loved films in which the subject was destroyed ['le sujet était détruit']."[34] For Godard, the very sense of the word *sujet* was to change radically, becoming the fulcrum for his rejection of the mythology of *A bout de souffle*.

The subject of *Pierrot le fou* dies twice. In reprising his role in *A bout de souffle,* Jean-Paul Belmondo, Godard's erstwhile protagonist, ends up repeating his demise, and in this sense *Pierrot* can be read as a repetition of the earlier film. But between the 1959 filming of *A bout de souffle* and the 1965 appearance of *Pierrot,* it is the very notion of subject that has died. For all his speed, uncertainty, and violent death, Michel, as character, enjoys a nonproblematical status guaranteed him by the warmed-over American essentialism of the film. That status is assured, even if ironically, by the many cinematic and literary intertexts employed to frame his identity. Even when he is (unknowingly) rejecting Faulkner's insistence on the integrating power of memory, he conforms to the patterns and behavior of the small-time American gangster. Thus, as *subject* of the film's consciousness he retains a kind of naive integrity to the bitter end.

The Belmondo who enters the fictional world of *Pierrot le fou,* however, finds that world so fragmented that he is unable to sustain either his own sense of integrity as subject or ours. As in his earlier role, Belmondo moves rapidly through a French landscape, steals cars, and ends up betrayed by the woman he loves. It is not the plot that has changed but Godard's own taste for quotation. It is precisely because of the many anecdotal similarities between the two films that we can appreciate the system of intertextual substitutions Godard has effected in his later film. Just as Anna Karina has been introduced to take the place of the American Jean Seberg, Aragon, Balzac, and Céline constitute the new intertextual "ABC of the French cinema,"[35] marshaled to screen out the American *B* Cinema of *A bout de souffle.* With this advent of the specifically French comes the transformation of character psychology and overall philosophy that herald Godard's future work.

To mark the undoing of this "Americanness," Godard chose Lionel White's *Obsession* for "adaptation." The success of this "undoing" is superficially measured by the dismissal given the novel by the critics who notice it at all. Gilles Jacob calls Lionel White "an unimportant point of departure for the film," while Jean-Louis Curtis notes that if "Godard took his story from the detective novel by Lionel White, the plot is totally mixed-up, a cat couldn't find its kittens in it ['une chatte n'y retrouverait pas ses petits']."[36] Curtis's complaint is significant in its entirety:

> Moreover, Godard really doesn't bother telling the story. The genre presupposes a rigor and logic which are foreign to the director's mind.

> Godard lifts from the novel a few violent scenes that he scatters here
> and there like a modern painter might splatter paint on a canvas, with-
> out the least regard for meaning. It has none. . . . I only wonder why
> he chose this detective material which he could just as well have done
> without.[37]

For the second time, Godard is accused of a move that "has no meaning." The rationale for the inclusion of White's novel is highly significant, however, for it leads to an understanding of an intricate set of
intertextual allusions in the film.

White's novel involves a man who, like Pierrot-Ferdinand, suddenly leaves his wife and runs off with the babysitter. On their first
night together, she cold-bloodedly murders a bookie and then leads
the narrator into an increasingly shady involvement with her "brother," a Vegas hood, and a major Mafia figurehead. Thus, Godard's
couple's flight, the scissor-punctured body in their room, the scenes
of underworld involvement, torture, and betrayal, and numerous
allusions to Las Vegas all stem directly from White's plot. This time,
however, the American literary antecedent holds no integral recuperative power for Godard's hero. White's hero, Conrad Madden
(one who plays at being mad?), starts out a loser: a heavy drinker, out
of a job, hating his wife and his two television-addict teenagers. But
the entire novel is dedicated to the emergence of a coherence,
thoughtfulness, and toughness in Madden that he lacked at the outset. In short, it fits the same *Bildungsroman* topos that so many of the
"série noire" films do.

White insists on Madden's coherent attitude through a series of
tautological musings that risk insulting his reader's intelligence. For
example: "I realized from the beginning that the longer we were able
to avoid arrest, the better our chances were for continued freedom."[38]
To avoid arrest, Conrad decides that the best plan is to replicate as
entirely as possible his previous bourgeois existence, but under assumed names. For this, he transforms his seventeen-year-old companion, Allie, into a replica of bourgeois respectability (which eventually
drives her to violent behavior):

> I knew that I must play a sort of Pygmalion game with Allie and al-
> ready I had started on the first stages. Certain things of course would
> be impossible, at least in the beginning. I couldn't give Allie the dic-
> tion and the words and phrases to fit in with her new personality over-
> night. It would take time. But I did what I could. (O, 69)

"What I could" involves first of all telling her not to speak, relegating her to the time-"honored" place of women in American B-movies: beautiful and dumb, or as he prefers to phrase it, "aloof and dumb."[39] Next she must wear a hat and high heels, eat sweetbreads, and own a toy poodle named Gigi. "I thought you liked me the way I am," she protests (O, 69). In vain. The price of "freedom" for her is enforced imitation of the very world she most abhors.

Just how coherent Conrad Madden is becomes evident in the following admission:

> It would be very convenient for me to believe that during those months I spent with Allie, I was actually living in a state of moral and emotional suspension—a sort of period of amnesia in which I really didn't understand what I was doing or why I was doing it. But this is not true. I remembered everything and I knew full well exactly what I was doing. I even believe I understood why I was doing what I was doing. (O, 86)

Like Faulkner, White associates integrity and responsibility with memory, and like Faulkner's Wilbourne (the creature born of will), White's Madden seeks to assert these qualities in the midst of what otherwise might be a tempting anarchy. He naively explains this sense of responsibility in paternal terms:

> It may be that Allie's very childishness, her lack of sophistication, appealed to me, made me want to protect her, to take care of her. It had been completely different with Martha. . . . I was obsessed with her and I was positive our destinies lay together. (O, 88)

Authority and paternity, bolstered by memory, precision, integrity, and responsibility, are the essence of this tale—right up until the decision to murder Allie for betraying him one time too many. It is precisely because Godard followed White's plot without conforming the least bit to the moral qualities of his character that we can appreciate that these are precisely the terms that are undermined in Godard's "version" of *Obsession*. A series of other, now French texts are used repeatedly in *Pierrot le fou* to screen out Lionel White, giving Godard's version an entirely different epistemological topos.

The first of these allusions confronts us visually before the first words of Ferdinand's monologue have time to sink in: during the opening credits, Godard places what look like random, and randomly colored, letters on the screen. For a long time this nonsensical alphabet remains puzzling, but gradually it seems to take on meaning as enough of the film's title and names of the actors are filled in. It is during this confusion that Belmondo reads the first sentence of Elie Faure's text on Velasquez: "Velasquez, after the age of fifty, never again painted sharply defined things ['ne peignait plus jamais une chose définie']."[40] In the first realistic images of the film an unidentified couple plays tennis as Ferdinand quotes, "He wandered around the objects with the air and the twilight ['Il errait autour des objets avec l'air et le crépuscule'], in the shadow and transparence of the backgrounds ['dans l'ombre et la transparence des fonds'] he surprised the colored palpitations ['des palpitations colorées'] . . . ," a text which begins to take on the role of the Godardian aesthetic defining the creation of the universe we are about to enter: a world without coherence, made of shadow and transparence, in which the image maker can only wander about among the colored palpitations in search of his subject.

At this point the image shifts, locating Ferdinand outside a bookstore called Le Meilleur des Mondes, obviously an allusion to Voltaire's *Candide,* one of the first works of the French Enlightenment to challenge the predominant Anglo-Saxon view of the world as a coherent system, made in the image of God. To accompany this literary allusion to skepticism, Ferdinand's voice-off continues his reading from Elie Faure's study of Velasquez: ". . . which he used as the invisible center of his silent symphony ['sa symphonie silencieuse']. He was no longer taking from the world anything more than the mysterious exchanges which cause forms and tones to interpenetrate one another in a secret and continuous progression ['les échanges mystérieux, qui font pénétrer les uns dans les autres les formes et les tons, par un progrès secret et continu']." Another abrupt shift of scene produces a vague nightscape, too obscure to decipher clearly, scanned by the words,

> whose course is not manifested or interrupted by any clash or any shock. . . . Space reigns ["L'espace règne"]. An aerial wave seems to glide over the surfaces, impregnating itself with the visible emanations in order to define and model them, and to carry away everywhere else a kind of perfume, a kind of echo of them which it disperses over all surrounding space as an imponderable dust ["poussière impondérable"].[41]

Only now does Godard's camera fix on Belmondo: he is sitting in his bathtub, reading to his little girl:

> The world where he lived was sad. A decadent king, sickly princes, idiots, dwarfs, invalids, certain monstrous jesters dressed like lords whose function it was to laugh at themselves and make others outside the law of life ["hors la loi vivante"], all bound up in etiquette, plots, and lies . . . the silence.[42]

We are about to enter into a similar world: the soirée to which Ferdinand's wife drags him corresponds only too directly to this sense of dispersal of the Spanish court. Ferdinand pauses to ask his daughter if she likes Faure's prose but hears "You're mad to read the children things like that!" from his wife (Grazielle Galvani). Mad indeed! More than his children's comprehension is threatened. As Ferdinand ends his reading with "A spirit of nostalgia floats in the air, one sees neither the ugliness nor the sadness nor the funereal and cruel direction given to that crushed childhood,"[43] the concreteness and precision of Lionel White's view of the world are dispersed like some imponderable dust, and not only by this reference to Velasquez. The French art historian Elie Faure's vision of painting in the Spanish golden age has a curiously modern, even postmodern, ring when inserted into Godard's montage. Godard heightens this sense of dispersal in the very title of the work and the resultant confusion of names that immediately assaults the viewer. That confusion increases, as does the character of Ferdinand-Pierrot, and so too the *sujet du film,* with every additional quotation woven into the film by its author.

The second of these is not long in coming. Although confronted with the threat of meeting the managing director of Standard Oil and spouting publicity slogans all evening with other like-minded Parisian *banlieusards,* Ferdinand is suddenly as if transformed the second he encounters the babysitter, Odile (Anna Karina). When Frank gives the phone number of their hosts for the evening as 225-70-01, Ferdinand playfully quips, "225—you can't say Balzac? You don't know Balzac? Read *César Birotteau*—and the three chords of the Fifth Symphony which thundered in his poor head."[44] *César Birotteau* is a queer choice, since it is one of the least read of Balzac's novels, but it is hardly an uncalculated choice by Godard. It is in some ways the least subversive of any of Balzac's works: composed almost as a Greek tragedy, complete with tragic hero (a perfume merchant!), hybris (Birotteau's lack of financial restraint), and tragic apotheosis (Birotteau's complete exoneration after quietly sacrificing everything to pay back all his creditors even though the laws of bankruptcy do not require such a step). It is, in short, a paean to the honesty of the rising French merchant class and to the emerging genius of that class, the *publicitaire* Gaudissart, an early avatar of the Madison Avenue fast-tracker. Indeed, Balzac's narrative is twice interrupted to collage two facsimiles of advertisements, one for Birotteau's "Superfine Pâte des Sultanes and Carminative Toilet Lotion," and a second for Popinot's "Cephalic Oil." Their position in Balzac's novel is exactly rendered by the series of publicity sound-bites emitted by Godard's partygoers:

> An Alfa-Romeo does the first kilometre from start in 34 seconds— fantastic braking power—four discs, marvelously comfortable, and, of course, what road holding! . . .

> Keeping fresh is easy. Lava soap, Eau de Cologne, scented perfume. To avoid all smell of perspiration I use Printil after washing and I'm absolutely perfect for the rest of the day. Printil comes in an atomiser, so fresh; or spray, stick or bottle.
> (PF, 27)

This latter discourse might well (barring its anachronisms) have been borrowed directly from Balzac's "Improved patents" ("Brevets d'invention et de perfectionnement")[45] and positions Ferdinand in diametric opposition to Birotteau's world of bourgeois integrity and optimism. In such a position, he imitates Birotteau's nemesis, Ferdinand du Tillet. Balzac's Ferdinand is, like his other diabolical creature, Vautrin, a master of duplicity, posing as Birotteau's friend and last resort while all the time planning his financial ruin. He is the evil genius who turns bourgeois capitalism on its ear and exploits the entire system for his own (unspecified) ends. He is not only duplicitous, he possesses a "double signature, one . . . a dead letter, the other living ['l'une morte, l'autre vivante']" (CB, 219/503–4), and sets in motion doubles of himself to carry out his schemes (CB, 268/538). Du Tillet's motto might well be, "It is better to be a criminal than a fool ['Il vaut mieux être criminel que sot']" (CB, 170/464). It would certainly be Ferdinand's in *Pierrot le fou.* Just as César Birotteau's great ball is the height of such *sottise,* so is the party that opens Godard's film. *His* Ferdinand exits protesting, "I'm worn out. I've a mechanism for seeing, called eyes, for listening, called ears, for speaking, called a mouth. I've got a feeling they're all going their separate ways. . . . There's no co-ordination. One should feel they're united. I feel they are deranged" (PF, 33, 34). Ferdinand's sense of fragmentation is a direct reaction to the social imbecility surrounding him just as his Balzacian namesake's is. Godard's particular genius here is to have set in motion a French literary subtext for Ferdinand that runs directly counter to the Lionel White novel on which the film is presumably based. That Godard finds elements of character dispersion and fragmentation in such canonical French texts as Faure and Balzac bodes ill for the coherence of his protagonist.

As they leave in Frank's big American sedan, Belmondo and Karina reveal that they have already met (though this is not the case in Lionel White's novel):

> MARIANNE: It's rather funny meeting each other again isn't it!
> FERDINAND: It must be four years.
> MARIANNE: No, five and a half. It was October.
> (PF, 35)

Marianne Renoir's correction places the date of their first meeting at *exactly* the time *A bout de souffle* was being filmed (October 1959). Her name, of course, constitutes a highly ironic allusion both to the woman who symbolizes the French nation and to the Renoir painting so admired and mirrored by Jean Seberg in the earlier film. Thus, on the one hand, they have outdone *A bout de souffle*'s meta-cinematic tendencies, for if Seberg apes Belmondo aping Bogart, the reference remains but an *allusion,* whereas Ferdinand and Marianne can locate their past *only* in previous films and thus function at the level of pure *illusion.* Moreover, in taking over the role of female protagonist, Anna Karina has effectively inserted her Frenchness in the place of Jean Seberg's Americanness in Godard's (and our) cinematic memory. To mark Jean Seberg's displacement, Godard introduces late in *Pierrot le fou* a reprise of this theme. In a movie theater, Jean-Paul Belmondo and Anna Karina now watch Jean Seberg with her inimitably American accent. We expect to see a scene from *A bout de souffle,* but instead she is collaged from Godard's short film *Le Grand Escroc,* and Belmondo holds up the Elie Faure text again, as if it were a sort of talisman brandished in order to blot her out via the new thematics and epistemology of *Pierrot le fou.* To complete the usurpation, she and Ferdinand paraphrase a conversation between Michel and Patricia during which she reproaches him for not being able to understand her. In *A bout de souffle* we remember the scene as follows:

> MICHEL: Me, I love you, and not like you believe.
> PATRICIA: How?
> MICHEL: Not like you believe.
> PATRICIA: You don't know what I believe.
> MICHEL: Yes, I do.

PATRICIA: You don't know what I think.

MICHEL: Yes, I do.

PATRICIA: No, it's impossible. I want to know what's behind your face. I've watched it for ten minutes and I see nothing . . . nothing . . . nothing! I'm not sad, but I'm afraid.

MICHEL: Sweet, gentle Patricia.

PATRICIA: Oh, no.

MICHEL: All right. Cruel, stupid . . . heartless, pitiful, cowardly, hateful . . .

PATRICIA: Yes, yes.

   (B, 86)

In *Pierrot le fou* that scene is reprised:

FERDINAND: Why do you look unhappy?

MARIANNE: Because you talk to me with words and I look at you with feelings.

FERDINAND: It's impossible to have a serious conversation with you. You never have ideas. Always feelings.

MARIANNE: But that's not true! There are ideas in feelings.

FERDINAND: Good. We will try to have a serious conversation. You are going to tell me what you love, what you desire . . . and then I'll do the same. Okay then, you start.

MARIANNE: Flowers . . . animals . . . the blue of the sky . . . music . . . I don't really know . . . everything . . . and you?

FERDINAND: Ambition . . . hope . . . the movement of things . . . accidents . . . and what else? I don't know . . . everything.

MARIANNE: You see *I was right five years ago.* We will never understand each other. What am I to do? . . . I don't know what to do. What can I do? . . . I don't know what to do. . . . What am I to do? I don't know what to do . . .

FERDINAND *(in diary):* Saturday . . . eroticism . . . it is possible to . . . approbation of life . . . death *(he crosses this word out)* . . . Sunday she opened the . . . and afterwards . . . Monday . . . very . . . I read very much. . . .

   (PF, 62–63, italics mine)

Marianne's repetition of the allusion to "five years ago" again effects a collage of this scene over the previous one. Although the two scenes have a similar feeling, the differences are radical: whereas Patricia wants to move behind Michel's expression, to understand his essence—she believes enough in this essence to be writing a novel—Marianne sees that they "will never understand each other," and Ferdinand agrees that now communication is "impossible." This realization leads immediately to a breakdown of the coherence of both characters' observations into a series of disconnected fragments. Thus Ferdinand notes, "In the end that is what it's all about. . . . You are waiting for me . . . I'm not there . . . I arrive . . . I come into the room. . . . I no longer really exist for you from that moment . . . whereas before I was alive . . . I was thinking . . . I was suffering perhaps" (PF, 62). This allusion to previous suffering harks back to Patricia's reading of Faulkner in *A bout de souffle*.

In pasting the present scene over the previous one, Marianne parallels Godard's decision to obliterate the quotation from Faulkner's *The Wild Palms* behind readings of, among other titles, Céline's *Voyage au bout de la nuit* and *Guignol's Band* (see plate 28):

> And then . . . I know nothing any more. . . . I go forward . . . inch by inch on my hands . . . and I dare . . . towards the right . . . I touch . . . I lightly stroke the hair of a fairy . . . of the wonderful, adored . . . Virginia! . . . Sublime happiness! Ah! . . . I found myself in an ecstasy so intense that I dared no longer move. Happy to the point of tears, numbed by happiness I am quivering . . . quivering. . . . How my heart is swelling, burning me. Unavoidably I burst into flames. I am in space . . . I cling to Virginia.
>
> You promised me China, Tibet, Mr. Sosthene . . . the island of Sonde, and magic exotic plants.[46]

As Marianne says when they first begin their adventure together, "What makes me sad is that life in novels is so very different. I'd like it to be the same, clear, logical, formal. But it's not like that at all" (PF, 36). And Ferdinand will write in his diary, "The language of poetry rises from the ruins" (PF, 59). The allusion to Céline follows directly on this poetic assertion, and for cause. In Céline's work, and in particular in *Guignol's Band,* the customary language and coherence of the traditional novel consistently break down into asyntagmatic bursts of poetry each time Ferdinand confronts violence or emotion of any kind. Thus, for example, when Boro begins to play the piano, Ferdinand's language goes haywire:

> it has to keep going! that's the big secret, never slow up never stop! perks you up with a trill . . . nicks you! . . . tinkles right into your worries . . . plays tricks with time, tickles your trouble, teases, pleases and tinkles your worries, and tum! tum! whirls you round . . . just a plugging . . . sleight of hand! . . . beat it, cheapjack! . . . Run-ti-ti-tum!

210

PLATE 28.   Ferdinand (Jean-Paul Belmondo) reads from Céline's *Guignol's Band* to Marianne (Anna Karina) in Godard's *Pierrot le fou.* (Courtesy of the Museum of Modern Art Film Stills Archive.)

il faut que ça tourne! . . . c'est le grand secret . . . jamais de ralenti jamais de cesse! d'un trille te la bouscule . . . sursaute! . . . encore un trille . . . frais mutin l'air anglais dévale . . . rigodon grêle! pédale tonne . . . jamais ne dédit . . . ne soupire . . . pose . . . pas autre chose à dire . . . et file et file . . . bouzille au fa . . . requinque. . . barre à bout de dièzes . . . riguedondonne!
(GB, 143/186)

Most of these passages could be rearranged on the page to assume their poetic function without any appreciable change in referentiality. Thus Céline moves constantly back and forth between the normal referential function of language (assumed to be at work in the realist novel) and a purely poetic function, just as Godard does in *Pierrot le fou* by increasing the fragmentation of his film. The effect on the narration and sense of character is devastating. The entire novel, awash in this poetic slang, meanders between exhibitions of extreme violence (brawls in bars, doped-out orgies that end in senseless murder, bloody fights between prostitutes) and brief respites in flight. No discernible direction nor development allows the reader any "comfort," nor does the narrator provide any useful commentary on these events other than the utterly trivial or cynical, such as "There goes another riot . . . " ("Voilà encore une autre salade . . . ") (GB, 188/248). Céline anticipated, in his epilogue, the public outcry against *Guignol's Band:*

> The pig! Ah! things are bad! . . . Unreadable! Sex-maniac! Damned loafer! Crook! . . . I don't understand it at all! It's terrible! impossible! It's not even a book! Neither head nor tail!

> Saligot! Ah! que ça va mal! . . . Pas lisible! Satyre! Jean-foutre! Escroc! . . . j'y comprends rien du tout! ah! mais c'est terrible! pas possible! C'est même pas un livre! . . . Ni queue ni tête!
> (GB, 1–2/380)

The reaction of Céline's fantasized critic ends up sounding remarkably like Jean-Louis Curtis's objections to Godard's use of Lionel White: "Un chat n'y retrouverait pas ses petits."[47]

Mirroring Céline's movement from a "prosaic" or linear structure to a "poetic," largely interchangeable one, Godard's cinematic narration becomes increasingly incoherent. In the Paris apartment to which Ferdinand and Marianne first flee, a never-to-be-explained body lies casually by, a pair of scissors embedded in its neck.[48] Using a Brechtian distanciation technique, Godard has Karina sing her way lightheartedly through a most pessimistic song about "love with no tomorrow" ("amour sans lendemain").[49] During their conversation in the apartment, the camera moves from a traditional shot-countershot grammar to focus on a Picasso portrait of a boy as Karina speaks, opposed by a pop-art figure of a woman as Belmondo's voice is heard. The destruction of normal cinematic cues has only begun, however. The next victim of Godard's meta-cinematic hijinks is the traditional authority of the voice-off narrator. In this scene, Godard has Belmondo and Karina articulate the voice-off narration, alternating every other word. Then images begin to be repeated, but not quite, suggesting not only that visual linearity has been forsaken but also that visual reliability has been compromised. It is as if the camera is trying to "get it right" by repeating their flight from this apartment in a variety of slightly different takes. Accompanying these flawed repetitions, the voice-off breaks down, repeating "Le lendemain" no less than four times. The spectator can only conclude that the film's narrative authority has collapsed or that time has sped up to create four tomorrows in rapid succession—in either case a serious destruction of linear credibility. This collapse of voice-off authority will recur at several other points in the film. Meanwhile, chronology and narrative authority, mirroring the breakdown of character, have been entirely compromised.

To further undo any semblance of narrative linearity, Godard both introduces and undermines the Brechtian technique of narrative signposts. Frequently, in their own film, Belmondo and Karina introduce chapters, usually with titles. But chapter 2 is followed by chapter 8, and chapter 8 is repeated and followed by chapter 7. It clearly no longer matters what the specific order of events is.

If unity of action is important to the detective novel, or *polard,* Godard constantly breaks down that unity by introducing, among other things, a series of interviews into the film, unrelated to any narrative development. In *A bout de souffle* Seberg played a journalism student and her interview of Parvulesco fit the narrative purpose of the film. In *Pierrot le fou* no justification can be found for the series of interviews given by Godard himself (rather than one of his characters), which includes Lazlo (from *A bout de souffle*) and another person who tells us that he is currently "un figurant de cinéma"—in *this* film, of course. At another moment an unidentified man approaches Belmondo in a café, reminds him that he (Belmondo) had borrowed a hundred thousand francs from him and slept with his wife, then agreeably bids him good day and exits.

Other traditional elements of film grammar are (un)systematically broken. Continuity is one of the first to go. Running through the French countryside, Anna Karina disappears from one frame wearing a white, rather formal dress and appears in the next inexplicably clothed in drab fatigues and army cap. The sound continuity is also constantly disrupted. Godard frequently adds extra-diegetic music but just as frequently interrupts it and then begins it anew, as if some accident *within* the film's diegesis had jarred the phonograph needle *outside* that topos. In a visual joke late in the film we see Belmondo and Karina in a sailboat accompanied by what appears to be extra-diegetic sound—and then we perceive a phonograph practically immersed by the spray from the bow. Size continuity is also to be distorted in a sequence in which Karina thrusts a pair of scissors at the camera and her arm appears entirely out of proportion to other elements in our view. In general, both sound and lighting are misused. Frequently the actors move into shaded areas and we lose the image of faces or bodies. Motors often drown out dialogue, and the voices on the walkie-talkies are so distorted as to be parodic.

All of this grammatical aporia, of course, reinforces the general breakdown of the coherence of the character subjects in the film. At numerous points in the film Marianne calls her companion Pierrot, and each time he responds, "My name is Ferdinand!" On the first occasion, she argues, "Ok, but one simply can't say, 'Mon ami Ferdinand'" (PF, 36–37). After a while, it no longer matters whether Marianne calls him Pierrot or Ferdinand, for his completely fragmented identity seems in either case to derive from literary models of fragmentation or pointlessness. Whether she refers to Céline's Ferdinand or Queneau's *Pierrot mon ami*,[50] the fruit of the allusion is largely the same: a bitter lemon. Queneau's character provides a model who is "lunaire":

> Pierrot was thinking . . . singularly about nothing in particular; there was nothing in his mind but a light and almost luminous mental cloud, like the fog on a beautiful winter's morning or a swarm of anonymous gnats ["une buée mentale, légère et presque lumineuse comme le brouillard d'un beau matin d'hiver, qu'un vol de moucherons anonymes"]. He had no unusual ideas about public morality or the future of civilization. No one had ever told him he was intelligent. He had been told instead that he behaved like an idiot and was a bit luney. In any case, here he was vaguely happy and content. (PMA, 22)

Pierrot's mind bears an uncanny resemblance to the allusions to Velasquez's later style that introduce Godard's film. In keeping with the directionlessness of his "protagonist," Queneau leads his reader through a series of episodes that seem always to verge on novelistic and romantic expectations but never to lead either to love, money, or closure. Pierrot loves a girl who recalls "quelques apparitions cinématographiques" (PMA, 76): "Quand je vous regarde," he tells Yvonne, "je me crois au cinéma" (PMA, 89). But he might as well be at the movies. None of his projects materializes, nor does he seem to care. In a novel full enough of coincidences to stock a surrealist magazine, Pierrot remains paradoxically the focus of the narration yet somehow always marginal. As Pierrot attempts to sum up his life, the narrator notes,

> When he thought about it with all the attention he could muster (a thing that rarely happened), he saw clearly how all the elements that made up his life could have been brought together into an adventure

that might have been worked into a murder mystery climaxing in a kind of algebraic problem with as many equations as unknowns and how none of this had worked out—he saw the novel it might have made . . . and the novel it *had* made . . . totally devoid of any of the pleasures that an activity of this kind normally brings ["il voyait le roman que cela aurait pu faire . . . et le roman que cela avait fait . . . parfaitement dégarni de tous les plaisirs que provoque le spectacle d'une activité de cet ordre"]. (PMA, 210–11)

When one of the other characters says to him, "But all of these silly stories probably don't interest you and you're very nice . . . to have listened so long to the ramblings of a jerk ['les bafouillages d'un couillonné']," we might well assume that Queneau is addressing *us*. An apt model for Godard's Pierrot, these "bafouillages d'un couillonné" pertinently lead nowhere, only to the sense that a more traditional and linear novel (film) *might have* been made of them. *Pierrot le fou* operates constantly at the level of a *potential* story, denied direction, development, and any real dénouement by the fragmentation at the root of the main characters.

When Godard's Ferdinand Griffon (whose name means "scribble") writes in his "journal," "We have entered the age of the Double-Man, one no longer needs a mirror to speak to oneself," he is quoting from Aragon's *La Mise à mort,* another major intertext of the film, one that entertains a particularly complex relationship to *Pierrot le fou.*[51] Although Godard quotes from Aragon's text, it is almost as though Aragon were quoting from *Pierrot,* putting a circular, almost specular spin on the notion of quotation!

Like Queneau's Pierrot (and, of course, Godard's), the narrator of *La Mise à mort* is constantly in search of a style and a story:

> You never have the idea of plagiarizing Gallimard, especially here, where all the elements are in place—the theme, the tone, the details—I could always claim that I hadn't read the book, who would believe me? It would only be more Balzac, youth, Balzacian youth! but a detective novel, especially me, I ask you again, who would believe it? And yet I swear to you that I haven't read it, or if I had, it was distractedly, as always, and I missed that particular passage. I was thinking about something more serious, about how I might make a commercial success out of my crime, make a film starring Belmondo . . . (MM, 388)

Clearly "crime" and "film avec Belmondo" focus the literary aspirations of Aragon's text on an undoing of everything that has traditionally held the realist novel together. His methods of composition feel very familiar to viewers of *Pierrot le fou:*

> If I put two and two together, if I backtrack, if I approach, inside out or right side in, I compose, oppose, chose, give up, reject, look around me, there are pieces missing, they don't get along, don't stick, don't fit, get stuck, overlap, bump about, I can't do it, I just can't do it.

> Si je mets un avec deux, si je reviens en arrière, si je rapproche, à l'envers, à l'endroit, je compose, j'oppose, je choisis, je renonce, rejette, regarde autour de moi, les morceaux, il en manque, ils ne bichent pas, collent mal, se calent, coincent, chevauchent, chahutent, je n'arrive pas, je n'arrive positivement pas.

> (MM, 346)

Elsewhere, Aragon's narrator (whose very existence is threatened by his own creations) writes anxiously, "Being is explained by its undoing" ("L'être est expliqué par comment il se défait") (MM, 137). Undoing is indeed the manner of (de)construction of this text composed in "the age of mirrors." The narrator, Antoine, differentiates himself from *his* narrator, Anthoine, who is often confused with Alfred—or Ferdinand (MM, 129) or Pierre (MM, 283) or Fernande, whose face is "red and white striped" (MM, 364, 366), and finally with intertextuality itself: "I am at once Iago, Vivien, Wilhelm Meister, Tchitchikov, Lancelot, myself, Julien Sorel, Dr. Jekyll, Petchorine, Gil Blas, Tom Jones, Prince Mychkine, Jehan de Saintré, Heathcliff, or whoever you want, the authentic facts appear to grow out of my madness" (MM, 230). The narrator finds it both difficult and frankly inevitable to "base a novel on an already written novel and characters on already imagined portraits ['bâtir un roman sur un roman déjà fait, des personnages sur le portrait déjà fait d'êtres imaginaires']" (MM, 335) and laments that having once begun to write, he is "innocently caught up in a game from which there is no escape . . . a crime" (MM, 398). We cannot help hearing Godard's voice here, defending the "pleasures" of quotation and anticipating the "crime" of killing off his protagonist.

All of these Ferdinands (Aragon's, Balzac's, Céline's) come to form the composite of yet another, whose work founds, if not their individual *literary* characteristics, then certainly the "positivement pas" of their individuation. Like his Swiss compatriot's, Ferdinand de Saussure's work anticipated Godard's narrative deconstruction at the level of language itself. It was Saussure, we remember, who ungrounded the linguistic sign from concrete reality, placing it in the circulation of "a concept and a sound-image."[52] Because of this move, Saussure saw the signifier as "unmotivated, i.e. arbitrary in that it actually has no natural connection with the signified" (CGL, 69). Based wholly on convention rather than teleology, arbitrary signs "realize better than the others the ideal of the semiological process; that is why language, the most complex and universal of all systems of expression, is also the most characteristic; in this sense linguistics can become the master-pattern for all branches of semiology" (CGL, 68). When Aragon writes, "Je n'arrive pas, je n'arrive *positivement* pas," he is bemoaning the fact that the elements necessary for the composition of his book, that is, signifiers, are merely

> independent terms in which the value of each term results solely from the simultaneous presence of the others . . . in which concepts are purely differential and defined not by their *positive* content but nega-tively by their relations with the other terms of the system. Their most precise characteristic is in being what the others are not. . . . [They] are characterized not, as one might think, by their own *positive* quality but simply by the fact that they are distinct. [They] are above all else opposing, relative and negative entities . . . in language there are only differences *without positive terms.* (CGL, 116–17, 119, 120, italics mine)

As "signifiers," the characters themselves become merely relative con-cepts in a larger system and so lose any *essential* value, retaining merely the negative value of who and what they are not. Thus, two characters with relatively little functional difference (e.g., narrator and protago-nist) encounter a degree of anxiety in Aragon's text that is entirely symptomatic. Just as in Saussure's system, where differences between signifiers may be minimal, Aragon's narrator manages only the slightest differentiation (an *h*—possibly suggesting the French for *axe*) between himself and his character: Antoine and Anthoine. The resultant sense of doubling leads to a loss of image: "Je devais sortir à ce point moi-même *un autre* que je ne me voie plus dans les miroirs" (MM, 18). For Céline and Queneau, characters become mere ciphers in a circulation of signs that does not valorize them in any a priori way. Godard's Ferdinand, merely the composite of so many intertextual others, may just as well be Pierrot. He may protest, "My name is Ferdinand!" but to no avail. In Aragon's "age of mirrors" the sense of self as always already Other is overwhelming.

Aragon's insistence, in the context of mirrors, on Gallicizing the name of Iago in Shakespeare's *Othello* to Jacques suggests, of course, the Jacques of mirrors (the Jacques of all "trades"), Jacques Lacan, the French Freud. "I will never cross the false mirror, which is only the screen between myself placed over there, where you are really what's happening ['Jamais je ne traverserai le faux miroir qui n'est que l'écran entre moi mis et là-bas où tu es vraiment ce qui se passe']," moans Aragon's narrator. "We are like the others, double beings ['Nous sommes comme les autres des êtres doubles']," writes Aragon's Ferdinand-Pierre (MM, 131, 85), in a gesture whose plagiarism doubly inscribes his own doubleness and recalls Lacan's *Stade du miroir*.[53] Whereas in *A bout de souffle* Michel can occasionally employ an alias (Lazlo) in pursuit of his project, the Godard of *Pierrot le fou* recognizes that Ferdinand-Pierrot is unassimilable to any single project. In moving from the American to the French mode, Godard recapitulates a process described by Jeffrey Mehlman in "French Freud":

> the establishment of a series of diacritical differences in meaning [between the Anglo-American and the French schools of psychoanalysis] operative within a number of crucial Freudian terms, and the delineation of the logic according to which those distinctions are (or are not) respected by Freud. . . . Suffice it for us to note that the prevailing *discontinuity*—cutting across such terms as ego, auto-eroticism . . . and the terms translated indifferently in English as instinct or drive—is between, on the one hand, a version of each notion suited to a biological, genetic, adaptive, or functional scheme, and, on the other, one which finds its place in the context of an articulation of the specific modes of *negativity* (censorship, repetition, displacement) of a transmissible unconscious structure. It is *a discontinuity then between the metaphorics of continuity . . . and one of discontinuity*.[54]

Pierrot le fou marks just such a step toward Gallic discontinuity in Godard's work. If *A bout de souffle* is nervous, jumpy, and uneven in style, its style itself is an "adaptive or functional scheme [in service of] a metaphorics of continuity" of portraiture. *Pierrot le fou*'s style may, at first glance, appear to be but an extension of Godard's earlier stylistic radicalism. Careful analysis has revealed that style no longer supports character development but itself fragments along with character and narrative coherence. We can no longer distinguish a "nuclear self" but are confronted by its replacement: "a *moi* that, paradoxically seeks the meaning of its own alienation through others' (ego ideals) and in language . . . forced to verify itself through others, despite the Real flux and instability of human response amid changing patterns of identifications and events. . . . The subject of reality reconstruction or subjective perception—the *moi*—is elusive, kaleidoscopic and evanescent."[55] If the "pieces" of the earlier film resemble the pieces of a puzzle, they can nevertheless easily be assembled into a coherent picture. The jigsaw of *Pierrot le fou,* as we have seen, simply cannot be reassembled into any coherent picture. Just as certain sequences, such as the flight from Marianne's apartment, are repeated in such a way as to defy any chronological definition, so Ferdinand's character defies development.[56] His journal does not "chart," it merely reflects the collage of fragments that surround him and enter helter-skelter his "mind." Stealing automobiles no longer feels like an adventure with a denouement, but simply a detour. But *ça ne vaut pas le détour.* It no longer really matters where the two actors go, since their fragmentation is total wherever they happen to be.

From the outset, Ferdinand laments his lack of unity and his sense of being "plusieurs." This splintering of the subject's unity recurs in many different forms in *Pierrot le fou.* For example, as Ferdinand and Marianne first drive away together, Godard uses the reflection of passing street lamps to suggest dispersion of pieces of themselves— Marianne gives the impression of erupting pieces of light out to the left, and Ferdinand off to the right, in a visually centrifugal sequence. Along with these pieces seems to go any connection between *intentionality* and *action.* Although Marianne says, "I'll put my hand on your knee . . . I'll kiss you all over" (PF, 37), she remains immobile. Ferdinand imitates both her statements of intention and her immobility. She repeats this failure to achieve unity later in the film when Ferdinand says, "You'll never leave me?" ("Tu ne me quitteras jamais?") and she answers, "Non. Oui" (PF, 61).[57]

When they agree to have a serious discussion and each enumerates the things he or she likes, their categories are mutually exclusive (as has often been noted), but each ends the list with "tout" (PF, 63). Although *everything* normally resumes and includes all categories, its meaning seeps away, paradoxically impoverished here: his "tout" and hers are clearly *not* in the same set. Soon he complains that he doesn't know what she means when she says, "Il fait beau." He ends up pronouncing oxymoronic statements, such as "I believe you, liar" ("Je te crois, menteuse") (PF, 90), and she ends up by giving up altogether on the signifying possibilities of language: "In the end words often mean the opposite to what they are supposed to mean. We say 'evident' about things which aren't evident at all" (PF, 99).

Neither can say what he or she means because neither knows how to mean what he or she says. Without a coherent sense of self, the world will never appear as a coherent or meaningful universe. Near the end of the film, we encounter the sad "musician" Devos (whose name suggests the Lacanian incorporation of the Other [*Je suis de vous* or *Je suis deux, vous*]), who simply cannot make others hear the music he believes he hears. He shouts to the departing Ferdinand, "You haven't understood a thing!" (PF, 102), an accusation that Godard and Ferdinand direct to us as spectators. When Ferdinand makes his last attempt to communicate with another being, he calls Paris but says, "C'est de la part de personne." By now he is no *one*. "What I wanted to tell you ['Ce que je voulais dire']," he begins as he ties the brightly colored dynamite to his head, but "he" cannot *want to mean* anything since "he" as subject is now thoroughly problematized. The word "dynamite" is visually reduced by the camera to a verb without subject—"am"—in our final view before the explosion obliterates this shimmering, highly unstable "meaning" of the verb "to be."

In an ironic reprise of his former cinematic aspirations, Godard had brought a "blind" Sam Fuller to his Parisian soirée in *Pierrot le fou.* Fuller's (American) definition of movies is: "A battleground. Love. Hate. Action. Violence. Death. In one word . . . Emotion." Godard may have shown us battlegrounds of love, hate, violence, and death in *Pierrot le fou,* but his film is singularly devoid of emotion, for there is no longer any real subject to emote or sympathize with. Instead, Godard's version of cinema begins, "We are made of dreams and dreams are made of us" ("Nous sommes faits de rêves et des rêves sont faits de nous"). All is fragmentation, breakdown of order, logic, linear time, and discourse into what Ferdinand calls "un mystère jamais résolu." "We are carefully looking for that moment when one abandons fictional character in order to discover the true one . . . if such a thing exists" (PF, 83). Ferdinand will announce, "I want to say at this precise moment before it's already in the past . . . I don't know. . . . The only thing I want is for time to stop. . . . I am only a huge question mark poised over the Mediterranean horizon" (PF, 90, 92). Michel may be shot by the Paris "flics" because he can no longer manage Patricia's trials, but Pierrot simply calls it quits because the film has run out. Or does he? Even in his final gesture he is "of two minds"—and soon to be of many more! In screening out the coherence of Faulkner and American *films noirs* behind Aragon, Balzac, and Céline, Godard has indeed effected a sea (transatlantic) change. The American Lionel White has ended up in *Pierrot le fou* on the moon trying (like *César Birotteau*'s Gaudissard, or the guests at Frank's party) to force Coca-cola down the throat of the man in the moon,[58] while Ferdinand copes with the disintegration of his character and his story, which progressively threatens coherence in the same way that Céline's anarchy increasingly usurps White's sense of paternal responsibility. Ultimately, the differences are much more than issues of nationalism: they are profound questions of epistemology ending in the metaphorics of radical discontinuity.

Conclusion

The Library as Psychic Labyrinth

> The frontiers of a book are never clear-cut . . . it is a
> node within a network.
> —*Michel Foucault*

As Godard's aesthetics of radical discontinuity once again illustrate, French new wave filmmakers embarked after 1958 on a new current, in ways entirely separate from each other yet surprisingly coherent. In striking out toward the unknown and against all traditions, these cineastes encountered the ultimate paradox of cinema and of being French. For however radical the notion of discontinuity may appear, it is *the* radical of cinema as well as of the Lacanian problematics of identity underlying so much of their work. Indeed, it is the genius of these artists to have linked these two domains. Just as the invention of art cinema lay in the discovery of the *intermittent* display of rapidly moving but disconnected images, and in the idea of *découpage*, so too does the ontology of the Lacanian *moi* lie in *émiettement* and alterity. And in that certain *je ne suis quoi* that is Frenchness, each has affirmed the deeper, often hidden connections between these two ontologies of discontinuity.

In *L'Année dernière à Marienbad*, for example, we discovered "a case of multiple motivations, in which a deeper motive comes into view behind the more superficial one." And as Freud goes on to explain, "Laws of poetic economy necessitate this way of presenting the situation; for this deeper motive could not be explicitly enunci-ated. It had to remain concealed, kept from easy perception of the spectator or reader; otherwise *serious resistances* . . . would have arisen

222

which might have imperilled the effect of the drama." However deeply hidden such a repressed element may be, Freud reminds us further that once activated, it cannot remain hidden, and "comes into view behind the more superficial motivation."[1]

It has been my contention throughout this study that such deeper motives are often brought into view via the screening of texts and/or references to literary texts. In many cases these texts have served as screens that simultaneously hide and reveal "multiple motivations," revealing libidinous elements such as repressed sexual and/or violent desires or tendencies otherwise hidden from explicit expression. Of course, these elements are what one would *expect* to find hidden in unconscious structures. And yet, another look at *Marienbad* would reveal that just beneath the "surface" of the entire film lies, like a palimpsest, Resnais's earlier short documentary *Toute la mémoire du monde*. Behind the images proffered, in other words, lie *other words*— an entire library of them. If Resnais's camera proceeds along labyrinths of corridors, searching out "answers" to the questions of identity and memory posed by *Marienbad*'s characters, it is merely retracing its "steps" of another year in another castle: France's Bibliothèque Nationale. In that earlier film the camera travels throughout the library, moving from the airy spaciousness of public rooms down into the suffocating "libido" of the Enfer. Thus, one of the elements screened in the later version of this film is revealed to be literature itself. No wonder, then, that *Marienbad* "hides" its "secret" in an intertextual configuration!

My analysis of each of these filmmakers, from Bresson to Truffaut, has brought to light much the same configuration, the "under"-riding and "under"-weaning involvement with "ma mère Littérature." Nowhere is this clearer, perhaps, than in Godard's reworking of his intertexts, substituting a more mature, Gallicized alphabet for the naively idealized American one of his earliest fascination with the movies. And yet, even where this Franco-American difference is not apparent *within* the problematics (and intertextuality) of the films analyzed here, it emerges from a comparison with American cousins. *Marienbad* offers yet again the case in point. If *Last Year at Marienbad* ends ambiguously in 1961, Hitchcock the next year has Marnie in bed with a proper husband, "cured" of the awful effects of her own incest trauma. For *Marnie* can, in many ways, be seen as the "Americanized" correction of *Marienbad*. Both films revolve around an unwanted seduction by a powerful male with a foreign accent. In both, the leading lady is sequestered in a huge country house, where she wrestles with her past. If DS's past remains allusive and elusive in *Marien-*

bad, suggesting throughout how incest trauma disrupts the very process of identity formation, Marnie's past is forcefully reactivated by her lover-psychiatrist, Mark Rutland (Sean Connery). His methods, though apparently easier to swallow than GA's, would sooner evoke for the French his Gallicized name (*connerie,* "sham") than any real success in this venture. Yet Hitchcock soothes his viewer (as Resnais will *not*) by "explaining" Marnie's original trauma in a series of explicit flashbacks and by reclaiming the incestuously abused Marnie from frigidity, returning her to a more comfortable version of sexuality with her leading man. The institution of marriage has been saved in the Anglo-American version, preserving Marnie for her culturally determined role as wife/mother of the very rich Rutlands. Money, heredity, and heterosexuality have all been neatly (almost magically) reasserted, or as Kaja Silverman terms it, "put back on the assembly line . . . in the true coherence of a patriarchy."[2]

One of the differences between the French original and its Anglo-American reworking lies in its drive for *coherence* and a happy ending. Indeed, Mark Crispin Miller has described the force of this difference in *Seeing Through Movies,* in which he laments "the transfer of creative authority out of the hands of filmmaking professionals and into the purely quantitative universe of the CEO's." Such a transfer, he concludes, "reduced, drastically, the movies' narrative potential . . . [and] all but wiped out that earlier diversity, coarsening a various and nuanced prior form into a poundingly hypnotic instrument—a mere *stimulus.*" Thus, "the convergence of the movies with both cartoons and ads, presents a fantasy of perfect wish-fulfillment . . . a narrative . . . finally nullified in an *all-healing,* all-inclusive merger—a rousing/tranquilizing moment of manifold collapse, [producing] the terminal erasure of all 'difference.'"[3] We are far indeed from Malle's version of *La Carte de Tendre,* which emphasizes *difference* in its evocation of, rather than repression of, "terres inconnues."

But we can perhaps best appreciate this particular difference between Anglo-American and French narrative when we compare *Marienbad* and *Marnie* to the third avatar of the story, *La Mariée était en noir.* Just as the term "riding coat" passed the channel into France as *redingote,* designating an indelibly Gallic version of the English sartorial piece, and then passed *back* to English soil as "redingot" to identify a ruthlessly Anglo-Saxon avatar of this garb, so have three versions of this film made their way back and forth across the Atlantic. If *Marnie* homogenizes Resnais's *Marienbad,* then Truffaut's *Mariée* simply removes the en(d) of the story. In a re-Gallicized version, *La*

Mariée offers "two essences, two centers, [where] the process of genre assignment is derailed . . . in an attempt at the repression of difference [which] is also necessarily an act of violence, produc[ing] its own black and blue marks in the text."[4] Peter Brunette and David Wills see *La Mariée* as "*two* parallel films which move forward simultaneously." The two films evoked may be *Marnie* and *Jules et Jim,* as the authors of *Screen/Play* suggest, but they might just as well be *Marnie* and *Marienbad.* Of course, the reason *La Mariée* invokes *Jules et Jim* lies in the way the film functions Gallically as "a screen . . . which shields both author and viewer from the powerful but potentially embarrassing spectacle of the true self in operation. . . . Thus the genre story seems there to provide some sort of *negative material base,* a necessary evil perhaps for the real story that must be both hidden and visible."[5] Jeanne Moreau will be "invaginated" back into *La Mariée* from *Jules et Jim* not only to undo Hitchcock but to allude to her thoroughly ambiguous role in Truffaut's earlier film.

Thus, with each move back and forth across the Atlantic, the oppositions between French and American cinema become more and more pronounced: the American desire for coherence and seamlessness will be consistently countered by an aesthetics of discontinuity and alienation. That very discontinuity in turn points to the abyssal structure of citation in French cinema.[6] Paraphrasing Derrida's notion that "we can only get to history through a process of textualization,"[7] we could say that the French filmmakers of the new wave could only get to the "subject" through the screen "mirror" of literature.

Evelyn Waugh wrote of Hollywood's relationship to literature: "Each book purchased for motion pictures has some individual quality, good or bad, that has made it remarkable. It is the work of a great array of highly paid and incompatible writers to distinguish the quality, separate it, and *obliterate* it."[8] If American moviemaking wants to forget that it is always written, French cinematography seems always to reach outward (or inward) toward other texts that both liberate and encapsulate its deeper levels of signification. By contrast with Hollywood's "bright erasure" of literature,[9] we can discern in the French new wave a tendency toward the "dark scripting" of intertexts from its own and many other literatures. One of the recent French imports to America, M. Deville's *La Lectrice,* so thoroughly exploits the inherent meta-literary fascination of French cinema that it reaches a kind of saturation point of intertextual complexity. Such complexities undoubtedly explain the recent tendency in Hollywood to "remake" French films rather than run the "risk" of importing them directly.

Ultimately, French cinema's fascination with a series of "marginal" texts suggests a cinematic ontology both circular and (not quite) hidden, always too close to—and too far from—the film's origins (not) to be noticed. Never comfortable, perhaps, but inevitably present.

Notes

Introduction: Screening the Text

1. Stanley Cavell, *The World Viewed* (Cambridge: Harvard University Press, 1979), 45. For a discussion of the relationship between primal scene and origins see Guy Rosolato, *Essais sur le symbolique* (Paris: Gallimard, 1969), 204–6. I also assume a familiarity with Christian Metz, *Le Signifiant imaginaire* (Paris: Union Générale d'Éditions, 1977).

2. See Jean-Louis Baudry, "Le Dispositif: approches métapsychologiques de l'impression de réalité," *Psychanalyse et cinéma,* special issue of *Communications,* 23 (1975): 56–72.

3. See Rebecca M. Pauly, *Le Berceau et la biliothèque* (Saratoga, Calif.: Amni, 1989), 2, 9, 63.

4. Jean Collet et al., "François Truffaut," *Cahiers du cinéma* 138 (December 1962): 55, translation mine.

5. Eric Rohmer, "Le Celluloid et le marbre," *Cahiers du cinéma* 44 (February 1955): 35, translation mine.

6. See Dudley Andrew, "The Impact of the Novel on French Cinema of the 30's," *L'Esprit Créateur* 30, no. 2 (Summer 1990): 3–13.

7. The bibliography on this subject is so large that I can only refer the reader to the selective bibliography on literature and film at the conclusion of the present work.

8. I use the term *nouvelle vague* with the usual precautions. By now, most historians have agreed that there was no movement per se, in the sense of a program, but rather a temporal coincidence of reaction. In this sense, perhaps *nouvelle vague* should be translated "vague news" rather than "new wave."

9. Helen Myers, "Introduction to The Ego and The Self," in *Psychoanalysis: Toward the Second Century,* ed. Arnold M. Cooper, Otto F. Kernberg, and Ethal Person (New Haven: Yale University Press, 1989), 38, 40.

10. Jeffrey Mehlman, "French Freud," *Yale French Studies* 48 (1972): 6.

11. Interview with Agnès Varda by Simone Dubreuilh cited by Gaston Bounoure in *Alain Resnais* (Paris: Seghers, 1962), 45. Cf. Jean-Luc Godard, "Je me considère comme un essayiste: je fais des essais en forme de romans ou des romans en forme d'essais: simplement je les filme au lieu de les écrire," cited in Pierre Gay, "Nouveau roman et cinéma nouveau," *Cinéma 70* 148 (July–August 1970): 65.

12. This is the subject, of course, of Harold Bloom's *The Anxiety of Influence* (New York: Oxford University Press, 1973).

13. François Ramasse, "La Règle du 'je': entretien avec Claude-Jean Philippe," in *La Nouvelle Vague 25 ans après*, ed. J. L. Douin (Paris: Cerf, 1983), 31, translation mine; François Truffaut, *Truffaut by Truffaut*, ed. Dominique Rabourdin, trans. Robert E. Wolf (New York: Abrams, 1987), 214.

14. The expression is borrowed from Emmanuel Decaux, "Images du livre," *Cinématographe* 31 (October 1977): 10. Decaux in fact argues, "Sacré ou massacré, rare ou omniprésent, le livre est irréductible *à sa forme de tombe*. Un livre, c'est beaucoup plus qu'un livre." For all her appreciation of the complexity of the problem, Marie-Claire Ropars consigns Maurice Sachs's *Abracadabra* the status of mere title and of graphic unconscious in Godard's *A bout de souffle* ("The Graphic in Filmic Writing: *A bout de souffle* or the Erratic Alphabet," *Enclitic* 5–6, nos. 1–2 [1981–82]: 147–61).

15. Freud, "Three Essays on the Theory of Sexuality," *The Standard Edition of the Complete Psychological Works of Sigmund Freud*, ed. and trans. James Strachey, 23 vols. (London: Hogarth, 1955–66), 7:154. Hereafter the *Standard Edition* will be cited as S.E.

16. Ellie Ragland-Sullivan, *Jacques Lacan and the Philosophy of Psychanalysis* (Urbana: University of Illinois Press, 1986), 180.

Chapter 1: Truffaut's *Jules et Jim*

1. J. B. Pontalis, *Entre le rêve et la douleur* (Paris: Gallimard, 1977), 136–37, translation mine.

2. Ibid., 76.

3. Truffaut, *Truffaut by Truffaut*, 201.

4. Ramasse, "La Règle du 'je,'" 31, translation mine.

5. Charles Rycroft, *A Critical Dictionary of Psychoanalysis* (Totowa, N.J.: Littlefield, Adams, 1973), 102, 104–5, s.v. "obsession."

6. Bloom, *The Anxiety of Influence*, 30. Henri-Pierre Roché, *Jules et Jim* (Paris: Gallimard, 1953), translation mine; all further references to this novel will be indicated in the text by R.

7. I have borrowed Eve Sedgwick's term, intended to describe "social bonds between persons of the same sex . . . a neologism obviously formed by analogy with 'homosexual' and just as obviously meant to be distinguished

from 'homosexual.' It is applied to such activities as 'male bonding.' To draw the 'homosocial' back into the orbit of 'desire' . . . is to hypothesize the potential unbrokenness of a continuum between homosocial and homosexual—a continuum whose visibility for men in our society is radically disrupted" (*Between Men: English Literature and Male Homosocial Desire* [New York: Columbia University Press, 1985], 1).

8. I have elected to concentrate on the intertextual and implicit "misprision" of Roché's text partly because it is the primary focus of this study but partly, too, because such an admirable study already exists of Truffaut's adaptation of Roché (see David I. Grossvogel, "Truffaut and Roché: Diverse Voices of the Novel and Film," *Diacritics* 3 [Spring 1973]: 47–52).

9. François Truffaut, *Jules et Jim* (Paris: Seuil, 1962), 27, translated by Norman Fry as *Jules and Jim* (New York: Simon & Schuster, 1968), 18. All further references to this text are indicated in the body of the essay as SC, followed by the pagination in the English and the French version, respectively.

10. Cf. Grossvogel, "Diverse Voices," 50: "In *Jules et Jim,* the dilemma is intensified through a doubling of the central character: Jules and Jim, physically complementary ('the small and round Jules and the tall and slender Jim'), are part of the discussion of Roché's central aphorism: 'maybe all men are like straw in the consuming fire of their women's beauty.'"

11. For a discussion of these aspects of Dostoevsky's *The Double* see my "Doubling *The Double:* Bertolucci's Strange Partnership with Dostoevsky," in *Bertolucci's Dream Loom: A Psychoanalytic Study of Cinema* (Amherst: University of Massachusetts Press, 1987), 41–63.

12. Roché, *Jules et Jim,* 17.

13. It may also evoke Ovid's Pygmalion (*The Metamorphoses,* trans. A. D. Melville [New York: Oxford University Press, 1986], 232–34), whose statue "fired him with love, . . . seemed to be alive," but this myth seems (literally) to pale before Mérimée's "darker" version, which has been *exhumed from underground* and is covered with a "blackish green color which time had bestowed," so appropriate to Truffaut's character (Prosper Mérimée, *La Vénus d'Ille,* in *Colomba* [1841; reprint, Paris: Garnier, 1962], 194, translation and italics mine; all further citations of this text will be indicated by VI).

14. Mérimée, *Vénus d'Ille,* 194. Tom Conley suggests (in a letter to the author) that given Mérimée's interest and expertise in Romanesque architecture, the story's Venus seems to be fashioned from a Romanesque model. This would have the effect of linking (indirectly to be sure) Truffaut with Rohmer. See chapter 5, on Rohmer, below.

15. Elaine Showalter, "Singles and Doubles: Gendering Jeckyll" (Paper delivered at the Boston University Lectures in Criticism, September 1987). See also idem, *The Female Malady: Women, Madness, and English Culture, 1830–1980* (New York: Penguin, 1985).

16. For corroboration of the lack of parallelism in the textual treatment of men and women, cf. *Le Petit Robert: dictionnaire de la langue française,* s.v. "femme" and "homme."

17. Alan Brody has suggested a parallel between Catherine and Ibsen's *Hedda Gabler* ("Jules and Catherine and Jim and Hedda," *Journal of Aesthetic Education* 5 [April 1971]: 91–101), which would further reinforce the tendency to see Catherine as simply strong-willed and free-minded rather than double. Brody may have been inspired to seek the Ibsen parallel because of the discussion of the play that precedes Catherine's leap into the Seine. Yet, although the heroine seems to fit the description ("she wants to be free . . . to invent her life at every moment" [SC, 36/49]), none of the other comments about the play fit Ibsen's work. The Ibsen parallel, however, in addition to the similarities perceived by Brody, emphasizes Hedda's (and by implication Catherine's) submission to male ownership rather than any deeper mysterious forces at work: Hedda says, "I often think there is only one thing in the world I have any time for . . . Boring myself to death." Instead, in desperation, she shoots herself (Ibsen, *Hedda Gabler,* in *The Plays of Henrik Ibsen* [New York: Tudor, 1934], 250).

18. Truffaut, "Edgar Ulmer: The Naked Dawn," in *The Films in My Life,* trans. Leonard Mayhew (New York: Simon & Schuster, 1978), 155–56. Several years before undertaking the film, Truffaut had written in his review of Edgar Ulmer's *The Naked Dawn,* "What counts are the delicate and ambiguous relationships among the three characters, the stuff of a good novel. One of the most beautiful modern novels I know is *Jules et Jim* by Henri-Pierre Roché, which shows how, over a lifetime, two friends and the woman companion they share love one another with tenderness and almost no harshness, thanks to an esthetic morality constantly reconsidered. *The Naked Dawn* is the first film that has made me think that *Jules et Jim* could be done as a film." The only suggestion of Truffaut's conflicts about this story is the word "ambiguous" in reference to relationships. Indeed, the transformation of the anecdotal material of the novel in the film serves to defuse the question of ambiguity by focusing on the figure of triangulation among the main characters.

19. See Sarah Kozloff's comments on this narrative voice in *Invisible Storytellers: Voice-over Narration in American Fiction Film* (Berkeley and Los Angeles: University of California Press, 1988), 112. See also Grossvogel, "Diverse Voices," 51.

20. Cf. Jacques Lacan's discussion of Freud's argument that only libido is masculine, which for Lacan implies that Freud has ignored all those who adopt the status of women (*Le Séminaire XX: encore* [Paris: Seuil, 1975], 75).

21. Alan Brody ("Jules and Catherine and Jim and Hedda," 100) makes the following comment in his essay on Truffaut and Ibsen: "The three-way focus becomes a central visual figure throughout the film. Thérèse forces her way into it and leaves when she is forced to the side in the cafe. After she is gone, Jules draws a woman's head on the tabletop with chalk. It is as though the two men must constantly have some female image between them in order to perpetuate the consciousness of their male friendship. . . . Every time Catherine struggles to break free she finds herself still serving only to deepen

and intensify the men's relationship to each other. The only way left is to destroy the possibility of any future triangle by taking Jim with her over the bridge."

22. Freud, "Three Essays on Sexuality," 154.

23. Gayle Rubin, "The Traffic in Women," in *Toward an Anthropology of Women,* ed. Rayna Teiter (New York: Monthly Review Press, 1975), 174.

24. Walter Benjamin, "The Work of Art in the Age of Mechanical Reproduction," in *Illuminations* (New York: Schocken Books, 1969), 236–37.

25. Roger Greenspun noted the presence of this insect and its "complementary movement" in *"Elective Affinities:* Aspects of *Jules et Jim," Sight and Sound,* 32, no. 2 (Spring 1963): 81.

26. It is worth noting at this juncture that David Lynch takes up this fascination with insects in *Blue Velvet*. Peter Brunette and David Wills (*Screen/Play: Derrida and Film Theory* [Princeton: Princeton University Press, 1989], 155) note that in Lynch's film "the bugs are in excess in terms of the diegetic structure of the film from the time the camera seeks them out in the grass immediately after the collapse of Jeffrey's father. But [that is] not to establish that they are excessive with respect to a psychoanalytic reading of that narrative." Notably, too, this analysis is printed on the page opposite their analysis of Truffaut's *La Mariée était en noir,* in which they discuss the "invagination" of Jeanne Moreau from *Jules et Jim* into the later film.

27. Cited in Annette Insdorf, *François Truffaut* (Boston: Twayne, 1978), 67.

28. See Tony Tanner's discussion of *Elective Affinities* in *Adultery in the Novel* (Baltimore: Johns Hopkins University Press, 1979).

29. J. W. Goethe, *Elective Affinities,* trans. R. J. Hollingdale (New York: Penguin, 1971), 248. All further references to this work will be indicated in the body of the essay by EA.

30. For another useful perspective on the male identification function in the triangle see René Girard, "Le Désir 'triangulaire,'" in *Mensonge romantique, vérité romanesque* (Paris: Grasset, 1961), 11–57.

31. Conley, "Vigo Van Gogh," *New York Literary Forum* 5 (1983): 153–54.

32. Ibid., 154. On the subject of collage, it is interesting to note that Truffaut refers to his adaptation of the Roché novel as "a text which I went over working with paste and scissors" (*Truffaut by Truffaut,* 76).

33. Greenspun, *"Elective Affinities,"* 81.

34. Quoted in Louis Marcorelles, "Interview with Truffaut," *Sight and Sound* 31, no. 1 (Winter 1961–62): 37.

35. Grossvogel ("Diverse Voices," 51) concurs, adding, "Truffaut reduces Kathe's desperation to find an equally-matched animal to a simple misunderstanding. . . . He began by smoothing over the asperities and complexity of Roché's characters. 'I wanted to equalize the characters so that they would elicit equal sympathy and one would be tempted to like them equally,' (*Le Monde,* January 24, 1962). . . . Gallicized in Truffaut's version as

Catherine, Kathe has none of the attributes implicit in the 'archaic' smile: the Germanic part is missing and, along with it the less 'likeable' but more earthy quality of the original character."

36. Pontalis, *Entre le rêve et la douleur,* 84.

Chapter 2: Louis Malle's *Lovers*

1. Cavell, *The World Viewed,* 45.

2. John McCarten, "The Current Cinema: Love at a Glance," *New Yorker,* 7 November 1959, 204.

3. Eugen Weber, "An Escapist Realism," *Film Quarterly,* 13, no. 2 (Winter 1959): 10.

4. Ellen Fitzpatrick, "The Lovers," *Films in Review* 10, no. 9 (November 1959): 561–62.

5. Richard Macksey, "Malle on Malle," *Post Script* 2, no. 1 (Fall 1982): 4.

6. McCarten, "The Current Cinema," 204; Hollis Alpert, "Love Story," *Saturday Review,* 8 August 1959, 24.

7. McCarten, "The Current Cinema," 204.

8. Vivant Denon, *Point de lendemain* (1777; reprint, Paris: Jean-Jacques Pauvert, 1959), 31, translation mine. All further references to this text will be indicated in the body of the essay by PL.

9. *Louis Malle par Louis Malle,* ed. Jacques Mallecot and Sarah Kant (Paris: Athanor, 1978), 64.

10. Noel Burch, "Qu'est-ce que La Nouvelle Vague?" *Film Quarterly* 13, no. 2 (Winter 1959): 20.

11. R. T. Rollet, "An Interview with Louis Malle," *Film Library Quarterly* 9, no. 4 (1977): 62.

12. *Louis Malle par Louis Malle,* 14. Cf. Gilles Jacob, "Entretien avec Louis Malle," *Positif* 157 (March 1974): 31, translation mine.

13. Jonathan Cott, "Fires Within: The Chaste Sensuality of Director Louis Malle," *Rolling Stone,* 6 April 1978, 43–44.

14. Jean Renoir, *The Rules of the Game* (New York: Simon & Schuster, 1970), 82.

15. Ibid., 9–12.

16. Malle himself uses this term to designate the musical score: "The Brahms Sextet in *The Lovers* is used in a conventional way because it brings a romantic mood into the love scene in that long, slow night shared by Jeanne Moreau and Jean-Marc Bory. It was beautiful, but its use was almost manipulative. I was certainly trying to convey certain emotions" (cited in Dan Yakir, "Louis Malle: An Interview from *The Lovers* to *Pretty Baby,*" *Film Quarterly* 31, no. 4 [Summer 1978]: 10).

17. I am thinking, for example, of films that not only permit interchangeability among women but encourage it, such as Hitchcock's *Vertigo,* where the male protagonist wants to remake his new girlfriend into an exact likeness of the former one.

18. Magritte's presence is unusually marked in this film. For example, the entire night sequence evokes a negative reproduction of Magritte's *Empire of Lights*.

19. *Louis Malle par Louis Malle*, 52. Cf.: "The cinema is a mediocre vehicle for ideas. It's often seen as lying in the wake of literature, but it should be compared instead to sculpture and to music. It is addressed to the senses and to our emotions. Reflection comes later" (ibid., 69). Compare these comments with Eisenstein's music-cinema metaphor in *The Film Sense* (New York: Harcourt, Brace & World, 1942, 1947), 157–216.

20. Yakir, "Louis Malle: An Interview," 7.

21. Cott, "Fires Within," 43.

22. Nor should my reference to *Beyond the Pleasure Principle*, for Magritte, as surrealist, was familiar with the preoccupation with Freudian thought in the group's early *Manifestoes*.

23. Cott, "Fires Within," 41, italics mine.

24. McCarten, "The Current Cinema," 204.

25. For a discussion of this aspect of the *précieux* movement see René Bray, *La Préciosité et les précieux* (Paris: Albin Michel, 1948), 136ff.

26. Richard Roud, "Les Amants," *Sight and Sound* 28, no. 1 (Winter 1958–59): 21, 22.

27. Joan de Jean, "The Salons, 'Preciosity,' and the Sphere of Women's Influence," in *A New History of French Literature,* ed. Denis Hollier (Cambridge: Harvard University Press, 1989), 297–303.

28. Louis Marin, *Utopics: Spatial Play,* trans. Robert A. Vollrath (Atlantic Highlands, N.J.: Humanities Press, 1984), 9.

29. Ibid., 9–10.

30. Ibid., 12–15. The entire passage reads, "Etymologically ne-uter, neither one nor the other, grammar defines it as neither masculine nor feminine. It is, rather, outside gender, neither active nor passive, but outside voice. . . . The neutral must be grasped as the transitory and passing term that allows movement from one contrary to another, but it would be the mediator between one and the other because its nature would be neither (for) one nor (for) the other. . . . The neutral will constitute the principle of the conjunction of contraries; it will join them in the very opposition, i.e. in a position or marked difference. *The neutral is the condition of possibility for producing and giving birth to the other side of the royal position of mastery and domination*" (italics mine).

31. Marin reminds us that "utopia is a figure produced by a practice that does not deny reality by changing it; instead it only indicates it by producing the *figure of its negative side.* . . . As strategy it groups operations aimed at . . . consciousness raising. The utopic discourse indicates within the ideological discourse . . . the theoretical and conceptual instruments that let us think about these contradictions" (ibid., 197–99).

32. Claude Filteau, "Le Pays de Tendre: l'enjeu d'une carte," *Littérature* 36 (December 1979): 40–43, translation mine. Cf. De Jean ("The Salons," 299–301): "It is fitting that these private academies were designated by

temporal and spatial terms, for the essence of the salon's importance in literary life was bound up with its status as a world apart, a parallel sphere with its own rules, activities and schedule. . . . To this blend of brilliant conversation, social refinement, and literary and linguistic deliberation was added the fourth component of the salon movement: political fermentation. Madame de Scudéry became the official novelist of the rebel camp, whose military and amorous exploits she *fictionalized* in *Artamene, ou le grand Cyrus.* The first volume of her new novel, *Clélie* has as its centerpiece the most celebrated document in salon literature, the *Carte de Tendre.*"

33. Conley, "Vigo Van Gogh," 153–54.

34. In this sense, Malle remains faithful to Scudéry's project, which was to find ways to reveal characters from within (see Jean Rousset, *Narcisse romancier* [Paris: José Corti, 1963], 40).

35. Filteau, "Le Pays de Tendre," 56–57.

36. Ibid., 52, 60. The author adds, "The unity of univocal representation of nature is no longer possible, for desire determines a relationship to nature that men and women express differently. In this sense, the map is a challenge laid down to men by the *précieuses*. The position of the (masculine) reader is linked to the strategy of the look, which designs its own itinerary of reading."

37. This reading is admittedly anachronistic vis-à-vis *la carte* itself, given the limited knowledge of the reproductive system's design available in the eighteenth century, but is entirely pertinent to Malle's appropriation of the map.

38. Kaja Silverman, *The Acoustic Mirror: The Female Voice in Psycho-analysis and Cinema* (Bloomington: Indiana University Press, 1988), 1, 67–69.

39. Ibid., 24.

40. Ibid., 30.

41. Silverman writes: "By isolating the female subject from the production of meaning, [Hollywood cinema] permits the male subject to pose as the voice that constrains and orchestrates the feminine 'performance' or 'strip-tease,' as enunciator rather than as himself an element of the *énoncé*. The identification of the female voice with the female body thus returns us definitively to the scene of castration. . . . Within this theoretical paradigm, female interiority is basically an extension of the female body, 'a stunted and inferior organ'" (ibid., 62, 67).

42. Silverman states: "Femininity turns on three things that are fundamental to all subjectivity, but whose disavowal and projection serve to define masculinity: castration, subordination to the gaze of the cultural Other, and 'discursive interiority' (i.e., insertion into the pre-existing symbolic order). . . . What poses for femininity is actually an inevitable part of all subjectivity. Since no one assumes identity except by being separated from the mother, losing access to the real, and entering into a field of preexisting meaning, and since no identity can be sustained in the absence of the gaze of

the other then what is needed is not so much a 'masculinization' of the female subject as a 'feminization' of the male subject—a much more generalized acknowledgement . . . of the necessary terms of cultural identity" (ibid., 149).

43. Pascal Bonitzer, *Le Regard et la voix* (Paris: Union Générale d'Éditions, 1976), 30, translation mine.

44. Silverman notes: "The implications for a female authoritative voice-off are staggering: To allow [woman] to be heard without being seen would be dangerous since it would disrupt the specular regime upon which dominant cinema relies; it would put her beyond reach of the male gaze (which stands in here for the cultural 'camera') and release her voice from the signifying obligations which the gaze enforces. It would liberate the female subject from the interrogation about her place, her time and her desires which constantly resecure her. Finally, to disembody the female voice would be to challenge every conception by means of which we have known woman within Hollywood film since it is precisely *as body* that she is constructed there" (*Acoustic Mirror,* 164).

45. Here again there is a strong degree of continuity with Madeleine de Scudéry's project in *Clélie,* in which characters avoid using the first person to present themselves (see Rousset, *Narcisse romancier,* 40ff.).

46. Stendhal's scene (*Le Rouge et le noir* [Paris: Garnier, n.d.], 53, trans. F. Scott Moncrieff as *The Red and the Black* [New York: Modern Library, 1926], 73) reads as follows: "Julien, ashamed of his cowardice, told himself: 'At the precise moment when ten o'clock strikes, I shall carry out the intention which, all day long, I have been promising myself that I would fulfill this evening, or I shall go up to my room and blow my brains out.' After a final interval of tension and anxiety, during which the excess of his emotion carried Julien almost out of his senses, the strokes of ten sounded. Finally, while the air was still throbbing with the last stroke of ten, he put out his hand and took that of Madame de Rênal."

47. See Bloom, *The Anxiety of Influence.*

48. See Leo Bersani, *Baudelaire and Freud* (Berkeley and Los Angeles: University of California Press, 1977), 106–24.

49. Baudry, "Le Dispositif."

50. This gesture may be interpreted as a casting off of the phallic net that thus far has covered the entire scenario.

51. As Filteau reminds us, "The univocal representation of nature no longer exists, for desire determines a relationship to nature that is different for men than for women. In this sense, the *Carte de Tendre* is a challenge presented to men by the *précieuses.* The position of the masculine reader is linked to the strategy of the look which designs his own itinerary as a reader" ("Le Pays de Tendre," 60).

52. Yet another rejection (cf. the liberated fish) of the defining power of the paternal logos (the phallic).

53. Marin, *Utopics,* 18.

54. *Louis Malle par Louis Malle,* 35–36, translation mine. All quotes in the remainder of this chapter are from this same source; all translations are mine.

Chapter 3: Resnais's *Marienbad*

1. Robbe-Grillet developed this idea first in an interview about the film with André Labarthe and Jacques Rivette, "Entretien avec Resnais et Robbe-Grillet," *Cahiers du cinéma* 123 (September 1961): 12–18.

2. Reported in Ragland-Sullivan, *Lacan and the Philosophy of Psychoanalysis,* 27–29.

3. Ibid., 27.

4. Jane Gallop, "Where to Begin?" in *Reading Lacan* (Ithaca: Cornell University Press, 1985), 75. All further references to this source will be indicated by RL.

5. Jacques Lacan, cited in RL, 86, italics mine.

6. Quoted in Latil-Le Dantec, "Notes sur la fiction et l'imaginaire chez Resnais et Robbe-Grillet," *Etudes cinématographiques* 100–103 (1974): 125, translation mine.

7. Alain Robbe-Grillet, *L'Année dernière à Marienbad* (Paris: Minuit, 1961), 22–23, trans. Richard Howard as *Last Year at Marienbad* (New York: Grove, 1962), 18. All further references to this text will be indicated by ADAM, followed by pagination in the English and the French version, respectively.

8. A sampling of critical positions includes: Jean Alter, "Alain Robbe-Grillet and the 'Cinematographic Style,'" *Modern Language Journal* 48, no. 6 (October 1964): 366, arguing that Robbe-Grillet's "anti-novelistic" stance endows the film with an "anti-cinematic" orientation; Geneviève Bollème, "*L'Année dernière à Marienbad:* essai d'interprétation," *Les Temps modernes* 183 (July 1961): 179, noting that "this meeting is . . . an untellable adventure which is lived in a present already doubled by the past, without future, with no tomorrow"; Burch, "Qu'est-ce que La Nouvelle Vague," 24, calling Resnais's work "hopelessly arbitrary" yet allowing that it contains "beautiful sequences"; and Raymond Durgnat, "Architecture in, and of, the Movies," in *Films and Feelings* (Cambridge: MIT Press, 1971), 110, calling it "a lattice of dislocations and contradictions." John Howard Lawson (*Film: The Creative Process* [New York: Hill & Wang, 1964], 237, 255) argues that "the characters move in patterns of baffling uncertainty, where there is no dividing line between dream and reality, or between past and present . . . the film is a brilliant distillation of the concept of alienation. The man and the woman [are] disjointed reflections of the incomplete reality around them."

9. Neal Oxenhandler, "Marienbad Revisited," *Film Quarterly* 17, no. 1 (Fall 1963): 33; William S. Pechter, "Last Night at Marienbad," *Kenyon Review* 25, no. 2 (Spring 1963): 343.

10. Marie-Claire Ropars-Wueilleumier, "L'Année dernière à Marienbad," in *L'Ecran de la mémoire* (Paris: Seuil, 1970), 117, 121.

11. In René Prédal, *Alain Resnais*, special issue of *Etudes cinématographiques* 64–68 (1968): 91–98.

12. Sigmund Freud, *The Interpretation of Dreams*, S.E. 4, 5 (see esp. 4:279ff.); Nick Browne, "Rhétorique du texte spéculaire," *Psychanalyse et cinéma*, special issue of *Communications*, 23 (1975): 202–12.

13. Some critics, such as Jacques Brunius ("Every Year in Marienbad, or the Discipline of Uncertainty," *Sight and Sound* 31, no. 3 [Summer 1962]: 123), go out of their way to insist on this male point of view as being necessary to interpreting the film. "The film," he claims, "is constructed in order to build up the gradual increase of his conviction, which is reflected by the weakening of the girl's [*sic*] resistance to persuasion."

14. In O. Revault d'Allonnes, "Alain Resnais, Antidoctrinaire," *Revue d'esthétique* 2–3 (1967): 126, translation mine.

15. Labarthe and Rivette, "Entretien avec Resnais et Robbe-Grillet," 2, translation mine. At least one critic, Solange Josa, agrees: "Peut-être est-ce A qui, loin d'être le personnage muet sur lequel se cristallise tout le discours intérieur de X est le personnage principal et le seul" (*"Marienbad:* ou peut-être . . . ," *Esprit* 30, no. 1 [January 1962]: 143).

16. Labarthe and Rivette, "Entretien avec Resnais et Robbe-Grillet," 5–6.

17. Reported by Robert Benayoun in *Alain Resnais: l'arpenteur de l'imaginaire* (Paris: Stock, 1980), 191. Elsewhere (Michele Manceaux, "A Munich avec Alain Resnais," *L'Express,* 20 October 1960, 39) Resnais is quoted as saying of his characters, "As in a puzzle, there are scattered pieces. From deep within, they call out to each other ['ils s'appellent les uns les autres'], but they must find the thread ['il faut trouver le fil']." In so stating, he raises a fundamental ambiguity: his sentence may signify either "they call to each other" or "they share each other's names."

18. From interview in *Cinéma 61* 61 (November 1961), quoted in Prédal, *Alain Resnais,* 37, translation mine.

19. Ragland-Sullivan, *Lacan and the Philosophy of Psychoanalysis,* 29.

20. Ibid., 38–43, italics mine.

21. Labarthe and Rivette, "Entretien avec Resnais et Robbe-Grillet," 2; Jean-Claude Bonnet, Emmanuel Decaux, and Bruno Villien, "Entretien avec Alain Resnais," *Cinématographe* 58 (1980): 20.

22. The game playing, tied as it is to the question of mirrors and identity, recalls, of course, Malle's allusions to *La Règle du jeu* in *Les Amants.*

23. Norman Holland, "Film, Metafilm, and Un-Film," *Hudson Review* 15, no. 3 (Fall 1962): 409.

24. Gérard Genette has argued ("Sur Robbe-Grillet," *Tel Quel* 8 [Winter 1962]: 42–43) that the very soul of Robbe-Grillet's work, far from presenting an equivalence of all images as simply present, presents "un mixte de Même et d'Autre: un Même reproduit, donc aliéné . . . par où l'identité tend

à l'altérité." A description that has very Lacanian overtones.

25. Notably, during the shooting of the film the actors told Michele Manceaux that "nous sommes dans ce film. . . émiettés par ce tournage en fragments" ("A Munich avec Alain Resnais," 39).

26. Janine Chasseguet-Smirgel, hardly a Lacanian, sees the role of mirrors in the film this way: "Mirrors, far from helping her recover her wholeness in the contemplation of her own image, merely infinitely multiply it, deepening the space in which it is lost. The object itself (in the vision of it available to this fractured Moi) is likewise multiplied (e.g., the photos in the drawer). . . . The reflection in a mirror, composed of two juxtaposed shots, breaks the character vertically, thus giving the image of a *divided* body. Later, a similar shot . . . confirms our belief that the object is only a reflection, merely a projection of the fragmented *moi*" ("A propos de *L'Année dernière à Marienbad*," in *Pour une psychanalyse de l'art* [Paris: Payot, 1971], 72–73, translation mine).

27. See Ragland-Sullivan, *Lacan and the Philosophy of Psychoanalysis,* 35–37.

28. Cited in d'Allonnes, "Alain Resnais, Antidoctrinaire," 123, translation mine.

29. Jacques Belmans, "Entretien avec Alain Resnais," *Etudes cinématographiques* 64–68 (1968): 187.

30. "Marienbad ou l'exception," *L'Arc* 31 (Winter 1967): 9, translation mine.

31. Cited in Benayoun, *Alain Resnais,* 101.

32. Belmans, "Entretien avec Alain Resnais," 187, translation mine.

33. Mireille Amiel and Jacques Petal, "Entretien avec Alain Resnais," *Cinéma 80* 259–60 (July–August 1980): 38, translation mine.

34. Bernard Pingaud, "Jouer avec le temps: entretien avec Alain Resnais," *L'Arc* 31 (Winter 1967): 93–96, translation mine.

35. E.g., "Having reached the first row of spectators, the camera continues its movement, passing in review, from almost directly in front now, the faces aligned, frozen with attention, and brightly illuminated by the light from the stage. But the camera's speed has gradually decreased and the image finally comes to rest on a few motionless heads" (ADAM, 24/29).

36. "Marienbad ou l'exception," 9.

37. Labarthe and Rivette, "Entretien avec Resnais et Robbe-Grillet," 6, translation and italics mine.

38. Alain Robbe-Grillet, "L'Année dernière à Marienbad," *Sight and Sound* 30, no. 4 (Fall 1961): 177, italics mine.

39. Ibid., 178–79.

40. Labarthe and Rivette, "Entretien avec Resnais et Robbe-Grillet," 4.

41. Serge Daney and Danièle Dubroux, "Entretien avec Alain Resnais," *Cahiers du cinéma* 347 (May 1983): 27–28, translation mine.

42. Adrian Maben, "Alain Resnais: *The War Is Over,*" *Films and Filming* 13, no. 1 (October 1966): 42.

43. Robbe-Grillet, "L'Année dernière à Marienbad," 179.

44. Labarthe and Rivette, "Entretien avec Resnais et Robbe-Grillet," 4. Some twenty years later, Resnais lashed out at "anti-psychology" (and by implication at Robbe-Grillet's position and the tendency to label Resnais's work by this term) saying, "Anti-psychology is only a kind of super-psychology!" (in Philippe Carcassonne, "Dix personnages en quête d'un film," *Cinématographe* 88 [April 1983]: 3, translation mine).

45. Robert Benayoun, "Sur *Mon oncle d'amerique:* entretien avec Alain Resnais," *Positif* 231 (June 1980): 40, translation mine.

46. "Entretien avec Resnais et Robbe-Grillet," 13, translation mine. Not surprisingly, Robbe-Grillet counters with his own discontent a few minutes later in this same interview: "Resnais knew he wasn't going to shoot what was in the script. He told me so. That was *the* point of friction between us. Resnais knew that for several seconds there would be something else" (16).

47. Brunius, "Every Year in Marienbad," 122.

48. Another common theme in Resnais's work, according to Peter Harcourt, is "his concern with sickness, often a moral sickness, and with degeneration and decline" ("Alain Resnais: Memory Is Kept Alive with Dreams," *Film Comment* 9, no. 6 [November–December 1973]: 48). Mireille Latil-Le Dantec characterizes Resnais's work as follows: "The essential thing is nostalgia, dreams of honor, remorse, friendship menaced by time and death, the feeling of guilt and lost love which every individual feels somehow secreted by time's invisible space and in which the individual attempts to get hold of his being outside the immediate present" ("Notes sur la fiction et l'imaginaire chez Resnais et Robbe-Grillet," 125).

49. Doris McGinty Davis, "*Le Voyeur* et *L'Année dernière à Marienbad,*" *French Review* 38, no. 4 (February 1965): 483.

50. See Latil-Le Dantec, "Notes sur la fiction et l'imaginaire chez Resnais et Robbe-Grillet," 132.

51. Ibid., 136, 138. This view is echoed by other critics, such as Neal Oxenhandler ("Marienbad Revisited," 33); Strother Purdy ("Gertrude Stein at Marienbad," *PMLA* 85, no. 5 [October 1970]: 1103); Ben Stoltzfus ("D'un langage a l'autre: les deux Robbe-Grillet," *Etudes cinématographiques* 100–103 [1974]: 94–95); Freddy Sweet (*The Film Narratives of Alain Resnais* [Ann Arbor: UMI Research Press, 1981], 52ff.); Geoffrey Wagner ("*Last Year at Marienbad* [1961]," in *The Novel and the Cinema* [Rutherford, N.J.: Fairleigh Dickinson University Press, 1975], 277–87); and Colin Westerbeck ("Infrastructures: The Films of Robbe-Grillet," *Artforum* 14, no. 7 [March 1976]: 54–57).

52. Wagner, "Last Year at Marienbad," 280.

53. Westerbeck, "Infrastructures," 57.

54. Belmans, "Entretien avec Alain Resnais," 191.

55. Amiel and Petal, "Entretien avec Alain Resnais," 43.

56. Sigmund Freud, *New Introductory Lectures,* quoted in Holland, "Film, Metafilm, and Un-Film," 408.

57. Labarthe and Rivette, "Entretien avec Resnais et Robbe-Grillet," 18.

58. Resnais states, "In *Marienbad* we improvised a lot" (in Pingaud, "Jouer avec le temps," 100).

59. Didier Goldschmidt, Jérôme Tonnerre, and Philippe Le Guay, "Deux entretiens avec Alain Resnais," *Cinématographe* 88 (April 1983): 24. Elsewhere Resnais says, "A character becomes a character when he begins to do things we don't approve," a claim that sounds very much like a projection of his own feelings vis-à-vis his scenario writer (cited by James Monaco, "Conversations with Resnais: There Isn't Enough Time," *Film Comment* 11, no. 4 [July–August 1975]: 40; see also Bonnet, Decaux, and Villien, "Entretien avec Alain Resnais," 20.

60. Roy Armes has demonstrated other, more subtle changes involving intercutting and sound techniques ("Robbe-Grillet, Ricardou and *Last Year at Marienbad*," *Quarterly Review of Film Studies* 5, no. 1 [1980]: 6ff., 12).

61. Benayoun, *Alain Resnais,* 95.

62. Quoted in ibid., 102.

63. In French, Ibsen's play is entitled *La Maison de Rosmer,* making the poster title more directly allusive than it might seem in English. Also, I am well aware that Bioy Casarès's *Invention of Morel* has been proposed as a useful intertext for *Marienbad,* and so it is. Yet it is a text that influenced Robbe-Grillet rather than Resnais (who did not know it at the time he made the film), and hence it seems of less pertinence to the current discussion of deviations from scenario to film.

64. Of the many essays devoted to this film, six have noted Resnais's allusion to Ibsen, yet only two critics, Jacques Brunius and Freddy Sweet, have attempted to spell out any of the implications of this choice for the film as a whole.

65. Delphine Seyrig, "Interview," *L'Arc* 31 (Winter 1967): 65.

66. Monaco, "Conversations with Resnais," 39, italics mine.

67. Even critics who did not see the specific allusion to Ibsen sensed it. René Prédal notes, for instance, "In *L'Année dernière à Marienbad,* the text and image don't signify the same thing . . . sometimes a detail differs between them. . . . The contradictions between text and image . . . constitute the very essence of the film. . . . The play in Marienbad plays the role of . . . psychological key of the film" (*Alain Resnais,* 41, 60); Daniel Rocher contends that the play is "against the dénouement of the film" and that the theater scene "falsifies the vision of numerous subsequent images" ("Le Symbolisme du noir et blanc dans *L'Année dernière à Marienbad,*" ibid. 100–103 [1974]: 39–43, translation mine; see also Ropars-Wueilleumier, "L'Année dernière à Marienbad," 115).

68. Quoted in Prédal, *Alain Resnais,* 32.

69. Henrik Ibsen, *Rosmersholm,* in *The Plays of Henrik Ibsen* (New York: Tudor, 1934), 252. All further references to this play will be indicated in the body of the text by R.

70. Pingaud, "Jouer avec le temps," 96–97.

71. Sigmund Freud, "Some Character Types Met With in Psycho-

analytic Work: Those Wrecked by Success (1916)," S.E. 14:316–31. All further references to this text will be indicated in the body of the essay as SF. There is an unusual footnote to this footnote: Janine Chasseguet-Smirgel's essay on the anal-sadistic motifs in *Marienbad* ("A propos de *L'Année dernière à Marienbad*") begins with the mention of Freud's writings on art, and she mentions, in passing, his thoughts on *Rosmersholm*. She failed to see the allusion in the film to this very text, however, and in my view her essay suffers from this "forgetting."

72. Freud, S.E. 3:204.

73. Quoted in Jeffrey Masson, *The Assault on Truth* (New York: Viking Penguin, 1984), 10.

74. Freud, S.E. 20:34, quoted in Dianne Hunter, "Introduction," in *Seduction and Theory* (Urbana: University of Illinois Press, 1989), 4. Hunter comments, "Freud's conclusion that 'these scenes of seduction had *never taken place*' constitutes, according to psychoanalytic orthodoxy, the founding moment of psychoanalysis; though ironically from the point of view of a major group of psychoanalytic commentators, it is in fact an unpsychoanalytic claim, since one of the central tenets of contemporary psychoanalysis is precisely the inextricability of fantasy and reality, and of perception and desire. . . . One can believe Freud's theory of the oedipus complex without concluding as Freud does that memories of being seduced in childhood by adults are *only* fantasies" (4–5).

75. For a discussion of the epidemic of incest see Judith Herman, "A Common Occurrence," in *Father-Daughter Incest* (Cambridge: Harvard University Press, 1981), 7–21.

76. Ibid., 29–31.

77. Janine Chasseguet-Smirgel confirms our sense of GA's behavior: "X's love, a sadistic, regressive love, is, simultaneously, quite full of culpability and anguish, for X is split between his desire to mutilate and kill the love object and the fear of seeing it disappear. . . . The fantasized attack gains even greater value when the victim is pure" ("A propos de *L'Année dernière à Marienbad*," 66–67).

78. Ibid., 65. What seems to me to be lacking in Chasseguet-Smirgel's treatment of the film is, ironically, any sense of the feminine point of view. Again (see n. 71 above), her limited point of view derives in part from her failure to appreciate the allusion to *Rosmersholm* and thus robs the film of a powerful countervalence to the purely male point of view, which otherwise seems to predominate.

79. For a discussion of Resnais's deconstruction of cinematic fetishism and the resultant unpleasure of the film see Diane Shoos, "Sexual Difference and Enunciation: Resnais's *Last Year at Marienbad*," *Literature and Psychology* 34, no. 3 (1988): 3–14.

80. The script refers in the first monologue to "black mirrors."

81. Cf. Resnais: "It seems to me that the ideal film would be one in which dream images would be mistaken for reality, and real ones for a sort of

confused bad dream ['une sorte de cauchemar confus']" (quoted in Latil-Le Dantec, "Notes sur la fiction et l'imaginaire chez Resnais et Robbe-Grillet," 125). Elsewhere (in Prédal, *Alain Resnais,* 97) Resnais spoke of *Marienbad* as an attempt to "sound the depths of the dream."

82. Herman, *Father-Daughter Incest,* 53, 96–97, italics mine.

83. Ibid., 103, 105.

84. Louise Wisechild, *The Obsidian Mirror* (Seattle: Seal, 1988), ii. All references to this text will be indicated as OM in the body of the essay.

85. Freud, *The Interpretation of Dreams.*

86. Chasseguet-Smirgel, "A propos de *L'Année dernière à Marienbad,*" 75–76.

87. Resnais in Manceaux, "A Munich avec Alain Resnais," 39.

88. Robert Benayoun, Michel Ciment, and Jean-Louis Pays, "*La Guerre est finie:* Entretien avec Alain Resnais," *Positif* 79 (October 1966): 19, 21.

89. Armes, "Robbe-Grillet, Ricardou, and *Last Year at Marienbad,*" 4.

90. Quoted in Prédal, "Des structures musicales," 32.

91. Freud, "Some Character Types Met With in Psycho-analytic Work," 329.

92. Pingaud, "Jouer avec le temps," 97.

93. Labarthe and Rivette, "Entretien avec Resnais et Robbe-Grillet"; Jean Carta and Michel Mesnil, "Un Cinéast stoicien: interview d'Alain Resnais," *Esprit* 28, no. 6 (June 1960): 943; Prédal, *Alain Resnais,* 164.

Chapter 4: Chabrol's Mirrored Films

1. Raymond Durgnat, "Le Beau Serge," *Films and Filming* 9, no. 4 (January 1963): 44.

2. Quoted in Gordon Gow, "When the New Wave Became Old Hat: The Films of Claude Chabrol," ibid. 13, no. 6 (March 1967): 21.

3. Jean-Claude Biette, "Claude Chabrol: l'homme centre," *Cahiers du cinéma* 323–24 (May 1981): 93, translation mine.

4. Philippe Carcassonne and Jacques Fieschi, "Claude Chabrol," *Cinématographe* 81 (September 1982): 12, translation mine. Chabrol refers to his *masque du pitre* as "rigolo."

5. Carlos Clarens, "*The Cousins* and *Le Beau Serge,*" *Films in Review* 10, no. 8 (October 1959): 496.

6. Robin Wood and Michael Walker, *Claude Chabrol* (New York: Praeger, 1970), 11.

7. For example: "In *Le Beau Serge* the village of Sardent is used primarily for its documentary reality" (ibid., 20).

8. For a discussion of the definition of realism see, e.g., George J. Becker, ed., *Modern Literary Realism* (Princeton: Princeton University Press, 1967).

9. See Joel Magny, *Claude Chabrol* (Paris: Cahiers du cinéma, 1987), 82–83, translation mine. Magny notes that "purely descriptive notations

turn out to be quite limited: a few place names . . . some emblematic characters . . . no economic activity whatsoever . . . practically no information on the past or the family of any of the characters" (ibid., 85).

10. Ibid., 85–86.

11. A similar problematic haunts Bresson's *Pickpocket,* as we shall appreciate in the next chapter.

12. Jean-Claude Bonnet, *"Inspecteur Lavardin:* entretien avec Claude Chabrol," *Cinématographe* 117 (March 1986): 17, translation mine.

13. Carcassonne and Fieschi, "Claude Chabrol," 9.

14. Durgnat, "Le Beau Serge," 44.

15. Horace, "The Country Mouse," trans. Hubert W. Wells, in *The Complete Works,* ed. Casper J. Kraemer, Jr. (New York: Modern Library, 1936), 70–75; Jean de La Fontaine, "Le Rat de ville et le rat des champs," in *Fables Choisies,* 2 vols. (Paris: Classiques Larousse, n.d.) 1:27ff. See also Tom Milne, "Chabrol's Schizophrenic Spider," *Sight and Sound* 39, no. 2 (Spring 1970): 59–60. R. H. Turner notes that "Horace's mouse and La Fontaine's rat escaped the perils of the city, and lived to point the moral" ("The Cousins," *Film Quarterly* 14, no. 1 [Fall 1960]: 42–43). Godard also suggested this fable in his review of *Les Cousins* ("Les Cousins," in *Godard on Godard,* trans. Tom Milne [New York: Da Capo Press, 1972], 128).

16. Quoted in Magny, *Claude Chabrol,* 29–30.

17. Cf. ibid., 59. In an earlier article on Chabrol, Magny noted, "It is significant that the greatest successes of Chabrol (both box office and critical) have been founded on misunderstandings" (*"La Musique douce* de Chabrol," *Cinéma 82* 285 [September 1982]: 40, translation mine).

18. I believe it is by now a commonplace that the film and the character played by James Stewart are emblematic of the voyeurism endemic to the cinematic experience itself.

19. All quotations from Chabrol's films are taken directly from the sound track, translations mine.

20. For example, Carlos Clarens calls *Les Cousins* "a Balzac-ian study of innocence corrupted by city life" (*"The Cousins* and *Le Beau Serge,"* 496). Rainer Werner Fassbinder, on the other hand, thinks the connection between Chabrol and Balzac evident yet hollow: "In Chabrol, France has no critic, no twentieth-century Balzac (the role in which these films indicate he would like to see himself), but France does have . . . a cynic with enormous nostalgia for the naive, for lost identity" ("Insects in a Glass Case: Random Thoughts on Claude Chabrol," *Sight and Sound* 45, no. 4 [Fall 1976]: 206).

21. See Honoré de Balzac, *Les Illusions perdues* (Paris: Garnier, 1961), 220, 463, translated by Ellen Marriage as *Lost Illusions* (Philadelphia: Gebbie, 1899). All further references to this text will be indicated in the body of the essay by IP, followed by pagination in the English and the French version, respectively.

22. See above, n. 12.

23. Several years later, Truffaut's heroine Adèle H. will refuse the gift of

a copy of her father's *Les Misérables* from another book dealer, a gesture that aligns her in an uncanny relationship with Truffaut's own relationship to "le père Hugo."

24. For an extended meditation on the authorial relationship between literature and film see my *Bertolucci's Dream Loom*.

25. Ovid, *Metamorphoses,* 177. All further references to this text will be indicated by OM.

26. For Apollodorus's version of the myth see Apollodorus, *Library of Greek Mythology,* trans. Keith Aldrich (Lawrence, Kans.: Coronado, 1975), 90.

27. Quoted in Magny, *Claude Chabrol,* 127.

28. Claude Chabrol, "Les Petits Sujets," in ibid., 191–92, translation mine.

29. Curiously, without ever evoking its mythic properties, Magny (*Claude Chabrol,* 103, 178–79) evokes the labyrinth as a metaphor for two of Chabrol's later films, *Le Scandale* and *Alice*.

30. Although the figure of incest is not immediately evident, I have always felt that the twin figures of Ariadne and Phedre sandwich Theseus in an incestuous impasse. Ariadne is obviously a maternal figure in offering the thread to Theseus, and his need to use, then reject her suggests his awareness of this. Phedre, her sister, will die because of her incestuous feelings for Theseus's son. On the development of the incest theme in French cinema see above, chap. 3.

31. Magny, *Claude Chabrol,* 59.

32. Françoise Calvez and Alain Carbonnier, "Question à Claude Chabrol et Paul Vecchiali," *Cinéma 82* 282 (June 1982): 69–74.

33. David Overbey, "Chabrol's Game of Mirrors," *Sight and Sound* 46, no. 2 (Spring 1977): 81.

34. Cited in Magny, *Claude Chabrol,* 198–99.

35. Cited in Joel Magny, "Le Joueur d'échecs," *Cahiers du cinéma* 390 (December 1986): 62–63, translation mine.

36. Bonnet, "Entretien avec Claude Chabrol," 16.

37. With his customary intuition, Jean-Luc Godard confirms this interpretation: "We can watch [Chabrol] taking his characters to their logical conclusion and making of their development the Ariadne's thread of his scenario. In *Le Beau Serge* this was already one of the film's principal features. But it is even more noticeable in *Les Cousins*. . . . Chabrol's big studio camera hunts the actors down, with both cruelty and tenderness, in all four corners of Bernard Evein's astonishing decor. Like some great beast it suspends an invisible menace over Juliette Mayniel's pretty head, forces Jean-Claude Brialy to unmask the great game, or imprisons Gérard Blain under double key with a fantastic circular movement of the camera" (*Godard on Godard,* 128–29).

38. André Malraux, *L'Espoir* (Paris: Gallimard, 1937), 95–96. For a discussion of this imagery see my *André Malraux and the Metamorphosis of Death* (New York: Columbia University Press, 1973), 107–11.

39. Fassbinder, "Insects," 205.

40. In *Les Cousins* the problem of time centers on Charles and Florence's misunderstanding about their rendezvous. He says, "See you after my three o'clock class." She arrives at three, he awaits her at five. This confusion of chronology is the motif that creates a breakdown of normal roles and coherences in the film.

41. Dominique Maillet, "Entretiens: Claude Chabrol," *Cinématographe* 24 February 1977): 28, translation mine.

42. If I insist on dream time here, it is because according to Freud, dreams scramble time, uniting present, immediate past, and remote past in a nexus of symbolically stratified meanings (see my *Bertolucci's Dream Loom*, chaps. 1 and 4).

43. Geza Roheim's work makes abundantly clear the deepest connections between myth and dream as psychic structures (see *The Gates of the Dream* [New York: International Universities Press, 1952], 423ff.).

44. I believe it is not unwarranted to see in Icarus a prefiguration of Hippolytus. Ovid (OM, 367) writes of the latter's death:

> And a fantastic mound of water swelled
> And towered mountain-high, with a loud noise
> Of bellowing, and then its crest split wide
> And out there burst, as the wave broke, a huge
> Horned bull, that reared breast-high into the air.

It is notable that both stories involve the breaking of paternal interdictions and of the oedipal bond.

45. Serge and Yvonne's first son, a *mongolien,* died at birth.

46. The word *malentendu* recalls Chabrol's discussion of his attitude toward Hitchcock.

47. See the discussion of transitional spaces and transgression in chap. 6, below.

48. In the myth his mother would be Pasiphae, she who slept with a bull.

49. And possibly suggesting cinema itself, given the "dark room" and the circular motif connected to the work of the camera. Cf. my discussion of the motifs of circularity and spinning in my *Bertolucci's Dream Loom*, chaps. 4 and 5.

50. A name originally coined by J. Hillis Miller in "Ariachne's Broken Woof," *Georgia Review,* 31, no. 1 (Spring 1977): 44–60. See also my chapter on *Spider's Stratagem* in *Bertolucci's Dream Loom.*

51. Milne, "Chabrol's Schizophrenic Spider," 60.

52. Chabrol once said, "I put a lot of projections in my films, but its not with an idea of having films within films. Perhaps I simply like projectors" (in Rui Nogueira and Nicoletta Zalaffi, "Chabrol," *Sight and Sound* 40, no. 1 [Winter 1970–71]: 4). Or perhaps he simply likes projection, as the comments below on autobiography will suggest.

53. In Carcassonne and Fieschi, "Claude Chabrol," 14.

54. Magny, *Claude Chabrol,* 17, 26.

55. Gilles Delavaud, "Chabrol Unlimited," *Cahiers du cinéma* 310 (April 1980): v. It is fascinating to note that Gide said of Balzac, "Balzac a trop de confiance en son génie; souvent, pressé par le besoin, sans doute, il bâcle ['Balzac had too much confidence in his genius; often, doubtless pressed by need, he rushed his work']."

56. Carcassonne and Fieschi, "Claude Chabrol," 9.

57. Magny notes, "The progress of Chabrol's films consists of moving from illusion to the beginnings of lucidity" (*Claude Chabrol,* 36), yet another allusion to *Les Illusions perdues.*

58. Overbey, "Chabrol's Game of Mirrors," 99.

59. Cited in Jan Dawson, "The Continental Divide," *Sight and Sound* 43, no. 1 (Winter 1973–74): 13, italics mine.

60. I am grateful to Joel Magny for disclosing the existence of these texts and for reporting on their content. The following synopsis is borrowed from his *Claude Chabrol,* 33, 34, and "*La Musique douce* de Chabrol," 49, 44.

61. Quoted in Magny, *Claude Chabrol,* 160.

62. In Alain Carbonnier, "Fritz Lang vu par . . . Claude Chabrol," *Cinéma 82* 282 (June 1982): 36.

63. Carcassonne and Fieschi, "Claude Chabrol," 6.

64. Joel Magny's conclusions about Chabrol's entire *oeuvre* generally confirm this distanciated style: "We always observe his characters from the outside . . . hence any identification is temporary and more dramatic than physical, more moral than affective. . . . The Chabrolien *mise en scène* works, not by a progressive deepening of anguish or suspense, but by a series of ruptures and reversals. . . . The Chabrolien *mise en scène* is based on a play of identification and detachment where a series of surprises breaks the illusion of the film and constantly reminds us that appearances are simultaneously deceiving and revealing. . . . What characterizes Chabrol is this deception of our senses, of the ultimate signifier, of the romantic message. Each of his films tries to be a round object, difficult to pick up. . . . The idea of repression is central to his poetic imagination" (*Claude Chabrol,* 38, 39, 49). Curiously, Magny's phrase "un objet . . . difficile à ramasser" is a quotation from Cocteau, who wanted *Orphée* to be so much an exploration of his unconscious that it should be perceived by his spectators as "un objet difficile à ramasser" (*Entretiens sur le cinématographe* [Paris: Pierre Belfond, 1973], 24).

65. Jean-Claude Bonnet, Philippe Carcassonne, and Jacques Fieschi, "*Violette Nozière:* Claude Chabrol," *Cinématographe* 39 (June 1978): 5, translation mine. Elsewhere he says, "When you look at people sometimes . . . for all you know, one of them might be a monster; and it's impossible to tell because he behaves like everybody else" (in Gordon Gow, "When the New Wave Became Old Hat," 20).

66. Carcassonne and Fieschi, "Claude Chabrol," 12–14.

67. Cited in Magny, *Claude Chabrol,* 211. Tom Milne adds, "It is characteristic of Chabrol that he should endorse the moral decisions of a man who appears indefensible. . . . Appearances have nothing to do with honesty,

sincerity or goodness in Chabrol's world. . . . Chabrol's air of calm beauty is simply a web woven by a schizophrenic spider to entrap the unwary, a mask which conceals, but never eliminates the abyss of reality underneath. . . . The strange vortex of passions which binds Chabrol's characters together makes their entanglements equally insoluble" ("Chabrol's Schizophrenic Spider," 60–61).

68. In Magny, *Claude Chabrol,* 117. Magny goes on that say that Landru is "une image bien proche de la personnalité de Chabrol."

69. Dan Yakir, "The Magical Mystery World of Claude Chabrol: An Interview," *Film Quarterly* 32, no. 3 (Spring 1979): 4.

70. Jean-Louis Comolli, "Claude Chabrol ou l'inconstance punie," in *La Femme infidèle, L'Avant-scène cinéma* 92 (May 1969): 3, translation mine.

71. Quoted in Nogueira and Zalaffi, "Chabrol," 4.

72. Yakir, "Magical Mystery World," 5.

Chapter 5: Rohmer's *Ma Nuit chez Maud*

1. Eric Rohmer, *Six contes moraux* (Paris: Editions de l'Herne, 1974), 68, trans. Sabine d'Estrée as *Six Moral Tales* (Surrey: Lorrimer, 1980), 64. All further references to this text will be indicated by SCM, followed by pagination in the English and the French edition, respectively.

2. Arthur Knight, "SR Goes to the Movies: M as in Mature," *Saturday Review,* 7 February 1970, 41.

3. See SCM, 64–65/68–69. Of course, to this view we must oppose Rohmer's own: "God save us from didactic cinema" (*Le Goût de la beauté,* ed. Jean Narboni [Paris: Flammarion, 1989], trans. Carol Volk as *The Taste for Beauty* [Cambridge: Cambridge University Press, 1989], 192).

4. Indeed, a recent essay on the film does just that. See Frank R. Cunningham, "Pascal's Wager and the Feminist Dilemma in Eric Rohmer's *My Night at Maud's,*" in *The Kingdom of Dreams in Literature and Film,* ed. Douglas Fowler (Tallahassee: Florida State University Press, 1986), 79–91. By quoting four of Pascal's major ideas without explaining how any of these illuminates the development of Rohmer's film, Cunningham illustrates the way the spectator may be seduced by the narrator's point of view and entirely miss the film's irony. See also Penelope Gilliatt, "The Current Cinema: A Good Night," *New Yorker,* 4 April 1970, 115–16.

5. I have borrowed Sara Kozloff's term from *Invisible Storytellers,* 44.

6. For a discussion of the term "enstasis" (a blind point around which the text turns) in a literary context see Claude-Gilbert Dubois, *L'Imaginaire de la renaissance* (Paris: Presses Universitaires Françaises, 1985), 223–25.

7. Rohmer expands on this idea: "There is a certainly literary material in my tales, a preestablished novelistic plot that could be developed in writing and that is, in fact, sometimes developed in the form of commentary. But neither the text of these commentaries nor that of my dialogues is my film: Rather, they are things that I film, just like the landscapes, faces, behavior,

and gestures. . . . After all, I do not say, I show" ("Letter to a Critic," in *The Taste for Beauty,* 80–81).

8. In the same way *Tous les garçons s'appellent Patrick,* made with Godard in 1956, anticipates *L'Ami de mon amie* of 1987 (see C. G. Crisp, *Eric Rohmer: Realist and Moralist* [Bloomington: Indiana University Press, 1988], 23).

9. Sara Kozloff discusses the presumed reliability of such narrators in *Invisible Storytellers.*

10. For clarity's sake, I will refer to the film's narrator as Jean-Louis and to the story's narrator as N.

11. Blaise Pascal, *Les Pensées* (1670; reprint, Paris: Seuil, 1962), trans. A. J. Krailsheimer as *Pensées* (Baltimore: Penguin, 1966), #423. Further references to Pascal's *Pensées* will be indicated by P, followed by the number of the *pensée.*

12. See Robbe-Grillet's *La Jalousie* for a continuous reinvention of the "events" of the story.

13. Rohmer, "In Search of Metaphor," in *The Taste for Beauty,* 109, italics mine.

14. See, e.g., Joel Magny, *Eric Rohmer* (Paris: Rivages, 1986), 56, 99; and Crisp, *Eric Rohmer,* 38.

15. I am thinking in particular of Proust and of the pages on Swann in *Du coté de chez Swann.*

16. Samuel Weber notes in this context, "The driving impulse of the child is toward a *particular kind of visual experience:* 'He wants to see the same thing in other people. . . . ' Perceptual recognition, the observation of what is already familiar—'the same thing'—is what the child desires, and this desire is strong enough to bend perceptual 'data' to its needs. The development of desire, as Freud describes it in *The Interpretation of Dreams,* is tied not to the perception of objects, but to their hallucination. The decisive modification implied by the 'castration complex' is that the deployment of desire implies not merely the production of hallucinations, but their *organization into a story. The story of castration* attempts to temporize the contradiction between 'perception' and 'prejudice' by temporalizing it. . . . Such a process seems to necessitate a form of articulation that is inevitably *narrative"* (*The Legend of Freud* [Minneapolis: University of Minnesota Press, 1982], 23–24).

17. Published in five parts in *Cahiers du cinéma* 44 (February 1955): 32–37; 49 (July 1955): 10–15; 51 (October 1955): 2–9; 52 (November 1955): 2–8; 53 (December 1955): 23–30. The series covers literature, painting, metaphor, music, and architecture. All translations are mine.

18. "Le Celluloid et le marbre: le siècle des peintres," *Cahiers du cinéma* 49 (July 1955): 10.

19. Rohmer's and Bresson's thinking are curiously parallel during this period. Bresson wrote, "Leonardo recommends thinking hard of the end, thinking first and foremost of the end. The end is the screen, which is only a surface. Submit your film to the reality of the screen, as a painter submits his picture to the reality of the canvas itself and of the colors applied on it, the

sculptor submits his figures to the reality of the *marble* or the bronze" (Robert Bresson, *Notes sur le cinématographe* [Paris: Gallimard, 1975], trans. Jonathan Griffin as *Notes on Cinematography* [New York: Urizen Books, 1977], 60). Rohmer in his essay "Le Celluloid et le marbre: le siècle des peintres" mentions Leonardo as well.

20. "Le Celluloid et le marbre: de la métaphore," *Cahiers du cinéma* 51 (October 1955): 6.

21. "Le Celluloid et le marbre: architecture d'apocalypse," *Cahiers du cinéma* 53 (December 1955): 23–24.

22. Ibid., 24–26. Ultimately, Rohmer saw it as the role of cinema to mediate between "two orders, one natural, the other human; one material, the other spiritual; one mechanical, the other free; one of the appetite, the other of heroism and grace—a classical opposition, but one that our art is privileged to be able to translate so well that the intermediary of the sign is replaced by immediate evidence" (*The Taste for Beauty,* ix). The immediate evidence of *Ma Nuit chez Maud* considerably muddles this opposition, as we shall see.

23. In his article on Hitchcock's *Vertigo* Rohmer made much of the opposition of two architectures, one modern, the other "turn-of-the-century homes," which create "an impression of disorientation in time. They symbolize the past." The eighteenth-century tower in the film "is linked to the major theme of the story, vertigo" (*The Taste for Beauty,* 168). Clearly, Rohmer is attentive to these architectural symbols.

24. See above, chap. 1.

25. "Le Celluloid et le marbre: architecture d'apocalypse," 25, italics mine.

26. For the role of the *deus absconditus* in Pascal see Lucien Goldmann, *Le Dieu caché* (Paris: Gallimard, 1959), trans. Philip Thody as *The Hidden God* (London: Routledge & Kegan Paul, 1964).

27. "Le Celluloid et le marbre: architecture d'apocalypse," 26.

28. *The Taste for Beauty,* 39, italics mine. Cf. "Cinema, the Art of Space," ibid., 19: "The motion picture uses a sequence of shots to help reinforce the expressive nature of each one. It does so, for example, by making slight movements perceptible (the batting of an eyelid, the clenching of a fist) or by allowing the viewer to follow the trajectories of movements that actually extend far beyond the breadth of its place of action."

29. Blaise Pascal, *Les Lettres provinciales,* in *Pascal,* ed. Louis Lafuma (Paris: Seuil, 1963), 412, trans. A. J. Krailsheimer as *The Provincial Letters* (Baltimore: Penguin, 1967), 145. All further references to this text are indicated by LP, followed by pagination in the English and the French version, respectively.

30. A distance that also measures Jean-Louis's separation from Pascal's "fire" of his conversion in the church.

31. These Marivaux titles are not gratuitous. Numerous critics of Rohmer have alluded to the presence of both Marivaux and Musset in his work. Alain Masson, for example, notes, "A paradoxical mind and friend of

the past, Rohmer judges modernity in the name of tradition: proverbs unmask comedy and comedians. This procedure is not foreign to Musset himself: Mariane's caprices or Perdican's sweet talk must both seem from a serious moral point of view, as grave problems, pathetic stammerings of a feminine liberty which can but barely reveal itself, the tragic pride of young men incapable of intimacy" ("Le Capricorne souverain de l'onde occidentale: sur les 'comédies et proverbes,'" *Positif* 307 [September 1986]: 43–45). See also Claude-Marie Trémous, "La Carte de Tendre," *Télérama,* 11 March 1981, 13; Gérard Legrand, "Notes pour *Les Aventures de Reinette et Mirabelle,*" *Positif* 309 (November 1986): 11–14; and Crisp, *Eric Rohmer,* 23.

32. Crisp, *Eric Rohmer,* 56.

33. Ibid., 57–59.

34. Crisp writes of Rohmer's *La Boulangère de Monceau,* "Both this epilogue and that of Maud can seem awkward and even superfluous, but they serve precisely to trigger off a re-evaluation and to suggest that reality is never so simple as we think" (ibid., 38). It is curious that he attempts no reevaluation of *Maud* given the irony of the epilogue.

35. It is important to note that Rohmer is at pains to clarify that the term "moral tale" refers, not to a lesson in morality, but rather to a tradition of sociological commentary in France. Rohmer had written, "In France we give the name 'moralist' to anyone who studies the ways of the heart—that is, of the personality, of social behavior, of the feelings. . . . A moralist is nearer to a psychologist than to a moralizer. But, that said, there is all the same in my Moral Tales a little morality in the traditional sense of the word; there is always a moment when the character has to make a decision of a moral nature, however high or low that 'morality' may be. . . . I chose the word 'moral' to contrast with the word 'physical,' simply as an indication that the whole point of the drama was in the evolution of the characters, not in the external events. In the six stories, there are no tragic or violent events. No deaths, no mysteries to solve. Everything is in the mind. Only the heroes' thoughts lend meaning to their acts" (cited in ibid., 32).

36. "Cinéma, art de l'espace," *Revue du cinéma* 14 (June 1948): 11, 13, cited in ibid., 3. Crisp's chapter on Rohmer's critical writings, entitled "Style and Ideology," has been immensely helpful in sorting out his evolving position on the question of realism.

37. "Vanité que la peinture," *Cahiers du cinéma* 3 (August 1951): 28, cited in Crisp, *Eric Rohmer,* 4.

38. Ibid., 22.

39. Crisp, *Eric Rohmer,* 5, 10–11.

40. Quoted in ibid., 11–12, from a survey of the relationship between film and novel published in *Cahiers du cinéma* 185 (December 1966): 123 and *Amis du film et de la télévision* 178 (March 1971).

41. See P, ##228, 242, 394, 418, 427, 429, 781, 793, 921; see also Goldmann, *Le Dieu caché.*

42. Goldmann, *Le Dieu caché,* 36–38/45–46.

43. Gérard Legrand, Hubert Niogret, and François Ramasse, "En-

tretien avec Eric Rohmer," *Positif* 309 (November 1986): 18.

44. The term is borrowed from Roland Barthes's *The Pleasure of the Text*, trans. R. Miller (New York: Hill & Wang, 1975), 64. Barthes notes, "Text means *Tissue;* but whereas hitherto we have always taken this tissue as a product, a ready-made veil, behind which lies, more or less hidden, meaning (truth), we are now emphasizing, in the tissue, the generative idea that the text is made, is worked out in a perpetual interweaving; lost in this tissue— this texture—the subject unmakes himself, like a spider dissolving in the constructive secretions of his web."

Chapter 6: Bresson's Sl(e)ight of Screen

1. Jean-Luc Godard and Michel Delahaye, "La Question: entretien avec Robert Bresson," *Cahiers du cinéma* 178 (May 1966): 69.

2. Cf. Jan Dawson, "The Invisible Enemy," *Film Comment* 13, no. 5 (September–October 1977): 24; and Gilles Gourdon, "Georges Bernanos," *Cinématographe* 41 (November 1978): 47. I except Mirella Jona Affron's essay ("Bresson and Pascal: Rhetorical Affinities," *Quarterly Review of Film Studies* 10, no. 2 [Spring 1985]: 118–34) on the parallels between the form and content of Bresson's *Notes sur le cinématographe* and Pascal's *Pensées*.

3. *Notes sur le cinématographe*, 85, 42, in English *Notes on Cinematography*, 40, 18. All further references to this text will be indicated by NC, followed by pagination in the English and the French edition, respectively. It is worth noting that the *Notes* constitutes a connection to Rohmer's work through the mediation of Pascal (see Affron, "Bresson and Pascal," which points up the many connections between Bresson's *Notes* and Pascal's *Pensées*).

4. Quoted in Rui Nogueira, "Burel and Bresson," *Sight and Sound* 46, no. 1 (1976–77): 21. Robert Vas confirms this sense of dismay, writing, "With the increasing familiarity of his methods goes a corresponding growing ambiguity of meaning, so that the ending seems as cursory as it is schematically striking. We are further from understanding Michel's pilgrimage and the forces behind it than we have ever been in the case of past Bresson heroes before" ("Pickpocket," *Monthly Film Bulletin* 27, no. 321 [October 1960]: 140).

5. E.g., in Jean-Paul Sartre's *La Nausée* (Paris: Gallimard, 1938).

6. The term "distanciation" is of course borrowed from Brecht. For a Brechtian analysis of Bresson see Susan Sontag, "Spiritual Style in the Films of Robert Bresson," in *Against Interpretation* (New York: Farrar, Straus & Giroux, 1961), 177–95.

7. Nick Browne, "Film Form/Voice-Over: Bresson's *Diary of a Country Priest*," *Yale French Studies* 60 (1980): 234.

8. Ibid., 235.

9. There is, as Browne thus notes (ibid., 239), a pairing of "written text"/"performance by voice" that focuses our attention on the battle for

supremacy of these two narrative techniques. But what is more important in *Pickpocket,* the narrative voice-off becomes a locus of conflict between what is said (or written) and what the viewer sees. Browne notes of *Diary,* "The relation between voice-over and image in the film is not essentially a difference in tenses, past and present. Within the framework of the film, there is a sense of movement between the pastness of the diary format and the presence of the unrolling image, whether accompanied by voice-over or not. . . . Within the narrative system of character, tense is only an aspect of the general problem of narrative distance. That linkage and control of two points-of-view is the underlying formal and compositional issue of the film and the basis of its power, becomes clear not so much in sequences accompanied by speech-narration that repeats what the scenes show (transparency) but in the scenes of explicit disjuncture, when the Priest says something to himself that is in conflict with what the image shows (character opaqueness)."

10. Here again I have borrowed the term "image maker" from Sarah Kozloff (see chap. 5, n. 5). For another "take" on these extra-diegetic elements see David Bordwell, *Narration in the Fiction Film* (Madison: University of Wisconsin Press, 1986), 289–310.

11. The character's facial expressionlessness is matched to the voice-off narrator's cold tone. Bresson argued (NC, 48/101) that "an ice-cold commentary can warm, by contrast, tepid ['tièdes'] dialogues in a film. Phenomenon analogous to that of hot and cold in painting." The term *tiède,* however, suggests that the dialogues themselves will hardly be lively, as indeed is the case in this film.

12. Alan Williams, "The Two Films," in *Max Ophuls and the Cinema of Desire* (New York: Arno, 1980), 17–42.

13. An accusation that might well be leveled at Bresson himself, a hypothesis whose implications I shall explore further on in this essay.

14. And a curious connection with *Les Amants,* where Jeanne and Raoul are pictured in a plane in this same amusement park.

15. Cf. André Targe, "Ici l'espace naît du temps," *Camera/Stylo* 68/69 (February 1989): 88–90, translation mine: "Far from erasing the traces of joins in the service of reinforcing narrative credibility, Bresson emphasizes them in raising the play that they introduce into the fictional continuity. . . . In place of identities or scenic tricks, the eye discerns only *functions.*" Targe evokes Eisenstein's famous comparison of montage and orchestral score in writing: "He has invented a new discourse of the image, derealizing its substance in favor of form, playing musically with rhythm and tempo" (98).

16. Ferdinand de Saussure, *Course in General Linguistics,* trans. Wade Baskin (New York: McGraw Hill, 1966), 114–16.

17. Ibid., 119–20.

18. Ibid., 116.

19. See André Bazin, "The Evolution of the Language of Cinema," in *Film Theory and Criticism,* ed. Gerald Mast and Marshall Cohen (New York: Oxford University Press, 1979), 126.

20. See Susan Sontag, *On Photography* (New York: Dell, 1973), 4–7,

111–22. Sontag's view of photography is closer to Bresson's other project of secrecy. She notes, "All that photography's program of realism actually implies is the belief that reality is hidden. And being hidden, is something to be unveiled . . . a disclosure. . . . Just to show something, anything, in the photographic view is to show that it is hidden" (120–21). See also Roland Barthes, *Camera Lucida,* trans. Richard Howard (New York: Hill & Wang, 1981).

21. Vincent Pinel notes that "the author's role consists in revealing the deeper personality of his actor. . . . To this end, Bresson uses a mechanical means: repetition. The actor, having reached a certain degree of saturation, forgets that he is 'playing' and becomes himself again. One must 'flatten the actor, make him die ["aplanir l'acteur, le faire mourir"]'" ("Le Paradoxe du non-comédien," *Etudes cinématographiques* 14–15 [1962]: 81–82, translation mine). For further discussions of Bresson's working methods with his "models" see Lars Helmstein, "Le Pont brûlé," *Camera/Stylo* 68/69 (February 1989): 28–46.

22. Marjorie Greene, "Robert Bresson," *Film Quarterly* 13, no. 2 (Winter 1959): 7.

23. See Pinel, "Le Paradoxe du non-comédien," 78–83; and Greene, "Robert Bresson," 5–10.

24. Godard, "La Question," 33–34.

25. Georges Sebbag, "Un Simple Crochet," *Camera/Stylo* 68/69 (February 1989): 5, translation mine. Sebbag adds, contrasting the usual use of actors with Bresson's, "He is seductive because he overcomes suicide, preserves appearances, and somehow manages to avoid the passage of time. But this long view of his is a disadvantage in the present moment: the current drama is somehow forgotten in the reconstitution of a trajectory that leads the actor outside the film to others he has done or will do. . . . By contrast, in Bresson's film an unknown profile, a strange body, neutralize these other voices that prevent us from authenticating a sequence and prolonging the action" (ibid.).

26. For a discussion of Brando's intertextuality, see my *Bertolucci's Dream Loom,* 120.

27. I am not the only viewer to see this allusion. Many of Bresson's critics have noted it in passing, among them René Cortade ("*Pickpocket* ou le roman russe à la glacière," *Arts, Lettres, Spectacles,* 23–29 December 1959, 7); Richard Roud ("The Redemption of Despair," *Film Comment* 13, no. 5 [September–October 1977]: 23–24); Lindley Hanlon (*Fragments: Bresson's Film Style* [Rutherford, N.J.: Fairleigh Dickinson University Press, 1986], 27ff.); Michel Estève (*Robert Bresson: la passion du cinématographe* [Paris: Albatros, 1983], 60ff.); and Mireille Latil-Le Dantec ("Bresson, Dostoievski," *Cinématographe* 73 [December 1981]: 11–17).

28. Fyodor Dostoevsky, *Crime and Punishment,* trans. Constance Garnett (New York: Modern Library, n.d.), 328–29. All further references to this novel will be indicated by CP.

29. The scene in *Crime and Punishment* (56–60) in which Raskolnikov

dreams that he witnessed the cruel bludgeoning of a little sorel horse bears striking similarities to the general theme of Bresson's film *Au hasard Balthazar,* about the donkey Balthazar.

30. André Bazin, "*Le Journal d'un curé de campagne* et la stylistique de Robert Bresson," in *Qu'est-ce que le cinéma* (Paris: Cerf, 1985), 114, 119, 126, translation mine.

31. Roger Tailleur, "*Pickpocket:* le pheaurme," *Positif* 33 (April 1960): 44. Colin Young argues that Bresson shows "only limited interest in the inspector/suspect relationship—he wishes us to see Michel alone" ("Conventional-Unconventional," *Film Quarterly* 17, no. 1 [Fall 1963]: 18). Only Latil-Le Dantec's "Bresson, Dostoievski" and Hanlon's *Fragments: Bresson's Film Style* develop the Bresson/Dostoevsky parallel to any great extent. I shall discuss their analyses below.

32. Paul Schrader, "Robert Bresson, Possibly," *Film Comment* 13, no. 5 (September–October 1977): 27.

33. Obviously these are Bakhtin's terms as used in *Problems of Dostoevsky's Poetics,* trans. R. W. Rotsel (New York: Ardis, 1973). I shall have occasion to return to them later in this essay.

34. Maurice Beebe, "The Three Motives of Raskolnikov," in *"Crime and Punishment" and the Critics,* ed. Edward Wasiolek (Belmont, Calif.: Wadsworth, 1961), 108.

35. Edward Wasiolek, "Structure and Detail," in ibid., 115.

36. Konstantin Mochulsky, *Dostoevsky: His Life and Work,* trans. Michael Minihan (Princeton: Princeton University Press, 1967), 312.

37. A. Boyce Gibson, *The Religion of Dostoevsky* (Philadelphia: Westminster, 1973), 92, 102.

38. Michael Holquist, *Dostoevsky and the Novel* (Princeton: Princeton University Press, 1977), 75, 100–101.

39. Philip Rahv, "Dostoevsky in *Crime and Punishment,*" in Wasiolek, *"Crime and Punishment" and the Critics,* 17. See also J. Middleton Murry, "Beyond Morality," in *Fyodor Dostoevsky: A Critical Study* (London: Martin Secker, 1916), reprinted in ibid., 47–53; Ernest J. Simmons, *Dostoevsky: The Making of a Novelist* (London: John Lehmann, 1950), 133; and Derek Offord, "The Causes of Crime and the Meaning of Law: *Crime and Punishment* and Contemporary Radical Thought," in *New Essays on Dostoevsky,* ed. Malcolm Jones and Garth Terry (Cambridge: Cambridge University Press, 1983), 41–65.

40. Jorge Luis Borges, "The Wall and the Books," in *Labyrinths* (New York: New Directions, 1962), 188.

41. Latil-Le Dantec, "Bresson, Dostoievski," 17. She is referring to the fact that after *Un Condamné à mort s'est echappé,* Bresson's work becomes increasingly bleak and pessimistic. His latest film, *Le Diable probablement,* is a misanthropic tale that ends in the suicide of its protagonist, Michel—the name of the hero of *Pickpocket* and of Gide's *L'Immoraliste,* another novel that resonates dramatically with this film. René Prédal adds, "The bleakness of

the last films of Bresson is equaled only by that of Godard's works. Enclosed in an armor of iron predestination, his characters find no escape from their despair and die miserable. . . . His heroes are unattached, incapable of forming attachments with others. . . . His condemnation is total, global" ("Bresson et son temps," *Cinéma 83* 294 [June 1983]: 10). See also Joel Magny, "L'Expérience intérieure de Robert Bresson," ibid. 23ff. Even a Christian writer like Jan Dawson concludes of Bresson, "His vision of Christ is a suicidal one. . . . If he has achieved a state of grace, it is a nihilistic grace" ("The Invisible Enemy," 25). Jean Sémolué adds, "To accomplish in front of us the action that will reveal their inner selves, Bresson's solitary characters emerge from the darkness only to disappear into darkness and silence once their action is accomplished" ("Les Personnages de Robert Bresson," *Cahiers du cinéma* 75 [October 1957]: 15). Calvin Green likewise concludes, "Bresson's films since *Pickpocket* have all emphasized the same mixed pessimism: grace alienates and mortifies" ("*Ars Theologica:* Man and God at the New York Film Festival," *Cinéaste* 3, no. 2 [Fall 1969]: 7). Cf. Estève, *Robert Bresson: la passion du cinématographe,* 134.

42. See Wasiolek, "Structure and Detail," 115; and Murry, "Beyond Morality," 47–53.

43. Paul Schrader, "Robert Bresson," in *Transcendental Style in Film: Ozu, Bresson, Dreyer* (Berkeley and Los Angeles: University of California Press, 1972), 93, 81.

44. Daniel Millar, "Pickpocket," in *The Films of Robert Bresson,* ed. Ian Cameron (New York: Praeger, 1969), 85; Richard Roud, "Novel Novel: Fable Fable?" *Sight and Sound* 31, no. 2 (Spring 1962): 86.

45. Amédée Ayfre, "The Universe of Robert Bresson," in Cameron, *The Films of Robert Bresson,* 23.

46. Michel Estève, "Permanence de Robert Bresson," *Etudes cinématographiques* 3–4 (1960): 227–28. Cf. Jean Wagner, "L'Homme derrière l'objet," *Cahiers du cinéma* 104 (February 1960): 50: "If there are bars separating the two heroes in the last scene, their souls are united: the wind listeth where it will."

47. Jean Sémolué, "Les Limites de la liberté," *Etudes cinématographiques* 3–4 (1960): 238–39, translation mine.

48. Allen Thiher writes, "In nearly all his works, be it *Au hasard Balthazar, Jeanne d'Arc, Pickpocket,* or *Une Femme douce,* Bresson's narrative turns in one way or another on isolation and humiliation, on estrangement and the impossibility of a desired community. Only in *Un Condamné à mort* does transcendence seem to be realized in the flesh" ("The Existentialist Moment: Bresson's *Un Condamné à mort:* The Semiotics of Grace," in *The Cinematic Muse: Critical Studies in the History of French Cinema* [Columbia: University of Missouri Press, 1979], 136).

49. Seguin, "Pickpocket," *Positif* 33 (April 1960): 41; Tailleur, "Pickpocket," 44.

50. Vas, "Pickpocket," 140. John Russel Taylor concludes, "There is no

sense of a process completed, but only of an inexplicable change of character" ("Robert Bresson," in *Cinema Eye, Cinema Ear: Some Key Filmmakers of the Sixties* [New York: Hill & Wang, 1964], 135).

51. See above, n. 33.

52. For a discussion of Chernyshevsky's role in Dostoevsky's work see Offord, "The Causes of Crime and the Meaning of Law."

53. The title of Camus's anthology of essays is *L'Envers et l'endroit*.

54. Certainly the theme of carnival goes back a long way. Bakhtin explores it in Rabelais's work, of course (see Mikhael Bakhtin, *Rabelais and His World,* trans. Helene Iswolsky [Cambridge: MIT Press, 1968]), but Curtius notes its presence already in the *Carmina Burana* as well as other works of antiquity (see Ernst Robert Curtius, *European Literature and the Latin Middle Ages* [New York: Harper & Row, 1953], 94–98).

55. Bakhtin, *Problems of Dostoevsky's Poetics,* 5.

56. Ibid., 87, 100–101.

57. A comparison of Nietzsche's *Beyond Good and Evil* with Michel's arguments to the police inspector reveals surprising coincidences (see *Beyond Good and Evil,* trans. Walter Kaufmann [New York: Vintage, 1966], 31, 37, 41–42, 44, 55ff.). I shall have more to say about Bresson's relationship to Camus below.

58. Bakhtin, *Problems of Dostoevsky's Poetics,* 142.

59. See Mireille Latil-le Dantec, "Le Diable probablement," *Cinématographe* 29 (July–August 1977): 32: "The negative gestural asceticism of *Pickpocket* subverts the accepted order of things, which it refuses because, in any case, the world is upside-down ['le monde est à l'envers']." And Jeanne will say to Michel, "You're not of this world ['Vous n'êtes pas dans la vie reelle']." I shall have more to say on this point below.

60. Edward Wasiolek, *Dostoevsky* (Cambridge: MIT Press, 1964), 83.

61. See Browne, "Film Form/Voice Over," 236. Browne writes of *Diary of a Country Priest,* "That linkage and control of two points-of-view is the underlying formal and compositional issue of the film, and the basis of its power, becomes clear not so much in sequences accompanied by speech-narration that repeats what the scenes show (transparence), but in the scenes of explicit disjuncture, when the Priest says something to himself that is in conflict with what the image shows (character opaqueness)."

62. This tendency has been noted by Patrick Bensard ("Notes sur *Pickpocket,*" in *Camera/Stylo* 69/69 [February 1989]: 113) and by Lindley Hanlon, (*Fragments,* 40, 114).

63. Richard S. Lambert, *The Prince of Pickpockets: A Study of George Barrington Who Left His Country For His Country's Good* (London: Faber & Faber, 1930), 34. Further quotations from this text will be indicated by PP.

64. Rahv, "Dostoevsky in *Crime and Punishment,*" 37. This is a feature, by the way, common to Dostoevsky, Bresson, and Camus, whose presence in this film is also remarkably complex.

65. Jacques Doniol-Valcroze and Jean-Luc Godard, "Entretien avec Robert Bresson," *Cahiers du cinéma* 104 (February 1960): 4.

66. The sense of Montaigne's text is, according to Tom Conley (unpublished letter to the author), rather the detached hand, the representation of an absence, following Christian iconography.

67. R. M. Arlaud et al., "Propos de Robert Bresson," *Cahiers du Cinéma* 75 (October 1957): 7.

68. *Arts*, 17 June 1959, quoted in Estève, *Robert Bresson: la passion du cinématographe*, 63.

69. Sémolué, "Les Limites de la liberté," 233. Lars Helmstein, "Le Pont brûlé," 36, is also quite explicit about the connection between Bresson's character of the pickpocket and his own approach to the cinema.

70. Doniol-Valcroze and Godard, "Entretien avec Robert Bresson," 6–7.

71. Pinel, "Le Paradoxe du non-comédien," 81.

72. Greene, "Robert Bresson," 7.

73. Magny, "L'Expérience intérieure," 22, translation mine.

74. Louis Malle, "Avec *Pickpocket* Bresson a trouvé," *Arts, Lettres, Spectacles*, 30 December 1959–5 January 1960, 1, 6. Patrick Bensard develops this angle, if obliquely, in "Notes sur *Pickpocket*," 111ff. They are not alone in this observation: Eric Rhode notes that Michel's robberies are for "erotic satisfaction" ("Pickpocket," *Sight and Sound* 29, no. 4 [Fall 1960]: 193). Magny comments cryptically, "Sexuality occupies a stronger place in the work of Robert Bresson the more his work becomes pessimistic" ("L'Expérience intérieure," 23).

75. Jacques Frenais notes that "*Pickpocket* is constructed like a sexual conquest, like a pick-up ['comme la drague']. In fact, the pickpocket Michel is Don Juan" ("Autour du *Pickpocket* de Robert Bresson," *Cinéma 78* 235 [July 1978]: 36).

76. Jean-Pierre Oudart, "Le Hors-champ de l'auteur," *Cahiers du cinéma* 236–37 (March–April 1972): 86.

77. Gide's *L'Immoraliste* provides one of the models for this film. Michel, the novel's narrator, watches, like Bresson, with quiet complicity and a secret voyeuristic pleasure, as an Arab youth steals a pair of scissors from him.

78. Patrick Bensard calls *Pickpocket* a "joyless Don-juanism" ("Notes sur *Pickpocket*," 113).

79. Not surprisingly, given the fact that he has been in analysis for many years. See Prédal, "Bresson et son temps," 10.

80. Jacques Frenais, "Autour du *Pickpocket*," 37.

81. Joyce McDougall, *Théâtres du Je* (Paris: Gallimard, 1982), 10, 36, translation mine.

82. Ibid., 56.

83. Pinel, "Le Paradoxe du non-comédien," 83. For other similar observations on Bresson's treatment of his actors see Jacques Laurans, "Le Choix d'un modèle," *Camera/Stylo* 68/69 (February 1989): 8–10; Helmstein, "Le Pont brûlé," 28–46; and Gourdon, "Georges Bernanos," 47.

84. Roland Monod, "Working with Bresson," *Sight and Sound* 27, no. 1 (Summer 1957): 32.

85. Cf. Joyce McDougall, *Plaidoyer pour une certaine anormalité* (Paris: Gallimard, 1978), 107: "Certain analysands . . . give the impression of repeating indefatigably an old situation in which the former child had to create a vacuum between himself and the Other, denying reality and eliminating unbearable affects"; see also ibid., 133ff., translation mine.

86. Oudart, "Le Hors-champ de l'auteur," 98, translation mine. See also Oudart's "Un Pouvoir qui ne pense, ne calcule, ni ne juge?" *Cahiers du cinéma* 258–59 (July–August 1975): 37. The ultimate repression of the actor, according to Marie-Claire Ropars-Wuilleumier ("Un Mauvais Rêve," in *L'Ecran de la mémoire* [Paris: Seuil, 1970], 178–81), occurs in Bresson's *Au hasard Balthazar.*

87. McDougall, *Plaidoyer pour une certaine anormalité*, 53. Elsewhere she notes, "It is no longer the disavowal of a *sensory perception* but something infinitely more elaborate and evolved, a disavowal, certainly, but of a different order" (52).

88. Ibid., 50. Cf. Bresson's statement: "Cinematography a military art. Prepare a film like a battle" (NC, 9/25). Cf. the following statement by André Targe: "In a universe entirely fragmented, devoid of any touchstone, filmic time breakdown loses the artificial coherence that editing normally gives it" ("Ici l'espace naît du temps," 90).

89. Cited in McDougall, *Plaidoyer pour une certaine anormalité*, 60.

90. Pierre Jouvet, "D'Homère à Proust: de Griffith à Bresson," *Cinématographe* 32 (November 1977): 9.

91. Marjorie Green, "Robert Bresson," 7.

Chapter 7: Godard's Quotations

1. Pamela Falkenberg, "'Hollywood' and the 'Art Cinema' as a Bipolar Modeling System: *A bout de souffle* and *Breathless*," *Wide Angle* 7, no. 3 (1985): 51.

2. Ibid., 52.

3. Cited in Jean-Marie Touratier and Daniel Busto, *Jean-Luc Godard: télévision/écritures* (Paris: Galilée, 1979), 122, translation mine.

4. I am not the first viewer to notice the similarities between these two films: see, e.g., Marie-Claire Ropars-Wuilleumier, "La Forme et le fond ou les avatars du récit," in *L'Ecran de la mémoire* (Paris: Seuil, 1970), 91ff.

5. Ibid., 91.

6. Mireille Latil-Le Dantec, "Jean-Luc Godard ou l'innocence perdue," *Etudes cinématographiques* 57–61 (1967): 50.

7. *Breathless*, ed. Dudley Andrew (New Brunswick: Rutgers University Press, 1987), 86; all further quotations from this film will be indicated by B. *Pierrot le fou*, trans. Peter Whitehead, rev. ed. (London: Lorrimer, 1984), 92; all further quotations from this film will be indicated by PF. Many of these parallels have been noted by Mireille Latil-Le Dantec in her essay, just quoted.

8. Gilles Jacob, "*Pierrot le fou:* sélection du Godard's Digest," *Cinéma 65* 101 (December 1965): 100–101, translation mine.

9. Ropars-Wuilleumier, "La Forme et le fond." As in all of her work, Ropars-Wuilleumier produces a perceptive, highly original reading of Godard's style(s) and in particular his "nouvelle forme de montage," which led to a new sense of poetry in his later films. Although I agree with the larger thrust of her essay, I will take issue here with her dismissal of the specific "significations" of Godard's citations.

10. Jacob, "Pierrot le fou," 100.

11. Dudley Andrew, "*Breathless:* Old as New," in *Breathless,* ed. Dudley Andrew (New Brunswick, N.J.: Rutgers University Press, 1987), 3–20; Ropars, "The Graphic in Film Writing."

12. Andrew, "Breathless," 17–20.

13. Jean Collet, Michel Delhaye, Jean-André Fieschi, André Labarthe, and Bertrand Tavernier, "François Truffaut," *Cahiers du cinéma* 138 (December 1962): 55.

14. Andrew, "Breathless," 15, 19.

15. Ropars-Wuilleumier, "La Forme et le fond," 96–97, translation mine.

16. Ropars, "The Graphic in Film Writing," 152, 153.

17. Jacques Belmans, "L'Ethique et l'esthétique du chaos," *Etudes cinématographiques* 57–61 (1967): 86, 94, adds yet another voice to this position.

18. Ropars-Wuilleumier, "La Forme et le fond," 100.

19. Ibid., 101.

20. Andrew, "Breathless," 10.

21. In *Godard on Godard,* 25, 27. All further references to this text will be indicated by G/G.

22. J. P. Telotte, *Voices in the Dark: The Narrative Patterns of Film Noir* (Urbana: University of Illinois Press, 1989), 26–27.

23. Roud writes in his footnote to Godard's "Defence and Illustration of Classical Construction" (G/G, 248–49): "The original title of this article (echoing the famous *Défense et illustration de la langue française,* a treatise by the sixteenth-century poet, Joachim du Bellay) is 'Défense et illustration du découpage classique.' *Découpage* is a difficult word to translate, usually rendered in multilingual vocabularies as either 'scenario' or 'shooting script.' 'Scenario' is misleading, since it usually implies no more than a story outline; 'shooting script' is better, but still not entirely satisfactory. The key idea in *découpage*—literally cutting up—is the break-down into scenes or shots, and their juxtaposition. Thus one can talk about the *découpage* of a comic strip. I have used 'construction' as a compromise, since English film vocabulary offers no word to serve as a link between the script and the editing stages."

24. Andrew, "Breathless," 11–15, italics mine.

25. Ibid., 11.

26. Dylan Thomas, *Portrait of the Artist as a Young Dog* (New York: New Directions, 1940), 91–92, italics mine.

27. Ropars, "The Graphic in Film Writing," 153.

28. Maurice Sachs, *Abracadabra* (Paris: Gallimard, 1952), 66, 68. All further references to this novel will be indicated by Aa; translations are mine.

29. Arlene Croce, "Breathless," *Film Quarterly* 14, no. 3 (Spring 1961): 56.

30. William Faulkner, *The Wild Palms* (New York: Random House, 1939), 24–25. All further references to this novel will be indicated by WP.

31. Dudley Andrew has also noted the significance of Melville in the film and revealed another allusion to Melville's *Bob le flambeur* in the scene in the travel agency ("Breathless," 13). Godard makes frequent references to cars in discussing cinema, e.g.: "One shouldn't admire Vadim simply because he does naturally what should long ago have been the ABC of the French cinema. We no longer admire a Maserati or the Leduc 022 for the same reasons that our grandparents admired a de Dion-Bouton" (G/G, 55).

32. Andrew, "Breathless," 13.

33. Ibid., 20.

34. Collet et al., "François Truffaut," 44.

35. Godard's term, used in an essay entitled "Sait-on jamais," in G/G, 55.

36. Jacob, "Pierrot le fou," 102; Jean-Louis Curtis, "Le Fou d'Anna," *La Nouvelle Revue française* 160 (April 1966): 689, translations mine.

37. Curtis, "Le Fou d'Anna," 689. See also Noel Burch, *Theory of Film Practice,* trans. Helen Lane (1973; reprint, Princeton: Princeton University Press, 1981), 148ff.

38. Lionel White, *Obsession* (New York: E. P. Dutton, 1962), 63. All further references to this text will be indicated by O. Godard parodies this redundancy in *Pierrot* when Belmondo jokes, "Its lucky I don't like spinach because I would crave it if I was deprived of it. I'd not be able to stand it."

39. See Silverman, *The Acoustic Mirror,* 1–69 passim, for remarks on the position of women in Hollywood cinema.

40. Elie Faure, *Histoire de l'Art,* vol. 1, *L'Art Moderne* (1924; reprint, Paris: Poche, 1964), trans. Walter Pach as *History of Art,* vol. 1, *Modern Art* (Garden City, N.Y.: Garden City Publishing, 1937), 124/167 (English and French pagination, respectively).

41. Ibid.

42. Ibid., 125/168.

43. Ibid., 126/171.

44. The Parisians usually spell out the first three numbers on the telephone dial, giving them cultural suffixes. Thus 225 reads, "BALzac." Godard is surely alluding here to the telephone number that used to ring out during every film presentation in Paris when it came time for the advertising "intermission." BALzac 0001 was the number of the ad agency responsible for these interludes.

45. Honoré de Balzac, *César Birotteau* (Paris: Editions de la Pléiade, 1936), 440, trans. Ellen Marriage as *The Rise and Fall of César Birotteau* (New York: Carroll & Graf, 1989), 141; see also 34ff./351ff. All further references

to this text will be indicated by CB, followed by pagination in the English and the French version, respectively.

46. See Louis-Ferdinand Céline, *Guignol's Band* (Paris: Gallimard, 1952), 331, trans. Bernard Frechtman and Jack T. Nile as *Guignol's Band* (New York: New Directions, 1954), 240. All further references to this novel will be indicated by GB, followed by pagination in the English and the French, respectively.

47. Curtis, "Le Fou d'Anna," 689.

48. Despite Gilles Jacob's confusions ("Pierrot le fou," 100–102), this dead man represents another allusion to Lionel White's *Obsession.*

49. Indeed, the entire sequence constitutes an ironic reprise of Malle's *Les Amants.*

50. Raymond Queneau, *Pierrot mon ami* (Paris: Gallimard, 1943). All references to this text will be indicated by PMA; translations are mine.

51. Louis Aragon, *La Mise à mort* (Paris: Gallimard, 1965), 86, 91. All further references to this novel will be indicated by MM; translations are mine.

52. Saussure, *Course in General Linguistics,* 66; further references will be indicated by CGL. See also the remarks on Saussure in chap. 6, above.

53. See Jacques Lacan, "Le Stade du miroir comme formateur de la fonction du Je," *Revue française de psychanalyse* 4 (October–December 1949): 449–55, trans. Alan Sheridan as "The Mirror Stage as Formative of the Function of the I as Revealed in Psychoanalytic Experience," in *Ecrits: A Selection* (New York: W. W. Norton, 1977), 1–7.

54. Mehlman, "French Freud," 6, italics mine.

55. Ragland-Sullivan, *Lacan and the Philosophy of Psychoanalysis,* 34, 39, 43. This idea has recently been reconfirmed by Helen Myers in "Introduction to the Ego and the Self," where she sees the ego as "a set of functions, more or less stable over time, containing both experiential and nonexperiential aspects [combining] adaptive and defensive functions . . . synthetic and integrative functions . . . from sensory-motor through symbolic to operational intelligence" (138) and "a center of initiative for action in the service of mastery, self-preservation, and internal balance," i.e., largely nonproblematical (140). See also Robert Michels, "The Mind and Its Occupants," in *Psychoanalysis: Toward the Second Century,* ed. Arnold M. Cooper, Otto F. Kernberg, and Ethal Person (New Haven: Yale University Press, 1989), 143–52; and Roy Schafer, "Narratives of the Self," ibid. 153–67. The Lacanian view is developed in Ragland-Sullivan, *Lacan and the Philosophy of Psychoanalysis,* 39–43ff.

56. This sequence has been dissected by David Bordwell in "Godard and Narration," in *Narration in the Fiction Film* (Madison: University of Wisconsin Press, 1985), 311–34.

57. An echo of Delphine Seyrig's sense of dispersion in *L'Année dernière à Marienbad.*

58. "It's the man in the moon," says Ferdinand. "And do you know what he's doing? He's crossing himself like mad. . . . Because he's fed up. When he

saw Leonov land on the moon, he was happy. At long last someone to talk to! Since the beginning of time he's been the only inhabitant of the moon. But Leonov tried as hard as he could to force the entire works of Lenin into his head. So, as soon as White landed, on his trip, he went for refuge with the American. He'd not had time to say hello, before White stuffed a bottle of Coca-Cola down his throat, demanding that he say thank you beforehand. No wonder he's fed up" (PF, 58).

Conclusion: The Library as Psychic Labyrinth

1. "Some Character Types Met With in Psycho-analytic Work," 329–31.
2. Kaja Silverman, *The Subject of Semiotics* (New York: Oxford University Press, 1983), 148, 221.
3. Mark Crispin Miller, "End of Story," in *Seeing Through Movies,* ed. Miller (New York: Pantheon, 1990), 198, 204, 213–38 passim.
4. Brunette and Wills, *Screen/Play: Derrida and Film Theory,* 144.
5. Ibid., 148.
6. The term was also used by Brunette and Wills in ibid., 123.
7. Quoted in ibid., 29.
8. Quoted in Miller, "End of Story," 221.
9. Ibid., 221.

Select Bibliography

François Truffaut

Works by Truffaut

Les Aventures d'Antoine Doinel. Paris: Mercure de France, 1970.

Le Cinéma selon François Truffaut. Edited by Anne Gillain. Paris: Flammarion, 1988.

Le Cinéma selon Hitchcock. Paris: Robert Laffont, 1966. Translated by Helen Scott as *Hitchcock*. New York: Simon & Schuster, 1983.

Les Films de ma vie. Paris: Flammarion, 1975. Translated by Leonard Mayhew as *The Films in My Life*. New York: Simon & Schuster, 1978.

Les 400 coups. Paris: Gallimard, 1960.

Jules et Jim. Paris: Seuil, 1962. Translated by Nicholas Fry as *Jules and Jim*. New York: Simon & Schuster, 1968.

"Jules et Jim: Sex and Life." *Films and Filming* 8, no. 10 (July 1962): 19.

Le Plaisir des yeux. Paris: Flammarion, 1987.

Truffaut by Truffaut. Edited by Dominique Rabourdin. Translated by Robert Wolf. New York: Abrams, 1987.

"Un Texte inédit sur Orson Welles." *Cinématographe* 15 (January 1977): 21–22.

Interviews

Carcassonne, Pierre. "Entretien avec François Truffaut." *Cinématographe* 44 (February 1979): 58–63.

Collet, Jean, Michel Delhaye, Jean-André Fieschi, André Labarthe, and Bertrand Tavernier. "François Truffaut." *Cahiers du cinéma* 138 (December 1962): 41–59.

Bibliography

Daney, Serge. "Entretien avec François Truffaut." *Cahiers du cinéma* 315 (September 1980): 7–17; 316 (October 1980): 21–30+.

Fieschi, Jacques. "François Truffaut." *Cinématographe* 27 (May 1977): 20–25.

Fieschi, Jacques, and Nestor Almendros. "Interview." *Cinématographe* 105 (December 1984): 34–38.

Insdorf, Annette. "Interview: François Truffaut, Feminist Filmmaker?" *Take One* 6, no. 2 (1978): 16–17.

"Interview." *New Yorker,* 20 February 1960, 36–37.

Kowinski, William. "François Truffaut: The Man Who Loved Movies." *Rolling Stone,* 14 June 1979, 43–44.

Marcorelles, Louis. "Interview with Truffaut." *Sight and Sound* 31, no. 1 (Winter 1961–62): 35–37, 48.

"Truffaut." *New Yorker,* 17 October 1970, 35–37.

Critical Works on Truffaut

Allen, Don. *Finally Truffaut*. New York: Beaufort Books, 1985.

———. "Truffaut Twenty Years After." *Sight and Sound* 48, no. 4 (Fall 1979): 224–28.

Almendros, Nestor. "Des solutions très claires." *Cahiers du cinéma,* special issue, December 1984, 70–72.

Armes, Roy. "François Truffaut." In *French Cinema since 1946,* 2:55–68. 2 vols. London: A. Zwemmer, 1966.

Baker, Peter. "Jules et Jim." *Films and Filming* 8, no. 9 (June 1962): 31.

Beylie, Claude. "L'Homme qui aimait les livres." *L'Avant-scène* 362–63 (July–August 1987): 3.

Bordwell, David. "François Truffaut: A Man Can Serve Two Masters." *Film Comment* 7, no. 1 (Spring 1971): 18–23.

Brody, Alan. "Jules and Catherine and Jim and Hedda." *Journal of Aesthetic Education* 5 (April 1971): 91–101.

Carcassonne, Pierre. "Dossier: cinéma et littérature: Truffaut le narrateur." *Cinématographe* 32 (November 1977): 15–17.

Coffee, Barbara. "Art and Film in François Truffaut's *Jules and Jim* and *Two English Girls*." *Film Heritage* 9, no. 3 (Spring 1974): 1–11.

Davidson, D. "From Virgin to Dynamo: The Amoral Woman in European Cinema." *Cinema Journal* 21, no. 1 (1981): 31–58.

Decaux, Emanuel. "L'Homme qui aimait les livres." *Cinématographe* 105 (December 1984): 45–47.

Fieschi, Jacques. "Truffaut critique." *Cinématographe* 25 (October–November 1975): 20.

Flauss, J. "Jules et Jim." *Film Journal* 22 (October 1963): 19–26.

Greenspun, Roger. "*Elective Affinities:* Aspects of *Jules et Jim*." *Sight and Sound* 32, no. 2 (Spring 1963): 78–82.

Grossvogel, David I. "Truffaut and Roché: Diverse Voices of the Novel and Film." *Diacritics* 3 (Spring 1973): 47–52.

Insdorf, Annette. *François Truffaut*. Boston: Twayne, 1978.

Klein, Michael. "The Literary Sophistication of François Truffaut." *Film Comment,* 3, no. 3 (Summer 1965): 24–29.

McDougal, Stuart. "Adaptation of an Auteur: Truffaut's *Jules and Jim.*" In *Modern European Filmmakers and the Art of Adaptation,* edited by Andrew Horton and Joan Magretta, 89–99. New York: Frederick Ungar, 1981.

Petrie, Graham. *The Cinema of François Truffaut*. New York: Barnes & Noble, 1970.

Roud, Richard. "Jules et Jim." *Sight and Sound* 31, no. 3 (Summer 1962): 142–43.

Sarris, Andrew. "Jules et Jim." *Village Voice,* 3 May 1962, 11–12.

Shatnoff, Judith. "The Anarchist Imagination." *Film Quarterly* 16, no. 3 (Spring 1963): 3–11.

Taylor, John Russel. "The New Wave." In *Cinema Eye, Cinema Ear,* 200–229. New York: Hill & Wang, 1964.

Thiher, Allen. "The Existential Play in Truffaut's Early Films." In *The Cinematic Muse: Critical Studies in the History of French Cinema,* 143–64. Columbia: University of Missouri Press, 1979.

Tintner, A. R. "Truffaut's *La Chambre Verte:* Hommage to Henry James." *Literature/Film Quarterly* 8, no. 2 (1980): 78–83.

Tyler, Parker. "Jules et Jim." *Film Culture* 25 (Summer 1962): 21–24.

Louis Malle

Works by Malle

Louis Malle par Louis Malle. Edited by Jacques Mallecot and Sarah Kant. Paris: Athanor, 1978.

Interviews

Braucourt, Gilles. "En direct avec Louis Malle." *Ecran* 25 (May 1974): 22–24.

Cott, Jonathan. "Fires Within: The Chaste Sensuality of Director Louis Malle." *Rolling Stone,* 6 April 1978, 38–41, 43–45.

Horton, Andrew. "An Interview with Louis Malle." *Literature/Film Quarterly* 7, no. 2 (1979): 86–98.

Jacob, Gilles. "Entretien avec Louis Malle." *Positif* 157 (March 1974): 28–35.

Macksey, R. "Malle on Malle." Pts. 1 and 2. *Post Script* 2, nos. 1, 2 (Fall 1982, Spring 1983): 2–12, 2–13.

Rollet, Ronald T. "An Interview with Louis Malle." *Film Library Quarterly* 9, no. 4 (1977): 45–47, 61–64.

Toubiana, Serge. "Souvenirs d'en France: entretien avec Louis Malle." *Cahiers du cinéma* 400 (October 1987): 21–22.

Yakir, Dan. "Louis Malle: An Interview from *The Lovers* to *Pretty Baby.*" *Film Quarterly* 31, no. 4 (Summer 1978): 2–10.

Critical Works on Malle

Alexander, A. J. "A Modern Hero: The Nongenue." *Film Culture* 22–23 (Summer 1961): 81–90.

Alpert, Hollis. "Love Story." *Saturday Review,* 8 August 1959, 24.

Armes, Roy. "Louis Malle." In *French Cinema since 1946,* 2:150–58. 2 vols. London: A. Zwemmer, 1966.

Burch, Noel. "Qu'est-ce que La Nouvelle Vague?" *Film Quarterly* 13, no. 2 (Winter 1959): 16–30.

Clarens, Carlos. "Fleurs de Malle." *Village Voice,* 28 February 1984, 58.

Collard, Charles. "Louis Malle." *Cinématographe* 113 (September 1985): 51–54.

Cott, Jonathan. "Louis Malle: Images of Decay and Change." *Rolling Stone,* 30 April 1981, 39.

Durgnat, Raymond. "Midnight Sun." *Films and Filming* 8, no. 8 (May 1962): 21–23, 46–48.

Fitzpatrick, Ellen. "The Lovers." *Films in Review* 10, no. 9 (November 1959): 561–62.

Gow, Gordon. "Louis Malle's France." *Films and Filming* 10, no. 11 (August 1964): 14–18.

Hartung, Philip. "What the Wave Brought." *Commonweal* 71 (November 1959): 265.

Lawson, John Howard. *Film: The Creative Process.* New York: Hill & Wang, 1964.

McCarten, John. "The Current Cinema: Love at a Glance." *New Yorker,* 7 November 1959, 204–5.

Meekas, Jonas. "Les Amants." *Village Voice,* 4 November 1959, 21.

R., E. H. "Les Amants." *BFI Monthly Bulletin* 26 (1959): 154.

Rollet, Ronald T. "The Documentary Films of Louis Malle." *Film Library Quarterly* 9, no. 4 (1977): 7–44.

Rotha, Paul. "Les Amants." *Films and Filming* 5, no. 9 (June 1959): 21.

Roud, Richard. "Les Amants." *Sight and Sound* 28, no. 1 (Winter 1958–59): 21–22.

Sabouraud, François. "L'Atomisation comme méthode." *Cahiers du cinéma* 398 (July–August 1987): 36–38.

Toubiana, Serge. "Regards d'enfants." *Cahiers du cinéma* 400 (October 1987): 19–20.

Weber, Eugen. "An Escapist Realism." *Film Quarterly* 13, no. 2 (Winter 1959): 9–16.

Alain Resnais and Alain Robbe-Grillet

Works by Resnais and Robbe-Grillet

Resnais, Alain. "Trying to Understand My Own Film." *Films and Filming* 8, no. 5 (February 1962): 9–10, 41.

Robbe-Grillet, Alain. "Alain Robbe-Grillet vous parle de *L'Année dernière à Marienbad.*" *Réalités* 184 (May 1961): 95–98, 111–15.

———. *L'Année dernière à Marienbad.* Paris: Minuit, 1961. Translated by Richard Howard as *Last Year at Marienbad.* New York: Grove, 1962.

———. "L'Année dernière à Marienbad." *Sight and Sound* 30, no. 4 (Fall 1961): 176–79.

———. "Brèves réflexions sur le fait de décrire une scène de cinéma." *Revue d'esthétique* 2–3 (1967): 131–38.

———. "Comment j'ai écrit *L'Année dernière à Marienbad.*" *Les Nouvelles littéraires,* 7 September 1961, 1.

Interviews

Amiel, Mireille, and Jacques Petal. "Entretien avec Alain Resnais." *Cinéma 80* 259–60 (July–August 1980): 37–46.

Belmans, Jacques. "Entretien avec Alain Resnais." *Etudes cinématographiques* 64–68 (1968): 185–91.

Benayoun, Robert. "Sur *Mon oncle d'amérique:* entretien avec Alain Resnais." *Positif* 231 (June 1980): 40–42.

Benayoun, Robert, Michel Ciment, and Jean-Louis Pays. "*La Guerre est finie:* Entretien avec Alain Resnais." *Positif* 79 (October 1966): 17–37.

Bonnet, Jean-Claude, Emmanuel Decaux, and Bruno Villien. "Entretien avec Alain Resnais." *Cinématographe* 58 (1980): 15–22.

Burch, Noel. "A Conversation with Alain Resnais." *Film Quarterly* 13, no. 3 (Spring 60): 27–29.

Carcassonne, Pierre. "Dix personnages en quête d'un film." *Cinématographe* 88 (April 1983): 3–12.

Carta, Jean, and Michel Mesnil. "Un Cinéaste stoicien: interview d'Alain Resnais." *Esprit* 28, no. 6 (June 1960): 934–45.

d'Allones, O. Revault. "Alain Resnais, Antidoctrinaire." *Revue d'esthétique* 2–3 (1967): 123–30.

Daney, Serge, and Danièle Dubroux. "Entretien avec Alain Resnais." *Cahiers du cinéma* 347 (May 1983): 27–36.

Durgnat, Raymond. "Last Words on *Last Year:* A Discussion with Alain Resnais and Alain Robbe-Grillet." *Films and Filming* 8, no. 6 (March 1962): 39–41.

Goldschmidt, Didier, Jérôme Tonnerre, and Philippe Le Guay. "Deux entretiens avec Alain Resnais." *Cinématographe* 88 (April 1983): 18–26.

Labarthe, André, and Jacques Rivette. "Entretien avec Resnais et Robbe-Grillet." *Cahiers du cinéma* 123 (September 1961): 1–18.

Maben, Adrian. "Alain Resnais: *The War Is Over.*" *Films and Filming* 13, no. 1 (October 1966): 40–42.

Maillet, Dominique, and Denis Offroy. "Entretien: Alain Resnais: 'Tout film doit être un piège à l'analyse.'" *Cinématographe* 8 (July–August 1974): 13–15.

Manceaux, Michele. "A Munich avec Alain Resnais." *L'Express,* 20 October 1960, 38–39.

"Marienbad ou l'exception." *L'Arc* 31 (Winter 1967): 8–9.

Masson, André, and François Thomas. "Entretien avec Alain Resnais sur l'amour à mort." *Positif* 284 (October 1984): 8–15.

Monaco, James. "Conversations with Resnais: There Isn't Enough Time." *Film Comment* 11, no. 4 (July–August 1975): 38–41.

Parra, Danièle. "Entretien avec Alain Resnais." *Revue du cinéma* 397 (September 1984): 51–54.

Philippon, André, and Serge Toubiana. "La Variation ajoutée: entretien avec Alain Resnais." *Cahiers du cinéma* 387 (September 1986): 17–21.

Pingaud, Bernard. "Jouer avec le temps: entretien avec Alain Resnais." *L'Arc* 31 (Winter 1967): 93–102.

Roud, Richard. "Memories of Resnais." *Sight and Sound* 38, no. 3 (Summer 1969): 124–29, 162.

Seaver, Richard. "Facts into Fiction." *Film Comment* 9, no. 4 (July–August 1975): 41–44.

Thomas, François. "Entretien avec Alain Resnais sur *Mélo.*" *Positif* 307 (September 1986): 7–12.

Critical Works on Resnais and Robbe-Grillet

Alexander, A. J. "A Modern Hero: The Nongenue." *Film Culture* 22–23 (Summer 1961): 81–90.

Alter, Jean. "Alain Robbe-Grillet and the 'Cinematographic Style.'" *Modern Language Journal* 48, no. 6 (October 1964): 363–66.

Armes, Roy. "Alain Resnais." In *French Cinema since 1946*, 2:108–26. 2 vols. London: A. Zwemmer, 1966.

———. *The Cinema of Alain Resnais.* New York: A. S. Barnes, 1968.

———. *The Films of Alain Robbe-Grillet.* Amsterdam: John Benjamins, 1981.

———. "Resnais and Reality." *Films and Filming* 16, no. 8 (May 1970): 12–14.

———. "Robbe-Grillet, Ricardou, and *Last Year at Marienbad.*" *Quarterly Review of Film Studies* 5, no. 1 (1980): 1–17.

Baker, Peter. "Venice Pictures." *Films and Filming* 8, no. 2 (November 1961): 31–32.

Bassan, Raphael. "Alain Resnais: l'art à la mémoire torturée." *Revue du cinéma* 381 (March 1983): 81–82.

Benayoun, Robert. *Alain Resnais: arpenteur de l'imaginaire.* Paris: Stock, 1980.

Beylie, Claude. "Le Meilleur des mondes possibles." *Cinématographe* 88 (April 1983): 13.

———. "L'Opéra du temps." *Cinéma 68* 128 (August–September 1968): 44–45.

Blumenberg, Richard M. "Ten Years after *Marienbad.*" *Cinema Journal* 10, no. 2 (1971): 40–43.

Bollème, Geneviève. "*L'Année dernière à Marienbad:* essai d'interprétation." *Les Temps modernes* 183 (July 1961): 177–79.

Bonnot, Gérard. "*Marienbad* ou le parti de Dieu." *Les Temps modernes* 187 (December 1961): 752–68.

Bounoure, Gaston. *Alain Resnais.* Paris: Seghers, 1962.

Brunius, Jacques. "Every Year in Marienbad, or the Discipline of Uncertainty." *Sight and Sound* 31, no. 3 (Summer 1962): 122–27, 153.

Burch, Noel. "Comment s'articule l'espace-temps." *Cahiers du cinéma* 188 (March 1967): 40–45.

———. "Four Recent French Documentaries." *Film Quarterly* 13, no. 1 (Fall 1959): 56–61.

———. "Qu'est-ce que La Nouvelle Vague." *Film Quarterly* 13, no. 2 (Winter 1959): 16–30.

———. "Réflections sur le sujet: sujets de fictions." *Cahiers du cinéma* 196 (December 1967): 52–59.

———. "Répertoire de structures simples." In *Praxis du cinéma,* 83–107. Paris: Gallimard, 1986. Translated by Helen R. Lane as "The Repertory of Simple Structures," in *Theory of Film Practice,* 51–69. Princeton: Princeton University Press, 1981.

———. "Vers un cinéma dialectique: répertoire des structures simples." *Cahiers du cinéma* 191 (June 1967): 54–60.

Burguet, Frantz-André. "L'Année dernière à Marienbad." *L'Arc* 16 (Fall 1961): 23–26.

Chasseguet-Smirgel, Janine. "A propos de *L'Année dernière à Marienbad.*" In *Pour une psychanalyse de l'art,* 49–80. Paris: Payot, 1971.

Crick, Philip. "Robbe-Grillet: Trans-Europ Express." *Cinema* 5 (February 1970): 37.

Davis, Doris McGinty. "*Le Voyeur* et *L'Année dernière à Marienbad.*" *French Review* 38, no. 4 (February 1965): 477–84.

Durgnat, Raymond. "Architecture in, and of, the Movies." In *Films and Feelings,* 99–114. Cambridge: MIT Press, 1971.

———. "Last Words on *Last Year:* A Discussion with Alain Resnais and Alain Robbe-Grillet." *Films and Filming* 8, no. 6 (March 1962): 39–41.

———. "Midnight Sun." *Films and Filming* 8, no. 8 (May 1962): 21–23.

Forbes, Jill. "Resnais in the 80's." *Sight and Sound* 56, no. 3 (Summer 1987): 212–14.

Frenkel, Lise. "Cinéma et psychanalyse." *Cinéma 71* 154 (March 1971): 73–93.

Gaggi, Silvio. "Marker and Resnais: Myth and Reality." *Literature/Film Quarterly* 7, no. 1 (1979): 11–15.

Gay, Pierre. "Nouveau roman et cinéma nouveau." *Cinéma 70* 148 (July–August 1970): 61–70.

Genette, Gérard. "Sur Robbe-Grillet." *Tel Quel* 8 (Winter 1962): 34–44.

Gili, Jean A. "*L'Homme qui ment:* le cinéma-mensonge." *Cinéma 68* 131 (December 1968): 135–36.

Gill, Brenden. "The Current Cinema: Dreamers." *New Yorker,* 10 March 1962, 89–90.

Glassman, D. "The Feminine Subject Written as History Writer in *Hiroshima mon amour.*" *Enclitic* 5, no. 1 (1981): 43–53.

Goldschmid, Didier. "Boulogne, mon amour." *Cinématographe* 88 (April 1983): 30–32.

Gollub, Judith. "French Writers Turned Film Makers." *Film Heritage* 4, no. 2 (Winter 1968–69): 19–25.

Gow, Gordon. "Travelling Fast: The Films of Alain Robbe-Grillet." *Films and Filming* 232 (January 1974): 54–56.

Hallier, Jean Edern. "Toute une vie à Marienbad." *Tel Quel* 7 (Fall 1961): 49–52.

Harcourt, Peter. "Alain Resnais: Memory Is Kept Alive with Dreams." *Film Comment* 9, no. 6 (November–December 1973): 47–50.

———. "Alain Resnais: Toward the Certainty of Doubt." *Film Comment* 10, no. 1 (January–February 1974): 23–29.

Holland, Norman. "Film, Metafilm, and Un-film." *Hudson Review* 15, no. 3 (Fall 1962): 406–12.

Houston, Penelope. "Resnais' *L'Année dernière à Marienbad.*" *Sight and Sound* 31, no. 1 (Winter 1961): 26–29.

Josa, Solange. "*Marienbad:* ou peut-être . . . " *Esprit* 30, no. 1 (January 1962): 142–44.

Kaiser, Grant E. "L'Amour et l'esthétique: *L'Année dernière à Marienbad.*" *South Atlantic Bulletin* 39, no. 4 (November 1974): 113–20.

Kennedy, Harlan. "The Time Machine." *Film Comment* 20, no. 1 (January–February 1984): 9–16.

Kreidl, John Francis. *Alain Resnais.* Boston: Twayne, 1977.

Kryou, Ado. "L'Année dernière à Marienbad." *Positif* 40 (July 1961): 65–67.

Labarthe, André S. "*Marienbad* Année Zéro." *Cahiers du cinéma* 123 (September 1961): 28–31.

Latil-Le Dantec, Mireille. "Notes sur la fiction et l'imaginaire chez Resnais et Robbe-Grillet." *Etudes cinématographiques* 100–103 (1974): 117–45.

Lawson, John Howard. *Film: The Creative Process.* New York: Hill & Wang, 1964.

Maakaroun, Elie. "Expériences et stylistiques du manque chez Resnais et Robbe-Grillet." *Etudes cinématographiques* 100–103 (1974): 105–16.

Magny, Joel. "De Resnais à Robbe-Grillet: l'instauration d'une écriture." *Etudes cinématographiques* 100–103 (1974): 146–58.

Menil, Alain. "Opus I." *Cinématographe* 88 (April 1983): 27–29.

Michalczyk, John. "Alain Resnais: Literary Origins from *Hiroshima* to *Providence*." *Literature/Film Quarterly* 7, no. 1 (1979): 16–25.

———. "Recurrent Imagery of the Labyrinth in Robbe-Grillet's Films." *Stanford French Review* 2 (1978): 115–28.

Mizrachi, François. "Thèmes surréalistes dans l'oeuvre d'Alain Resnais." *Etudes cinématographiques* 40–42 (1965): 199–207.

Monaco, James. *Alain Resnais.* New York: Oxford University Press, 1979.

Morrissette, Bruce. "Games and Game Structures in Robbe-Grillet." *Yale French Studies* 41 (1968): 159–67.

———. *Novel and Film.* Chicago: University of Chicago Press, 1985.

———. *Les Romans de Robbe-Grillet.* Paris: Minuit, 1963.

Murray, Edward. "Alain Robbe-Grillet, the New Novel, and the New Cinema." In *The Cinematic Imagination*, 280–90. New York: Frederick Ungar, 1972.

Ollier, Claude. "Ce Soir à Marienbad." *La Nouvelle Revue française* 106, 107 (October, November 1961): 711–19, 906–12.

Oxenhandler, Neal. "Marienbad Revisited." *Film Quarterly* 17, no. 1 (Fall 1963): 30–35.

Pechter, William S. "Last Night at Marienbad." *Kenyon Review* 25, no. 2 (Spring 1963): 337–43.

Pingaud, Bernard. "Le Cinéma: dans le labyrinthe." *Preuves* 128 (October 1961): 65–69.

Prédal, René. *Alain Resnais.* Special issue of *Etudes cinématographiques* 64–68 (1968).

Purdy, Strother. "Gertrude Stein at Marienbad." *PMLA* 85, no. 5 (October 1970): 1096–1105.

Rhode, Eric. "Alain Resnais." In *Tower of Babel: Speculations on the Cinema,* 137–58. New York: Chilton Books, 1965.

Rocher, Daniel. "Le Symbolisme du noir et blanc dans *L'Année dernière à Marienbad*." *Etudes cinématographiques* 100–103 (1974): 87–104.

Ropars-Wuilleumier, Marie-Claire. "L'Année dernière à Marienbad." In *L'Ecran de la mémoire,* 114–21. Paris: Seuil, 1970.

Roud, Richard. "Novel Novel: Fable Fable?" *Sight and Sound* 31, no. 2 (Spring 1962): 84–88.

Roulet, Claude. "D'un récit à l'autre." *Cinématographe* 31 (October 1977): 7–9.

Samson, Pierre. "Le Lyrisme critique d'Alain Resnais." *L'Arc* 31 (Winter 1967): 103–11.

Seyrig, Delphine. "Interview." *L'Arc* 31 (Winter 1967): 65–69.

Shoos, Diane. "Sexual Difference and Enunciation: Resnais's *Last Year at Marienbad*." *Literature and Psychology* 34, no. 3 (1988): 1–15.

Sontag, Susan. "Resnais's *Muriel*." In *Against Interpretation,* 232–41. New York: Farrar, Straus & Giroux, 1961.

Stanbrook, Alan. "The Time and Space of Alain Resnais." *Films and Filming* 10, no. 4 (January 1964): 35–38.

Stoltzfus, Ben F. *Alain Robbe-Grillet and the New French Novel*. Carbondale: Southern Illinois University Press, 1964.

———. "D'un langage à l'autre: les deux Robbe-Grillet." *Etudes cinématographiques* 100–103 (1974): 87–103.

Sweet, Freddy. *The Film Narratives of Alain Resnais*. Ann Arbor: UMI Research Press, 1981.

Tailleur, Roger. "*L'Année dernière à Marienbad* d'Alain Resnais." *Les Lettres nouvelles* 16 (July–September 1961): 164–69.

Taylor, John Russel. "The New Wave." In *Cinema Eye, Cinema Ear: Some Key Filmmakers of the Sixties*, 200–229. New York: Hill & Wang, 1964.

Thiher, Allen. "*L'Année dernière à Marienbad:* The Narration of Narration." In *The Cinematic Muse: Critical Studies in the History of French Cinema*, 166–79. Columbia: University of Missouri Press, 1979.

Thivel, Caroline. "Monsieur Resnais." *Cinématographe* 116 (February 1986): 52–4.

Tilliette, Xavier. "Les Inconnus de Marienbad." *Etudes* 312, no. 1 (January 1962): 79–87.

Tonnerre, Jérôme. "Le Roi de l'or." *Cinématographe* 88 (April 1983): 14–15.

Van Wert, William. *The Film Career of Alain Robbe-Grillet*. Boston: G. K. Hall, 1977.

———. "Intertextuality and Redundant Coherence in Robbe-Grillet." *Romanic Review* 73, no. 2 (March 1982): 249–57.

Wagner, Geoffrey. "*Last Year at Marienbad* (1961)." In *The Novel and the Cinema*, 277–87. Rutherford, N.J.: Fairleigh Dickinson University Press, 1975.

Ward, John. *Alain Resnais or the Theme of Time*. New York: Doubleday, 1968.

Westerbeck, Colin L. "Intrastructures: The Films of Alain Robbe-Grillet." *Artforum* 14, no. 7 (March 1976): 54–57.

Weyergans, François. "Dans le dédale." *Cahiers du cinéma* 123 (September 1961): 22–27.

Williams, Linda. "Hiroshima and Marienbad: Metaphor and Metonymy." *Screen* 17, no. 1 (Spring 1976): 34–39.

Claude Chabrol

Works by Chabrol

Chabrol, Claude. "Le Dernier jour de souffrances." *Mystère-Magazine* 109 (February 1957): 47–61.

———. "Hitchcock Confronts Evil." *Cahiers du Cinema in English* 2 (1966): 67–71.

———. "Musique douce." *Mystère-Magazine* 70 (November 1953): 12–25.

———. "Les Petits sujets." *Cahiers du cinéma* 100 (October 1959): 31–32.

Translated as "Big Subjects, Little Subjects," in *Movie* 1 (June 1962): 12–13.

Chabrol, Claude, and Eric Rohmer. *Hitchcock*. Paris: Editions universitaires, 1957.

Interviews

Bonnet, Jean-Claude. "*Inspecteur Lavardin:* entretien avec Claude Chabrol." *Cinématographe* 117 (March 1986): 15–18, 26–27.

Bonnet, Jean-Claude, Philippe Carcassonne, and Jacques Fieschi. "*Violette Nozière:* Claude Chabrol." *Cinématographe* 39 (June 1978): 2–6.

Calvez, Françoise, and Alain Carbonnier. "Question à Claude Chabrol et Paul Vecchiali." *Cinéma 82* 282 (June 1982): 69–74.

Carbonnier, Alain. "Fritz Lang vu par . . . Claude Chabrol." *Cinéma 82* 282 (June 1982): 35, 36.

Carbonnier, Alain, and Joel Magny. "Entretien avec Claude Chabrol." *Cinéma 82* 285 (September 1982): 51–59.

Carcassonne, Philippe. "Entretien avec Claude Chabrol." *Cinématographe* 59 (July–August 1980): 35–38.

Carcassonne, Philippe, and Jacques Fieschi. "Claude Chabrol." *Cinématographe* 81 (September 1982): 3–15.

Debiesse, François, and Denis Offroy. "Claude Chabrol: 'Ce qui m'intéresse c'est l'imbécillité.'" *Cinématographe* 6 (February–March 1974): 4–5.

Le Guay, Philippe. "Les Professionnels: Claude Chabrol." *Cinématographe* 80 (July–August 1982): 6–7.

Maillet, Dominique. "Entretiens: Claude Chabrol." *Cinématographe* 24 (February 1977): 28–30.

Nogueira, Rui, and Nicoletta Zalaffi. "Chabrol." *Sight and Sound* 40, no. 1 (Winter 1970–71): 2–6.

Sarris, Andrew. "Claude Chabrol." In *Interviews with Film Directors,* 75–85. New York: Avon Books, 1967.

Toubiana, Serge. "Entretien avec Claude Chabrol." *Cahiers du cinéma* 339 (September 1982): 4–14, 63–65.

———. "Isabelle Huppert—Claude Chabrol." *Cahiers du cinéma* 407–8 (May 1988): 4–10.

Yakir, Dan. "Innocents with Dirty Hands: Claude Chabrol on Violence and *Violette*." *Village Voice,* 23 October 1978, 67–68.

———. "The Magical Mystery World of Claude Chabrol: An Interview." *Film Quarterly* 32, no. 3 (Spring 1979): 2–14.

Critical Works on Chabrol

Appel, Alfred. "The Eyehole of Knowledge: Voyeuristic Games in Film and Literature." *Film Comment* 9, no. 3 (May–June 1973): 20–26.

Bibliography

Armes, Roy. "Claude Chabrol." In *French Cinema since 1946*, 2:46–54. 2 vols. London: A. Zwemmer, 1966.

Bergan, R. "Directors of the Decade—Claude Chabrol." *Films and Filming* 351 (December 1983): 28–30.

Biette, J. C. "Claude Chabrol: l'homme centre." *Cahiers du cinéma* 323–24 (May 1981): 93.

Bonitzer, Pascal. "Jeu de massacre." *Cahiers du cinéma* 381 (March 1987): 2–5.

Bonnet, Jean Claude. "Chabrol mis en scène." *Cinématographe* 117 (March 1986): 38.

Carbonnier, Alain. "Poulet à la diable." *Cinéma 85* 329 (November 1985): 2.

Clarens, Carlos. "*The Cousins* and *Le Beau Serge*." *Films in Review* 10, no. 8 (October 1959): 495–96.

Comolli, Jean-Louis. "Claude Chabrol ou l'inconstance punie." *La Femme infidèle, L'Avant-scène cinéma* 92 (May 1969): 3.

Dawson, Jan. "The Continental Divide." *Sight and Sound* 43, no. 1 (Winter 1973–74): 12–15.

Delavaud, Gilles. "Chabrol Unlimited." *Cahiers du cinéma* 310 (April 1980): v–vi.

Durgnat, Raymond. "Le Beau Serge." *Films and Filming* 9, no. 4 (January 1963): 44.

Fassbinder, R. W. "Insects in a Glass Case: Random Thoughts on Claude Chabrol." *Sight and Sound* 45, no. 4 (Fall 1976): 205–6, 252.

Gow, Gordon. "When the New Wave Became Old Hat: The Films of Claude Chabrol." *Films and Filming* 13, nos. 6, 7 (March, April 1967): 20–26, 26–31.

Lawson, John Howard. *Film: The Creative Process*. New York: Hill & Wang, 1964.

Magny, Joel. *Claude Chabrol*. Paris: Cahiers du cinéma, 1987.

———. "Le Joueur d'échecs." *Cahiers du cinéma* 390 (December 1986): 60–64.

———. "*La Musique douce* de Chabrol." *Cinéma 82* 285 (September 1982): 38–50.

Marcorelles, Louis. "Les Cousins." *Sight and Sound* 28, no. 3 (Fall 1959): 169–70.

Milne, Tom. "Chabrol's Schizophrenic Spider." *Sight and Sound* 39, no. 2 (Spring 1970): 58–62.

Overbey, David. "Chabrol's Game of Mirrors." *Sight and Sound* 46, no. 2 (Spring 1977): 78–81, 99.

Renaud, Tristan. "Le Cas Chabrol." *Cinéma 74* 189 (July–August 1974): 41–45.

Toubiana, Serge. "Le Secret derrière Chabrol." *Cahiers du cinéma* 339 (September 1982): 4.

Turner, R. H. "The Cousins." *Film Quarterly* 14, no. 1 (Fall 1960): 42–43.

Wood, Robin, and Michael Walker. *Claude Chabrol*. New York: Praeger, 1970.

Eric Rohmer

Works by Rohmer

Rohmer, Eric. "Le Celluloid et le marbre." *Cahiers du cinéma* 44 (February 1955): 32–37.

———. "Le Celluloid et le marbre: le siècle des peintres." *Cahiers du cinéma* 49 (July 1955): 10–15.

———. "Le Celluloid et le marbre: de la Métaphore." *Cahiers du cinéma* 51 (October 1955): 2–9.

———. "Le Celluloid et le marbre: beau comme la musique." *Cahiers du cinéma* 52 (November 1955): 4–12.

———. "Le Celluloid et le marbre: architecture d'apocalypse." *Cahiers du cinéma* 53 (December 1955): 22–30.

———. "Deux extraits d'*Une Femme douce*." *Cinématographe* 73 (December 1981): 19–20.

———. "Faust." *L'Avant-scène cinéma* 190–91 (July–September 1977): 7–41.

———. *Le Goût de la beauté*. Edited by Jean Narboni. Paris: Flammarion, 1989. Translated by Carol Volk as *The Taste for Beauty*. Cambridge: Cambridge University Press, 1989.

———. "L'Hélice et l'idée." *Cahiers du cinéma* 357 (March 1984): 24–27.

———. "Hommage à H. Hawks: la plus haute idée du cinéma." *Cinéma 78* 231 (March 1978): 60–63.

———. "Notes sur la mise en scène." *L'Avant-scène cinéma* 173 (October 1976): 5–6.

———. *L'Organization de l'espace dans le "Faust" de Murnau*. Paris: Union Générale d'Éditions, 1977.

———. "Redécouvrir l'amérique." *Cahiers du cinéma* 54 (December 1955): 11–16.

———. "Réponse aux questions aux cinéastes." *Cahiers du cinéma* 185 (December 1966): 113, 123.

———. *Six contes moraux*. Paris: Editions de l'Herne, 1974. Translated by Sabine d'Estrée as *Six Moral Tales*. Surrey: Lorrimer, 1980.

———. "Les Trois Faust." *L'Avant-scène cinéma* 190–91 (July–September 1977): 6.

———. "Note sur la traduction et sur la mise en scène de Perceval." *L'Avant-scène cinéma* 221 (February 1979): 6–7.

———. "Notes sur *Le Petit Théâtre de Jean Renoir*." *Cinéma 79* 244 (April 1979): 20–24.

———. "La Vie c'était l'écran." *Cahiers du cinéma*, special issue, December 1984, 16–24.

Rohmer, Eric, and Claude Chabrol. "Une Allégorie policière." *L'Avant-scène cinéma* 249 (June 1980): 4–5.

———. *Hitchcock*. Paris: Editions universitaires, 1957.

Bibliography

Interviews

Barron, Fred. "Eric Rohmer: An Interview." *Take One*, September–October 1972, 8–10.

Bergala, Alain, and Alain Phillippon. "Eric Rohmer: la grace et la rigueur." *Cahiers du cinéma* 364 (October 1984): 8–15.

Beylie, Claude, and Alain Carbonnier. "Le Celluloid et la pierre: entretien avec Eric Rohmer." *L'Avant-scène cinéma* 336 (January 1985): 4–10.

Biette, Jean-Claude, Jacques Bontemps, and Jean-Louis Comolli. "L'Ancien et le nouveau: entretien avec Eric Rohmer." *Cahiers du cinéma* 172 (November 1965): 33–59.

Bonitzer, Pascal, and Michel Chion. "Entretien avec Eric Rohmer." *Cahiers du cinéma* 346 (April 1983): 18–24, 28.

Bonitzer, Pascal, Jean-Louis Comolli, Serge Daney, and Jean Narboni. "Nouvel entretien avec Eric Rohmer." *Cahiers du cinéma* 219 (April 1970): 46–55.

Bonitzer, Pascal, and Serge Daney. "Entretien avec Eric Rohmer." *Cahiers du cinéma* 323–24 (May 1981): 26–39.

———. "Rohmer sur Rohmer." *Cinéma Forum* 23, no. 225 (June 1983): 61–62.

Carbonnier, Alain, and Joel Magny. "Jean Douchet et Eric Rohmer." *Cinéma 84* 301 (January 1984): 11–15.

Carcassonne, Philippe, and Jacques Fieschi. "Eric Rohmer." *Cinématographe* 67 (May 1981): 28–35.

———. "Eric Rohmer: entretien." *Cinématographe* 73 (December 1981): 18–19.

Douchet, Jean. "Entretien . . . Eric Rohmer." *Cinéma 84* 301 (January 1984): 11–15.

Fieschi, Jacques. "Eric Rohmer: 'J'ai voulu mettre en scène un texte.'" *Cinématographe* 19 (June 1976): 9–11.

Hammond, Robert, and Jean-Pierre Pagliano. "Eric Rohmer on Film Scripts and Film Plans." *Literature/Film Quarterly* 10, no. 4 (1982): 219–25.

Legrand, Gérard, Hubert Niogret, and François Ramasse. "Entretien avec Eric Rohmer." *Positif* 309 (November 1986): 15–23.

Magny, Joel, and Dominique Rabourdin. "Entretien avec Eric Rohmer." *Cinéma 79* 242 (February 1979): 11–19.

Mauro, Florence. "Secret de laboratoire: entretien avec Eric Rohmer." *Cahiers du cinéma* 371–72 (May 1985): 90–93.

Narboni, Jean. "Le Temps de la critique: entretien avec Eric Rohmer." *Cahiers du cinéma* 357 (March 1984): 28–29.

Nogueira, Rui, and Carlos Clarens. "Eric Rohmer: Choice and Chance." *Sight and Sound* 40, no. 3 (Summer 1971): 118–24.

Ostria, Vincent. "A l'improviste: entretien avec Eric Rohmer." *Cinématographe* 122 (September 1986): 32–37.

Petrie, Graham. "Eric Rohmer: An Interview." *Film Quarterly* 24, no. 4 (Summer 1971): 34–41.

Philippon, Alain, and Serge Toubiana. "Le Cinéma au risque de l'imperfection." *Cahiers du cinéma* 392 (February 1987): 8–14.

Yakir, Dan. "Rohmer Talks about Beauty and Box Office." *Village Voice,* 25 October 1976, 49–52.

Ziolkowski, Fabrice. "Comedies and Proverbs: An Interview with Eric Rohmer." *Wide Angle* 5, no. 1 (1982): 62–67.

Critical Works on Rohmer

Arnaud, Claude. "L'Eternelle jeunesse d'Eric Rohmer." *L'Avant-scène cinéma* 355 (December 1986): 2–5.

Beylie, Claude. "Les 'Petits Riens' d'Eric Rohmer." *L'Avant-scène cinéma* 336 (January 1985): 14–15.

Borchardt, Edith. "Eric Rohmer's *Marquise of O* and the Theory of the German Novella." *Literature/Film Quarterly* 12, no. 2 (1984): 129–35.

Canby, Vincent. "*Claire's Knee:* Close to a Perfect Movie." *New York Times,* 7 March 1971, sec. 2.

———. "Eloquent *Ma Nuit chez Maud*." *New York Times,* 24 September 1969.

Carbonnier, Alain. "Un Art tendant vers l'épure." *L'Avant-scène cinéma* 336 (January 1985): 11–13.

———. "L'Illusion de la liberté." *L'Avant-scène cinéma* 293 (October 1982): 5–6.

Chevallier, Jacques. "Eric Rohmer par Joel Magny." *Revue du cinéma* 429 (July–August 1987): 13.

Clarens, Carlos. "L'Amour sage." *Sight and Sound* 39, no. 1 (Winter 1969–70): 6–9.

Cowie, Peter. "Ma Nuit chez Maud." *Focus on Film* 1 (January–February 1970): 11–13.

Crisp, C. G. *Eric Rohmer: Realist and Moralist.* Bloomington: Indiana University Press, 1988.

Cunningham, Frank R. "Pascal's Wager and the Feminist Dilemma in Eric Rohmer's *My Night at Maud's.*" In *The Kingdom of Dreams in Literature and Film,* edited by Douglas Fowler, 79–91. Tallahassee: Florida State University Press, 1986.

Dawson, Jan. "Ma Nuit chez Maud." *Monthly Film Bulletin* 37, no. 432 (January 1970): 6–7.

Fieschi, Jacques. "*La Marquise d'O* de Eric Rohmer." *Cinématographe* 19 (June 1976): 9–11.

Gilliatt, Penelope. "The Current Cinema: A Good Night." *New Yorker,* 4 April 1970, 115–16.

Gow, Gordon. "My Night with Maud." *Films and Filming* 16, no. 7 (April 1970): 54.

Green, Calvin. "*Ars Theologica:* Man and God at the New York Film Festival." *Cinéaste* 3, no. 2 (Fall 1969): 6–10, 36.

Hart, Henry. "My Night at Maud's." *Films in Review* 21, no. 5 (May 1970): 307–8.

Hatch, Robert. "Films." *Nation,* 27 April 1970, 509–10.

Kauffman, Stanley. "A Theoretical Auteur." *American Film* 5, no. 4 (January–February 1980): 65–67.

Knight, Arthur. "SR Goes to the Movies: M as in Mature." *Saturday Review,* 7 February 1970, 41.

Latil-Le Dantec, Mireille. "De Murnau à Rohmer: les pièges de la beauté." *Cinématographe* 23, 24 (January, February 1977): 13–14, 18–20.

Legrand, Gérard. "Notes pour *Les Aventures de Reinette et Mirabelle.*" *Positif* 309 (November 1986): 11–14.

Le Guay, Philippe. "La Jeune Fille et Rohmer." *Cinématographe* 122 (September 1986): 38.

———. "Le Scenario d'abord." *Cinématographe* 108 (March 1985): 36–37.

Magny, Joel. *Eric Rohmer.* Paris: Rivages, 1986.

Masson, Alain. "Le Capricorne souverain de l'onde occidentale: sur les 'comédies et proverbes.'" *Positif* 307 (September 1986): 43–45.

———. "Magny (Joel): Eric Rohmer." *Positif* 320 (October 1987): 78–79.

Meekas, Jonas. "Ma Nuit chez Maud." *Village Voice,* 2 April 1970, 59.

Milne, Tom. "Rohmer's Siege Perilous." *Sight and Sound* 50, no. 3 (1981): 192–95.

Morgenstern, Joseph. "Movies: Bride Shopping." *Newsweek,* 23 February 1970, 100.

Pechter, William S. "The Reputation of Eric Rohmer." *Commentary* 52, no. 2 (August 1971): 84–86.

Petrie, Graham. "Ma Nuit chez Maud." *Film Quarterly* 23, no. 2 (Winter 1969–70): 57–59.

Sarris, Andrew. "Films in Focus: And Now a Few Films for Grown-ups." *Village Voice,* 26 June 1984, 49.

———. "Ma Nuit at Maud's." *Village Voice,* 4 September 1969, 43.

———. "Rohmer Reflects the Virtue of Repression." *Village Voice,* 25 October 1976, 49.

Schickel, Richard. "My Night at Maud's." In *Second Sight: Notes on Some Movies, 1965–1970,* 306–8. New York: Simon & Schuster, 1973.

Simon, John. "Why Do They Rave So Over Rohmer?" *New York Times,* 29 October 1972, sec. 2.

Tremous, Claude-Marie. "La Carte de Tendre." *Télérama,* 11 March 1981, 13.

Tucker, Martin. "Maud's Place." *Commonweal* 92 (May 1970): 169–70.

Vidal, Marion. "La Séductrice et l'élue." *Positif* 300 (February 1986): 48–51.

Walsh, Moira. "My Night at Maud's." *America* 122, no. 14 (11 April 1970): 378–79.

———. "Structured Ambiguity in the Films of Eric Rohmer." *Film Criticism* 1, no. 2 (1976): 30–36.

Westerbeck, Colin. "The Rohmerantic Tradition." *Commonweal* 103 (December 1976): 816–17.

———. "Rohmer Renewed." *Commonweal* 104 (January 1977): 21–23.
Williams, Linda. "Eric Rohmer and the Holy Grail." *Literature/Film Quarterly* 11, no. 2 (1983): 71–82.

Robert Bresson

Works by Bresson

Notes sur le cinématographe. Paris: Gallimard, 1975. Translated by Jonathan Griffin as *Notes on Cinematography.* New York: Urizen Books, 1977.

Interviews

Amengual, Barthélémy. "Les Affaires publiques." *Cinéma 83* 94 (June 1983): 18.
Arlaud, R. M., et al. "Propos de Robert Bresson." *Cahiers du cinéma* 75 (October 1957): 3–9.
Cameron, Ian. "Interview." In *The Films of Robert Bresson,* edited by Ian Cameron, 134–37. New York: Praeger, 1969.
Daney, Serge. "Rencontre avec Robert Bresson." *Cahiers du cinéma* 333 (March 1982): 34–35.
Daney, Serge, and Serge Toubiana. "Entretien avec Robert Bresson." *Cahiers du cinéma* 348–49 (June–July 1983): 13–14.
Doniol-Valcroze, Jacques, and Jean-Luc Godard. "Entretien avec Robert Bresson." *Cahiers du cinéma* 104 (February 1960): 3–9.
Estève, Michel. "Jeanne d'arc à l'écran." *Etudes cinématographiques* 18–19 (1962): 79–87.
Fieschi, Jacques. "Entretiens: Robert Bresson." *Cinématographe* 29 (July–August 1977): 28–30.
Godard, Jean-Luc, and Michel Delahaye. "La Question: entretien avec Robert Bresson." *Cahiers du cinéma* 178 (May 1966): 26–35, 67–71.
Guitton, Jean. "Entretien avec Robert Bresson." *Etudes cinématographiques* 18–19 (1962): 85–97.
Kovacs, Yves. "Entretien avec Robert Bresson." *Cahiers du cinéma* 140 (February 1963): 4–10.
Sadoul, Georges. "Robert Bresson à Georges Sadoul." *Les Lettres françaises,* 7 March 1963, 1, 9.
Schrader, Paul. "Robert Bresson, Possibly." *Film Comment* 13, no. 5 (September–October 1977): 26–30.

Critical Works on Bresson

Affron, Mirella Jona. "Bresson and Pascal: Rhetorical Affinities." *Quarterly Review of Film Studies* 10, no. 2 (1985): 118–31.
Agel, Henri. "L'Ascèse liturgique." In *Le Cinéma et le sacré,* 29–42. Paris: Cerf, 1954.

Bibliography

————. *Robert Bresson*. Brussels: Club du livre de cinema, 1957.

Armes, Roy. "Robert Bresson: An Anachronistic Universe." In *The Ambiguous Image: Narrative Style in Modern European Cinema*, 82–94. Bloomington: Indiana University Press, 1976.

Ayfre, Amédée. "The Universe of Robert Bresson." In *The Films of Robert Bresson*, edited by Ian Cameron, 6–24. New York: Praeger, 1970.

Bazin, André. *"Le Journal d'un curé de campagne* et la stylistique de Robert Bresson." In *Qu'est-ce que le cinéma*, 107–28. Paris: Cerf, 1985.

Bensard, Patrick. "Notes sur *Pickpocket.*" *Camera/Stylo* 68/69 (February 1989): 111–14.

Briot, René. *Robert Bresson*. Paris: Cerf, 1957.

Browne, Nick. "Film Form/Voice-Over: Bresson's *Diary of a Country Priest.*" *Yale French Studies* 60 (1980): 233–40.

————. "Narrative Point of View: The Rhetoric of *Au Hasard Balthazar.*" *Film Quarterly* 31, no. 1 (Fall 1977): 23–31.

Burch, Noel. *Praxis du cinéma*. Paris: Gallimard, 1969.

Cameron, Ian, ed. *The Films of Robert Bresson*. New York: Praeger, 1969.

Charensol, Georges. "Le Chef d'oeuvre de Robert Bresson." *Les Nouvelles littéraires*, 24 December 1959, 10.

Clouzot, Claire. *Le Cinéma français depuis la nouvelle vague*. Paris: Fernand Nathan, 1972.

Cortade, René. *"Pickpocket* ou le roman russe à la glacière." *Arts, Lettres, Spectacles*, 23–29 December 1959, 7.

Dawson, Jan. "The Invisible Enemy." *Film Comment* 13, no. 5 (September–October 1977): 24–25.

Delahaye, Michel. "Pickpocket." *Cinéma 60* 43 (February 1960): 116–17.

Doniol-Valcroze, Jaques. "De l'avant-garde." In *Sept ans du cinéma français*, edited by Henri Agel, 14–16. Paris: Cerf, 1953.

Duca, Lo. "Un Acte de foi." *Cahiers du cinéma* 1 (April 1951): 45–47.

Durgnat, Raymond. "Diary of a Country Priest." *Films and Filming* 13, no. 3 (December 1966): 28–32.

————. "Pickpocket." *Films and Filming* 7, no. 1 (October 1960): 25.

Estève, Michel. "Le Dieu caché de Bernanos et de Bresson: *Journal d'un curé de campagne.*" In *Cinéma français et condition humaine*, 211–17. Paris: Albatros, 1978.

————. "Permanence de Robert Bresson." *Etudes cinématographiques* 3–4 (1960): 225–31.

————. *Robert Bresson*. Paris: Seghers, 1974.

————. *Robert Bresson: la passion du cinématographe*. Paris: Albatros, 1983.

Frenais, Jacques. "Autour du *Pickpocket* de Robert Bresson." *Cinéma 78* 235 (July 1978): 35–37.

Gill, Brendan. "The Current Cinema: *Pickpocket.*" *New Yorker*, 25 May 1963, 154.

Gilles, Paul. "Robert Bresson: une patience d'âne." *Arts*, 3–9 November 1965, 40–41.

Gilson, René. "Pickpocket." *Cinéma 60* 43 (February 1960): 117–18.

Gourdon, Gilles. "Georges Bernanos." *Cinématographe* 41 (November 1978): 47.

Green, Calvin. "Ars Theologica: Man and God at the N.Y. Film Festival." *Cinéaste* 3, no. 2 (Fall 1969): 6–9, 36–37.

Greene, Marjorie. "Robert Bresson." *Film Quarterly* 13, no. 2 (Winter 1959): 4–10.

Hanlon, Lindley. *Fragments: Bresson's Film Style.* Rutherford, N.J.: Fairleigh Dickinson University Press, 1986.

Helmstein, Lars. "Le Pont brûle." *Camera/Stylo* 68/69 (February 1989): 28–46.

Hurley, Neil P. "Pickpocket." In *Theology through Film.* New York: Harper & Row, 1970.

Jouvet, Pierre. "L'Acteur mode d'emploi." *Cinématographe* 61 (October 1980): 4–7.

———. "D'Homère à Proust: de Griffith à Bresson." *Cinématographe* 32 (November 1977): 7–10.

———. "Je déteste la vie . . . " *Cinématographe* 29 (July–August 1977): 35.

Kelman, Ken. "The Structure of Fate: Bresson's *Pickpocket.*" In *The Essential Cinema,* edited by P. Adams Sitney, 208–15. Anthology of Film Archives. New York: New York Univeristy Press, 1975.

Lambert, Gavin. "Un Condamné à mort s'est échappé." *Sight and Sound* 27, no. 1 (Summer 1957): 32–33, 53.

———. "Notes on Robert Bresson." *Sight and Sound* 23, no. 1 (July–September 1953): 35–39.

Latil-Le Dantec, Mireille. "Bresson, Dostoievski." *Cinématographe* 73 (December 1981): 11–17.

———. "Le Diable probablement." *Cinématographe* 29 (July–August 1977): 31–35.

———. "Dossier: l'argent au cinéma: Bresson et l'argent." *Cinématographe* 27 (May 1977): 15–19.

Laurans, Jacques. "Le Choix d'un modèle." *Camera/Stylo* 68/69 (February 1989): 8–10.

Leprophon, Pierre. "Robert Bresson." In *Présences contemporaines du cinéma,* 358–72. Paris: Nouvelles Editions Debresse, 1957.

Leterrier, François. "Robert Bresson, l'insaissisable." *Cahiers du cinéma* 66 (December 1956): 34–36.

Magny, Joel. "L'Expérience intérieure de Robert Bresson." *Cinéma 83* 294 (June 1983): 19–26.

Malle, Louis. "Avec *Pickpocket* Bresson a trouvé." *Arts, Lettres, Spectacles,* 30 December 1959–5 January 1960, 1, 6.

Mauriac, Claude. "Robert Bresson." In *Petite littérature du cinéma,* 65–73. Paris: Cerf, 1957.

Millar, Daniel. "Pickpocket." In *The Films of Robert Bresson,* edited by Ian Cameron, 82–89. New York: Praeger, 1969.

Monod, Roland. "Working with Bresson." *Sight and Sound* 27, no. 1 (Summer 1957): 30–32.

Nogueira, Rui. "Burel and Bresson." *Sight and Sound* 46, no. 1 (1976–77): 18–21.

Oudart, Jean-Pierre. "Bresson et la vérité." *Cahiers du cinéma* 216 (October 1969): 53- 56.

———. "Un Discours en défaut." *Cahiers du cinéma* 232 (October 1971): 4–12.

———. "Le Hors-champ de l'auteur." *Cahiers du cinéma* 236–37 (March–April 1972): 86–89.

———. "L'Idéologie moderniste dans quelques films récents." *Cahiers du cinéma* 236–37 (March–April 1972): 83–86.

———. "Modernité de Robert Bresson." *Cahiers du cinéma* 279–80 (August–September 1977): 27–30.

———. "Un Pouvoir qui ne pense, ne calcule, ni ne juge." *Cahiers du cinéma* 258–59 (July–August 1975): 36–41.

———. "La Suture." *Cahiers du cinéma* 211 (April 1969): 36–39.

Petric, Vlada. "For a Close Cinematic Analysis." *Quarterly Review of Film Studies* 1, no. 4 (1976): 453–77.

Pinel, Vincent. "Le Paradoxe du non-comédien." *Etudes cinématographiques* 14–15 (1962): 78–84.

Prédal, René. "Bresson et son temps." *Cinéma 83* 294 (June 1983): 4–11.

Prokosch, Mike. "Bresson's Stylistics Revisited." *Film Quarterly* 25, no. 2 (Winter 1971–72): 30–32.

Rhode, Eric. "Correspondence: *Pickpocket*." *Sight and Sound* 31, no. 3 (Summer 1962): 154.

———. "Dostoevsky and Bresson." *Sight and Sound* 39, no. 2 (Spring 1970): 82–83.

———. "Pickpocket." *Sight and Sound* 29, no. 4 (Fall 1960): 193–94.

———. "Robert Bresson." In *Tower of Babel: Speculations on the Cinema*, 33–47. New York: Chilton Books, 1967.

Rohmer, Eric. "Le Miracle des objets." *Cahiers du cinéma* 65 (December 1956): 42–45.

Ropars-Wuilleumier, Marie-Claire. "Un Mauvais Rêve." In *L'Ecran de la mémoire*, 178–81. Paris: Seuil, 1970.

———. "Robert Bresson." In *De la littérature au cinéma: genese d'une écriture*, 96–104. Paris: Armand Colin, 1983.

Roud, Richard. "Novel, Novel: Fable Fable?" *Sight and Sound* 31, no. 2 (Spring 1962): 84–88.

———. "The Redemption of Despair." *Film Comment* 13, no. 5 (September–October 1977): 23–24.

Sadoul, Georges. "Délits et chatiment." *Les Lettres françaises,* 24 December 1959, 7.

———. "Robert Bresson, janséniste." *Les Lettres françaises,* 22 February 1951, 6.

Sarris, Andrew. "Pickpocket." *Village Voice,* 23 May 1963, 15.

Schrader, Paul. "Robert Bresson." In *Transcendental Style in Film: Ozu, Bresson, Dreyer*, 64–105. Berkeley and Los Angeles: University of California Press, 1972.

Sebbag, Georges, ed. *Robert Bresson*. Paris: Ramsay, 1989.
———. "Un Simple Crochet." *Camera/Stylo* 68/69 (February 1989): 5–7.
Seguin, Louis. "Pickpocket." *Positif* 33 (April 1960): 40–41.
Sémolué, Jean. "L'Argent: note pour une approche." *Cinéma 83* 294 (June 1983): 27–30.
———. "Les Limites de la liberté." *Etudes cinématographiques* 3–4 (1960): 230–40.
———. "Les Personnages de Robert Bresson." *Cahiers du cinéma* 75 (October 1957): 10–15.
———. *Robert Bresson*. Paris: Editions universitaires, 1959.
Sitney, P. Adams. "The Rhetoric of Robert Bresson." In *The Essential Cinema*, 182–207. Anthology of Film Archives. New York: New York University Press, 1975.
Skoller, Donald S. "Praxis as a Cinematic Principle in the Films of Robert Bresson." *Cinema Journal* 9, no. 1 (Fall 1969): 13–22.
Sloan, Jane. *Robert Bresson: A Guide to References and Sources*. Boston: G. K. Hall, 1983.
Sontag, Susan. "Spritual Style in the Films of Robert Bresson." In *Against Interpretation*, 177–95. New York: Farrar, Straus & Giroux, 1961.
Tailleur, Roger. "*Pickpocket:* le pheaurme." *Positif* 33 (April 1960): 41–44.
Targe, André. "Ici l'espace naît du temps." *Camera/Stylo* 68/69 (February 1989): 87–99.
Taylor, John Russell. "Robert Bresson." In *Cinema Eye, Cinema Ear: Some Key Filmmakers of the Sixties,* 115–37. New York: Hill & Wang, 1964.
Thiher, Allen. "The Existentialist Moment: Bresson's *Un Condamné à mort:* The Semiotics of Grace." In *The Cinematic Muse: Critical Studies in the History of French Cinema,* 130–42. Columbia: University of Missouri Press, 1979.
Truffaut, François. "Robert Bresson." In *The Films of My Life,* 188–96. New York: Simon & Schuster, 1978.
Vas, Robert. "Pickpocket." *Monthly Film Bulletin* 27, no. 321 (October 1960): 139–40.
Wagner, Jean. "L'Homme derrière l'objet." *Cahiers du cinéma* 104 (February 1960): 49–50.
Young, Colin. "Conventional-Unconventional." *Film Quarterly* 17, no. 1 (Fall 1963): 14–30.

Godard

Works by Godard

Breathless. Edited by Dudley Andrew. New Brunswick, N.J.: Rutgers University Press, 1987.
"But 'Wave' Adds Brightness." *Films and Filming* 7, no. 12 (September 1961): 7, 36.
Godard par Godard. 2 vols. Edited by Alain Bergala. Paris: Editions Belfond,

1968. Reprint. Paris: Flammarion, 1985. Translated by Tom Milne as *Godard on Godard.* New York: Da Capo Press, 1972.

Introduction à une véritable histoire du cinéma. Paris: Editions Albatros, 1980.

Pierrot le fou. Translated by Peter Whitehead. 1969. Rev. ed. London: Lorrimer, 1984.

"Sauve qui peut (la vie): quelques remarques sur la réalisation et la production du film." *Revue Belge du cinéma* 22–23 (Summer 1986): 117–20.

Interviews

Baby, Yvonne. "Entretien avec Jean-Luc Godard: dresser des embuscades dans la planification." *Le Monde,* 6 May 1965, 16.

———. "Un Entretien avec J.-L. Godard, le réalisateur du 'Petit Soldat.'" *Le Monde,* 13 September 1960, 13.

———. "Mon film est un documentaire sur Jean Seberg et J-P. Belmondo." *Le Monde,* 18 March 1960, 12.

———. "Shipwrecked People from the Modern World: Interview with Jean-Luc Godard." In *Focus on Godard,* edited by Royal S. Brown, 37–39. Englewood Cliffs: Prentice Hall, 1971.

Bachman, Gideon. "The Carrots Are Cooked: A Conversation with Jean-Luc Godard." *Film Quarterly* 37, no. 3 (Spring 1984): 13–19.

Bellour, Raymond. "Jean-Luc Godard s'explique." *Les Lettres françaises,* 14 May 1964, 8–9.

Bontemps, Jacques. "Struggle on Two Fronts: A Conversation with Jean-Luc Godard." *Film Quarterly* 22, no. 2 (Winter 1968): 20–35.

Carroll, Kent E. "Film and Revolution: An Interview with Jean-Luc Godard." *Evergreen Review* 14, no. 83 (October 1970): 47–51, 66–68.

Collet, Jean. "Entretien avec Jean-Luc Godard." *Cahiers du cinéma* 138 (December 1962): 21–39.

———. "No Questions Asked: Conversation with Jean-Luc Godard." In *Focus on Godard,* edited by Royal S. Brown, 40–45. Englewood Cliffs: Prentice Hall, 1971.

Comolli, Jean Louis. "Parlons de *Pierrot:* nouvel entretien avec Jean-Luc Godard." *Cahiers du cinéma* 171 (October 1965): 18–35.

Cott, Jonathan. "Interview with Godard." *Rolling Stone,* 14 June 1969, 21–23.

Cournot, M. "Quelques évidentes incertitudes: entretien avec J.-L. Godard." *Revue d'esthétique* 2–3 (1967): 115–22.

Dieckman, Katherine. "Godard in His Fifth Period." *Film Quarterly* 39, no. 4 (Winter 1985–86): 2–6.

Feinstein, Herbert. "An Interview with Jean-Luc Godard." *Film Quarterly* 17, no. 3 (Spring 1964): 8–10.

Guegan, Gérard. "Entretien avec Jean-Luc Godard." *Les Lettres françaises,* 19 November 1964, 1, 8, 9.

———. "Plein sud." *Cahiers du cinéma* 169 (August 1965): 7.

"Jean-Luc Godard: 'Je ne suis pas à bout de souffle.'" *Arts,* 23 March 1960, 1–2.

Manceaux, Michele. "Learning Not to Be Bitter: Interview with Jean-Luc Godard." In *Focus on Godard,* edited by Royal S. Brown, 25–35. Englewood Cliffs: Prentice Hall, 1971.

Mieville, Anne-Marie. "Soft and Hard: Soft Talk on a Hard Subject between Two Friends." *Revue Belge du cinéma* 22–23 (Summer 1986): 161–67.

Touratier, Jean-Marie, and Daniel Busto. *Jean-Luc Godard: télévision/écritures.* Paris: Galilée, 1979.

Critical Works on Godard

Alpert, Hollis. "The Conscienceless Hero." *Saturday Review,* 11 March 1961, 39.

Amengual, Barthélemy. "Destruction du 'Musée imaginaire': *Pierrot le fou.*" *Etudes cinématographiques* 57–61 (1967): 146–77.

———. "Jean-Luc Godard et la remise en cause de notre civilisation de l'image." *Jean-Luc Godard: au dela du récit.* Special issue of *Etudes cinématographiques* 57–61 (1967): 113–17.

Andrew, Dudley. "Au début du souffle: le culte et la culture d'*A bout de souffle.*" *Revue Belge du cinéma* 22–23 (Summer 1986): 10–21.

———. "*Breathless:* Old as New." In *Breathless,* edited by Andrew Dudley, 3–20. New Brunswick, N.J.: Rutgers University Press, 1987.

Aragon, Louis. "Collages dans le roman et dans le film." In *Collages,* 107–29. Paris: Hermann, 1965.

———. "Qu'est-ce que l'art, Jean-Luc Godard?" *Les Lettres françaises,* 9–15 September 1965, 1, 8.

Aristarco, Guido. "Langage et idéologie dans quelques films de Godard." *Etudes cinématographiques* 57–61 (1967): 7–15.

Armes, Roy. "Jean-Luc Godard." In *French Cinema since 1946,* 2:69–92. 2 vols. London: A. Zwemmer, 1966.

Barr, Charles. *The Films of Jean-Luc Godard.* New York: Praeger, 1970.

Bechtold, Charles. "A bout de souffle." *Cinématographe* 13 (May–June 1975): 40–42.

Bellour, Raymond. "Godard or not Godard." *Les Lettres françaises,* 14 May 1964, 8.

———. "Le Miroir critique." *La Nouvelle Revue française* 152 (August 1965): 305–17.

Belmans, Jacques. "L'Ethique et l'esthétique du chaos." *Etudes cinématographiques* 57–61 (1967): 83–99.

Benayoun, Robert. "Dictionnaire du cinéma français: Godard, Jean-Luc." *Positif* 46 (June 1962): 27.

———. "*Pierrot le fou:* la machine à décerveler." *Positif* 73 (February 1966): 93–96.

Bertolucci, Bernardo. "Versus Godard." *Cahiers du cinéma* 186 (January 1967): 29–30.

Bonitzer, Pascal. "J-M. S. et J-L. G." *Cahiers du cinéma* 264 (February 1976): 5–10.

Bibliography

Bonnot, Gérard. "Un Naïf au cinéma: Jean-Luc Godard." *Les Temps modernes* 186 (November 1961): 566–75.

Bordwell, David. "Godard and Narration." In *Narration in the Fiction Film*, 311–35. Madison: University of Wisconsin Press, 1985.

———. "Jump Cuts and Blind Spots." *Wide Angle* 6, no. 1 (1984): 4–11.

———. "La Saute et l'ellipse." *Revue Belge du cinéma* 22–23 (Summer 1986): 85–90.

Bory, Jean Louis. "Terrible!" *Arts,* 12–18 May 1965, 10.

Braucourt, Guy. "*Pierrot le fou* ou les héros de Jean-Luc Godard." *Etudes cinématographiques* 57–61 (1967): 101–12.

Brown, Royal S., ed. *Focus on Godard.* Englewood Cliffs: Prentice Hall, 1971.

———. "Jean-Luc Godard: Nihilism versus Aesthetic Distantiation." In *Focus on Godard,* edited by Royal S. Brown, 109–21. Englewood Cliffs: Prentice Hall, 1971.

Burch, Noel. "Fonctions de l'alea." In *Praxis du cinéma,* 154–76. Paris: Gallimard, 1986.

Burgoyne, R. "The Political Topology of Montage: The Conflict of Genres in the Films of Godard." *Enclitic* 7, no. 1 (1983): 14–23.

Caen, Michael. "*Pierrot le fou:* l'oeil du cyclone." *Cahiers du cinéma* 174 (January 1966): 74.

Cameron, Ian, ed. *The Films of Jean-Luc Godard.* New York: Praeger, 1970.

Casebier, Allan. "Exploiting Expectation: Audience Capacities." In *Film Appreciation,* 62–73. New York: Harcourt, Brace, Jovanovich, 1978.

Cluny, Claude Michel. "Les Mégots de Godard." *La Nouvelle Revue française* 191 (August 1968): 668–72.

Collet, Jean. *Jean-Luc Godard.* Paris: Seghers, 1968.

Comolli, Jean-Louis. "A rebours?" *Cahiers du cinéma* 168 (July 1965): 86–87.

———. "La Présence et l'absence." *Cahiers du cinéma* 141 (March 1963): 54–58.

Croce, Arlene. "Breathless." *Film Quarterly* 14, no. 3 (Spring 1961): 54–56.

Crofts, Stephen. "The Films of Jean-Luc Godard." *Cinema* 3 (June 1969): 27–32.

Crowther, Bosley. "Breathless." *New York Times,* 8 February 1961, sec. 2.

———. "Cubist Crime." *Time,* 17 February 1961, 62.

Curtis, Jean-Louis. "Le Fou d'Anna." *La Nouvelle Revue française* 160 (April 1966): 689–94.

Daney, Serge. "The T(h)errorized (Godardian Pedagogy)." *Thousand Eyes* 2 (1977): 33–43.

Delahaye, Michel. "Jean-Luc Godard et l'enfance de l'art." *Cahiers du cinéma* 179 (June 1966): 65–70, 77.

———. "Jean-Luc Godard ou l'urgence de l'art." *Cahiers du cinéma* 187 (February 1967): 29–33.

Deleuze, Gilles. "A propos de 'Sur et sous la communication': trois questions sur *Six fois deux.*" *Cahiers du cinéma* 271 (November 1976): 5–12.

de Mourgues, Nicole. "Godard et Véronique: une histoire de noms propres . . ." *Revue Belge du cinéma* 22–23 (Summer 1986): 95–101.

Dort, Bernard. "Godard ou le romantique abusif." *Les Temps modernes* 235 (December 1965): 1118–28.

———. "Le Star et le comedien." *Etudes cinématographiques* 14–15 (1962): 5–11.

Duras, Marguerite. "Godard." *Cahiers du cinéma* 312–13 (June 1980): 25–26.

Durgnat, Raymond. "Some Mad Love and the Sweet Life." *Films and Filming* 8, no. 6 (March 1962): 16–18, 42.

Egly, Max. "Jean-Luc Godard: *A bout de souffle,* 1969." In *Regards neufs sur le cinéma,* 216–23. Paris: Seuil, 1965.

Estève, Michel, ed. *Jean-Luc Godard: au delà du récit.* Special issue of *Etudes cinématographiques* 57–61 (1967).

Falkenberg, Pamela. "'Hollywood' and the 'Art Cinema' as a Bipolar Modeling System: *A bout de souffle* and *Breathless.*" *Wide Angle* 7, no. 3 (1985): 44–53.

Farber, Manny. "The Films of Jean-Luc Godard and Americanism." *Artforum* 7, no. 2 (October 1968): 58–61.

Fieschi, Jean-André. "Après." *Cahiers du cinéma* 168 (July 1965): 87.

———. "Dossier: cinéma et littérature." *Cinématographe* 32 (November 1977): 18–21.

Fieschi, Jean-André, and André Téchiné. "Fable sur *Pierrot.*" *Cahiers du cinéma* 171 (October 1965): 35–36.

Goldman, Judith. "Godard: Cult or culture?" *Films and Filming* 12, no. 9 (June 1966): 36–37.

Goldmann, Annie. "Jean-Luc Godard: un nouveau réalisme." *La Nouvelle Revue française* 165 (September 1966): 558–65.

Gow, Gordon. "Breathless." *Films and Filming* 7, no. 11 (August 1961): 25.

Greene, Naomi, "Brecht, Godard, and Epic Cinema." *Praxis: A Journal of Radical Perspectives on the Arts* 1, no. 1 (Spring 1975): 19–24.

Guegan, Gérard. "Plein sud." *Cahiers du cinéma* 169 (August 1965): 7.

Guest, Harry. "Godard Quotation." *Sight and Sound* 35, no. 4 (Fall 1966): 207.

Henderson, Brian. "Godard on Godard: Notes for a Reading." *Film Quarterly* 27, no. 4 (Summer 1974): 34–36.

———. "Toward a Non-Bourgeois Camera Style." *Film Quarterly* 24, no. 2 (Winter 1970): 2–14.

Jacob, Gilles. "*Pierrot le fou:* sélection du Godard's Digest." *Cinéma 65* 101 (December 1965): 100–104.

Kael, Pauline. "*Breathless* and the Daisy Miller Doll." *New Yorker,* 11 February 1961, 101–6.

Kauffmann, Stanley. "Adventures of an Anti-Hero." *New Republic,* 13 February 1961, 20–21.

Kavanagh, Thomas M. "Le Gai Savoir." *Film Quarterly* 25, no. 1 (Fall 1971): 51–52.

Klein, Michael. "Pierrot le fou." *Film Quarterly* 19, no. 3 (Spring 1966): 46–48.

Latil-Le Dantec, Mireille. "Jean-Luc Godard ou l'innocence perdue." *Etudes cinématographiques* 57–61 (1967): 49–70.

Lawson, John Howard. "A bout de Souffle." In *Film: The Creative Process,* 239–40. New York: Hill & Wang, 1964.

Lefevre, Raymond. *Jean-Luc Godard.* Paris: Eidilig, 1983.

Lesage, Julia. "Visual Distancing in Godard." *Wide Angle* 1, no. 3 (1976): 4–13.

Lockerbie, S. I. "Apollinaire au cinéma." *Guillaume Apollinaire* 5 (1966): 106–9.

Macbean, James Roy. "Filming the Inside of His Own Head: Godard's Cerebral Passion." *Film Quarterly* 38, no. 1 (Fall 1984): 16–24.

———. "Godard Seen through a Camera Obscura, Darkly." *Quarterly Review of Film Studies* 9, no. 4 (1984): 341–45.

McCabe, Colin. *Godard: Images, Sounds, Politics.* Bloomington: Indiana University Press, 1980.

Marcorelles, Louis. "Godard's Half-Truths." *Film Quarterly* 17, no. 3 (Spring 1964): 4–7.

———. "Views of the New Wave." *Sight and Sound* 29, no. 2 (Spring 1960): 84–85.

Martin, Marcel. "Pierrot le fou." *Cinéma 65* 99 (August 1965): 5–6.

Metz, Christian. "Le Cinéma moderne et la narrativité." *Cahiers du cinéma* 185 (December 1966): 43–68.

Michaelson, Annette. "Film and the Radical Aspiration." In *Film Culture Reader,* edited by P. Adams Sitney, 404–22. New York: Praeger, 1970.

Milne, Tom. "Jean-Luc Godard, ou La Raison Ardente." In *Focus on Godard,* edited by Royal S. Brown, 123–34. Englewood Cliffs: Prentice Hall, 1972.

———. "Pierrot le fou." *Sight and Sound* 35, no. 1 (Winter 1965): 6–7.

Moullet, Luc. "Jean-Luc Godard." *Cahiers du cinéma* 106 (April 1960): 25–26.

Mussman, Toby, ed. *Jean-Luc Godard: A Critical Anthology.* New York: Dutton, 1968.

Narboni, Jean, ed. *Jean-Luc Godard par Jean-Luc Godard.* Paris: Pierre Belfond, 1968.

Nourissier, François. "Le Second Souffle." *La Nouvelle Revue française* 92 (August 1960): 321–27.

Pollack-Lederer, Jacques. "Jean-Luc Godard dans la modernité." *Les Temps modernes* 262 (March 1968): 1558–89.

Ropars, Marie-Claire. "The Graphic in Film Writing: *A bout de souffle* or the Erratic Alphabet." *Enclitic* 5–6, nos. 1–2 (1981–82): 147–61.

———. "La Perte du langage." *Esprit* 33, no. 9 (September 1965): 315–17. Translated as "Loss of Language." *Wide Angle* 1, no. 3 (1976): 17–19.

———. "Pierrot le fou." *Esprit* 34, no. 2 (February 1966): 302–4.

Ropars-Wuilleumier, Marie-Claire. "La Forme et le fond ou les avatars du récit." In *L'Ecran de la mémoire,* 91–113. Paris: Seuil, 1970.

Rosenbaum, Jonathan. "Theory and Practice: The Criticism of Jean-Luc Godard." *Sight and Sound* 41, no. 3 (Summer 1972): 124–26.

Roud, Richard. *Jean-Luc Godard.* London: Thames & Hudson, 1970.

Siclier, Jacques. *Nouvelle Vague?* Paris: Cerf, 1961.

Simon, John. "Godard and the Godardians." In *Private Screenings,* 272–96. New York: Macmillan, 1971.

Sontag, Susan. "Godard." In *Styles of Radical Will,* 147–89. New York: Farrar, Straus & Giroux, 1966.

Taylor, John Russell. "The New Wave: J-L Godard." In *Cinema Eye: Cinema Ear: Some Key Filmmakers of the Sixties,* 211–20. New York: Hill & Wang, 1964.

Thiher, Allen. "Postmodern Dilemmas: Godard's *Alphaville* and *Deux ou trois choses que je sais d'elle.*" In *The Cinematic Muse: Critical Studies in the History of French Cinema,* 180–98. Columbia: University of Missouri Press, 1979.

Vianey, Michel. *En Attendant Godard.* Paris: Bernard Grasset, 1966.

Whitehead, Peter. "Pierrot le fou." *Films and Filming* 12, no. 9 (June 1966): 16, 51–52.

Williams, Alan. "Godard's Use of Sound." In *Film Sound: Theory and Practice,* edited by Elisabeth Weis and John Belton, 332–45. New York: Columbia University Press, 1985.

———. "Is Sound Recording Like a Language?" *Yale French Studies* 60 (1980): 51–66.

General Bibliography of Works Cited

Andrew, Dudley. *Film in the Aura of Art.* Princeton: Princeton University Press, 1984.

———. "The Impact of the Novel on French Cinema of the 30's." *L'Esprit Créateur* 30, no. 2 (Summer 1990): 3–13.

———. *The Major Film Theories: An Introduction.* London: Oxford University Press, 1976.

Apollodorus. *Library of Greek Mythology.* Translated by Keith Aldrich. Lawrence, Kans.: Coronado, 1975.

Aragon, Louis. *La Mise à mort.* Paris: Gallimard, 1965.

Armes, Roy. *French Cinema.* New York: Oxford University Press, 1985.

———. *French Cinema since 1946.* Vol. 2. London: A. Zwemmer, 1966.

Arnheim, Rudolf. *Film as Art.* Berkeley: University of California Press, 1957.

Bakhtin, Mikhael. *Problems of Dostoevsky's Poetics.* Translated by R. W. Rotsel. New York: Ardis, 1973.

———. *Rabelais and His World.* Translated by Helene Iswolsky. Cambridge: MIT Press, 1968.

Balazs, Bela. *Theory of the Film.* New York: Dover, 1970.

Bibliography

Balzac, Honoré de. *César Birotteau*. Paris: Editions de la Pléiade, 1936. Translated by Ellen Marriage as *The Rise and Fall of Cesar Birotteau*. New York: Carroll & Graf, 1989.

———. *Les Illusions perdues*. Paris: Garnier, 1961. Translated by Ellen Marriage as *Lost Illusions*. Philadelphia: Gebbie, 1899.

Barthes, Roland. *Camera Lucida*. Translated by Richard Howard. New York: Hill & Wang, 1981.

———. *The Pleasure of the Text*. Translated by R. Miller. New York: Hill & Wang, 1975.

Baudry, Jean-Louis. "Le Dispositif: approches métapsychologiques de l'impression de réalité." *Psychanalyse et cinéma*. Special issue of *Communications*, 23 (1975): 56–72.

Bazin, André. "The Evolution of the Language of Cinema." In *Film Theory and Criticism*, edited by Gerald Mast and Marshall Cohen, 124–38. New York: Oxford University Press, 1979.

———. *Qu'est-ce que le cinéma?* Paris: Cerf, 1985.

Becker, George J., ed. *Modern Literary Realism*. Princeton: Princeton University Press, 1967.

Beebe, Maurice. "The Three Motives of Raskolnikov." In *"Crime and Punishment" and the Critics*, edited by Edward Wasiolek, 98–108. Belmont, Calif.: Wadsworth, 1961.

Beja, Morris. *Film and Literature*. New York: Longman, 1979.

Benjamin, Walter. *Illuminations*. New York: Schocken Books, 1969.

Bersani, Leo. *Baudelaire and Freud*. Berkeley and Los Angeles: University of California Press, 1977.

———. *The Freudian Body*. New York: Columbia University Press, 1986.

Bloom, Harold. *The Anxiety of Influence*. New York: Oxford University Press, 1973.

Bluestone, George. *Novels into Film*. Berkeley: University of California Press, 1968.

Bonitzer, Pascal. *Le Regard et la voix*. Paris: Union Générale d'Éditions, 1976.

Bonnet, Jean-Claude. "Trois cinéastes du texte." *Cinématographe* 31 (October 1977): 2–6.

Bordwell, David. *Narration in the Fiction Film*. Madison: University of Wisconsin Press, 1986.

Borges, Jorge Luis. *Labyrinths*. New York: New Directions, 1962.

Bray, René. *La Préciosité et les précieux*. Paris: Albin Michel, 1948.

Browne, Nick. "Rhétorique du texte spéculaire." In *Psychanalyse et cinéma*. Special issue of *Communications*, 23 (1975): 202–12.

Brunette, Peter, and David Wills. *Screen/Play: Derrida and Film Theory*. Princeton: Princeton University Press, 1989.

Burch, Noel. *Praxis du cinéma*. Paris: Gallimard, 1969. Translated by Helen Lane as *Theory of Film Practice*. 1973. Reprint. Princeton: Princeton University Press, 1981.

———. "Qu'est-ce que la nouvelle vague?" *Film Quarterly* 13, no. 2 (Winter 1959): 16–30.

Carrière, Jean-Claude. "Le Cinéma, à force d'influencer la littérature finit par la tuer." *Cinéma 70* 148 (July–August 1970): 61–64.

Casarès, Bioy. *The Invention of Morel and Other Stories*. Translated by Ruth Sims. Austin: University of Texas Press, 1964.

Cavell, Stanley. *The World Viewed*. Cambridge: Harvard University Press, 1979.

Céline, Louis-Ferdinand. *Guignol's Band*. Paris: Gallimard, 1952. Translated by Bernard Frechtman and Jack T. Nile as *Guignol's Band*. New York: New Directions, 1954.

Chasseguet-Smirgel, Janine. *Pour une psychanalyse de l'art*. Paris: Payot, 1971.

Chatman, Seymour. *Story and Discourse: Narrative Structure in Fiction and Film*. Ithaca: Cornell University Press, 1978.

Clouzot, Claire. *Le Cinéma français depuis la nouvelle vague*. Paris: Fernand Nathan, 1972.

Cocteau, Jean. *Entretiens sur le cinématographe*. Paris: Pierre Belfond, 1973.

Cohen, Keith. *Film and Fiction: The Dynamics of Exchange*. New Haven: Yale University Press, 1979.

Conley, Tom. "Vigo Van Gogh." *New York Literary Forum* 5 (1983): 153–65.

Cooper, Arnold M., Otto F. Kernberg, and Ethal Person, eds. *Psychoanalysis: Toward the Second Century*. New Haven: Yale University Press, 1989.

Curtius, Ernst Robert. *European Literature and the Latin Middle Ages*. New York: Harper & Row, 1953.

Daney, Serge. "Les Cahiers du cinéma, 1968–1977." *Thousand Eyes* 2 (1977): 18–32.

Decaux, Emmanuel. "Images du livre." *Cinématographe* 31 (October 1977): 10–12.

De Jean, Joan. "The Salons, 'Preciosity,' and the Sphere of Women's Influence." In *A New History of French Literature*, edited by Denis Hollier, 297–303. Cambridge: Harvard University Press, 1989.

Denon, Vivant. *Point de lendemain*. 1777. Reprint. Paris: Jean-Jacques Pauvert, 1959.

Dostoevsky, Fyodor. *Crime and Punishment*. Translated by Constance Garnett. New York: Modern Library, n.d.

Douin, Jean-Luc, ed. *La Nouvelle Vague 25 ans après*. Paris: Cerf, 1983.

Dubois, Claude-Gilbert. *L'Imaginaire de la renaissance*. Paris: Presses Universitaires Françaises, 1985.

Durgnat, Raymond. *Films and Feelings*. Cambridge: MIT Press, 1967.

Eisenstein, S. *The Film Sense*. New York: Harcourt, Brace & World, 1942.

Faulkner, William. *The Wild Palms*. New York: Random House, 1939.

Faure, Elie. *Histoire de l'Art*. Vol. 1. *L'Art Moderne*. 1924. Reprint. Paris: Poche, 1964. Translated by Walter Pach as *History of Art*. Vol. 1. *Modern Art*. Garden City, N.Y.: Garden City Publishing, 1937.

Bibliography

Filteau, Claude. "Le Pays de Tendre: l'enjeu d'une carte." *Littérature* 36 (December 1979): 37–60.

French, T. L. "The Tinkerers." *Thousand Eyes* 2 (1977): 4–17.

Freud, Sigmund. *The Standard Edition of the Complete Psychological Works of Sigmund Freud.* Edited and translated by James Strachey. 23 vols. London: Hogarth, 1955–66.

Gallop, Jane. *Reading Lacan.* Ithaca: Cornell University Press, 1985.

Gibson, A. Boyce. *The Religion of Dostoevsky.* Philadelphia: Westminster, 1973.

Girard, René. *Mensonge romantique, vérité romanesque.* Paris: Grasset, 1961.

Goethe, J. W. *Elective Affinities.* Translated by R. J. Hollingdale. New York: Penguin, 1971.

Goldmann, Lucien. *Le Dieu caché.* Paris: Gallimard, 1959. Translated by Philip Thody as *The Hidden God.* London: Routledge & Kegan Paul, 1964.

Gollup, Judith. "French Writers Turned Film Makers." *Film Heritage* 4, no. 2 (Winter 1968–69): 19–25.

Graham, Peter, ed. *The New Wave.* Garden City, N.Y.: Doubleday, 1968.

Harrington, John. *Film and/as Literature.* Englewood Cliffs: Prentice Hall, 1977.

Hayward, Susan, and Ginette Vincendeau, eds. *French Film: Texts and Contexts.* London: Routledge, 1990.

Heath, Stephen. *Questions of Cinema.* Bloomington: Indiana University Press, 1981.

Henderson, Brian. *A Critique of Film Theory.* New York: Dutton, 1980.

Herman, Judith. *Father-Daughter Incest.* Cambrige: Harvard University Press, 1981.

Holquist, Michael. *Dostoevsky and the Novel.* Princeton: Princeton University Press, 1977.

Horace. *The Complete Works.* Edited by Casper J. Kraemer, Jr. New York: Modern Library, 1936.

Hunter, Diane. *Seduction and Theory.* Urbana: University of Illinois Press, 1989.

Ibsen, Henrik. *Hedda Gabler.* In *The Plays of Henrik Ibsen.* New York: Tudor, 1934.

———. *Rosmersholm.* In *The Plays of Henrik Ibsen.* New York: Tudor, 1934.

Jost, François. *L'Oeil/Caméra: entre film et roman.* Lyon: Presses Universitaires de Lyon, 1987.

Kaplan, E. Ann, ed. *Psychoanalysis and Cinema.* New York: Routledge, 1990.

Kawain, Bruce. *Telling It Again and Again: Repetition in Literature and Film.* Ithaca: Cornell University Press, 1972.

Kline, T. Jefferson. *André Malraux and the Metamorphosis of Death.* New York: Columbia University Press, 1973.

———. *Bertolucci's Dream Loom: A Psychoanalytic Study of Cinema.* Amherst: University of Massachusetts Press, 1987.

Kozloff, Sarah. *Invisible Storytellers: Voice-over Narration in American Fiction*

Film. Berkeley and Los Angeles: University of California Press, 1988.

Lacan, Jacques. "Le Stade du miroir comme formateur de la fonction du Je." *Revue française de psychanalyse* 4 (October–December 1949): 449–55. Translated by Alan Sheridan as "The Mirror Stage as Formative of the Function of the I as Revealed in Psychoanalytic Experience." In *Ecrits: A Selection*, 1–7. New York: W. W. Norton, 1977.

———. *Le Séminaire XX: encore*. Paris: Seuil, 1975.

La Fontaine, Jean de. *Fables Choisies*. 2 vols. Paris: Classiques Larousse, n.d.

Lambert, Richard S. *The Prince of Pickpockets: A Study of George Barrington who left his country for his country's good*. London: Faber & Faber, 1930.

Leutrat, Jean-Louis. *Kaleidoscope: analyses de films*. Lyon: Presses Universitaires de Lyon, 1988.

McDougall, Joyce. *Plaidoyer pour une certaine anormalité*. Paris: Gallimard, 1978.

———. *Théâtres du Je*. Paris: Gallimard, 1982.

Malraux, André. *L'Espoir*. Paris: Gallimard, 1937.

Marcus, Fred. *Film and Literature: Contrasts in Media*. Scranton, Pa.: Chandler, 1971.

Marin, Louis. *Utopics: Spatial Play*. Translated by Robert A. Vollrath. Atlantic Highlands, N.J.: Humanities Press, 1984.

Masson, Jeffrey. *The Assault on Truth*. New York: Viking Penguin, 1984.

Mauss, Marcel. *The Gift: Forms and Functions of Exchange in Archaic Societies*. Translated by Ian Cunnison. New York: W. W. Norton, 1967.

Mehlman, Jeffrey. "French Freud." *Yale French Studies* 48 (1972): 5–9.

Mérimée, Prosper. *La Vénus d'Ille*. In *Colomba*, 181–219. 1841. Reprint. Paris: Garnier, 1962.

Metz, Christian. *Langage et cinéma*. Paris: Larousse, 1971.

———. *Le Signifiant imaginaire*. Paris: Union Générale d'Éditions, 1977.

Michalczyk, John. *The French Literary Filmmakers*. Philadelphia: Art Alliance Press, 1980.

Michels, Robert. "The Mind and Its Occupants." In *Psychoanalysis: Toward the Second Century*, edited by Arnold M. Cooper, Otto F. Kernberg, and Ethal Person, 143–52. New Haven: Yale University Press, 1989.

Miller, J. Hillis. "Ariachne's Broken Woof." *Georgia Review* 31, no. 1 (Spring 1977): 44–60.

Miller, Mark Crispin, ed. *Seeing Through Movies*. New York: Pantheon, 1990.

Mochulsky, Konstantin. *Dostoevsky: His Life and Work*. Translated by Michael Minihan. Princeton: Princeton University Press, 1967.

Monaco, James. *The New Wave*. New York: Oxford University Press, 1976.

Morin, Jacques. "Pour en finir avec l'adaptation." *Cinéma 70* 148 (July–August 1970): 45–51.

Morrissette, Bruce. *Novel and Film*. Chicago: University of Chicago Press, 1985.

Murry, J. Middleton. "Beyond Morality." *Fyodor Dostoevsky: A Critical Study*. London: Martin Secker, 1916.

Myers, Helen. "Introduction to The Ego and The Self." In *Psychoanalysis:*

Toward the Second Century, edited by Arnold M. Cooper, Otto F. Kernberg, and Ethal Person, 135–42. New Haven: Yale University Press, 1989.

Nietzsche, Friedrich. *Beyond Good and Evil.* Translated by Walter Kaufmann. New York: Vintage, 1966.

Offord, Derek. "The Causes of Crime and the Meaning of Law: *Crime and Punishment* and Contemporary Radical Thought." In *New Essays on Dostoevsky,* edited by Malcolm Jones and Garth Terry, 41–65. Cambridge: Cambridge University Press, 1983.

Ovid. *The Metamorphoses.* Translated by A. D. Melville. New York: Oxford University Press, 1986.

Pascal, Blaise. *Les Lettres provinciales.* In *Pascal,* edited by Louis Lafuma, 371–469. Paris: Seuil, 1963. Translated by A. J. Krailsheimer as *The Provincial Letters.* Baltimore, Penguin, 1967.

———. *Les Pensées.* 1670. Reprint. Paris: Seuil, 1962. Translated by A. J. Krailsheimer as *Pensées.* Baltimore: Penguin, 1966.

Pauly, Rebecca M. *Le Berceau et la bibliothèque.* Saratoga, Calif.: Amni, 1989.

Pingaud, Bernard. "Nouveau roman et nouveau cinéma." *Cahiers du cinéma* 185 (December 1966): 27–40.

Pontalis, J. B. *Entre le rêve et la douleur.* Paris: Gallimard, 1977.

Queneau, Raymond. *Pierrot mon ami.* Paris: Gallimard, 1943.

Ragland-Sullivan, Ellie. *Jacques Lacan and the Philosophy of Psychoanalysis.* Urbana: University of Illinois Press, 1986.

Rahv, Philip. "Dostoevsky in *Crime and Punishment.*" In *"Crime and Punishment" and the Critics,* edited by Edward Wasiolek, 16–38. Belmont, Calif.: Wadsworth, 1961.

Ramasse, François. "La Règle du 'je': entretien avec Claude-Jean Philippe." In *La Nouvelle Vague 25 ans après,* edited by J. L. Douin, 29–38. Paris: Cerf, 1983.

Rank, Otto. *Das Inzest-Motiv in Dictung und Sage.* Berlin, 1912.

Renoir, Jean. *The Rules of the Game.* New York: Simon & Schuster, 1970.

Ricardou, Jean. "Page, film, récit." *Cahiers du cinéma* 185 (December 1966): 71–74.

Richardson, Robert. *Literature and Film.* Bloomington: Indiana University Press, 1969.

Roché, Henri-Pierre. *Jules et Jim.* Paris: Gallimard, 1953.

Roheim, Geza. *The Gates of the Dream.* New York: International Universities Press, 1952.

Ropars-Wuilleumier, Marie-Claire. *De la littérature au cinéma.* Paris: Armand Colin, 1970.

———. *L'Ecran de la mémoire.* Paris: Seuil, 1970.

———. "Un Langage cinématographique." *Esprit* 28, no. 6 (June 1960): 960–67.

Rose, Jacqueline. *Sexuality in the Field of Vision.* London: Verso, 1986.

Rosolato, Guy. *Essais sur le symbolique.* Paris: Gallimard, 1969.

Ross, Harris. *Film as Literature: Literature as Film*. New York: Greenwood, 1987.

Rousset, Jean. *Narcisse romancier*. Paris: José Corti, 1963.

Rubin, Gayle. "The Traffic in Women." In *Toward an Anthropology of Women*, edited by Rayna Teiter, 157–210. New York: Monthly Review Press, 1975.

Rycroft, Charles. *A Critical Dictionary of Psychoanalysis*. Totowa, N.J.: Littlefield, Adams, 1973.

Sachs, Maurice. *Abracadabra*. Paris: Gallimard, 1952.

Sartre, Jean-Paul. *La Nausée*. Paris: Gallimard, 1938.

Saussure, Ferdinand de. *Course in General Linguistics*. Translated by Wade Baskin. New York: McGraw Hill, 1966.

Schafer, Roy. "Narratives of the Self." In *Psychoanalysis: Toward the Second Century*, edited by Arnold M. Cooper, Otto F. Kernberg, and Ethal Person, 153–67. New Haven: Yale University Press, 1989.

Schrader, Paul. *The Transcendental Style in Film: Ozu, Bresson, Dreyer*. Berkeley and Los Angeles: University of California Press, 1972.

Sedgwick, Eve. *Between Men: English Literature and Male Homosocial Desire*. New York: Columbia University Press, 1985.

Showalter, Elaine. *The Female Malady: Women, Madness, and English Culture, 1830–1980*. New York: Penguin, 1985.

———. "Singles and Doubles: Gendering Jeckyll." Paper delivered at the Boston University Lectures in Criticism, September 1987.

Silverman, Kaja. *The Acoustic Mirror: The Female Voice in Psychoanalysis and Cinema*. Bloomington: Indiana University Press, 1988.

———. *The Subject of Semiotics*. New York: Oxford University Press, 1983.

Simmons, Ernest J. *Dostoevsky: The Making of a Novelist*. London: John Lehmann, 1950.

Sontag, Susan. *Against Interpretation*. New York: Farrar, Strauss & Giroux, 1961.

———. *On Photography*. New York: Dell, 1973.

Spiegel, Alan. *Fiction and the Camera Eye: Visual Consciousness in Film and Modern Novel*. Charlottesville: University of Virginia Press, 1976.

Stendhal. *Le Rouge et le noir*. Paris: Garnier, n.d. Translated by F. Scott Moncrieff as *The Red and the Black*. New York: Modern Library, 1926.

Tanner, Tony. *Adultery in the Novel*. Baltimore: Johns Hopkins University Press, 1979.

Telotte, J. P. *Voices in the Dark: The Narrative Patterns of Film Noir*. Urbana: University of Illinois Press, 1989.

Thiher, Allen. *The Cinematic Muse: Critical Studies in the History of French Cinema*. Columbia: University of Missouri Press, 1979.

Thomas, Dylan. *Portrait of the Artist as a Young Dog*. New York: New Directions, 1940.

Van Wert, William. *The Theory and Practice of the Ciné-Roman*. New York: Arno, 1978.

Wagner, Geoffrey. *The Novel and Cinema*. Rutherford, N.J.: Fairleigh Dickinson University Press, 1975.

Wasiolek, Edward. *Dostoevsky*. Cambridge: MIT Press, 1964.

———. "Structure and Detail." In *"Crime and Punishment" and the Critics*, edited by Edward Wasiolek, 109–17. Belmont, Calif.: Wadsworth, 1961.

Weber, Samuel. *The Legend of Freud*. Minneapolis: University of Minnesota Press, 1982.

White, Lionel. *Obsession*. New York: E. P. Dutton, 1962.

Williams, Alan. *Max Ophuls and the Cinema of Desire*. New York: Arno, 1980.

Wisechild, Louise. *The Obsidian Mirror*. Seattle: Seal, 1988.

Wollen, Peter. *Signs and Meaning in the Cinema*. Bloomington: Indiana University Press, 1972.

Select Filmography

Jules et Jim

Les Films du Carosse. 1961.
Director: François Truffaut.
Producer: Marcel Berbert.
Screenplay: François Truffaut and Jean Gruault. Based on the novel by
  Henri-Pierre Roché.
Photography: Raoul Coutard.
Music: Georges Delerue.
Cast: Jeanne Moreau (Catherine), Oskar Werner (Jules), Henri Serre (Jim),
  Marie Dubois (Thérèse), Boris Bassiak (Albert), Vanna Urbino
  (Gilberte), Sabine Haudepin (Sabine). Narrator: Michel Subor.

Les Amants

Nouvelles Editions des Films. 1958.
Director: Louis Malle.
Producer: Irène Leriche.
Screenplay: Louis Malle and Louise de Vilmorin.
Photography: Henri Decae.
Music: Johannes Brahms.
Cast: Jeanne Moreau (Jeanne Tournier), Alain Cuny (Monsieur Tournier),
  Judith Magre (Maggie), José Villalonga (Raoul), Jean-Marc Bory (the
  lover), Gaston Modot (the butler).

L'Année dernière à Marienbad

Terra-Film, Cormoran, Précitel, Argos-Films. 1961.
Director: Alain Resnais.
Producers: Pierre Courau and Raymond Froment.
Screenplay: Alain Robbe-Grillet.
Photography: Sacha Vierny.
Music: Francis Seyrig.
Cast: Delphine Seyrig (A), Giorgio Albertazzi (X), Sacha Pitoeff (M).

Le Beau Serge

AJYM. 1958.
Director: Claude Chabrol.
Producer: Claude Chabrol.
Screenplay: Claude Chabrol.
Photography: Henri Decae.
Music: Emile Delpierre.
Cast: Gérard Blain (Serge), Jean-Claude Brialy (François), Michèle Meritz
    (Yvonne), Bernadette Lafont (Marie), Claude Cerval (the priest).

Les Cousins

AJYM. 1959.
Director: Claude Chabrol.
Producer: Claude Chabrol.
Screenplay: Paul Gégauff.
Photography: Henri Decae.
Music: Paul Misraki.
Cast: Jean-Claude Brialy (Paul), Gérard Blain (Charles), Claude Cerval
    (Clovis), Juliette Mayniel (Florence).

Ma Nuit chez Maud

Les Films du Losange. 1969.
Director: Eric Rohmer.
Producers: Barbet Schoeder and Pierre Cotrell.
Screenplay: Eric Rohmer.
Photography: Nestor Almendros.
Music: Mozart.
Cast: Jean-Louis Trintignant (the narrator), Françoise Fabian (Maud),
    Marie-Christine Barrault (Françoise), Antoine Vitez (Vidal).

Pickpocket

Productions Agnès Delahaie. 1959.
Director: Robert Bresson.
Producer: Agnès Delahaie.
Screenplay: Robert Bresson.
Photography: Léonce-Henry Burel.
Music: Lulli.
Cast: Martin Lassalle (Michel), Marika Green (Jeanne), Pierre Leymarie
(Jacques), Jean Pélégri (the inspector), Kassagi (the initiator), Pierre
Etaix (the second accomplice).

A bout de souffle

Impéria Films, Société Nouvelle de Cinéma. 1959.
Director: Jean-Luc Godard.
Producer: Georges de Beauregard.
Screenplay: Jean-Luc Godard. Based on a text by François Truffaut.
Photography: Raoul Coutard.
Music: Martial Solal, Mozart.
Cast: Jean-Paul Belmondo (Lazlo Kovacs, alias Michel Poiccard), Jean
Seberg (Patricia), Daniel Boulanger (Vital), Henri-Jacques Huet (Ber-
ruti), Jean-Pierre Melville (Parvulesco), Jean-Luc Godard (the in-
formant).

Pierrot le fou

Rome-Paris-Films. 1965.
Director: Jean-Luc Godard.
Producers: Georges de Beauregard and Dino de Laurentis.
Screenplay: Jean-Luc Godard. Adapted from Lionel White's *Obsession*.
Photography: Raoul Coutard.
Music: Antoine Duhamel.
Cast: Jean-Paul Belmondo (Ferdinand, Pierrot), Anna Karina (Marianne),
Dirk Sanders (the brother, Fred), Samuel Fuller (the director), Roget
Dutoit (the gangster), Graziella Galvani (the wife), Jean-Pierre Léaud
(young man in cinema).

Index

to *Sunday Bloody Sunday,* 14; repression in, 9, 19; repression of women's sexuality in, 12; role of Henri Serre in, 9; triangular relationships in, 18, 230–31n.21; use of voice-over in, 12–13, 60

Kahn, Masud, 182
Kleist, Heinrich von: *Penthesilea,* 21
Kovacs, Lazlo, 200
Kuleshov, Lev, 155

Labyrinth: in Chabrol's work, 91, 95–99, 103, 107, 110–18 passim, 244n.29; in Denon's work, 49; library as, 222, 223; in Resnais's work, 67, 79
Lacan, Jacques: *Ecrits,* 55, 65; on loss, 41; on mirror stage, 55–56, 59, 64, 70, 78, 86, 218; overtones of in *Marienbad,* 237–38n.24; on paternal signifier, 43; and problematics of identity, 222; theory of in Godard's work, 220; and view of the ego, 3, 51
La Fontaine, Jean de, 90
Lambert, Richard: *Prince of Pickpockets,* 173–76
Latil-Le Dantec, Mireille: on *Marienbad,* 69–70; on *Pickpocket,* 165–66
Lawrence, D. H., 189
Lenin, Vladimir Ilyich, 196, 261–62n.58
Lewis, C. S., 96
Lovers, The. See Amants, Les
Lynch, David, 231n.26

McBride, Jim, 184, 185, 189, 192
McDougall, Joyce, 180–82
Magny, Joel: on Bresson's films, 177; on Chabrol's films, 89, 99, 114
Magritte, René: and Malle's *Les Amants,* 31, 39, 44, 47. Works: *Les Amants,* 31, 33; *Empire of Lights,* 233n.18; *La Representation,* 39, 44, 51, 233nn. 18, 22; *Le Viol,* 39
Malle, Louis: *Les Amants,* 24–53; on Bresson, 178; compared to Chabrol, 87; on montage, 31; range of canon of, 5; on repetition, 31; work com-

pared to *L'Année dernière à Marienbad,* 60; version of *La Carte de Tendre,* 224
Malraux, André, 189; *L'Espoir,* 4, 101
Mann, Anthony: *Man of the West,* 192, 194
Ma Nuit chez Maud: analyzed, 119–47; blindness in, 134–35, 141; Jansenism in, 120–21, 128, 135, 139; Marxism in, 120–21; Pascal's *deus absconditus* in, 145–46, 249n.26; role of Françoise Fabian in, 126–47; role of probabilism in, 122, 124, 133, 136–37, 147; role of Antoine Vitez in, 119; Romanesque art in, 130, 132–33, 143; voyeurism in, 132
Marin, Louis, 36–38, 43, 52
Marivaux, 140, 249–50n.31
Marx, Karl, 169
Masson, Jeffrey, 76
Mehlman, Jeffrey, 3, 218
Melville, Jean-Pierre: *Bob le Flambeur,* 260n.31; *Le Doulos,* 200; role in *A bout de souffle,* 186
Mérimée, Prosper: *La Venus d'Ille,* 9–12
Metacinema: as concern of new wave, 4; in Godard's work, 200, 208; in Resnais's work, 58
Metaphor: and collage, 19; defined by Rohmer, 129–30; equivalent in film, 127
Miller, Mark Crisipin, 224
Mirror: in Aragon's *Mise à mort,* 217–18; in Chabrol's work, 91, 92, 99, 105; in Cocteau's *Orphée,* 33; in Godard's work, 213; and identity in *Les Amants,* 32–33, 45, 52–53; of literature by film, 225; in *Marienbad,* 54–57, 59, 61–63, 68, 70, 81–83, 86, 238n.26; as prison in Denon, 49; of spectator in cinema, 7; stage in psychoanalysis, 41, 54–64, 86
Misprision: in Chabrol's films, 114; in *Jules et Jim,* 9, 18; in the new wave, 5
Molière: *Les Précieuses ridicules,* 34